ESSENTIALS
OF
MANAGERIAL ECONOMICS

(For M.B.A., M.Com. Courses)

Dr. P.N. Reddy
Ph.D.
Director, K.K.E.C.S. Institute of Management Bangalore.
Former Dean & Chairman, Department of P.G. Studies in Commerce and Management, Bangalore University.

Prof. H.R. Appannaiah
M.Com.
Dean of Studies, Surana P.G. Centre, Kengare Bangalore-60.
Former Principal, P.A. College, Tiptur, Founder President, Federation of Teachers' Councils of Commerce and Management in Karnataka

Asha Ganesh
M.A.
Head, Economics Department, Surana College of Management, Basavanaguid, Banggalore-560 004

Himalaya Publishing House

ISO 9001:2015 CERTIFIED

First Edition : 1995
Second Edition : 1997
Third Revised &
Millennium Edition : 2000
Reprint : 2002, 2004, 2011, 2019
Edition : 2025

Published by : Mrs. Meena Pandey
for **HIMALAYA PUBLISHING HOUSE PVT. LTD.,**
"Ramdoot", Dr. Bhalerao Marg, Girgaon, Mumbai - 400 004.
Phone: 022-23860170, 23863863; **Fax:** 022-23877178
E-mail: himpub@bharatmail.co.in; **Website:** www.himpub.com

Branch Offices :

New Delhi : "Pooja Apartments", 4-B, Murari Lal Street, Ansari Road, Darya Ganj, New Delhi - 110 002. Phone: 011-23270392, 23278631; Fax: 011-23256286

Nagpur : Kundanlal Chandak Industrial Estate, Ghat Road, Nagpur - 440 018. Mobile: 09325409992, 09325908881

Bengaluru : Plot No. 91-33, 2nd Main Road, Seshadripuram, Behind Nataraja Theatre, Bengaluru - 560 020. Phone: 080-41138821; Mobile: 09379847017, 09379847005

Hyderabad : No. 3-4-184, Lingampally, Besides Raghavendra Swamy Matham, Kachiguda, Hyderabad - 500 027. Phone: 040-27560041, 27550139

Chennai : No. 34/44, Motilal Street, T. Nagar, Chennai - 600 017. Mobile: 09380460419

Pune : "Laksha" Apartment, First Floor, No. 527, Mehunpura, Shaniwarpeth (Near Prabhat Theatre), Pune - 411 030. Phone: 020-24496323, 24496333; Mobile: 09370579333

Cuttack : Plot No 5F-755/4, Sector-9, CDA Markat Nagar, Cuttack - 753 014, Odisha. Mobile: 09338746007

Kolkata : 3, S.M. Bose Road, Near Gate No. 5, Agarpara Railway Station, North 24 Parganas, West Bengal - 700109. Mobile: 09674536325

Printed at : A to Z Printers, New Delhi. On behalf of HPH.

PREFACE

We are pleased to place in the hands of our readers the revised edition of *Essentials Managerial Economics*. Managerial Economics has become a specialised branch of study as principles and methodologies of economics are increasingly applied in managerial decision-making.

Besides providing basic aspects of economics, information is provided on, issues concerning profit measurement, and economic optimisation. Other macro economic aspects like Fiscal and Monetary Policies, Balance of Payments are also added to the text, keeping in view the changes in curriculum of M.B.A. and M.Com. courses of different universities. The book is comprehensive in analysis and is written in easy and understandable style. Study questions are given in the end of each chapter. We invite readers to inform us the deficiencies of the book for improve the quality of the book subsequent edition.

We thank, Shri D.P. Pandey, Shri K.N. Pandey and Shri Neeraj Pandey, for their co-operation in publishing this title. We also thank, S. Ganesh the area Representative and the staff of HPH for their co-operation.

AUTHORS

PREFACE TO THE FIRST EDITION

With the increase in technology and innovations, the business world today is fast growing and has also posed several managerial problems to the top management. Particularly the top executives of business enterprises have to solve many business problems by taking appropriate managerial decisions. Decision-making will be a tough job, unless they are provided with certain tools. Even forecasting of the demand or turnover, profit planning, production planning etc., needs certain tools to take sound managerial decisions. The top management will have alternative solutions to a problem and the managers and top executives have to choose the best solution for solving the problem. "Managerial Economics" provides certain tools and techniques which facilitate the management to formulate and adopt a sound business policy. This discipline is the combination of pure economic theory and quantitative techniques. Economic theory in combination with statistical and mathematical equations can provide some solutions to solve business problems. Hence the discipline "Managerial Economics" has come into business scene.

Many books are available on this subject. But in this volume we have tried to put the tools and techniques in a simple and direct style, which facilitates the readers to understand them easily. This title acts as a course book for learners and also provide sufficient material for the students who take to M.B.A. and M.Com. courses. This can also be a base book for B.Com. and B.B.M. students of Indian Universities. Intelligent study questions are provided at the end of each chapter. We welcome the healthy criticisms from our readers. This helps us in improving the subsequent edition.

We are thankful to Shri D.P. Pandey of Himalaya Publishing House, Mumbai for having nearly brought out this edition. Our thanks are also due to Shri S. Ganesh, area Representative of HPH for having done the liason work.

P. N. Reddy
H. R. Appannaiah
Asha Ganesh

CONTENTS

CHAPTER 1

MEANING AND SCOPE OF MANAGERIAL ECONOMICS

INTRODUCTION

Managerial Economics is a science concerned with managing the economic organisations of our society. When we say economic organisations, they include the micro and macro units of the economy. There are millions of firms both big and small, which are concerned with manufacturing of various outputs and services for the sake of making profit. It is essential for the survival and continuity of the business organisations. Knowledge of managerial economics is of immense help in solving various problems which arise in the functioning of business enterprises. Every business organisation is expected to commence its functions only after formulating business policies. Modern business organisations have to chalk out the programme systematically in which the resources are converted into objects which satisfy the people. It is the function of the management to use resources such as raw materials, energy, manpower and so on for the realisation of results in such a way that the business firm is not only able to pay its way, but is also able to earn some surplus to meet the needs of growth and expansion.

Managerial economics is concerned with the application of economic theory and methodology to the decision making processes of the enterprise. In other words, managerial economics is concerned with the using of those aspects of economic theory which would help in maximising profit through an increase in the production and marketing of the product. The process of application of economic analysis to the management of the firm is that of using various concepts and techniques which enable the decision maker to achieve his goal in business.

Managerial economics is a powerful mechanism of theoretical knowledge to the business executives in managing their organisations systematically and effectively.

MEANING AND NATURE OF MANAGERIAL ECONOMICS

Economics is a science of management of limited resources with unlimited wants of human beings. The development and happiness of human beings depend upon the production, distribution and consumption of various goods and services. Man wants food, shelter and clothing primarily. These are for his existence. He needs more in order to make his life comfortable and joyful. These lead to exploration of various resources, materials and techniques of production, movement and consumption of various types of goods. Man is confronted with various problems like what to produce, how to produce, for whom to produce, are the resources economically used, are the products so produced within the reach of men, etc. Knowledge of economics helps to solve all these problems. Here lies the importance of managerial economics.

As population and per capita income go on increasing, the demand for goods and services also increases. These developments in human civilization inspire the leaders in production, trade and commerce to take up new economic activities. With the expansion and diversification of human wants, various economic activities will result and here comes the role of managerial economics in order to direct the utilisation of natural and man-made resources in a desired manner for the production of various goods and services. Managerial economics is now derived as a body of organised and systematised knowledge comprising of theories. Economics is often defined as the science of management of economic institutions which engage in the conversion and transformation of raw-resources into consumable products. The modern society with its complex character, exercises tremendous influence through tastes and attitudes on the production and marketing of innumerable types of goods and services. Ever increasing and changing of human wants and the existence of limited volume of resources give rise to many problems such as what to produce, how to produce and how much to produce and where to produce. In this game, managerial economics assumes the central role. The men behind organizing production and marketing of the products are called the business people or business executives. The business executives now turn to economics to get knowledge which would help in formulating business policies. Thus, a new branch of economics called Managerial Economics emerged in the fifties of this century. Managerial Economics is thus a ready-made tool for the business people in shaping their business decisions. Managerial economics is an indispensable tool for the business people to make proper decisions. Thus, Managerial Economics is the application of economic theory and methodology to decision making processes within the enterprise. In other words, it refers to these aspects of economic analysis which are relevant to the practice of management processes in the business organisation.

Decision Making

Modern business organisations are very much concerned with decision making and forward planning. Decision making means the process of selecting the suitable action from among several alternative courses of action. The modern business is confronted with various intricate problems such as - what goods to be produced. Here the problem is selecting from among various models. Secondly, there is another problem regarding the quality of the products to be produced. Then again, selecting the proper technology of production, such as labour saving technology or labour using technology, which energy resource is to be used - gas, diesel, coal-based or electricity, etc. Then comes another problem - how to obtain resources or what alternative resources are there for these resources and the cost aspects. Finally, the determination of prices which would give the business people a reasonable amount of profit. Thus, decision making is the central objective of managerial economics.

Forward Planning

Forward planning means preparing the perspective plan of development of the organisation. This involves capital budgeting, obtaining land for future expansion, the availability of technology, cost reduction programmes etc. As the production of the quantity of the output increases, the unit cost is required to fall gradually. Future expansions will have to be done from the surplus derived from annual profit. Forward planning also involves plans for mobilising raw-materials, labour, pricing, etc. Thus, forward planning and decision making go hand in hand.

Present day business functions with the cloud of uncertainty. This makes decision making and forward planning difficult and complicated. If the knowledge of the future is certain, then the formulation of business plans is not difficult. But today, since the business functions with too much of uncertainty, the knowledge of managerial economics helps it to incorporate suitable changes whenever necessary.

In managerial economics, the approach methodology is obtained from economic theory. In other words, economic theory in the service of business executives is known as *managerial economics.* Managerial economics is developed to bridge the gap between economic theory as taught in universities and as practiced in business organisations. Managerial economics employs multi-disciplinary approach utilising analytical and decision making tools derived from accounting, finance, marketing and administrative theory as well as from economic theory and quantitative analysis. In other words, managerial economics shows how economic analysis can be useful in formulating business policies.

Definitions

Some of the management economists have defined the term 'Managerial Economics' in various ways. Some of the definitions are really illustrative. Spencer and Siegelman defined Managerial Economics as 'the integration of economic theory with business practice for the purpose of facilitating decision making and forward planning by the management'. According to them, the decision making and forward planning are the important fields of the study of managerial economics.

McNair and Merian* say that managerial economics consists of the use of economic modes of thought to analyse business situations. According to them, managerial economics becomes applied economics since economic theory is invoked in solving business problems. In other words, it also means integration of economic theory with business practice. The linkage between economics and management will help the business people to run the organisations effectively and smoothly. Economics advocates rational utilisation of resources since they are scarce and have alternative uses. The business people are aware of these problems and hence they decide to set up priorities and on the basis decide the utilisation of resources. They also explore various alternatives before deciding on a particular resource. If a manager decides to increase the output of one commodity from a given resource, it means this resource is not available to produce other products. This economic problem will compel the managers to take a realistic decision. Economics broadly sets out the theory of pricing of a product. This theory is put into application by the manager in deciding the selling price of the product or products, while the economist views the problem in a broader angle which the manager uses it to a particular situation. The general laws propounded by economists are put into particular situations by the manager. Economists develop tools and techniques to study and solve various general problems. The business managers use the same tools and techniques to solve specific problems of their enterprises. Economists are concerned with elucidating general theories while, the business economists use them for organisations.

Managerial economics does not cover all aspects of either management or economics. It covers only those aspects which are useful in business matters. The managerial economists have to make proper planning for the growth of the organisation. They have to make realistic forecasts regarding the future demand, competition, availability of resources and also the mode

* Malcolm P. McNair and Richard S. Merian : Problems in Business Economics.

of profit. He has to secure cooperation and coordination from departments of his organisation in order to make his planning effective. Thus, Managerial Economics covers only those aspects of economics which are relevant to the decision making process of the firm. Managerial Economics is purely micro-economics. It will not bother about macro-economic aspects.

For the demand forecasting to be realistic, the managerial economists are required to use concepts like elasticity of demand. The business manager uses various techniques such as Critical Path Method (CPM) and Programme Evaluation and Review Technique (PERT) in order to find out whether the firm is going on the desired path of progress.

Prediction is another characteristic of Economics. Assuming certain variables as constant, the economist propounds laws. He uses the same techniques in order to predict profit, demand, production, costs, pricing and capital in certain quantities. Since the business works under the cloud of uncertainty, the economist has to predict the future in as realistic terms as possible.

The main goal of Managerial Economics is to solve practical problems. Study of Managerial Economics is for getting knowledge to address practical problems of business. It is pragmatic. It avoids abstract ideas. It considers only the concrete issues pertaining to business. Business is not restricted to private sector. The scope of Managerial Economics extends to public enterprises as well.

Micro and Macro-Economics

The study of economics is divided by modern economists into two parts, micro-economics and macro-economics. The terms micro-economics and macro-economics were first used by Swedish Economist Ragnar Frisch in the 1920s. An economic system may be looked at as a whole or in terns of various decision making units such as individual consumers or households, producing units such as firms, business concerns, individual factors of production such as land, labour, capital and entrepreneurs and individual industries such as iron and steel, cotton textiles, automobiles etc. When we are analysing the problems of economy as a whole, it is macro-economics, while an analysis of the behaviour of any particular decision making unit such as firm, an industry, or a consumer constitutes micro-economics.

Micro-economics is also called Price Theory while Macro-economics is called Income Theory. 'Price theory' explains the composition and allocation of total production, why more of some things are produced than others. 'Income Theory' explains the level of total production and why the level of production rises or falls.

Micro-Economics

Prof. Boulding defines Micro-economics as the study of a particular firm, particular household, individual price, wage, income, industry and particular commodity. It is defined as a study of economic activities of such units as consumers, resource owners and business firms.

The word 'micro' means a millionth part. It forms only a small part or component of the whole economy. The study of the behaviour of individual consumer of a product or the study of an individual firm or the individual industry is micro-economics. Micro-economic theory studies the behaviour of individual decision-making units, such as individual consumers, firms, resource-owners, etc. Micro-economics studies how the resources flow from resource owners to individual business units and the flow of goods and services from individual firms to households. It studies the composition of such flows and how prices of goods and services in the flow are determined. The subject matter of micro-economics is individual consumer and a firm or an industry. It explains how and in what manner the price of a commodity is determined. It studies how an individual consumer attains equilibrium. It also studies the processes of equilibrium of these entities and their implication on resource allocation. Thus, micro-economics involves the study of economic motive and behaviour of individual consumers and producers and the principles underlying the organisation and operation of firms and industries.

Macro-Economics

Prof. Boulding defines that ' Macro-economics deals not with individual quantities as such, but with aggregates of these quantities, not with individual income but with national income, not with individual prices but with price levels, not with individual outputs but with national output.'

'Macro-economics is concerned with such variables as the aggregate volume of output of the economy, with the extent to which its resources are employed, with the size of the national income and with the general price levels', says Gardner Ackley. The study of totals of important variables in the economic system such as income, consumption, saving, investment, employment forms the subject matter of macro-economics.

Macro-economics is also called aggregative economics. Macro-economics is concerned with aggregates and averages of the entire economy. It deals with economic affairs 'in the large'. It concerns the overall dimensions of economic life. It deals with how economy grows. It establishes an important relationship between movements of income, employment and price level.

Difference between Micro-Economics and Macro-Economics

The main differences between micro-economics and macro-economics are as follows:

(i) *Differences in Aggregation*

Micro-economics studies the functions and problems of individual units like a firm, while Macro-economics studies that of aggregate of firms or an industry. Economic development as a whole is the function of macro-economics.

(ii) *Difference in Objective*

The objective of micro-economics is maximisation of profits of an individual firm. Macro-economics studies the problems, policies and principles relating to full employment, growth, etc.

(iii) *Operations of the Economy*

Micro-economics is concerned with the working of a firm. It tells us how the individual units in the economy are functioning, whether they are earning maximum profit. On the other hand, macro-economics studies the movements of national income, etc. Micro-economics deals with price determination by a firm. Macro-economics is concerned with price stabilisation. Micro-economics is applicable to the various branches of economics such as public finance, international trade etc. Macro-economics is applicable to the economy as a whole. and how individual units work together to produce economic stability and reasonable growth.

(iv) *Macro-economic Paradoxes*

Economists like Prof. Boulding and Prof. Samuelson have pointed out the risks of the distinction between these two branches. The set of errors arising out of this distinction is known as 'Macro-economic Paradoxes' or the fallacy of aggregation. What it means is that what benefits the individual, may cause harm to aggregates. For example: If the demand for a commodity is sluggish, a decrease in price may result in the increase in the demand for that product. The same principle if applied to macro-economics, leads to disastrous consequences. If the general price level is allowed to fall, this may result in depression, fall in income and employment in the economy as a whole. Therefore, when there is fall in the general price level, the policy is that it should be stabilised. In the same way, individual saving results in capital formation. If the people as a whole save by reducing the consumption, it results in fall in the aggregate demand and results in depression. In this way, these micro-economic decisions cannot be applied to the economy as a whole.

Prof. Boulding has shown the differences between these two types of analysis with an example of a forest. Just as the forest consists of different types of trees, society also consists of different groups of individuals. The difference between the individual and society is similar to the difference between individual trees and a forest. The difference between a tree and a forest is as follows: An individual tree may die while the forest continues. An individual tree grows to a limit and then decays, but the forest continues growing. If old trees fall, new trees grow in their places. It is difficult to put a single tree on fire, but the fire in the forest spreads very quickly. A single tree has no effect on climate, while a forest has a cooling effect on the climate. In this way, micro-economics and macro-economics differ from each other. Micro-economics proves wrong when applied to macro-economics. Concluding, Prof. Boulding says that it must not be thought, because of differences, that micro and macro-economics study different phenomena. They are different ways of studying the same set of phenomena.

Importance of Micro-economics

Micro-economics occupies a very important place in the study of economic principles. It has both theoretical and practical importance. Micro-economics is applied in solving economic problems concerning the individual units in the economy. Keynes said that micro-economics is a necessary part of one's apparatus of thought. Micro-economics helps us to understand the operations of the economy. Since it forms the study of individual units in the economy, it helps to have a clear understanding of individual units which form the basis of the whole economy. The problems of the economy are analysed on the basis of the individual units of the economy. It tells us how millions of consumers and producers in an economy take decisions about the allocation of productive resources among millions of goods and services. It explains how through the market mechanism, prices of individual goods and services are determined and the goods and services are produced and distributed. It explains the condition of efficiency both in consumption and production and departure from the optimum.

Economic policies are formulated with the help of micro-economics. In other words, micro-economics is used in formulating economic policies. For example, when a government wants to impose new taxes, it can make necessary changes in it by knowing the reactions of the people regarding the new taxes. This knowledge of individual reactions can be obtained from the micro-economics. Micro-economics is useful in removing difficulties which may arise in the working of a firm in the industry. To improve the difficulties of a firm, there is no need to study macro-economics. The study of working of a firm or that industry is sufficient.

The role of micro-economics is both positive and normative. It not only tells us how the economy operates but also how it should be run to promote well-being of the people of the country. The main objective of any production is to provide for consumption. Therefore, the product so produced must satisfy the needs of consumers. It should be so priced such that the entire product must be utilised for consumption. Prof. Lerner observes, 'Micro- economic theory facilitates the understanding of what would be a hopelessly complicated confusion of billions of facts by constructing simplified models of behaviour'.

Limitations of Micro-Economics

Micro-economics thus is very useful in studying the functioning of individual units of the economy. Yet, it suffers from certain limitations. Since it is confined to the study of individual units, it cannot give us any idea of functioning of the economy as a whole. If an industry is flourishing, it cannot be concluded that the whole industrial economy is flourishing. Therefore, micro-economics is limited to a narrow sphere of the economy. Secondly, micro-economics is applicable only to a full employment economy. It is rare to come across the existence of a full employment economy. Prof. Keynes has said that to assume a full employment, economy is to assume our difficulties away. Both these limitations are quite significant and they reduce the usefulness of micro-economics.

Importance of Macro-Economics

As already pointed out, Macro-economics studies the aggregate and averages of the entire economy such as national income, aggregate output, total employment etc. Macro-economics is useful in several ways. Macro-economics helps us to get a clear idea of functioning of the whole economic system. Modern economic system is very complex in view of the existence of innumerable number of facts which are inter-dependent and as such it is very difficult to get a clear idea of the functioning of the economy on the basis of micro-economics. Therefore, the study of macro-economics is necessary. Macro-economics gives a bird's eye view of the economic world. The study of individual entities of the economy will lead us nowhere. The whole economy is more important than the individual unit.

Macro-economics is of great importance in formulating economic policies. Government which is a policy making body is concerned with the whole and not individual units. It is concerned with the stabilisation of price level and not that of a price of any individual commodity. It is concerned with the national income, not with individual income. Economic policies cannot be obviously based on the basis of fortunes of a single firm or even a single industry or the price of an individual commodity. It is very important to regulate full employment, national income and the price level, etc.

Macro-economics is very useful in solving many economic problems. Whenever there is recession or depression in the economy, it is macro-economics that suggests suitable remedial measures. In the same way, to curb inflation, macro-economic policies are useful.

Limitations of Macro-Economics

Macro-economics tends to generalise the reasoning and conclusions derived from micro-economics. Many things can be done by individuals without any difficulty and without any adverse consequences. If it is attempted by all, then disastrous conclusions will follow. For example, if all depositors start withdrawing from the bank, the bank will collapse. That is why Dr. Keynes said that saving by the community may prove a calamity. If people increase saving, no doubt, it results in increased capital accumulation. But it, at the same time, reduces aggregate demand leading to fall in production, employment etc. As such, to generalise from individual experience, is one of the greatest dangers of macro-economic theory.

Macro-economics overlooks individual differences. For example, general price level may be stable, but the price of foodgrains increase. It causes hardships to common people. A steep rise in the manufactured products may conceal a calamitous fall in the agricultural prices, while the average prices were steady. The agriculturists may be ruined. While speaking of aggregate, it is necessary to remember the nature, composition and structure of the components.

Inter-dependence of the Micro-Macro Approaches

It may appear to common minds that Micro-economics and Macro-economics are unrelated and independent. In fact, it is not so. Neither approach is complete without the other.

Every micro-economic problem involves macro-economic thought. How much a firm should pay for a labour no doubt comes within the purview of micro-economy. But the wages of one firm are related to the wages of other firms in the locality. Thus, every price, every wage and every income is dependent directly or indirectly upon the prices, wages, incomes of all other products, of all other workers and of all individuals in the community. It is thus clear that every micro-economic problem involves macro-economic analysis.

Macro-economic analysis requires micro-economic analysis. A society consists of individuals. Individuals collectively make up society. In the same way, many firms constitute the industry and many industries collectively make up the economy. Therefore, to get a clear idea of working of our economy, we are required to know the working of individual units. The total production of individual firms make up the output of the entire economy. The sum total of individual income is the national income. Therefore, to understand the working of the economy, we have to study the theory of individual firms. Thus, a study of macro-economics necessarily involves the study of micro-economics.

Integration of these Two Approaches

What is needed is a proper integration of the micro and macro approaches to such problems. In fact, there are a few macro problems which have no micro elements involved and a few micro problems that are without macro aspects. It is therefore proper to integrate both in analysing the economic problems and prescribing policy measures for solving them. Ignoring one and concentrating on the other gives rise to incomplete results.

Is Managerial Economics Micro-Economics or Macro-Economics ?

Managerial economics essentially is micro-economics. It is concerned with business firms. It studies the problems of a business firm such as forecasting the demand for its product, calculating the cost of production, fixation of price, profit planning and capital management.

Though basically being micro-economics, Managerial Economics seeks the help of macro-economics. It is because that individual units function in an environment in which all firms work. If it has to survive, it has to modify its objectives, plans and programmes so as to conform with the whole economy. The firm has to function in a macro-economic environment and therefore it has to adjust its pricing policy and profit policy to national economic policies. Therefore, Managerial Economics cannot be exclusively micro-economics in character. It has to face macro-economic issues like, tax policies, business cycles, wage policies, industrial relations, pricing and distribution policies and anti-monopoly policies of the government. Managerial Economics in this respect becomes macro-economics. The importance that macro-economics has come to acquire is not without reasons. Macro-economics helps in understanding the economic environment in which the individual unit works. Therefore, if the individual units are studied under the broader macro perspective, suitable decisions can be taken to correct if there are any imbalances. Further, macro-economics is useful in formulating policies applicable to a whole nation. It is not at all possible to frame policies to individual units. Under the guidelines shown by macro-economists, individual units can function effectively. A clear understanding of both the individual units and the whole environment is necessary to produce the best results.

Positive and Normative Economics

Economics as a Science

While discussing the nature and scope of Managerial Economics, we observed that it is more a science than an art. It is a science because it studies the subject matter comprehensively and systematically, which explains the cause and effect relationship. According to Poincare, 'Science is built of facts as a house is built of stones; but an accumulation of facts is no more a science than a heap of stones in a house'. If a subject is to be called a science, it should have the following features: i. Science is a systematised body of knowledge, ii. Science establishes the relationship between cause and effect of a fact. and iii. Laws of science are universal.

Economics is a science for it fulfils all the above conditions. In economics, facts are collected in a systematised manner and they are analysed properly and conclusions which are universal in character are drawn. Conclusions are drawn with a view to apply them to solve problems in various situations and laws are propounded. The laws of economics are similar to laws of sciences. In laws, the relationship between cause and effect are established. Many economic laws have been experimented and tested to get out of any evils. The scope of experiments of economic laws is very wide and the laboratory for these experiments is the world with human beings.

Economists possess the measuring rod of money to measure the economic facts. Alfred Marshal said that the instrument of money has made economics a more certain science than any other social science. Therefore, economics has the quality of quantitative measurement of science. Money is a good measuring rod to measure the economic motives of man. Further, it is concluded that most of the economic laws are universal. Basic laws are applicable not only in a socialist society but also in a capitalist society. On the basis of these arguments, managerial economics may be called a science.

According to some economists, Economics cannot be considered as a pure science like Physics and Chemistry. The only difference between physical science and economics is that economics is very much concerned with animate beings. In economic science, man is the central figure, while in other physical science, matter is the central figure. Matter is used in such a manner so as to satisfy the wants of man. Since man is the central figure, economic science has to regard the feelings of man. Therefore, while analysing economic laws, a condition namely 'other things remaining the same' is used. Economics is thus called a *social science*.

Economics has a utilitarian value. The science of economics is very much used to promote well-being of man. It studies the human behaviour as a relationship between ends and scarce means which have alternative uses. Economics is not only light giving but also fruit bearing. In this context, economics is regarded as an art. It can be called a human science. Modern economists are using knowledge, energy and time to study various problems with a view to establish a human kingdom where everyone lives in happiness.

It is in this context, modern economists have further explored to know whether economics is a positive science or a normative science.

Positive Science

Positive science explains and explores the economic subject. It establishes the relationship between cause and effect of a particular event as it happens. Positive science confirms itself to accurate description of a phenomenon. It explains what it is, how it works and what are its effects. For example, we say that light travels in a straight line. The science which studies the fact is known as a positive science. Economics is also a positive science. It also explains and explores an economic phenomenon. For example, when prices rise, demand for the products fall. If the demand for labourers increase, wages also rise. In India, general wage rate is 'ower than that of western countries. Some economists maintain that the function of economics is that of positive science. The function of the economist is to explore and explain and not to advocate or condemn. As a positive science, economics can show the merits and demerits of deficit financing. According to some economists, economics has no place to offer value judgements regarding the merits and demerits of the facts.

There are economists who say that economics cannot be disassociated from ethics. There is an economic thought. Having analysed the causes of maldistribution of wealth, why should the economist feel shy of telling that the consequences of such a thing is injurious to the health of the economy. Equitable distribution of wealth promotes happiness in society. Therefore, from this point of view, economics is called a normative science.

Normative Science

Normative science is one which explains the events or facts as they ought to be. Normative science answers the questions 'what should be or what should not be'. A normative science is defined as a body of knowledge relating to the criteria of what ought to be and concerned with ideal as distinguished from actual, said Lord Keynes. Normative science is called the science of ethics. 'The real function of a science is in the use we can make of it to promote the ends of human welfare', quoted R.T. Bye. Another thinker Arthus Smithies has said that the economist should diagnose and prescribe for economic health of society. Prof. Pigo says that 'Economics is chiefly valuable not as an intellectual gymnastic nor as a means of winning truth for its own sake but as a handmaid of ethics and a servant of practice'. Therefore, according to these economists, economics is more a normative science than a positive science.

Economics is both Positive and Normative

Economics associates with ethics. For example, maldistribution of wealth is dangerous. It creates tug of war between the rich and the poor. Therefore, the purpose of economics is to promote welfare and as such it is a normative science. Mahatma Gandhi said, 'Economics which disregards moral and sentimental considerations is like wax works that being life like, still lacks the life of a living flesh'. In order to pass value judgement, it is necessary that the problems are to be explored and explained. Since people approach economics for a fruit, economics should provide solutions which are beneficial to mankind. It is in this regard economics is called both a positive and a normative science.

Economics is regarded as a normative science due to the fact that economics is an engine of social betterment. Economists, since time immemorial, have been giving suggestions regarding the welfare of human beings. For example, Adam Smith advocated the Taxation Policy, Malthus advocated population control and suggested how to control it, J.S. Mill suggested imposition of taxes on unearned income. Keynes suggested measures to remove unemployment. In this way, economists have been advocating various measures to promote human welfare.

Hence, economics consists not merely allocating scarce resources among competing ends but is maximising total satisfaction according to one's own judgement. The choice resulting from subjecting competing desires to judgement makes economics obviously a normative science.

Managerial economics is a normative science because it deals with problems of modern business organisations and offers solutions. It tells us what should be under a particular circumstance. A managerial economist tells the management what should be done to achieve the business objectives. It tells us, the businessmen, what should be done in order to get results.

Managerial economics is considered as applied economics. It suggests how the economic principles are applied to the formulation of policies and programmes. It tells the business executives how to achieve the business objectives.

In order to pass judgements, managerial economics has to explore and explain the issues. It has to describe the state of operation of the firm or the economy at a point of time or during a period of time. It also develops hypothesis and explains why it has happened. Along with it, it also suggests how to overcome problems. In the case of normative micro-economics, one is concerned with problems like what the objectives and policies of business ought to be and how to go about them. In the macro-economic level too, managerial economics behaves in a normative way.

In conclusion, it can be said that Managerial Economics is essentially micro-economics. It studies an individual unit namely a business firm. It is concerned with normative micro-economics. In normative micro-economics, the economist says what ought to happen rather than what happens. In attempting to study the various connected problems, he has to take up positive economics.

Conclusion

The main goal of Managerial Economics is to solve practical problems. The study of Managerial Economics is for getting knowledge to solve practical problems in business. It is pragmatic. It avoids abstract ideas. It considers only the concrete issues pertaining to business. Business is not restricted to private sector alone. The scope of Managerial Economics extends to public sector enterprises as well.

Managerial economics is a scientific art too. Art is a system in which the rules and regulations so formulated are put into successful application. Managerial economics helps the management in better utilisation of scarce resources for the production of commodities which are going to satisfy the needs of man.

Managerial Economics and Other Subjects

Managerial Economics is closely related with other subjects like pure economics, statistics, mathematics and accounting.

Its Relationship with Economics

In fact, managerial economics is applied economics. Managerial economics depends entirely on economic analysis for getting theoretical knowledge, tools and instruments for decision making and forward planning. It bridges the gulf between pure economics and management practice. The important subjects of study of Managerial Economics are demand, cost of production, pricing of products in different market structures, profit maximisation, etc. In order to fully understand the above concepts, it is necessary to have a thorough knowledge of economic analysis. In order to estimate demand for products, the Managerial Economics relies on elasticity of demand. At the same time, the incomes of the individuals, the production and distribution of wealth in the economy, the tastes of the people, etc. are taken into consideration. On the basis of the above, demand forecasting is made. The income and employment theory of modern economics helps the managerial economics to make demand forecast as accurate as possible. The prospects of the individual firms depends on the general prosperity of the economy as a whole. As such, the knowledge of pure economics is indispensable to analyse the economic prospects of individual firms. The major fields of economics which are useful to management economists are the following:

(i) Demand theory,

(ii) Theory of the firm-price-output and investment decisions,

(iii) Business financing,

(iv) Public finance and fiscal policy,

(v) Money and Banking,

(vi) National Income and Social Accounting, Theory of International Trade and Economic Development.

Thus, Managerial Economics derives insight and guidance from economics.

Managerial Economics and Statistics

Managerial Economics is not a mere theoretical exposition. In fact, it is concerned with practical problems which are stated in quantitative data (In fact after the II World War, the business people are using the knowledge and the analytical techniques of behavioural science). The data so collected applied and presented helps the management to take appropriate decisions whenever possible.

Managerial Economics uses statistical methods to test the economic generalisations and conclusions. When the data are checked in the respective fields, the business managers will be able to take correct decisions.

Statistical data are collected frequently in order to reduce the danger of uncertainty in the minds of business people.

Managerial Economics and Mathematics

Mathematics is another important tool used in Managerial Economics. It is stated that managerial economics is both conceptual and metrical for, without measurement, the theory will be misleading in taking decisions. Mathematics helps in estimating various economic relationships, predicting relevant economic quantities and using them in decision taking and forward planning. Managerial economics uses considerable amount of geometry, algebra and calculus in deriving solutions. Further, operational research is used in estimating demand and determining the prices of the products.

Then there is Operational Research (OR) which is closely related to Managerial Economics. Operational Research is the application of mathematical techniques to solving business problems. It provides all the data required for business decisions and forward planning. Techniques such as linear programming, game theory, etc. are due to the works of operational research. Linear Programming is extensively used in decision taking. Managerial Economics is concerned with efficient use of scarce resources. Operational research is concerned with efficient use of scarce resources. There is close affinity between Managerial Economics and Operational Research. Managerial economics gives special emphasis to problems involving maximisation of profit and minimisation of costs, while operational research focusses attention on the concept of optimization. Managerial Economics has made much use of optimisation concept but initially started with marginal analysis taken from economics. Managerial Economics uses the logic of Economics, Mathematics and Statistics for undertaking effective decisions, while Operational Research techniques based on these ways of thinking are being used to solve decision making problems in business. Again, both Operational Research and Managerial Economics are concerned with taking effective decisions.

Operational research is a tool in the hands of managerial economics to solve day to day business problems. Managerial Economics is an academic subject which aims to understand and analyse problems and decision making by a firm. Thus, Operational Research is a functional activity pursued by specialists within the firm. Though it is expensive, it helps to make accurate solutions by means of providing necessary data.

Managerial Economics and Accounting

Management Accounting provides necessary financial data for suitable decisions in business. The business decisions are generally based on accounting data. For example, the profit and loss statement of the firm for a specific period will reveal how the firm has performed. The managerial economist will now form future course of action, namely, whether to continue in the existing manner or to make proper improvements etc. Accounting information supplies necessary information needed for business decision making. Manager of a business concern needs market information, production information and accounting information for taking effective business decisions. Thus, there exists a close link between managerial economics and management accounting. The main task of management accounting is to provide the sort of data which managers need to solve some business problems accurately. The accounting data are also to be provided in such a manner so as to help the managerial economist to take correct decisions in business.

Conclusion

Thus, Managerial Economics is concerned with determining the means of achieving given objectives in the most efficient manner while considering both explicit and implicit constraints on the application of the means. The major areas of Managerial Economics are:

(i) Decision making,
(ii) Demand analysis and forecasting,
(iii) Production and cost,
(iv) Pricing and market structure, and
(v) Capital budgeting and profits.

Managerial economics is firmly rooted on the foundation provided by economics and is enriched by the growing influence of Mathematics, Statistics or Management Accounting.

Scope of Managerial Economics

The scope of Managerial Economics extends to those fields of activity which are carried out by business organisations. Managerial Economics is concerned with solving all problems pertaining to business affairs. It refers to policies of planning and development of business. The subject matter of Managerial Economics is classified under the following broad heads :-

(a) Consumption Analysis with special emphasis on Demand Analysis and forecasting.
(b) Production and Cost Analysis.
(c) Pricing decisions, policies and practices
(d) Profit Management.
(e) Capital Management and
(f) Decision - Making.

(a) Demand Analysis : Spencer and Siegelman defined a business firm as an economic organism which transforms productive resources into consummable goods which are meant for sale in the market. As such, a firm before producing any consummable commodity, must assess the nature of demand for the product. It has to search out and measure the forces that determine sales. In order to estimate the future demand, the manager has to take into consideration the Income Elasticity, Price Elasticity, and Substitution Elasticity of Demand. Demand analysis covers Demand

Determinants, Demand Distinctions and Demand Forecasting. Demand analysis is an important benchmark for appraising saleman's performance and for setting up sales quotas.

(b) Production and cost analysis : The production and cost analysis is another field of study of managerial economics. It helps the manager to attain efficient allocation of productive resources which are scarce. The Production and Cost Analysis is essential for effective project planning. The costs of production of a firm are estimated from the accounting records. From these records, the business manager will be in a position to compare costs of production of different periods and thereby evolves suitable policies in controlling costs and deriving suitable profits.

The production analysis is concerned with proper product mix and what factors are to be combined in what manner to produce a given product. It is done in physical terms while cost analysis is done in financial terms. The important topics discussed in this field are cost concepts, classifications, cost input relationships. economies and diseconomies of scale, production function and cost control.

(c) Pricing decisions, policies and practices : Pricing of the product or products produced by the firm is a very important field of managerial economics. The chief function of the firm is pricing. This depends upon the cost of production and at the same time, the prices of substitutes and the nature of competition. Price affects profits which in turn determine the existence and growth of the firm. The Manager is required to have a thorough knowledge of the theories of production and the pricing in order to make sure that the firm gets profit continuously. The Manager has to determine suitable price policies applicable to short and long-term production.

(d) Capital Management : A business firm is organised with a view to make profit. In order to organise a business firm, the most important requirement is capital. Capital management is efficient use of scarce capital. Capital management is done by means of preparing a Capital budget. It includes both Investment Capital and Working Capital. It also involves short term and long-term requirement. Further it deals with three things - Cost of capital, Rate of return and Selection of project.

(e) Profit Management : Profit Management is central matter in Managerial Economics. A business firm is an organisation designed to make profit and profits are the primary measure of success. Social criteria of business relate to the quality of the product, rate of progress and the behaviour of prices. But these are tests of the desirability of the whole profit system. Within this system, profits are acid test of the individual firm's performance.

The business firm's sacred objective is to make profit but it has to make profit under the situation of uncertainty. This is due to various factors like the prices of resources, the cost of production etc. Since the firms have to work in a world of uncertainty, profit planning becomes very difficult. Yet, it is necessary to plan the future profits in a realistic manner, taking into consideration the element of uncertainty. Profit planning, profit management, profit measurement are the important areas of managerial economics.

(f) Decision making : Decision making is the most important function of the Business Manager. Faced with scarce resources and competing ends, the choice of a final end is to pass value judgment. To try to achieve optimum satisfaction is to realise the objective which may be considered good and reasonable. The economic agent has to act on the principle that scarce resources are put into best advantage and should not be wasted. This is obviously a 'universal human value' affecting all economic behaviour. It is in this context that decision making occupies a central place in management.

Methods of Managerial Economics

Since Economics is recognised as a science, it follows certain methodologies. A systematic way of approach to any problem is called methodology. In fact, method means the mode of rule of accomplishing an end. It is a procedure of examining any economic problem. Some tools are employed to arrive at a solution. These tools are used in a systematic way in managerial economics. A business manager is confronted with many problems. In order to solve these problems, he is required to use some tools of investigation. In other words, he uses certain methods which would help him to understand the problems. These methods are: i. Internal data, ii. The data given by associations, iii. Published data, iv. Field investigations and assistance of specialised agencies. They let us know the details of these methods.

(i) Internal Data

Internal data refers to facts and figures available with the company or a business organisation. When a manager wants to solve the problem, he should have complete knowledge of things going on in his company. He gets the latest figures and facts regarding production, inventory, sales etc. In a modern business organisation, all major departments are expected to maintain complete records. Nowadays they are all computerised. He can get any information within minutes. Let us now see how he can use these figures in order to take a decision. Supposing the sales of a company producing soaps fell down in the previous month. In order to find out the reason and to arrive at a solution, he takes the data of several months of the year. The data from three departments such as production, inventory and sales is as follows :-

Data on Production, Inventory and Sales

Month	*Production*	*Inventory*	*Sales (in tonnes)*
January	3000	2000	4000
February	3100	1000	3100
March	2900	1000	3000
April	2800	900	3000
May	3200	700	3000
June	3000	900	3000
July	3000	900	3000
August	2000	900	2800
September	2000	100	2100
October	2000	Nil	2000
November	2100	100	3000
December	3000	200	2900

With this data, the manager is required to analyze the cause for downward trend in sales, particularly during September and October. From the table, it can be seen that sales actually fell down during September and October. Rest of the months, the sales were normal except in January. A look at the production level will reveal that in months of August, September and October production was only 2000 tonnes. The question is that why the stocks could not be met from the inventory. A look at the inventory position also reveals that the stocks of finished goods fell down from 2000 tonnes to nil in October. This means that the inventory department met the demand of sales department to the maximum extent. In the month of September, the stock fell down to 100 tonnes and in October to nil and hence could not meet the requirement of sales department. Therefore, the problem is with the production department. The solution lies in tackling the causes for decreased production. The manager now takes up measures of increasing production. Thus, internal data is of great help in solving business problems. He will now closely follow the trend in production and inventory management. Huge stocks of inventory means blocking of working capital. A meagre stock or huge stock of finished goods would have a telling effect on sales.

(ii) Associations

Manufacturers form association in order to promote their interests. Association will help the producers in obtaining raw materials, movement of finished goods etc. The members of the association are required to furnish various data, which will compile it and publish it in their annual reports. Members of the association can study these figures supplied by the association. This reveals whether a company is selling more or less. The data is useful in knowing where the company stands in the market. He can now take up suitable measures in improving the sales of its product.

(iii) Published Data

The data furnished by the associations does not give a correct picture of the industry as a whole. It is only partial. In order to get the information at the national level, he has to depend upon the published data brought out either by the government or by research bodies including data published by Planning Commission, Centre for Monitoring Economy, National Council of Applied Economic Research. The D.G.T.D. publishes two books, Annual Report and The Handbook of Statistics. Annual Report contains the data of production of both agricultural and industrial products. The Handbook of Statistics furnishes advance information. From these documents, the business managers can know as to how many units are manufacturing various industrial products, their installed capacity and percentage of utilisation, etc. The Centre of Monitoring Indian Economy brings out several publications periodically. These publications will help in arriving at two important points, namely the production trend over the years and percentage of capacity utilisation. From this, present supply of products can be estimated. On the demand side, the journals like Fortnightly Journal of Indian Economy publishes current as well as future demand. From this, the managers can draw the production schedule of their products.

Besides these, factors like seasonal, economic and climatic are also to be known. The Association of Indian Engineering Industry publishes bulletins to reveal the demand and supply pattern of engineering goods. A managerial economist can arrive at an agreeable conclusion as regards production, inventory and sales.

(iv) Field Investigation

In addition to the above mentioned methods, it is necessary to undertake field investigation. The company can take up this work by itself sending sales executives or personnel to the required areas. Supposing the sales of the product of a particular company in a particular area is sluggish, then the company can take up special investigation. This enquiry may be conducted to find out the various facts, such as number of rival products sold in the region, their prices, their demand, the nature of sales campaign by the rivals, etc. To get answers to these questions, one has to go to the specific area for detailed investigation. The company takes up market survey by itself. On the basis of the survey report, the company can take suitable measures to face the competition.

(iv) Specialised Agencies

If the company finds that its officers are not equipped to undertake this type of enquiry, it can entrust this work to specialised consultancies. Market Survey is a technical job, which only experts can do it efficiently. The consultancy may also furnish many related matters such as potential buyers, their income and their consumption pattern etc. It is also better to entrust such specially technical enquiries to those agencies.

Economic Theories Applied to Managerial Economics

Several concepts and tools are in use in economic theory to analyse various problems concerned with production and consumption. These concepts and tools are very much used in managerial economics too. In fact, economics does not provide ready-made answers to all problems but it offers a variety of broad principles which can be applied with modifications wherever necessary to solve economic problems. In applying economic principles for solving various business problems, the managerial economist has to use additional skills and tools to bridge the gap between economic theory and business practices. It is because, that in actual practice, there exists great disparity between economic principles and actually observed practices in business. The basic principle tools which are used in managerial economics are as follows:

(i) The Opportunity Cost Principle,

(ii) The Incremental Principle,

(iii) The Principle of Time Perspective,

(iv) The Discounting Principle,

(v) The Equi-marginal Principle.

(i) The Opportunity Cost Principle

By opportunity cost, we mean the cost involved in any decision consists of sacrifices of alternatives required by that decision. If there are no sacrifices, there are no costs. The opportunity costs are measured by the sacrifices made in the decision. This can be very well understood by the following examples. The opportunity costs of funds employed in one's own business is the amount of interest income earned if the amount had been used in other projects.

The opportunity cost of using a machine to produce one product is the income forgone which would have been possible from other products. If the machine has only one use, it has no opportunity cost. If the machine has a number of uses, opportunity cost of a product is measured in terms of cost of producing an alternative product. Similarly, the opportunity cost of time an entrepreneur devotes to his own business is the salary that he could earn if he would take up a job with someone else. For decision making, application of opportunity cost principle is very much useful. It is because that it is the only relevant cost.

(ii) The Incremental Principle

Economists use the incremental principle in Consumption, Production, Pricing and Distribution. Incremental concept is closely related to marginal cost and marginal revenue in the theory of pricing. Incremental cost involves estimating the impact of decision alternatives on costs and revenue, emphasising the changes in the total cost and total revenue resulting from changes in prices, products, procedures, investments etc. The two basic components of incremental principle are incremental cost and incremental revenue. Incremental cost is the change in the total cost as a result of new decisions. The incremental principle is useful when the firm wants to expand the production of a commodity. If the incremental revenue is higher than incremental cost, then it is profitable for the manager to expand the business. The moment the incremental revenue is equal to incremental cost, the manager is required to stop further expansion. Incremental principle is very much used in decision taking.

(iii) The Principle of Time Perspective

The Time perspective such as short run and long run or market period, short period, long period and secular period is useful in determining prices of products. Economists have established through analysis, that short term costs and prices are higher than long run prices and costs. In this connection, they have maintained an argument that in the short term, average prices may not cover average costs, but in the long run, they must be equal. The most important aspect in decision taking is that the firm must maintain right balances between short term and long term considerations. Modern economists have introduced a new time perspective called 'intermediate run' between short term and long term in order to explain price and output behaviour of the firm under oligopoly. The principle of time preference can be stated as 'a decision should take into account both the short run and the long run effects on revenues and costs and maintain a right balance between short run and long run perspectives'.

This principle can be explained with the following illustration. If a company has idle capacity, to make use of this idle capacity, it may offer the product at a price lower than the cost. This may be alright in the short period.

Supposing the demand for the product rises, then the firm comes into the problem of building sufficient capacity to increase production. This will result in increased incremental cost. In the long run, the prices will have to equal cost. It is therefore necessary to give due consideration to the time perspective. Haynes, Mote and Paul mentioned an example of a company which followed the stable price policy, even though there was idle capacity. The reason was that the management realised that long run repercussions of pricing below the full cost would be more than offset any short term gain.

(iv) Discounting Principle

Discounting principle occupies a very important place in managerial economics. It is because the future is uncertain. The costs and revenues may change in the future. Whenever the present value of a business is to be known, the future values will have to be discounted. For example, suppose a person is offered to make a choice to make an investment on shares of a company, he will prefer the present value more than the future value. It is because of the uncertainty of the future. If the share is worth Rs. 100, he will prefer Rs.100 today to Rs.100 next year. Even if he is sure to receive Rs. 100 next year, one would do well to receive Rs.100 now and invest it for one year and earn a rate of interest on Rs. 100 for one year. To find out its worth, we have to find out what rate of interest he is going to earn in one year. Suppose the rate of interest is 10 percent. Then we have to discount Rs.100 at 8% in order to find out its present value. The relevant formula for finding out is :

$$PW = \frac{Rs.100}{1+i} \qquad \text{where 'i' is the rate of interest}$$

Present Worth of Rs 100 is $100 \div 1 + 8\% = 100 \div 1.08 = 92.59$

The same logic applies to longer periods. A sum of Rs100 after two years will have a present worth :

$$\frac{Rs.100}{(1+i)^2} = \frac{Rs.100}{(1.08)^2} = \frac{Rs.100}{1.1664} = Rs.\ 85.73$$

The discounting principle is thus stated as follows :

If a decision affects costs and revenues of future dates, it is necessary to discount those costs and revenues to obtain the present values of both before a valid comparison of alternatives can be made.

(v) The Equimarginal Principle

The equimarginal principle is one of the widely used concepts in economics. The law of equimarginal principle states that an input should be allocated in such a way that the value added by the unit of the input is the same in all its uses. This law can be explained with the following illustration.

Suppose a firm has to employ 50 workers in three departments such as spinning, weaving and printing. The firm has to allocate the workers in such a way that the marginal productivity of the last worker employed is the same. Supposing the marginal productivity of labour in spinning is Rs. 20 and in weaving Rs. 30, it is profitable to shift labour from spinning to weaving, thereby there is expansion in B and reduction in A. The optimum is reached when the value of marginal product is equal in all the twin activities. The formula is as follows:

$$VMP_A = VNW_B = VMP_C \text{ etc.}$$

In applying the equimarginal principle or make it more practicable, certain aspects will have to be looked into. Firstly, we have to find out the net value of the marginal products before resorting to comparison. It is because, when a worker is to be added to an activity, it necessitates adding other inputs like machinery. And to find out the net marginal value of the workers, we must deduct from his VMP, the value of additional materials used in the process of production. Supposing the value of the additional material used is Rs.10, then the VMP of the worker is 30 – 10 = 20.

Secondly, the future prices of the products produced by additional labour input is also to be considered. If, as a result of increased production, the price falls, the additional revenue earned by the firm will be less. Then we have to subtract the reduction in revenue from the VMP of the worker in order to get net marginal revenue product of the labour.

Thirdly, it is necessary to discount the revenues made available to the firm from the sale of additional production in the future. Labour is to be paid today, while the output will be sold in future. If a year is required to sell the output, we have to discount the net product for one year.

It should be noted that equimarginal principle works only under ideal conditions. For example, due to non-economic pulls and pressures, an economic activity will have to be carried on, even though additional revenue is negative. This happens especially when the government wants to keep up employment generation programme. There are also certain instances where firms want to expand, managers may resort to spend more than necessary. Managements may not agree to retrench workers even after the introduction of automation, simply because of maintaining good labour relations. In such cases, the equimanagerial principle has to be rendered unworkable.

Summing up, it can be seen that principles and theories of economics are of considerable interest to modern business enterprises. Economic theories as such cannot be directly applied to draw conclusions. Economic theory is meant for generalised study and for applications to practical situations, some modifications have to be made. There is a great need for modification of the assumptions in managerial economics. For example, there is an assumption in the theory of a firm where the entrepreneur saves to maximise his profit. But in actual practice, the businessmen strive to attain a level of profit holding a certain share of the market for his product. Prof. Baumol is of the opinion that firms do not devote all their energies to maximising profit but they seek to maximise the sales revenue. Thus, suitable modifications have to be made to the assumptions of pure economic theory.

Role and Responsibilities of a Managerial Economist

A managerial economist is one who has specialised in basic economic theory and with this knowledge, he applies it to business prosperity. He is very well called an adviser to a firm since the firm takes several economic decisions which are vital to the growth of a firm. He has to study cost - price - output relationship and advise the business in fixing the prices of the making and forward planning. Nowadays, all big business organisations are utilising the services of managerial economists. The managerial economist, by virtue of his expert knowledge, can help the businessmen to take correct decisions.

The managerial economist can help the Board of Management in several ways. He can assist the management in decision making process of what commodities to be produced, how are prices determined and to determine marketing strategy. These are external factors to the firm and are said to constitute the business environment. He can also assist the management in business operations. That is, the firm has to take several decisions as regards the amount of capital to be invested and at what price, the capital has to be modilised and to procure factors of production and at what prices and finally at what price the commodities can be sold etc. These are very complicated and the managerial economist can help the management in solving these issues. To solve these problems, a number of micro and macro variables will have to be studied and this can be done only by the managerial economist. In fact, he has to analyse and forecast external factors which affect the business prosperity. They are certain macro-variables such as the national income, its distribution, volume of both internal and external trade, the monetary and fiscal policies of the Government etc. This is because modern industrial organisations operate in the general economic and institutional framework of the whole economy and the Government policies create a profound impact on business. Therefore, the managerial economist is required to provide necessary information and guidance to tackle problems both during inflation and deflation. The managerial economist has also got to analyse the balance of payments position of the country, exchange rate, import and export policies of the government, etc. so that the industry which is exporting the products can very well make necessary adjustments. The managerial economist is required to tackle various questions which are referred to him. Some of the basic questions which are referred to the managerial economist are:

(i) The present and future outlook of the national economy. The present phase of growth taking place in the economy whether the economy is facing inflation or recession.

(ii) The growth rate of population and the occupational distribution of population and the income pattern of various categories of population.

(iii) The demand pattern of industrial products in internal and external markets - the changes and fashions of the people in different regions of the country and the impact of these on the production and sale of durable goods.

(iv) The consumption pattern of people abroad and the scope of foreign trade of products produced by the firms.

(v) Financial aspect namely the availability and cost of capital both in the country and outside.

(vi) The foreign exchange regulations and sources of foreign capital for the expansion and modernisation of the firms.

In this context, the managerial economist has to acquire knowledge with regard to foreign collaboration.

(vii) The problems of institutional finance for the firms and ways of obtaining institutional finance for the development of the firm.

(viii) Price variations of both raw materials, finished products and the extent of competition that the firm has to face.

(ix) The sectional outlay of five-year plans and its effect on the production and sale of company's product. Supposing the outlay on agricultural mechanisation is increased by 10 or 15 per cent over the previous plan's outlay, then producers of machineries are required to formulate plans of development, such as quantity of steel and other materials required and fixation of prices for different categories of agricultural machineries.

(x) The economic policies of Government and how far they are helpful for affecting the growth of the activities of the firm.

(xi) The policies concerning the company taxation, general excise duties, import and export duties etc.

(xii) The decisions of the Central Bank of the country with regard to interest rates on short term and long term borrowing and their rules and regulations etc.

Thus, the field of enquiry of the managerial economist is so vast that he is required to have up-to-date knowledge of economic trends at the macro level in order to offer required advice to the industry. These are relating to external operations of the firm for which the managerial economist has a greater role to play in the firm. Professors K.J.W. Alexander and Alexander G. Kemp have outlined specific functions of the managerial economist in an industrial organisation, which are as follows :

(i) Sales forecasting,
(ii) Industrial market research,
(iii) Economic analysis of competitors,
(iv) Pricing of industrial products,
(v) Capital budgeting,
(vi) Production programmes,
(vii) Future investment programmes,
(viii) Advice on trade and public relations,
(ix) Advice on the purchase of raw materials,
(x) Advice on inventory building,
(xi) Advice on the use and conservation of foreign exchange earnings,
(xii) Market survey to determine the nature and extent of competition,
(xiii) Environmental aspects.

The fields of enquiry of the managerial economist are so exhaustive that he becomes a key person in an industrial organisation.

The managerial economist has to keep an eye on the fast changing technological developments. An economic decision is taken within the framework of technological developments. Therefore, he has to make a continuous assessment of the impact of technological changes. If the firm does not make suitable changes in the production and marketing strategies, it fails to face competition of the rival firms. In this context, he has to find out ways and means of economising and thereby minimise the cost of production.

Above all, the managerial economist has to help the management in business planning by offering guidance for the correct running of the industrial organisation. Organisationally, the managerial economist has to work in harmony with the policymakers of the industry, for the successful functioning of the firms.

The managerial economists perform varied functions. Apart from sales forecasting and market research, they have to maintain statistical records of sales performance not only of their industrial organisations, but also the rival firms. Every firm wants to sell more and capture a greater portion of industry sales and for this purpose, the managerial economist is required to guide them.

The fundamental function of the managerial economist in an industrial organisation is to supply economic information to the management. The information includes the prices of the rivals of the products, the consumers' attitude towards the price and quality of the products, tax rates, tariffs rates etc. He is required to collect all the information, analyse them and present them to the management.

In India

Managerial economists in India are required to perform the following functions. The main fields of activity of the managerial economists in this context are as follows :-

(i) Macro forecasting of demand and supply. The Planning Commission projects future demand and supply of various commodities. The managerial economists are required to modify them in the light of past performance .

(ii) Micro and Macro level production planning. Macro level production planning is made by the Planning Commission and also National Council of Applied Economic Research. The managerial economists are required to project the production trends of their units taking into consideration their production capacities and normal constraints such as transport bottlenecks, fuel and power shortage, working capital constraints and market absorption.

(iii) Planning of capacity production and determination of product mix.

(iv) Preparing economic feasibility of new production processes, diversification of production etc.

(v) Participating in the planning process of company's development.

(vi) Preparing periodical economic reports on company's product sales, of rival products, consumers' preferences, future growth opportunities, general price trends and national and international factors affecting the prospects of industry as well as the units concerned.

(vii) Participating in seminars, conferences, workshops organised by Chambers of Commerce or Industry's Association.

(viii) Preparing rules and principles which facilitate in attaining the goals and objectives of the company. These goals relate to costs, revenues and profits áre important within both the business and non-business institutions.

(ix) Suggesting how economic theories and methodologies can be applied in the decision making process of the firm.

Responsibilities of the Managerial Economist

Managerial economics is a composite discipline. It contains quantitative statements as well as statements touching ethical aspects. Managerial economics is more practical than theoretical and as such the managerial economist has to study practical economic implications of any decision taking. The main responsibilities of the managerial economist are as follows:

(i) Better Management of Resources

Though managerial economics is normative, it cannot ignore the positive aspect. Positive economics is a scientific discipline while normative economics is a branch of ethics. If the firm is to attain success in business, it has to produce products of exceptionally high quality and sell it at reasonable prices. This requires better management of men and resources. The utilisation of optimum production capacity, the exploitation of hidden talents in the manpower, better financial management are *sine qua non* for success in business. It is said that the opinion of the managerial economist on a normative question is of no more value than guessing the result of a football match. This field rests with management itself. But the role of the managerial economist in the organisation is that of a pure scientist leaving the normative aspect to the management.

(ii) Economic Forecast

The firms function in certain social, economic and political systems. For example, we assume the existence of mixed economy in which individuals enjoy right to property. We also assume that law and order prevails in the country and every one is subordinate to rule of law and there exists stable political system. The existence of free markets is assumed. The markets keep buyers and sellers of a commodity in touch with one another. That is how prices are determined and a uniform price prevails for a product in the market. The managerial economist functions in such at social and political environment and thus manages the affairs in perfect coordination and understanding. He cannot function in an ivory tower. He functions in realities. Therefore, economists have to function in an environment where resources are scarce and technical factors put a limitation on industrial output etc. Though the managerial economist works in an uncertain environment, he is required to forecast the demand for the product, the sales turnover, the net profits etc as realistic as possible. His analysis should indicate the risks that the company may experience in varied situations. The economic forecast is like weather forecast, as such, in the midst of uncertainties, the forecast should suggest how the management can adjust the production and marketing of the product and withstand the economic fluctuations.

The managerial economist is required to watch carefully the happenings of his forecast, he is required to alert the management at the earliest possible time.

The managerial economist is a thinker. He is a friend and philosopher of the industrialists. He should, therefore, be both conceptual as well as practical. He must possess a good knowledge of working of the individual units as well as the industry as a whole and the behaviour of the market and business conditions and likely changes that take place in the economy. Then only he can successfully function as an economic adviser.

Apart from being an adviser of the organisation, he is also a researcher. Economic research is an effective tool for any realistic forecasting. Therefore, he is required to come in contact with data sources and collect the essential data pertaining to his field, to use it whenever necessary.

To conclude, the managerial economist has an important role to play by helping the management in decision making and forward planning. He has to recognise his responsibilities and obligations in the firm, if he has to perform an effective role.

Questions

1. "Business Economics has a close connection with micro-economic theory and macro-economic theory of decision making and forward planning". Elucidate.
2. Define Managerial Economics and discuss its scope.
3. Discuss the functions and responsibilities of Managerial Economist.
4. Explain the fundamental concepts of Managerial Economics.
5. "Managerial Economics is economics applied to decision-making". Explain.
6. Explain how managerial economics is related to Economics, Mathematics, Statistics and Accounting.

Short answer questions

1. Is Managerial Economics a positive science or normative science.
2. Is Managerial Economics prescriptive or descriptive.
3. Explain the uses of operational research in Managerial Economics.
4. What are the limitations of Managerial Economics.
5. What is the significance of forward planning to a firm.
6. Mention the functions of Managerial Economist.

❖❋❖❋❖

CHAPTER 2

OBJECTIVES OF THE FIRM

Meaning of the Firm

A *firm* is defined as an organisation carrying on economic activities like production, distribution and marketing of goods and services with a view to earn profit. In traditional economic theory, a firm is defined as an organisation of an individual or a group of individuals formed to achieve economic objectives. A firm in modern period is defined as a joint stock company in which decisions are taken by the shareholders and they are executed by the Company Officers.

Whether the firm is owned by an individual or by groups of persons, the goal is to make profit. Once this goal is ensured, the next goal, namely the expansion of the firm comes into existence. The traditional economists keeping profit maximisation as the goal of the firm, formulated a theory which is called *equilibrium* of a firm. They said that when a firm is in equilibrium position, it is earning maximum money profits.

As regards the objectives of a firm, Prof. Galbraith in his book *'The Goals of Industrial System'* says, 'Any organisation, as for any organism, the goal has a natural assumption of pre-eminence', it is the survival of the organisation". Survival here refers to obtain normal earnings. Once a firm accomplishes this objective, it plans to expand the activities of the firm, which means assuming more resposibilities in the organisation. The goals of expansion are followed by growth and then by technological development. This means taking up of innovation. In course of time, a business firm with a simple objective grows to a goal institution with multiple objectives.

The goals of a business firm are classified under five heads such as production goal, inventory goal, the sales goal, the market share goal and the profit goal.

Profit - Making Objective

The producer in a modern business firm is interested in maximising profits. The term *profit maximisation* means generation of largest absolute amount of profits over a period of time. Here the term period `time' is used to refer to both short period and long period. The term profit maximisation refers not to normal profit but to super-normal profit. The normal profits are minimum income which the entrepeneur must get if he wants to stay in business. The normal profit is a fixed amount independent of the level of the output that a firm earns. Since the normal profit is included in average cost, it does not come under the principle of profit maximisation. It is the super-normal profit maximisation. Therefore, it is the super-normal profits which is the residual income of the entrepreneur which he aims at maximising.

There has been a controversy regarding this objective. Some economists stick to this assumption while some others oppose it tooth and nail. Some economists hold the view that businessmen are interested in maximising the profit for each accounting period. For them, immediate profit is more important than future profit. But there are some economists who object to this view say, that businessmen emphasise on the future in the concept of profits. According to them, profit is defined as the maximum dividend that a company can pay without impairing its ability to pay the same dividend in the subsequent years.

A Reality

A doubt has been expressed by many regarding the reality of the concept of maximising profit. In fact, profit maximisation theory justifies its stand on the ground that it is necessary for a business to meet the social welfare obligation. Secondly, the goal of profit maximisation is forced on him by the impact of competing firms, namely, if he can make profit, he survives; otherwise, he will have to disappear from business. These justifications of profit maximisation have been criticised on the following grounds.

Criticism

Enlightened businessmen vehemently oppose the concept of profit maximisation as their business objective. They say that service of society rather than personal profit is their aim. In an modern industrial organisation, decisions are taken by salaried executives rather than owners of the firm. They aim at sales maximisation. So long as competition is keen, the demand for the product is high, and any firm, however inefficient, can make profit. Profit maximisation in such circumstances will not be the objective. Then, the objective of profit maximisation is difficult to realise. If a businessman wants to maximise his profit, he has to fix a price, so as to equalise marginal cost and marginal revenue. This means that he must be able to estimate the demand at all prices and marginal cost at all outputs. This is a very difficult task and it is not practiced anywhere.

Further, some have considered profit maximisation as immoral. Thoms J. Hailstones in his book *'Readings in Economics'* observes, "Profit maximisation requires the businessmen to use every trick he can think of to keep wages and fringe benefits down to extract the last possible dollar from the consumer to sell low quality merchandise as he can legally hoodwink the customer into buying, to use income solely for the benefits of the stock holder, to disclaim any responsibility to the community, to wrangle the lowest possible price from his vendors regardless of its effect on them" and so on.

It is also a fact that business practices followed by the businessmen are not consistent with the profit maximisation principle. Businessmen are also guided by a sense of fairness, adequacy etc. in fixing the prices for their products. If they get a certain percentage of profit, they are highly satisfied.

Thus, profit maximisation is far from the realistic objective of business firms. We can conclude by quoting Dorfman, "on balance, the maximisation hypothesis is not as firmly grounded in the facts of life as a fundamental scientific hypothesis should be. But substantial and prolonged divergences from the behaviour, it implies, are rare particularly in industries with many participants. It therefore can still be entertained as a sound working hypothesis".

Long term survival

The theory of long term survival as an objective of business was developed by Prof.Rothschild.

It is stated that when a businessman fixes the price for his product, his aim is not to get maximum profit but to satisfy his sense of security. It means that he aims at getting good income for many years to come, so that he does not suffer from insecurity. In other words, the objective of the entrepreneur is to get a steady flow of profit for a long time to come. What Prof.Rothschild says in this connection is worth to ponder over. "Profit maximisation has until now served as the wounderful master-key that opened all the doors leading to an understanding of the entrepreneur's behaviour...". But there is another motive which cannot be so lightly dismissed and which is probably of a similar order of magnitude as the desire for maximum profit, the desire to secure profits.

In a market structure like imperfect competition and monopolistic competition, where there are large number of firms operating, profit maximisation may become valid objective. But under perfect competition, where the price is fixed by the industry and the individual firm has to accept the prevailing price, but has no option, the question of profit maximisation does not arise. In the case of monopolistic competition and absolute monopoly, the entrepreneurs are in a position to fix the price and hence is not possible. The oligopolist has both desire and the power to achieve a secure position. In such a market situation, the desire for security is more desirable than profit maximisation.

Sales Maximisation

Prof. Baumol has developed a model in which he says maximisation of sales revenue is an alternative goal of maximisation. He says that maximisation of sale rather than maximisation of profit is the ultimate objective of the entrepreneur. He has added, that sales have become an end of themselves and not merely as a means of improving operational efficiency and profit. Baumol regards sales maximiisation as the most valid assumption governing the behaviour of the firm. Sales maximisation means maximum revenue from sales. The objective of the firm is to sell as high as possible, so that the firm gets more revenue. Prof.Baumol also calls his model 'Revenue Maximisation Hypothesis'.

Prof. Baumol in his book *`Business Behaviour, Value and Growth'* expounds his approach. He says, when the sales of the firm increase, the profits of the firm will also increase. Therefore, by increasing the sales, the firm is fulfilling the objective of profit maximisation. He makes his position very clear by analysing this concept that the entrepeneurs promote sales without incurring additional costs so that his determined rate of return of investment is not affected. He maintains that the firm is not going to sacrifice its assumed profit if sales were to increase. So, he observed, "So long as profits are high enough to keep stockholders satisified and contribute adequately to the firnancing of company's growth, management will bend its efforts to the augmentation of sales revenue rather than to further increase its proifts".

The sales maximisation hypothesis is explained with the help of the following diagram :

In this diagram, the firm aims at selling a maximum output with earning minimum profit. TR is the total revenue from the sales of the product. TC is the total cost incurred for producing the output. TP curve represents the total cost incurred for producing the output. TP curve represents the total profit. At the output OA, the profits is the maximum. If the firm aims at producing the output OD, the sales revenue is DR3. At this, total profit is less. Hence, the firm sells OB output and at this output, the total sales revenue is BR1 and the firm is earning minimum profits. Thus Prof. Baumol concludes that the firm maximises total revenue without incurring any loss, but his minimum profit is maintained.

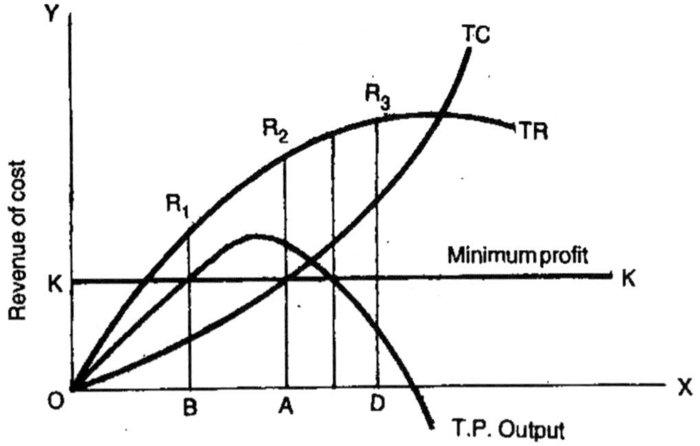

Maximisation of balanced rate of growth

The balanced rate growth model is propounded by Prof. Morris. He suggested a variation to Baumol's model of sales maximisation and called it maxmisation of growth. According to Prof.Morris, the objective of the firm is the maximisation of balanced rate of growth of the firm. The executives of the firm are interested in salary, status, power, prestige and security, while the owners(shareholders)are concerned about profit, market share and output, etc. Thus, the goals of the shareholders differ from that of the manager. Prof.Morris correlating the goals of the owners and the managers, reduced the variable to a single variable, namely the size of the firm. Thus, he concluded that the managers are concerned with the rate of growth of the size of the firm. Morris defined the size of the firm in terms of Corporate Capital which is equivalent to sum of the value of the assets, the inventories and the cash at the office.

Prof. Morris added that the balance of growth model is not without constraints. He says that the firm has to face two constraints. Firstly, the constraint comes from the limit of the expansion of managerial skill. Secondly, it comes from finances.

Keeping the above constraints in mind, Prof. Morris has argued that the managers aim to have a balanced growth of demand for the product and supply of capital. If the managers decide to expand the firm too rapidly by establishing risky projects, then the balanced rate of growth concept will be defeated. The balanced rate of growth involves not only bringing sufficient profits to the shareholders, but also safeguarding the interests of managers.

Thus, the rationale for this objective is that by combining the objective of shareholders and the managers in a suitable manner, the balanced rate of growth of the firm can be achieved.

Satisfying Model

The satisfying objective has been put forth by Prof. Simon. He put forth the behavioural theory of the firm in1955 itself. Behaviour theory is purely psychological in character but it combines with industrial economics. This approach centres round on the decision making process of the large multi-product firm under uncertainty in an imperfect market. Prof. Simon calls his model satisfying behaviour of the managers in such type a of firm. The managers in such firms take decisions for the future on the basis of the information they get. This information might not be accurate. As a result of this, any decision taken might not be practicable. Management under such uncertainty and incomplete information, takes decisions which satisfies their calculations. In fact, the management determines a `satisfactory aspiration level' on the basis of past experience and judgement determines about the uncertainty of the future. If the aspiration is fulfilled easily, the future operations are revised upwards, and if the aspiration is not fulfilled, then the future operations are revised downwards. In these calculations, the management is satisfied with the deicision taken.

The management tries to satisfy, but not to maximise either profits or sales. In other words, the firm wants to see that the overall performance is executed in accordance with the desired goals.

The satisfying behaviour concept also suffers from certain flaws. Prof. Simon talks about the nature of information and says that it is generally incomplete and imperfect. It is not clear, how information supplied by the organisation is imperfect. The important fact in Simon's approach is that the management is required to adjust to the changing conditions. Prof. Simon makes an ambitious aim, namely co-ordinating the objectives of both the owners and the managers.

The behaviour model of Prof. Simon was subsequently modified by Cyert and March. According to them, assuming that the world is uncertain and changing the market conditions is imperfect, the absence of accurate information about changed conditions are imperfect in the industry or the economy and with limited ability of managers, the firm cannot work with global rationality. Under these conditions, the firms aspire for a reasonable profit and a reasonable sales of the product or products.

Before any firm can arrive at a decision, it has to keep in mind the restrictions that it has to contend with. These restrictions can arise in two ways. Sometimes, they may come from within the organisation i.e. they are internal to the firm. For example, a firm, which has every capital at its disposal need not explore all alternative possibilities of goods and services that it can produce. Knowing that it has limited capital, it may explore only a few possibilities and decide to produce one of the goods. Here, capital is the constraint which has to be kept in mind before arriving at the decision of what to produce.

Conversely, sometimes there are restrictions such as making by external factors quantity, unavailability of sufficient quantity of raw materials, or restrictions imposed by laws and regulations etc. Some of the important external restrictions are discussed below:

(i) Restrictions Relating to Output

In case of most of the commodities, the quantity that has to be produced by the firms is determined by an external authority. This authority has the liberty to specify how much has to be produced and this can act as a restriction to the producing firm.

Again, the licensing authority can specify the rules relating to the quantity of the commodity and the firm is expected to abide by it. This can also act as a constraint to the producing firm. For example, the firm producing baby foods may be expected to meet certain nutritional requirements specified by the competent authority.

(ii) Restrictions Relating to Resources

Quantity of resources available to a firm may be fined or limted, keeping the availability of resources, on the basis of which the firm will have to take the appropriate decision. Especially in a developing country like India, scarcity of resources acts as a major obstruction to the firm's production levels.

(iii) Restrictions Imposed by Law

The government may impose certain restrictions on the firm's activities. It may define specifically the level of wages and bonus, or the measures to be taken to maintain the health and safety of employees. Restrictions may also take the form of taxes, subsidies, quotas, differential rates of interest on loans etc. Before the firm can arrive at any decision, it has to consider all these legally imposed restrictions.

(iv) Restrictions Imposed by Environmental Factors

All firms have to operate within the framework of a given economic, social and political environment. These environments may vary from country to country. The decision making firm, therefore, needs to have a clear knowledge of these environments both within the domestic economy and also outside it, because today no economy is a closed economy.

The decision maker must have a thorough knowledge about all aspects relating to objectives and policies of the government. such as plan objectives, industrial policies, fiscal and monetary policies, foreign trade policy etc. He is also expected to have a fair idea in all the relevant macro-economic trends such as national income, money supply, levels of poverty and unemployment etc. It is necessary for him to keep track of the changing social and political environment in the country.

It is in these matters that the service of economists and analysts can be of great use to the producers. They and specialists who are in constant touch with the changes that are occuring in the economy is their responsibility to keep the top level management well informed about the forthcoming changes.

Decision Process

The goal of managerial economics is to solve practical problems of business. This requires decision making at the level of the firm. Decision making is the process of selecting the appropriate action from among various alternative actions. Decisions have far reaching effects on the firm and are often easy to make. The following steps should be followed to arrive at right decisions:

(a) To establish objectives,
(b) To express the decision-problem,
(c) To identify alternatives,
(d) To assess alternatives,
(e) To select the best possible alternative,
(f) To implement the decision,
(g) To monitor the performance.

At the outset, it is necessary to be clear about the objectives of a firm. In today's complex world, there are many alternatives available to a firm and also several constraints facing them. In order to have a clear understanding of these, a through examination of the environment-opportunities and constraints is necessary. An evaluation of alternatives involves collection of all relevant data and their analysis through appropriate techiques. Once the above four steps are completed, it is simple to choose an alternative on the basis of the objective. However, implementation of the decision taken requires resources, an explanation to those who are affected by it and the ability to face the consequences. After implementing the decision, its performance must be monitored in comparison with expectations, so that errors are minimised in the future.

Ours is a dynamic economy and decisions have to be made within time constraint. Things change over time and an undue delay in decision-making may turn opportunities into risks.

Conclusion

The business firms have certain goals to be fulfilled. The main goal is to produce and market the goods and services which satisfy the buyers and thereby earn a profit sufficient for the survival and growth of business. While discussing about the business objective, Peter Drucker says that the objectives of the firm are market standing, innovation, productivity, economical use of productive resources including finance, improved performance of men and machinery, co-operation and public responsibility. He says that a firm has to earn profit and also meet the social objectives.

Profit making is no doubt an essential function of a business firm. Adam Smith considered that profit is a device which transforms the selfishess of mankind into channels of useful service. Prof. Drucker also holds the same view. According to him, profit serves three main objectives:

(i) It measures the effectiveness and soundness of the business enterprise.

(ii) It helps to cover the risk in business.

(iii) It ensures supply of future capital for invasion, expansion and thus enhance the wealth of the society.

Profit as such is not at all a defective objective. The future growth of the economy depends upon generation and reinvestment of profit. Profit serves as a motivation for expansion, diversification and lastly innovation.

Questions

1. "Among the multiplicity of objectives that a modern firm has, profit maximisation continues to be the most important". Comment .
2. How far is profit maximisation relevant to a modern business organisation. Explain it to a modern business organisation.
3. Explain the concept of sales maximisation as an objective of a firm.
4. What do you mean by revenue maximisation. How is it different from profit maximisation.

Short Answer Questions

1. Define the firm and state its objectives.

❖✻❖✻❖

CHAPTER 3

DEMAND ANALYSIS

THE THEORY OF CONSUMER BEHAVIOUR

The Utility Concept

People buy goods because they satisfy the wants of the people. Utility means the want satisfying power of a commodity. Utility is defined as a property of the commodity which satisfies the wants of the consumers. Utility is purely subjective in character. It depends upon the mental attitude of the consumers. Being subjective, it varies from individual to individual. It means, different persons derive different utilities for the same product. People know utility of goods by means of introspection. The desire for a commodity by a person depends upon the utility he expects from a commodity. If the desire for the commodity is greater, then its utility to the person is also higher. It should be noted that the question of morality does not influence the utility. The commodity may not be useful in the ordinary sense of the term, even then it may provide utility to some people. For example, cigarettes have no utility for non-smokers. But for the smokers, cigarettes bring utility. Thus, the concept of utility is ethically neutral.

Total Utility

Utility of a commodity or commodities are additive. It means utility of various goods or different quantities of the same goods can be added to obtain total utility. Total utility refers to the sum total of satisfaction which a consumer receives by consuming various units of the same commodity. The more units of a commodity that a consumer consumes, his total utility of that commodity is high. As a consumer goes on consuming more and more units of a commodity, he eventually reaches the maximum level of satisfaction, that is the total utility reaches the maximum point and if the consumption increases beyond this point, total utility also diminishes.

Marginal Utility

There is another concept in theory of consumption namely the marginal utility. Marginal utility refers to the utility of every additional unit of a commodity consumed. Mariginal utility can be defined as a change in total utility resulting from a one unit change in the consumption of a commodity at a particular point of time. Normally, when a person is buying a commodity, he consciously or unconsciously weighs the utility he is going to offer. He will continue buying different units of a commodity till the marginal utility of the unit is equal to the price. This concept is very well explained by Stonier and Hague as "A consumer will exchange money for units of a commodity A up to the point where last (marginal) unit of A which he buys has for him a marginal significance in terms of money just equal to its money price.' Let us take up the following example :

Units of a Commodity (Apple)	Total Utility	Marginal Utility
1	20	20
2	37	17
3	51	14
4	62	11
5	68	6
6	68	0
7	64	-4
8	50	-14

In the above example, total utility goes on increasing until the consumption of 5th unit. It is very important to note that the increase is in the diminishing rate. The total utility is the maximum at 6th unit (68), then afterwards it falls.

In the case of marginal utility, it is 20 for the first unit and goes on decreasing with every additional unit consumed. It becomes zero for the 6th unit and becomes negative for the subsequent unit. If the table is converted into a graph, the diagram appears as follows :

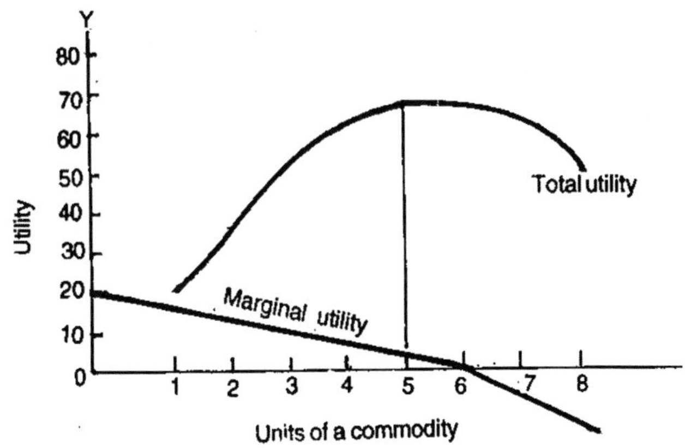

The total utility curve rises gradually and reaches the maximum at the 6th unit of a commodity and afterwards diminishes. Marginal utility curve slopes downwards from left to right from the first unit onwards. Marginal utility curve cuts OX axis at the 6th unit and falls below the axis afterwards. It shows that as the quantity of the commodity with the consumer increases, its marginal utility decreases. This is called the Theory of *Diminishing Marginal Utility*. The question now to be solved is why does marginal utility fall when the quantity of the commodity with the consumer increases. The reasons for this phenomena are- even though human wants in the aggregate are unlimited, yet a particular want can be satisfied fully. Therefore, when a person consumes more and more units of a commodity, his want is satisfied and that he does not want any more. Thus, his marginal utility decreases as consumption of that commodity increases. A stage is reached that further consumption brings marginal utility to zero.

Another reason is that goods are imperfect substitutes to one another. Different commodities satisfy different wants. When a person goes on consuming more and more units of a commodity, the marginal utility falls as his want is satisfied. But, if the commodity could be substituted for other commodities, it would have satisfied other wants. Hence, its marginal utility would not have decreased even though its quantity increases.

The Law of Diminishing Marginal Utility

Marshall, who was the famous exponent of the theory of marginal utility, defines the law of diminishing marginal utility as follows: "The additional benefit which a person derives from a given increase of his stock of a thing diminishes with every increase in the stock that he already has'. Prof. Lipsey defines it as "For any individual consumer, the value that he attaches to successive units of a particular commodity will diminish steadily as his total consumption of that commodity increases".

This means that as the consumer consumes more of a commodity, the utility of every additional unit consumed diminishes.

Assumptions of the Law of Diminishing Marginal Utility

1. Various units of a commodity are homogeneous.
2. There is no time gap between the consumption of different units.
3. Every consumer wants to maximise utility.
4. The tastes and preferences of the consumer remains the same during the period of consumption.
5. Marginal utility of money remains the same.

Limitations of the Law

The law of diminishing marginal utility suffers from certain limitations. These are discussed below:-

(i) ***Homogeneity***

It is assumed that the units of the commodity consumed must be homogeneous.The size of the unit and the quality of the unit must be the same. Normally, this is very difficult to fulfil. For example, if we take an apple, the taste, the size, etc. differ from unit to unit.Unless the units are of suitable size and quality, the law will not hold good. The initial quantity must be greater than the critical minimum.

(ii) ***Suitable Time***

The time of consumption should not vary. The commodity is consumed within a certain time. If you take the first cup of coffee at 8.a.m and the next cup at 3 p.m., there is no reason why the utility of the second cup of coffee is less. If the second cup of coffee is taken at 8.10 am., the third cup at 8.20 a.m., and the fourth cup at 8.30 a.m, then the law of diminishing marginal utility will definitely operate.

(iii) ***No Change in the Taste of the Consumer***

This is an important assumption in which the character of the consumer should not change. After taking a cup of coffee at 8 am., he takes a cup of tea at 9 a.m., the utility increases. In fact, if one hears more music, reads more literature and earns more and more, utility will increase in each case. On the other hand, if a person hears the same song, reads the same book, utility is bound to diminish. If a person earns more and more money, the utility of additional earnings will definitely be less. But it is not so in the case of a miser.

(iv) ***Normal Persons***

The law of diminishing marginal utility applies to normal persons and not to eccentric or abnormal persons. The law assumes that the consumer behaves rationally. If he behaves in an irrational manner, the law does not operate.

(v) ***Constant income***

The law assumes that the income of the consumer remains the same during the period of consumption. Any change in income will falsify the law. If the income of a consumer rises in the course of a given consumption time, the presently consumed commodity becomes inferior and he goes in for a superior commodity. Even here if the person buys more and more units of a superior good, then the additional units of commodity brings less utility.

Thus, the law of diminishing marginal utility is a statement of tendency. It depends upon so many conditions - if these conditions are not fulfilled, law does not operate.

It is worth noting that the law of diminishing utility does not operate because, the successive units of the commodity are inferior. In fact, utility is less in the case of inferior commodities.

It follows from this law that more urgent wants are satisfied first. As stock increases, it will be put to less urgent uses and the reduction in stock would mean reversing the process.

Uses of the Law

The law of diminishing utility is very much useful in both economic theory and policy. In determining the price of a commodity, the concept of marginal utility plays a crucial role. The law has helped in explaining paradox of value - namely water-diamond paradox. Though water is essential for life it has no price. On the other hand, diamond is not essential, but has a high price. According to modern economists, total utility of a commodity does not determine the price but the marginal utility of a commodity determines the prices. Water on account of its plentiful supply, its relative marginal utility is less.Therefore, it has less price. On the other hand, diamonds are scarce and its marginal utility is very high and hence it commands a high price.

The law of diminishing marginal utility explains the reason for the downward sloping of a demand curve. Further, the concept of consumer surplus is based upon the law of diminishing marginal utility.

Another important use of this concept is in the field of direct taxation. For the rich people with higher income, marginal utility of money is low. On the other hand, the poor people with less income find marginal utility of money very high. Hence, higher direct taxes are levied on the rich while the poor are exempted.

Consumer's Equilibrium

Consumer's equilibrium is explained with the help of the law of marginal utility. The consumer with a given outlay of money, has to spend on various goods and services. Now, the question is, how he should allocate the given money among various goods.

Supposing he has to buy only one commodity, he will attain equilibrium at a point of units of the commodity where the marginal utility equals price. In the case of more than one commodity, the same principle is extended. It means the marginal utilities of goods and their prices should be equal. This is called the Law of Equi-marginal Utility. The Law of Equimarginal Utility states that the consumer would distribute his money income between the goods in such a way that the utility derived from the last rupee spent on each good is equal. In other words, a consumer attains equilibrium when marginal utility of money expenditure on each goods is the same. In other words,

$$\frac{\text{Marginal utility of `X' commodity}}{\text{Price of that commodity}} = \frac{\text{Marginal utility of `Y' commodity}}{\text{Price of `Y' Commodity}}$$

Let us take up the following example in order to understand this principle clearly.

Marginal utility of X and Y goods

Units	Marginal utility of X Commodity	Marginal utility of Y Commodity
1	20	24
2	18	21
3	16	18
4	14	15
5	12	9
6	10	3

Let us assume that price of X commodity is Rs. 2 per unit and that of Y is Rs. 3 per unit. Reconstructing the above table by dividing them with price, the reconstructed table will be as follows:-

Units	Mu of X Commodity'/ Price of X	Mu of Y Commodity'/ Price of Y
1	10	8
2	9	7
3	8	6
4	7	5
5	6	3
6	5	1

Now, with a given money income, i.e. he allots Rs. 19 to buy these goods, he will purchase 5 units of X commodity and 3 units of Y commodity and attains equilibrium. At 5th unit of X commodity, $\frac{\text{mu of X}}{\text{price of X}}$ is equal to $\frac{\text{mu of Y}}{\text{price of Y}}$ of 3rd unit of Y commodity.

The diagrammatic expression of the theory of consumer's equilibrium is as follows:

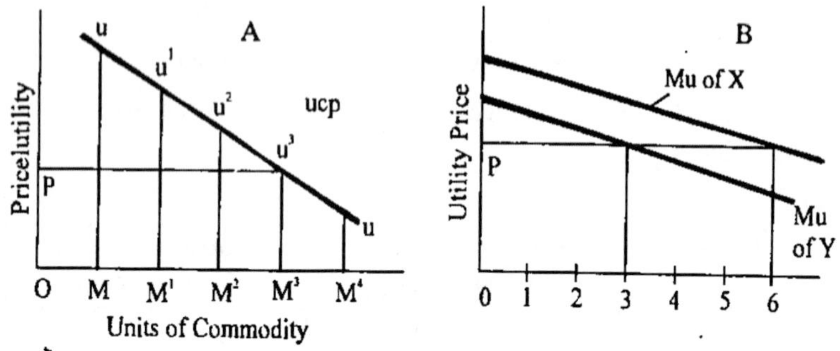

In the case of one commodity, the consumers buy (A) 4 units of X commodity because the price is equal to utility of the 4th unit. In the 'B' diagram, consumer buys two commodities X and Y. He buys 6 units of X and 3 units of Y commodity and attains equilibrium.

Importance of Utility Analysis

Utility analysis is the basis of demand theory. With the help of law of diminishing marginal utility, the law of demand is formulated. As stated above, the law of demand or demand curve shows the relationship between the price of the commodity and its quantity demanded. Marshall derived the demand curve for a commodity from its utility function. The law of demand can be derived in two ways: firstly, with the aid of law of diminishing marginal utility and secondly, with the help of equimarginal utility.

The law of marginal utility states that as the quantity of a good increases, marginal utility of the goods falls. In other words, marginal utility curve is downward sloping. Now the consumer goes on purchasing goods but the marginal utility of goods equal the price. He will be at equilibrium. His satisfaction will be maximum when marginal utility equals price. When the price of a good falls, its utility also falls. It therefore follows that diminishing marginal utility curve implies downward sloping demand curve.

According to the law of equimarginal utility, the consumer is in equilibrium in regard to his purchases of various goods when marginal utilities of goods are proportional to their prices. Thus, the consumer is in equilibrium when he is buying the quantities of two goods in such a way that it satisfies the following rule of proportion.

$$\frac{\text{mu of X}}{\text{price of X}} = \frac{\text{mu of Y}}{\text{price of Y}} \text{etc,}$$ where Mu stands for marginal utility of price of that commodity.

The consumer will be in equilibrium when he equalises mariginal utility of money expectations with the ratio of marginal utility and the price of each commodity. Supposing the price of X commodity falls and price of Y commodity and consumer's money income remain the same, then the equilibrium position also is disturbed. With the lower price, $\frac{\text{Mu X}}{\text{P X}}$ will be greater than $\frac{\text{Mu X}}{\text{P X}}$. In order to restore equilibrium, marginal utility of X must be reduced by buying more of X goods. It is thus clear when the price of a good falls, the quantity demanded of that commodity rises.

THE LAW OF DEMAND

INTRODUCTION

People are talking about consumption and production of goods and services for centuries. Producers make goods in order to satisfy the consumption of wants of the people. If no one consumes, there will be no production at all. Consumption is thus, the end of productive activity. What goods are to be produced and in what quantities depend on what is demanded by the people. Thus, the knowledge of demand is indispensable for managers to determine what to be produced and how much to be produced. Here also lies the important thing, namely the price of the product. Demand analysis is concerned with the size of the demand for the product.There are three managerial aspects of demand - one is the Analysis and Forecasting of Demand, second is the Effect of Demand on the activities of the firm. Then the third is the Positive Approach of meeting the demand.

Demand Analysis has two main managerial purposes: 1) Forecasting sales 2) Manipulating demand. The first is passive managerial aspects of demand because it represents factors which influence the firm, the second is active which represents what the firm can influence. Forecasting implies knowledge of the factors likely to affect demand in a given situation. Sales forecasting is only passive because it estimates external economic factors and predicts the amount of sales that the firm can do. But in a free economy, since consumers enjoy absolute freedom to consume, the producers have to take up production of those commodities which people expect to buy. The demand analysis unearths the main issue of what people want and how much do they want.

DEMAND DETERMINANTS

The demand for the product is essentially the attitude of consumers towards the product. The consumer's attitude gives rise to actions in buying so many units of a product at different prices. Precisely stated, the demand for a commodity is the amount of it that a consumer will purchase or will be ready to take off from the market at various prices at a given time. Thus, demand in economics implies both the desire to buy and ability to pay for a product. It is to be noted that mere desire does not constitute demand, if it is not supported by the ability to pay for it. For example, a poor man wants to have a car, but this does not constitute demand, because he has not got the necessary money to buy it. Again, a miser has plenty of money but he has not got the necessary desire to have a car. These do not constitute demand. Thus, demand in economics means desire backed up by adequate purchasing power to pay for the product when demanded.

Demand for the product is determined by several factors like price of the product, taste and desires of the consumers for commodity, income of the consumer, the prices of related goods such as substitutes and complements, advertising and sales promotion. These factors have the greatest influence on sales of the products. Let us discuss fully these variables which influence demand.

(i) **Price of a Commodity** This is the basic factor in determining demand. There is a definite relationship between the quantity demanded and the price of the product. If a person wants to pay a certain price to the commodity, he must get satisfaction which is equivalent to the payment of price. No rational human being will pay for a product more than what it is worth to him in terms of utility. If the price is high, the individual has to sacrifice much, therefore he buys less. If the price falls, his sacrifice is less, he buys more. This inverse relationship between the price and the quantity demanded is called the *Law of Demand.*

(ii) **Consumer's Income** The income of the consumer is another important variable which influences demand. The ability to buy a commodity depends upon the income of the consumer. The higher the income, larger is the quantity of a product that the consumer will buy. For example, a rich man can afford to buy more because his purchasing power is high. When the income of consumers increases, they buy more at a given price or at a higher price. When the income falls, the consumers are forced to buy less.

(iii) **Tastes and Preferences of Consumers** The demand for a commodity depends upon tastes and preferences of consumers. These depend upon the cultural and social standard of consumers. If the consumers develop taste

for a commodity, they buy whatever may be the price. The particular life style influences the consumers to buy luxury goods and quality products. For example, a few years back, the demand for soft drinks was very low. But now the demand for soft drinks has increased very significantly, which is due to change in taste. Advertisement and sales campaign and improved knowledge are some of the factors which cause changes in consumers' tastes and preferences.

(iv) **Prices of Related Goods** The demand for a product is also affected by the prices of substitutes and complements. Generally, commodities have alternatives and also they are used as complements. For example, coffee and tea are substitutes. Ink and pen are complements. When coffee becomes cheaper, the consumers substitute coffee for tea and as a result the demand for coffee increases and that of tea decreases. If the price of ink rises, the demand for pen falls. Likewise, when the price of cars falls, the demand for them would increase which in turn will increase the demand for petrol.

(v) **Advertisement and Sales Campaign** In these days of modern civilisation, the advertisements and sales campaign in newspapers and television influence the demand for products very significantly. They can change the demand pattern of the upper class people.

Thus, all these factors contribute for the demand for a commodity. We can analyse the concept of demand in the form of a formula as $q = f(py\ pr^{w})$, where q stands for quantity demanded, p stands for the price of the commodity, y stands for income of the consumers, pr stands for price of the related goods and w stands for tastes and preferences. If income, price of related goods, tastes and preferences are assumed to be constant, the quantity demand for a commodity depends upon the price. Then, the formula for demand is $q = f(p)$.

(vi) **Demand schedule** Demand schedule is a statement showing the relationship between the price and the quantity demanded. The following illustration shows price-quantity relation.

Table 1

Price	Indivdual Demand Schedule Quantity demanded
Rs.10	I Units
Rs. 8	2 Units
Rs. 6	4 Units
Rs. 4	8 Units
Rs. 2	14 Units

Table 2

Price	Market demand schedule assuming there are many buyers with different income and tastes
Rs. 10	10,000Units
Rs. 8	20,000Units
Rs. 6	40,000Units
Rs. 4	80,000Units
Rs. 2	14,00,000Units

The demand schedule shown above reveals the relationship between the price and the quantity of the commodity bought. If the price is Rs. 2, 14 units of the commodity are purchased. If the price rises to Rs. 6, only 4 units of the commodity are demanded. If the price rises to Rs. 10, then only I unit is demanded. It shows that lower the price higher the amount of the commodity are demanded, higher the price, lower the amount of the commodity are demanded. Assuming there are many consumers with different incomes and tastes, by adding up all the individual demand schedules, a market demand schedule is obtained. The demand schedule if plotted on a graph map, a demand curve is obtained which is shown below:

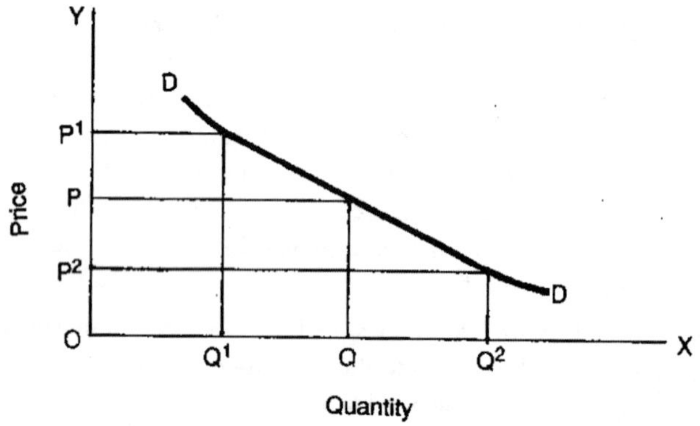

The demand curve (DD) simply shows the relationship between the price, and the quantity of the commodity demanded. The demand curve slopes left to right downwards, indicating that when price rises, lower amount of the commodity is purchased and when price falls, more is demanded. The slope of the demand curve is negative because as price declines, more units of the commodity are bought. It is conventional to show, the quantity demanded on the X axis and the price on the Y axis. The demand curve is also known as Average Revenue Curve (AR) because the price paid by the consumer is revenue per unit for the seller.

Chief Characteristics of Law of Demand

(1) The law states that demand varies inversely with price, not necessarily proportionately. If the price falls by 10 per cent, it does not follow that demand will rise exactly by 10 per cent. It may be more than 10 percent or less than 10 percent.

(2) Price is an independent variable while the quantity demanded is a dependent variable. It means that demand is entirely dependent on the price.

(3) The law of demand depends upon certain conditions such as constancy of tastes and preferences, incomes of the individuals, prices of substitutes, etc. If these change, demand also changes.

Income and Substitution Effects of Law of Demand

The law of demand states that if the price of a commodity falls, the demand for the commodity rises and vice-versa. It means that demand responds to the price in the reverse direction. This aspect can be explained with reference to the behaviour of buyers. The buyers are classified into marginal buyers and intra-marginal buyers. Intra-marginal buyers are those who increase or decrease their consumption of a good but do not start or stop their consumption when faced with price variations. The behaviour of mariginal buyers can be explained in terms of income and substitution effects.

(i) Income effect

The fall in the price of a commodity is equivalent to an increase in income of the consumer, because he spends less while buying the same quantity of the commodity as before. A part of the money so gained can be used to buy more of the same commodity. When the price rises, the consumer's income is reduced since he has to spend more money to buy the same units of the commodity, by curtailing the consumption of other commodities. If the consumer does not want to buy more units of the same commodity when price falls, he may use the surplus money to buy some units of a superior commodity. The reverse takes place when price rises. Thus, income effect of a change in price is negative for superior goods and positive for inferior goods.

(ii) Substitution effect

When the price of a commodity falls, the consumers can buy more units of the same commodity or they can substitute that commodity for some other commodity or commodities which have now become relatively dear. If the price of tea falls, the consumers will now buy less of tea and more of coffee. It is also possible that if the price of coffee falls, others may now use coffee in place of tea. When the price of tea rises, more of tea will be used while consumption of other commodities is reduced. This is 'substitution effect'.

A change in price gives rise to both substitution effect and income effect. Income effect is positive and substitution effect is negative. The sum of income and substitution effects measure the price effect. For superior goods, both the income and substitution effects work in the same direction, while for inferior goods they work in opposite direction.

Exceptions to the Law of Demand

The demand curve generally slopes left to right downwards. But sometimes, it may rise from left to right upwards. This is called exceptions to the law of demand. It means, when prices rise, more units of a commodity may be demanded. If price falls, less units of the commodity may be demanded. This is shown in the form of a rising demand curve. Such cases are very rare. However, there are some cases in our every day life. They are often referred to *Giffen* goods. Giffen goods are those inferior goods on which consumers spend a large part of their incomes. Giffen paradox states that the demand is strengthened with a rise or weakened with a fall in price.

(i) In a poor community, people spend a major portion of their income on staple foods like wheat, jowar, etc. If the price of wheat or jowar falls, the people are forced to give up buying of these goods and buy more of rice and other superior goods. When the price of wheat or jowar rises, the consumers buy more of wheat or jowar and forego the buying of other goods. Sir Robert Giffen found that in the nineteenth century in Ireland, the people were so poor that they spent a major portion of income on bread and a small amount on meat. Bread was so cheap while meat was very costly then. When the price of bread rose, they spent their entire income on bread and abandoned meat. Thus, a rise in the price of bread resulted in increased sales of bread. This phenomenon happens in all communities when they spend a major portion of their income on staple commodities.

(ii) When a shortage is feared, people become panicky and buy more even though the price is rising.

(iii) There are some commodities which are purchased by the upper sections of the society for their 'snob appeal' or ostentation. If price of goods of ostentation rise, some people buy more units of these goods. Veblen calls this conspicuous consumption. For example, diamond. When the price of diamond rises, rich people buy more in order to exhibit their superiority in society. When the price of diamond falls, its demand will also fall for it loses its prestige.

(iv) Sometimes people buy at a higher price in sheer ignorance.

(v) In the speculative market, a rise in price of shares and stocks is followed by large purchases, while a fall in their prices is followed by less purchase. When the prices of shares rise, people expect that their prices would rise further and rush to buy. When the price falls, they anticipate further fall in the price and stop buying.

Basis of the Law of Demand - Diminishing Marginal Utility

The fundamental question in the demand analysis is, why do consumers buy more when the price falls and vice versa. The answer is that the consumer acting rationally, calculates deliberately the satisfaction he gets from the consumption of various units of a commodity at a given time. The goal of a consumer is to derive maximum satisfaction or utility from the purchase of various units of a commodity. In order to maximise satisfaction or utility, the consumer allocates his expenditure on a commodity in such a way that he receives the same marginal utility for the last unit of money spent on that commodity.

The peculiar characteristic of the law of utility is its diminishing character. The law of diminishing marginal utility states that as a consumer goes on buying more and more units of a commodity, the utility from every additional unit also decreases. The purchases of most of the people are governed by this law. For example, the utility of a text book on Managerial Economics will be higher to a student who does not possess the book. After having bought the book, he does not need the second book of the same title. If he buys the second book, the utility from that book will be less than the first book. This means that utility of several units of a commodity to an individual diminishes with every increase in his stock of that commodity. This is called the *law of diminishing marginal utility.* When he is forced to buy the second, the third and the fourth unit of the same commodity, he is not prepared to pay the same price for the succeeding units. Since he derives diminishing marginal utility from every succeeding units, he offers lower prices to those units. Otherwise, he will not derive maximum satisfaction from every unit of money spent on the commodity. It means, the consumer will not pay for a commodity more than the money value of its marginal utility to him. Larger the units of the commodity purchased, lower the result of marginal utility. Therefore, the consumer will not buy more units of a commodity unless its price is low. This behaviour of the consumer will make him attain equilibrium. Consumer's equilibrium will be at a point where the utility from a unit of a commodity is equal to money value spent on that commodity. A formula is worked out as follows:

$$\frac{\text{Mu of a}}{\text{Price of a}} = \frac{\text{Mu of b}}{\text{Price of b}} = \frac{\text{Mu of c}}{\text{Pr ice of c}} \text{ etc.}$$

If this condition is not satisfied, then he will not attain equilibrium. If $\frac{\text{Mu of a}}{\text{Price of a}} > \frac{\text{Mu of b}}{\text{Price of b}}$, then the consumer will transfer money from b to a which will result in an increase in total utility, since utility received from a exceeds the utility from b.

Thus, the basis of law of demand is operation of the law of diminishing marginal utility. The consumer will buy more only if the price falls, because the more he buys, the lower is the marginal utility.

Market Research and Law of Demand

It is stated that the consumer behaves in a rational manner and implicitly follows the law of demand in most cases. Marketing executives have often found that the law of demand is not relevant to them in organising the sales of the commodities. Therefore, market research is now required to propound a viable theory of consumer behaviour relevant to marketing executives.

Market research consists of consumer surveys, i.e., studies of buyers' motives, attitudes, preferences and purchasing habits. Information is gathered from personal interviews and mailed questionnaires and the same is supplemented by indirect study such as interviews with market observers who study the behaviours of the buyers through observation. When such surveys are studied, they throw light on the characteristics of demand for various products. It can bring about the sharpening of marketing targets, improvement of distribution methods and adoption of sales improvement techniques.

In a free economy with exposed competition, the consumer is a king. Neither the price nor the quality can influence him in buying the product. The demand analysis is used to determine exactly what kind of product he wants. Whenever a new product is introduced, it should be made acceptable to people. The product has to be improved on the basis of market research.

Economic analysis takes little interest in classification and sumarization of past sales. But producers may formulate their production, and pricing policies on the basis of past sales.

Some of the researches have found that the sales of the commodity are associated with single price. They found, in respect of some commodities, though they were the best, they were not being sold as made in the forecast because of low price. Since the prices were low, they thought the quality of their products was low. When the producers increased their prices, they found that sales increased very significantly. One researcher found that many consumers feel that it is risky and uncertain to go in for a low priced product. The customer who purchased high priced products was cautious. Thus, it can be concluded that the consumer behaviour is not so simple that buyers do not behave according to the law of demand.

Changes in Demand

The demand curve shows the inverse relationship between the price and quantity demanded, i.e., how various quantities of a commodity can be sold at different prices assuming other things such as tastes and preferences, prices of the related goods and consumer's money income are remaining constant. Classical economists were quite aware that price is not the sole factor determining sales and changes in other things may change the demand schedule. The effect of changes in demand consequent on changes in other things is called *shift* in demand schedule. It means that quantity sold at each price will be different because incomes are greater or lower.

The factors that affect the demand schedule are the following:

Tastes and preferences of the customers
Incomes of the people
Change in the prices of related goods
The number of consumers in the market
Changes in the propensity to consume
Consumer's expectation with regard to future prices
Income distribution.

Some explanations to the above factors :

(i) Tastes and preferences of the consumers

Whenever there arises changes in fashion, due to the pressure of advertisements in mass media, it will affect the demand. In the sixties of the present century, when Coca-Cola was introduced to the market, the demand was very conservative. Even though the price of Coca-Cola was low, the demand was not high. But now, people's taste for Coca-Cola has undergone tremendous changes. Even though its price is high, demand is high. In economics, we would say that the demand curve for Coca-Cola has shifted upwards. On the contrary, when any goods go out of fashion, the demand for them decreases. Then the demand curve shifts downward.

(ii) Incomes of the people

The demand for a commodity also depends upon the money incomes of the people. When their money earnings are high, their demand for goods and services also will be high. For example, after planning was introduced in India, money earnings of the people have started increasing and consequently, the demand is rising even where prices are rising. Then the demand curve shifts upward.

(iii) Changes in the prices of the related goods

The related goods are complements and substitutes. When the price of a substitute good falls, the demand for it also falls and vice-versa. For example, if the price of tea falls, demand for it also falls but demand for the substitute, the price of which has not changed, rises. Then the demand for coffee increases. The same things happen in the case of complementary goods. For example, when the price of cars falls, the demand for them would increase, which in turn will increase the demand for petrol.

(iv) The number of customers in the market

In a country like India and China, the number of consumers is vastly increasing owing to an alarming increase in population. Consequently, the demand for essential goods is also high. It is also easy for the sellers to find market for their goods in such thickly populated countries. Thus, the greater the number of buyers for a product, the greater the market demand for it.

(v) Changes in the propensity to consume

Propensity to consume is another important factor in determining the demand for a commodity. During the period of inflation, propensity to consume is high. Consequently, the demand for goods is also high. During the depression, the propensity is low owing to fall in income and gloom about the future. The propensity is low. Then the demand curve shifts downward. Changes in propensity to consume will bring about changes in the demand schedule.

(vi) Consumer's expectation of future prices of goods

This is another important factor which affects demand. If due to some reason, the future prices would rise, the demand for many goods also will rise. During inflation, people expect the future prices will be high and start buying larger quantities at the prevailing prices. Then the demand curve shifts upward and vice-versa.

(vii) Income distribution

Income distribution refers to the equitable distribution of income among people by a Govemment's tax and public expenditure policies. When distribution of income is equal among the people, then the propensity to consume by the society as a whole increases and consequently the demand will be high. For example, if progressive taxes are levied on high income groups of people and the same revenue is spent on the betterment of poor people, their incomes rise and which in turn increases the demand for goods and services. If the growth of wealth and income is concentrated in the hands of the rich people, their number being small in a society, the purchasing power of a large percentage of the people will remain low and the demand for goods also will be low. Then the demand curve shifts downward.

The increase and decrease in demand are shown in the shifting of demand schedules. In the following diagram, the changes in demand schedules are shown.

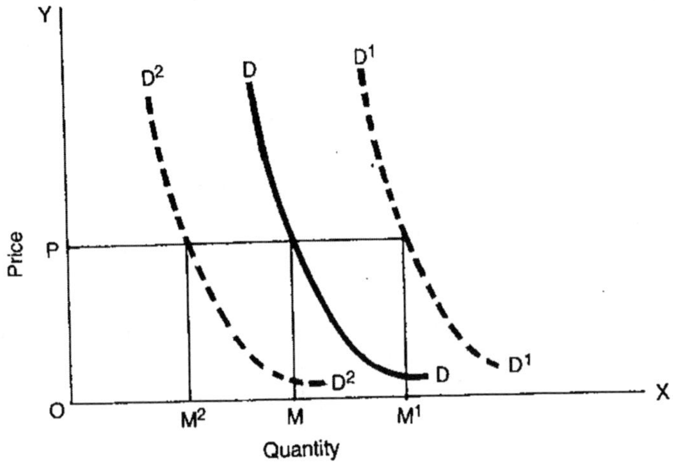

In the beginning, DD is the demand curve. If there are favourable changes in the factors determining demand, the demand curve (DD) shifts upward to D^1D^1. At price OP, the consumers will buy more, i.e. from OM to OM^1. When the other factors become unfavourable, the demand curve shifts downward to D^2D^2. Then the demand falls to OM^2.

The increase in demand occurs due to the following factors -

(a) The fashion for goods increases or people's tastes and preference become more favourable for goods.

(b) Consumer's income increases.

(c) Price of substitutes of a commodity in question rises.

(d) Price of complementary goods have fallen.

(e) Propensity of the consumption of people increases

(f) Increase in the number of consumers owing to increase in population.

(g) Transfer of income in favour of middle and low income groups of people.

In all the above cases, the demand curve shifts upwards. Decrease in demand occurs when the following situations arise:

(a) A good goes out of fashion or the people may develop distaste for the goods.

(b) Incomes of the people fall.

(c) Prices of substitutes fall.

(d) The prices of complements rise.
(e) There arises decline in the propensity to consume by the people. and
(f) Income is transferred in favour of rich people.

Conclusion

From the above analysis, it becomes clear that increase and decrease in demand arises when the assumptions change. This is also called shifts in demand.

The determinants of demand depend upon the product and on the demand situations such as income, sales promotion, product improvement and the price.

The Indifference Curve Approach

The utility analysis suffers from certain shortcomings. It assumes that utility is measurable cardinally, i.e., it can be assigned definite numbers. Since utility is a mental concept, it cannot be measured cardinally. Instead we can have ordinal measure which means that satisfaction can be compared and say that it is more or less.

Further, marginal utility analysis boasts too much and explains too little. Hence, an alternative analysis was propounded by Prof. Hicks and Allen and called *'Indifference Curve Analysis'*.

In indifference curve analysis, the consumer compares the satisfactions obtained from different combinations of goods. If the various combinations are marked A, B, C, D and E, the consumer can tell whether he prefers A to B, B to C and so on. Similarly, he can indicate his preference or indifference between any other combinations. The concept of ordinal utility implies that the consumer cannot go beyond stating his preference or indifference.

What are Indifference Curves?

An indifference curve represents satisfaction of a consumer from two or more combinations of commodities. Since all combinations of two commodities give the consumer equal satisfaction, he will be indifferent between them, that is, he will not bother about the specific combination. He is prepared to accept any combination so long as all combinations give the consumer equal satisfaction.

Let us start the analysis by considering that the consumer buys two commodities, namely apples and mangoes. He does not make the purchase of these two goods arbitrarily. If he buys six apples, he does not buy any mangoes. If he buys five apples, he buys two mangoes. If he buys three apples, he buys six mangoes and so on. It is only in this way of selecting combination of goods, the consumer derives equal satisfaction. If he buys more units of these two combinations, he derives higher satisfaction. Let us have an indifference schedule.

Combination	Apples	Mangoes
1	15	0
2	11	2
3	8	3
4	6	4
5	5	5

When the schedule of indifference analysis is depicted in the form of a diagram, it will be as follows :

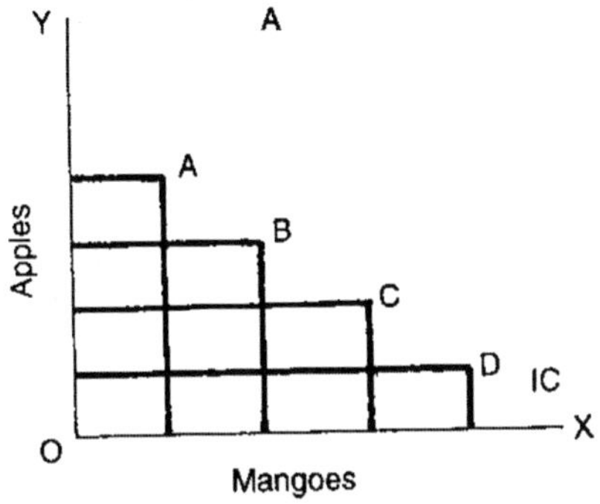

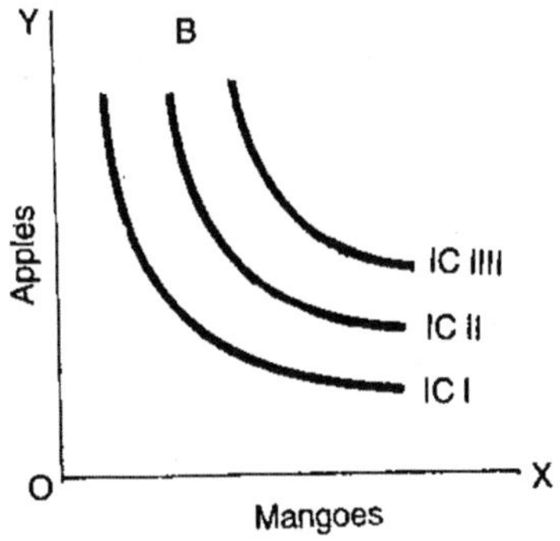

In the diagram A, there are four combinations of two commodities. All these combinations give the consumer equal satisfaction. IC is an indifference curve with several combinations showing equal satisfaction.

In the diagram B, there are three indifference curves. No doubt, an indifference curve represents a level of satisfaction obtained by the consumption of these two commodities. The three indifference curves represent three levels of satisfaction.

IC_1 represents a lower level of satisfaction while IC_3 represents higher level of satisfaction. Indifference curves remind us of a weather map showing lines of equal pressure of the contour lines on a topographical map. A set of indifference curves in a diagram is called an indifference map. In other words, a higher indifference curve represents a higher level of satisfaction than a lower indifference curve but how much higher cannot be indicated. This is because the indifference curve system is based upon the concept of ordinal utility, according to which the consumer is able to state only the qualitative difference in his various levels of satisfaction.

An indifference map of a consumer portrays consumer's scale of preferences.

Let us now understand the properties or attributes of indifference curves. The assumptions made in this technique are as follows -

(i) It is assumed that consumer will always prefer large amount of goods to a smaller amount of goods provided that the amount of other goods at his disposal remain unchanged.

(ii) The tastes of the consumer remain unchanged during the period of consumption.

(iii) In indifference curve analysis, the principle of diminishing rate of substitution is assumed. In other words, if a consumer prefers more and more units of one commodity, he will forego fewer units of the other commodity. The concept of marginal rate of substitution is a tool of indifference curve technique and is parallel to the concept of marginal utility in the Marshallian analysis of demand.

Properties of Indifference Curves

A. Indifference curves slope downward to the right. This property implies that an indifference curve has a negative slope. When the indifference curve being downward sloping means that when the amount of one good in the combination is increased, the amount of the other good is reduced. This must be so, if the level of satisfaction is to remain on the same indifference curve. The diagram A in the previous page makes this point very clear.

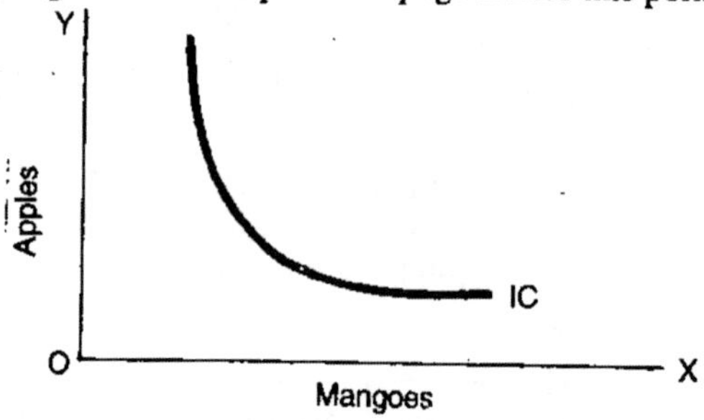

B. Indifference curves are convex to the origin. The implication of this rule is that as the consumer has more and more of X goods he takes less and less of Y goods. The marginal rate of substitution goes on falling. In the table mentioned in the previous page, it can be seen that for the second combination, the consumer for goes 4 apples for one mango. In the third combination, he sacrifices 3 apples to one more mango. Like this, the rate of substitution between apples and mangoes goes on falling with the movement from one combination to another combination. Thus, the normal shape of the indifference curve is convex to the origin as shown in the diagram A. The curvature of the indifference curves reflects the degree of substitutability between the two commodities. If the indifference curve is flat or straight, it indicates that the two commodities are perfect substitutes. In the case of perfect substitutes, the indifference curves are downward sloping straight line(as shown in the diagram C.) If the consumer is not willing to substitute one commodity for another, the indifference curve will either be vertical or horizontal as shown in the diagrams D and E.

Goods which can be substituted are represented by the indifference curve which is convex to the origin.

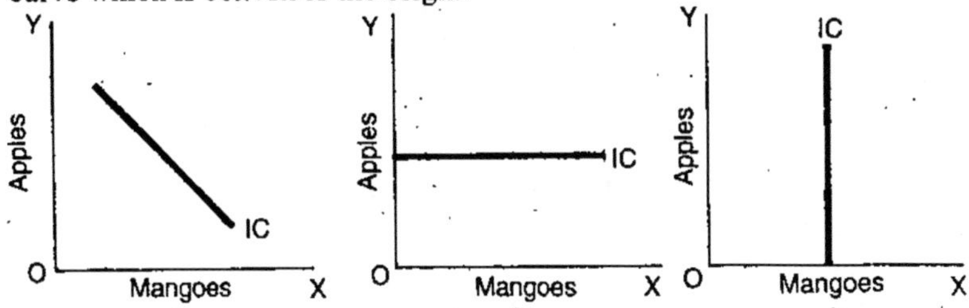

C D E

C. Indifference curves cannot intersect each other. In other words, only one indifference curve will pass through a point in the indifference map. This property follows from the assumption 1 and 2. Supposing two indifferences intersect each other, then the whole theory becomes absurd. Let us study the following diagram keeping in mind the qualification of indifference curve.

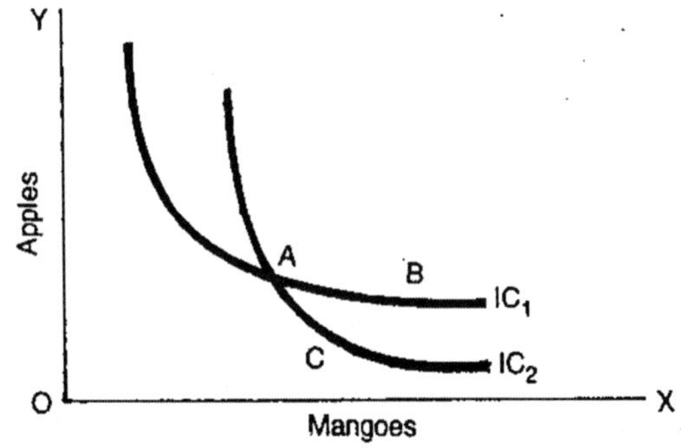

Indifference curves represent different levels of safisfaction. IC_1 is higher than IC_2 in the above diagram. The two indifference curves cut each other at the point A. At the point B, the consumer is on the higher indifference curve and at the point C, he is on the lower indifference curve. The point A is on both the indifference curves, which in turn means that A is at once equal to B and C which as seen, represent two indifference curves. Then the question arises whether higher indifference curve (IC_1) is equal to lower indifference curve (IC_2). As such, a thing cannot be and as such two indifference curves cannot intersect each other. Further, indifference curves can neither touch nor be tangent to each other.

Consumer's Equilibrium

As we have seen in the utility analysis, the consumer will attain equilibrium when the utility from a particular unit of the commodity is equal to its price. (marginal utility = price). In indifference curve analysis, the procedure of equilibrium is somewhat different. In order to find out the equilibrium position of the consumer, we have to draw the price line. The price line is also called the *budget* line or outlay line.

Price line

Understanding of price line is very essential in understanding the theory of consumer's equilibrium. The indifference curve is formed out of several combinations of the goods which give the consumer the equal level of satisfaction. Supposing as shown in the diagram A, there are four combinations of two commodities which are giving the consumer same level of satisfaction. It is because of this, he is indifferent to any of the combination. But there is one particular combination which gives him maximum level of satisfaction. To find out that combination, understanding of price line is very important.

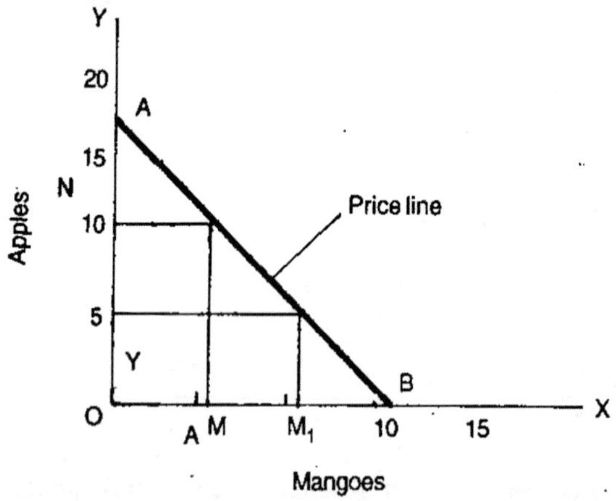

In order to determine the price line, we have to know the prices of the two commodities and the money outlay to buy these goods. Supposing the consumer has set apart Rs. 30 from his total income to buy these two commodities. If we assume that the price of apple is Rs. 2 and that of the mango is Rs. 3 and if he spends Rs. 30 on apple, he gets 15 apples or OA and on mangoes he gets 10 mangoes or OB. These points are shown in the following diagram.

AB points in the diagram are connected by a line and this is called *price line.* This line shows all the possible combinations of two goods that the consumer can buy if he spends the whole of his outlay, prices being unchanged.

Supposing he buys ON of apples, he has to buy OM of mangoes. If he prefers to buy OM of mangoes, he has to buy ON[1] of apples.

Shifting of the Price Line

If the prices of the two goods remained unchanged and his income or outlay increases, then the new price line will lie parallel to the old price line. Supposing the price of apples remain unchanged and that of mangoes fall, then the price line changes. These aspects are shown in the following diagrams.

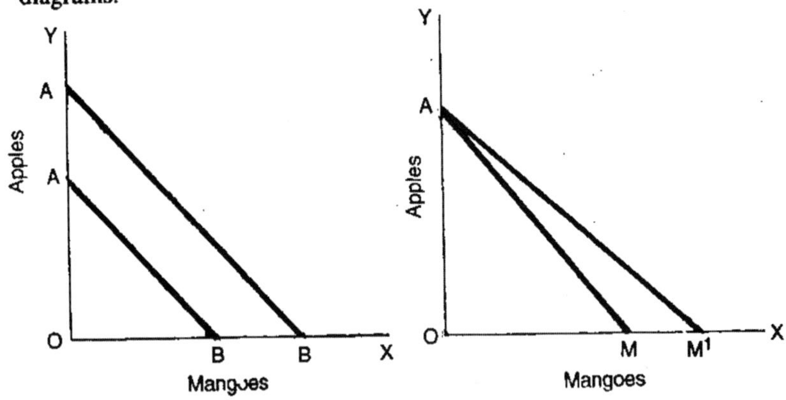

The diagram 'X' indicates change in money outlay (income) while the prices of the two goods remain unchanged. In the 'Y' diagram, the money outlay remains unchanged. The price of apples is the same and the price of mangoes falls. In the case of change in money income, a new price line parallel to the original price line comes into being. In the case of price line where the price of one commodity is constant and the price of the other commodity changes, the slope of the price line changes. The concept of price line is an important tool in the determination of consumer's equilibrium.

Consumer's equilibrium

We are now in a position to explain with the help of price line, how a consumer reaches equilibrium position. A consumer is said to be in equilibrium when he is buying such a combination of goods, as leaves him with no tendency to rearrange his purchases of goods. He is then in a balance position in regard to the allocation of money on various goods. In the Indifference curve analysis, the consumer's equilibrium is determined in respect of the purchases of two goods only.

The consumer has before him the indifference map showing three or four indifference curves. He has also a price line before him. In the diagram below, the process of consumer's equilibrium is explained.

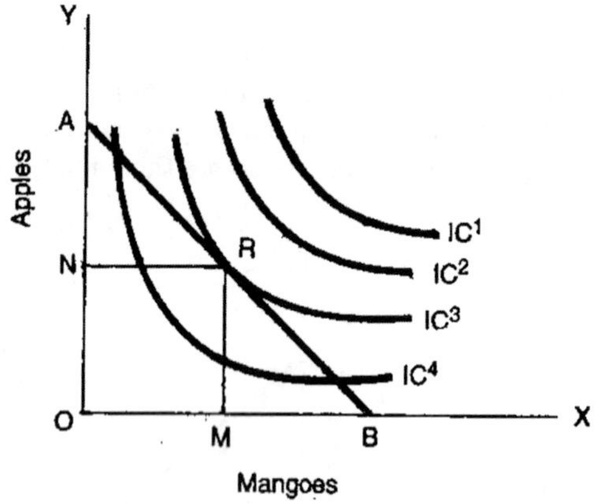

There are four indifference curves showing different levels of satisfaction. Price line AB is shown to represent the money expenditure on two goods. The price line AB contains all the possible opportunities of combining the two goods that are open to the consumer. Any point of the indifference curve lying on the price line is the combination of two goods which give the consumer maximum satisfaction. This is called *equilibrium* position.. Any point not lying on the price line cannot be an equilibrium point The consumer will be in equilibrium at a point R, i.e., he will be buying OM of mangoes and ON of apples. Thus, it can be stated that the consumer will maximise his satisfaction and be in equilibrium at a point where the price line is tangent to an indifference curve. In the above diagram, the price line AB is tangent to indifference curve 3 at a point R. Any combination of two goods other than the above cannot give the consumer maximum satisfaction and equilibrium.

Conditions of Equilibrium

We can state the condition for equilibrium by saying that the given price line must be tangent to the indifference curve. The same may be stated as equality between marginal rate of substitution and the ratio between the prices of these two goods. This is no doubt a necessary condition for equilibrium. For attaining equilibrium, there is another condition which must be equally fulfilled. That is at the point of equilibrium, the marginal rate of substitution must be falling. It means that indifference curve is convex to origin. If the indifference curve is convex to the origin at the point of equilibrium, it means that at that point, the marginal rate of substitution of mangoes for apples is falling.

Conclusion

Thus, the point of consumer's equilibrium may be defined by the condition that the marginal rate of substitution between any pair of two commodities will be equal to the ratio of the prices of the two commodities. In other words, the marginal rate of substitution of money for any commodity must be equal to the price of that commodity. The slope of the price line and that of indifference curve must coincide.

Income Effect or Income Consumption Curve

In the above analysis, we have made two assumptions, namely the money income of the consumer is given and the prices of the two goods in combinations are also constant. Normally, either the money income of the consumer changes or prices of these goods change. The consequences of such changes are studied here under. Let us now take up the effect of consumer's change in money income on consumer's equilibrium. Whenever his money income rises, prices of goods and tastes of the consumer remaining the same, he will buy more quantities of these goods. This is known as income effect. Income effect shows this reaction of the consumer. The income effect means the change in consumer's purchases of the goods as a result of increase in his money income. This is shown in the following diagram.

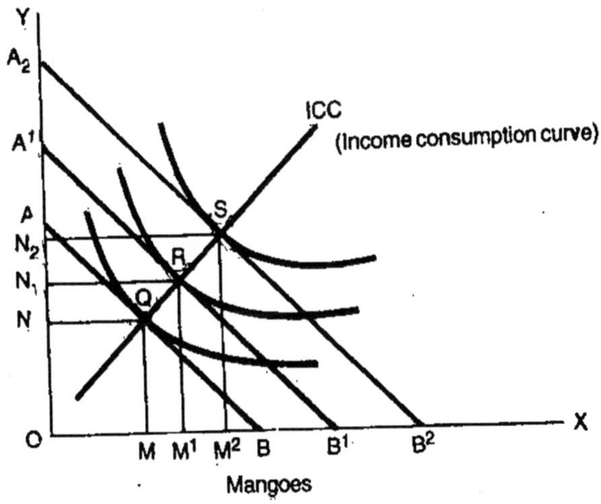

With given money income and prices of the two commodities as indicated in the price line AB, the consumer will be in equilibrium at a point of Q on the indifference curve (IC_1), buying ON of apples and OM of mangoes. Now his money income increases. The prices of the two goods are remaining the same. Then a new price line A_1B_1 comes into being. As a result of this change in money income and buying more units of the two goods, he goes to a higher indifference curve namely IC_2. The price line A^1B^1 is tangent to new indifference curve IC_2 at R. As a result of his increase in income, he buys ON_1 of apples and OM_1 of mangoes. If his income increases still further, then the price line moves further up to A_2B_2. He goes to a higher indifference curve IC_3. The consumer will be in equilibrium at point of S where the price line A_2B_2 is tangent to IC_3 at a point S. If the points Q, R and S are connected, we get a line called the *income consumption line.* The income consumption curve is the locus of equilibrium points at various levels of consumer's income. Income consumption curve traces out the income effect on the quantity consumed by the people.

Types of Income Effect

Most of the income consumption curves slope upwards to the right. This means as income increases, consumer buys more of each of any two goods he is consuming. This is the usual shape of the income consumption curve. The effect of income consumption curve may be positive or negative. If the consumption of goods increases with the increase in income, the income effect for the goods is positive. For example, if the income of wage earned i.e. factory workers increases, their consumption of superior goods rises. This is the positive effect of the income consumption curve. However, for the same goods, the income effect is negative. Income effect for goods is said to be negative where, with the increase in income, the consumer reduces his consumption of goods. Such goods for which income effect is negative, we call them *inferior* goods. This is because the goods whose consumption falls as income increases are considered to be inferior goods by the consumer and he substitutes superior goods for them. Therefore, with increase in income, consumption of superior goods rises while the consumption of inferior goods falls. When the people are poor, they consume coarse grains such as maize, jowar, bajra, etc. When they become richer, they buy superior grains such as wheat, rice, etc. In the case of inferior goods, the income consumption curve slopes backwards to the left. If the income effect is positive, it slopes upwards to the right.

Price Effect - Price Consumption Curve

We have now analysed as to what happens to the consumer's

equilibrium when his money income changes. We will now explain how the consumer reacts to changes in the price of goods, his money income, the price of other goods and his taste remaining unchanged. Price effect shows the reaction of the consumer, whenever the price of one commodity falls. When the price of a good changes, the consumer would be better off or worse off than before, depending upon whether the price falls or rises. In other words, as a result of change in the price of the goods, his equilibrium position would also change. Let us study the following diagram.

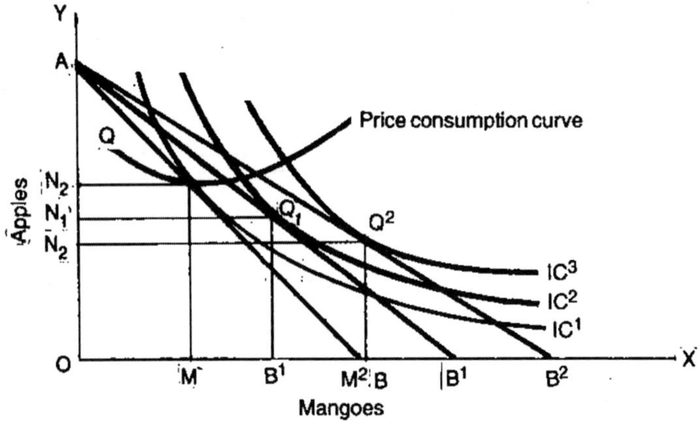

AB is the original price line and is tangent to IC_1, at Q. The consumer is in equilibrium buying ON of apples and OM of mangoes. The price of mangoes falls while the price of apples remain the same. As a result of this, the new price line AB_1 is formed. Since the consumer gets more units of mangoes for the same money expenditure, he goes to a higher indifference curve. The new price line AB, is tangent to IC_2 at Q_1, and the consumer is in equilibrium buying ON_1 of apples and OM_1 of mangoes. He has thus become better off, i.e.,his level of satisfaction has increased as a consequence of fall in the price of mangoes. Suppose the price of mangoes falls still further, so that AB_2 is now the relevant price line. With the price line AB_2, the consumer is in equilibrium at Q_2 on the indifference curve IC_2, where he has OM_2 of mangoes and ON_2 of apples. When all the equilibrium points Q, Q_1, and Q_2 are joined together, we get what is called price consumption curve. *Price consumption* curve traces the effect of change in the price of a commodity. It shows how the changes in the price of mangoes will affect the consumer's purchases of mangoes, price of apples, his tastes and money income remaining constant.

The price consumption curve is downward sloping. It indicates as price of a commodity falls, more units of that commodity are bought.

Two Components of Price Effect

When the price of a good falls, the consumer feels better off. There is an increase in the potential purchasing power of the consumer's income following a relative fall in the price of one commodity. This is called *income* effect. It is as if his income has increased and the prices of both the goods have remained the same. The income effect is the first component of the price effect. The consumer is moving along the income consumption curve.

The income effect will lead to the purchase of a better commodity. This is called *substitution* effect. Since the price of X has fallen, it becomes cheaper. Since the price of Y has remained unchanged, it becomes dearer. So, a tendency arises in the mind of the consumer to buy more units of a commodity for which the price has not fallen. In other words, he will substitute cheaper goods for the dearer one. Thus, the second component of price effect is the substitution effect. The following diagram illustrates the two components of price effect.

Initially, the consumer is in equilibrium, price line AB is tangent to the indifference curve 1. With a fall in price of X goods, a new price line comes into existence.

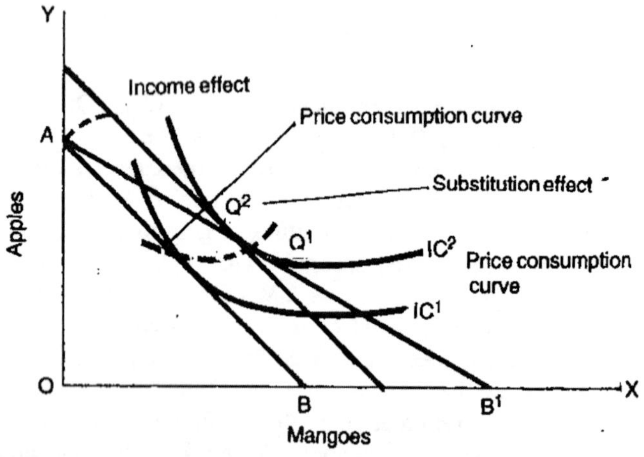

Income effect and substitution effect of the fall in the price of one commodity differs while the price of other commodity is remaining the same.

The splitting up of price effect into income effect and substitution effect is advantageous in bringing out clearly the response of a consumer to a change in price of a commodity. The response to a change in price of a commodity will reveal in terms of income effect and substitution effect. In the case of most of the goods, the income effect and substitution effect will work in the same direction. But, in some cases, they operate in a different direction. The direction of substitution effect is quite certain. A fall in the relative price of goods always leads to an increase in the quantity demanded of the goods. In other words, substitution effect always induces the consumer to buy more of the cheaper goods. But the direction of income effect is not certain. With a rise in income, the individual will generally buy more of goods. But with the rise in income, the individual will buy less of goods if it happens to be inferior goods for him, since he will use better or superior substitutes in place of inferior goods when his income rises. Thus, the income effect may be either positive or negative. In the case of superior goods, income effect is positive while it is negative in the case of inferior goods.

Substitution effect is always positive. That is, if the price of goods falls, more of it will be purchased and substituted for other goods whose prices have not fallen. If the substitution effect is positive, the income effect is negative. It means that the demand for the commodity, whose price has fallen may not increase much or it may diminish as in the case of Giffen Goods.

Giffen Goods

Giffen goods are inferior goods. In the case of Giffen goods, the income effect is negative.

Derivation of Individual Demand Curve

The price consumption curve traces the effect of a change on the quantity demanded of a good. The price consumption curve does not directly relate price with quantity demanded. In the indifference curve diagram, price is not shown in the Y axis. On the other hand, demand curve directly relates to price and quantity demanded, price being shown on the Y axis and quantity being shown on the X axis. The demand curve can be drawn from the price consumption curve. For this, we have to assume price in the Y axis. Then the downward sloping demand curve comes into existence (The detailed discussion is made in the demand analysis).

Demand Distinctions

Demand analysis is studied for specific purposes. The main purpose is for the business objectives. The business people are required to make a thorough study of demand analysis with a view to solve business problems and to make business decisions. The business people have to produce goods which have great demand 'in the market. In order to study the demand potential for goods, they are classified into several types. They are as follows-

Producers' goods and consumer goods,
Durable and non-durable goods,
Derived demand and autonomous demand,
Industry demand and company demand,
Short run demand and long term demand,
Short term demand fluctuations and long term demand trends
Market demand and market segments.

Producers Goods and Consumers Goods

Producers' goods are those goods which are used in the production of goods which may be consumer goods or producers' goods. Examples: machines, tools and implements, ships, locomotives etc. Consumers' goods are those goods which are in use in the final consumption. Examples of consumer goods can be given any number-food items, ready made clothes, utensils and so on and so forth. There are intermediate goods such as yarn to produce cloth, steel to produce machinery which are producers' goods. There are single use goods and durable use goods. Manufactured food items are single use consumption goods. Sewing machines are a single use, durable use goods. A car, a refrigerator are consumer durable goods.

The reasons for the demand for producers' goods are the following

Buyers of produce goods are professionals. They are experts and they can make discrimination pricewise, qualitywise and are sensitive to substitutes.

Their motives are purely profit. Products are bought not for the product sake but for making profit. Their purchases are not at all influenced by advertisement, but more sensitive to price differences.

Demand for producers' goods fluctuate more dramatically than consumer goods.

The distinction between consumer goods and producers' goods though serves a useful purpose, is purely arbitrary. Whether goods are producers' goods or consumers' goods, it is based on (i) who buys (ii) why he buys. For example, if coal is used for cooking, it is a consumers' good- if the same coal is used in a railway engine, it is a producers' good. If the car is used by a retired executive, it is a consumers' good and if the same car is used by a marketing executive, it is a producers' good.

Durable Goods and Perishable Goods

Durable goods are those which satisfy their owners for a long time to come if they are maintained properly. Perishable goods or non-durable goods are goods which can be consumed only once. In other words, perishable goods are themselves consumed, while in durable goods, the services are consumed.

Durable products present more complicated problems of demand analysis than the non-durable goods or perishable goods. Sale of perishable goods are made to meet the current demand which depends upon current conditions. while the sale of durable goods add to the stock of existing goods which are still serviceable. Therefore, it is necessary to segregate current demand for durable goods with that of existing goods.

One characteristic of demand for durable goods is the volatile relation to business conditions, since the current production of durable goods is only a fraction of the products which are in current use. For example, normal production of automobiles is used - (i) to replace 10 per cent of the existing cars and (ii).to expand car production by 5 per cent, then a 3 per cent increase in demand for cars will raise the new car demand by 20 percent. To put it more clearly, let us assume that there are 20,000 cars in use. The replacement demand at the rate of 10% means 2000 cars. (Supposing there is expansion in demand for cars by 5%, it means 1500. Then the existing total production would be 3000. If there is an extra 3% rise, then it means 600 additional cars, i.e. 20% of the existing production of 3000 cars).

Demand analysis for durable goods is not simple. Both replacement and expansion have manifold sets of demand determinants. Replacement demand depends on the value of existing cars as transportation relative to their scrap value. When the existing demand rises up suddenly, the prices of used cars go up higher than the scrap value, as a result, the scrapping rate falls (replacement demand falls). If the expansion demand falls, the scrappage rate will be higher than the level of new car production. The most important determinant for replacement is obsolescence due to technological developments. Obsolescence is pervasive and strategic in American economy in determining the level of business activity. Physical deterioration is rarely a deciding factor in replacement of durable goods. For durable goods, both consumers' and producers' goods, style, convenience and income play a dominant role in demand.

Occasionally, technological upheaval can produce a blast of obsolescence that wipes out any distinction between expansion and replacement. For such innovation, demand depends upon cultural tags, financial agencies and rivalry of alternate investments.

While buying durable goods, the buyers, apart from their incomes and current prices of the products, look into other things such as maintenance and operating costs in relation to their future income and other demands. They may look into the future sale prices of these products. They consider carefully whether to buy now or postpone the purchase … for durable goods, not only present prices and incomes, but their cu… trends and states of optimism are proper variables to include in demand functions. Expectation of proper improved designs are also important.

Derived Demand and Autonomous Demand

When the demand for a product is tied with another product, it is called *derived* demand. For example, demand for steel is related to the production of machinery. Demand for all producer's goods, raw-materials and components are derived demand. Demand for building materials like doors and windows, cement, sand etc. is derived from demand for houses. It is difficult to find recently products whose demand is all demand.In fact, independent demand is derived. There is no autonomous demand. Derived demand is supposed to have less price elasticity than autonomous demand, assuming that subs…es are equally available. For a 10% cut in the price of steel would cause only one percent cut in the cost of a car, assuming prices of all other components are the same.

Some products are tied to others in their uses and they have no independent demand. For example, television antennas. If a commodity has a number of uses, it is difficult to tie demand down to parent products.

Derived demand facilitates forecasting when proportions of the two products are fixed. In some cases, demand may not provide a very reliable basis. For example, demand for looms in Cotton Textile Industry would normally be determined by the demand for cotton textiles. Yet, it may not give the current indicator as the looms may be used in double or triple shifts and the number of looms required may be reduced by half or one third. The recession in motor car industry forced tyre manufacturers to cut production and reduce stocks.

When the proportion between the parent and dependent goods is not fixed it is very difficult to determine demand for dependent goods on the basis of the demand for parent goods. If the number of uses to which a particular product can be put fluctuates, it is difficult to estimate the derived demand on the basis of the demand for the parent product. Electric motors and sulphuric acid are good examples for they can be used in any number of industries.

Industry Demand and Company Demand

Industry demand refers to the demand for the products used by all firms in a particular industry. For example, total demand for cotton, jute, steel etc. in an economy. Industry is composed of a group of closely associated firms. All firms manufacturing cloth are put together in order to form a cotton textile industry. The firms in the cotton textile industry are buying the same product namely yarn and selling the product (cloth) which are close substitutes. When there is considerable product differentiation within the industry and substitutes compete with other industries, then the concept of industry demand becomes irrelevant. For example, jaggery and sugar are distant substitutes excluded in the sugar industry.

An industry demand schedule represents the relation of the price of the product to the quantity that will be bought by all firms. It has a clear meaning when the firms are producing cloth substitutes. It has no meaning when the products produced by the firms differ markedly. Adding Ambassador and Premier cars and averaging their prices does not produce a meaningful demand schedule.

Industry's demand schedule can be classified into customers groupwise. For example, steel required for building construction and manufacture of machinery, etc. From the managerial point of view, mere industry's demand does not serve any purpose. What is to be recognised is to know the company's share in the industry's demand.

Company demand refers to the demand for the products of a particular company. Demand for Ambassador cars refers to the demand for the product of that company. while demand for cars refers to the total demand for cars of all firms put together. In order to understand the relation between company demand and industry demand, it is necessary to know the characteristics of different market structures. There are different market structures, such as monopoly, perfect competition, monopolistic competition and oligopoly. In the case of monopoly, there is a single firm and hence there is no difference between company demand and industry demand. In other words, company demand curve would be the same as the industry demand curve. In the case of perfect competition, the industry demand curve is completely divorced from company demand curve. The company in this market situation has no independent price since all firms are selling the identical product. In the case of company, the demand curve is a horizontal straight line, while the industry demand curve is negative sloped.

In the case of oligopoly, there are two types - one is homogeneous oligopoly and the other is differentiated oligopoly. In the case of homogenous oligopoly, sellers are few and their products are standardised, the business is highly transferable among themselves. Example: aluminium, steel and cement. There is competition among rivals. The company's own demand curve is uncertain, for it depends on the rivals. What is generally done is that the sellers charge the same price to stay on in the market, since the product produced by all firms is identical. If a firm would reduce the price, this would lead to a chain of reactions in the industry. In many manufacturing industries, a few large firms dominate and account for substantial portions of the industry's output. But most products are not uniform and hence there is a small price variation.

There is differentiated oligopoly - few sellers with differentiated products. (for example, motor cars, refrigerators, television sets, etc.). The products of the rival companies differ physically, the company's demand is less closely inter-dependent to industry's demand, since the consumers express preferences. The individual companies have got more leeway in manipulating their prices. The company may have an independent demand function, depending upon the superiority of the product and advertisement effect.

In the case of monopolistic competition, the individual companies have their own demand curves and the industry demand curve has no meaning. The products of different firms are considered as different products and so for each product, there is a demand curve as in monopoly. It differs from the monopolist in that, company demand may be affected by the competitions of the rivals. Hence the demand curve of the firm in monopolistic competition is more price elastic.

Demand Analysis in Terms of Market Share

The market share concept of company demand is now being used in demand analysis. The market demand for a product may be 10 million tonnes of steel. But a company's output may be 2 million tonnes. Then the company's share in the market demand is 20 per cent. It is stated that some companies control 60 to 70 per cent of the product market, which are called *dominant* companies. The concept of market share becomes important because of the entire demand being the result of vast impersonal economic forces and is usually beyond the capacity of an individual company to control it. For example, an X company which produced say 60 per cent of the market share, cannot control the entire market but the market share enjoyed by it can be manipulated. Market share information may help in persuading people to buy the product of that company. This concept of demand indirectly is useful for the company either to increase its market share or try to retain it at least for which the company has to improve the product or change the market strategy.

The factors that determine the market share are - (1) The price differentials, (2) Promotional expenditure and, (3) Product improvement.

The price differential or price spread for product in the market determines the market share of the company. If a company's price is lower than the price charged by other companies, then that company would be able to capture a greater market share. If there is still competition in the market, a company may resort to increased promotional campaign, or it may take up product improvement by using latest technology. Thus, market share concept influences the individual companies to improve their respective positions in the market. In this cultural setting, market share objectives are often defensive.

Short Run Demand and Long Run Demand

Short run demand refers to existing or current demand. Further, there is immediate reaction to price changes, income fluctuation, etc. whereas long-term demand refers to demand which ultimately exists due to changes in prices or promotion of product improvement. For example, a cut in price of electricity will induce the existing users of electrical appliances to make greater use of them. This is short term change in demand. In the long run more people will be induced to buy them, ultimately leading to a greater demand for electricity. Thus, a temporary price cut cannot be viewed in the same light as one that is expected to stick. Competition among the producers will result in cut in the prices in the short run. This will lead to the entry of new competitors and exploration of substitutes in the long run.

Factors that cause this distinction are - (1) Cultural lags in information and experience, (2) Capital investments required on the part of consumers to change their consumption patterns.

A price change today will result in a chain of adjustments in customer's attitudes and competitor's prices. There may be delayed action on the part of the buyers in response to price changes, because in practice, the consumers' use patterns are sticky. In the case of new products, price changes may not induce the buyers to buy them more. In the long run, price cuts may accelerate growth considerably, because by that time, there will have been adjustments in the use patterns.

Another factor is with regard to the new investments that will have to be made in order to take advantage of price cuts. In order to buy electrical appliances like refrigerators, T.V. sets, washing machines, etc., a huge investment will have to be made, which may not be possible for many people. Thus, long run growth is not entirely dependent on price-cuts. Yet, price cuts influence the increase in demand considerably.

Demand Fluctuations and Long Trends

Fluctuations in demand cause more problems to producers since demand shifts in passage of time. There are several kinds of time patterns such as of day, month, seasonal and cyclical trends. Forecasting brief of time patterns does not pose serious problems to businessmen. But the forecasting as to how sales fluctuate from year to year and projecting long term trends in demand pose difficulties. In year to year fluctuations, much of the setting namely competitive structure, market position, quality and even prices remain constant. For long term, the trend is different, for everything is uncertain. There might be changes in tastes, technology and way of life.

Forecasts of year to year changes provide for programming firm's production plans, such as man-power requirement, raw materials requirement, inventory, cash etc. Projection of long range demand trends are useful for planning investments, choosing location, etc. Joel Dean observes that in the atomic age, long run forecast is necessarily a speculation.

Total Market and Market Segment

Total market for a product refers to its total demand. When the total market for toilet soaps is referred, it includes all the brands or substitutes of toilet soaps. Market segment refers to the part of the total market such as foreign market, local market, regional market and national market. Market segment may also be carved out by sub-products, the uses of products, sensitivity to price, etc. When demand is divided into different segments, this gives rise to the market segment. Total market includes all segments.

When demand forecasting is to be made, total market has to be taken into consideration. When pricing, distribution and promotion is to be taken up, their market segment is preferred. Each of these market segments may differ in prices, packaging, promotion etc. For manipulating price, promotion, production and distribution, a segment concept of demand is appropriate.

ELASTICITY OF DEMAND

Elasticity of demand is a common device for describing the shape of the demand function. It is a measurable concept which measures the response to change in demand. The law of demand indicates the direction of change in the quantity demanded in response to a change in price while elasticity of demand refers to the degree of responsiveness of quantity demanded to a change in its price, income of the consumer and prices of related goods. Alfred Marshall who developed this concept defined it as 'The elasticity (or responsiveness) of demand in a market is great or small according to the amount demanded increases, much or little for a given fall in price and diminishes much or little for a given rise in price'. Thus, elasticity of demand refers very much to price changes only. It is also defined as *'The contraction and extension attribute of demand by virtue of which it stretches or contracts under the pressure of a change in price is called elasticity of demand'*. Thus, the term elasticity refers to the degree of correlation between price and demand. Elasticity of demand is the measure of the responsiveness to a change in the price. Prof. Joan Robinson defines it as *'The elasticity of demand at any price or at any output, which is the proportional change of amount purchased in response to a small change in price divided by the proportional change of price'.* In simple language, price elasticity is the ratio of relative change in quantity to a relative change in price. The terms demand elasticity and price elasticity are used in the same sense.

Various Concepts of Elasticity

The quantity demanded of a commodity may change as a result of changes in the determinants such as price, incomes of the consumer and prices of the related goods. The concept of elasticity of demand therefore refers to the degree of responsiveness of quantity demanded of goods to a change in its price, income and prices of related goods. Accordingly, there are three kinds of elasticity namely price elasticity, income elasticity and cross elasticity or elasticity of substitution. Joel Dean introduced another kind of elasticity namely promotional elasticity.

Price Elasticity of Demand

The concept of price elasticity of demand has an important practical application in decision making. Many a times, the producers are involved in a controversy whether to lower the price, to increase the sales or not. If he would come to know that a 5 percent reduction in price will lead to a 20 percent rise in the quantity demanded, he takes a decision of lowering of the price. Here the concept of elasticity becomes crucial.

The price elasticity of demand refers to the response of quantity demanded of a commodity to a change in its price, given the consumer's income, his tastes and price of all other goods. Thus, price elasticity means the degree of responsiveness or sensitiveness of quantity demanded of a commodity to a change in price. It can be precisely defined as proportionate change in quantity demanded in response to a small change in price divided by proportionate change in price.

$$\text{Thus, price elasticity} = \frac{\text{Proportionate change in quantity demanded}}{\text{Proportionate change in price}}$$

$$= \frac{\dfrac{\text{Change in quantity demanded}}{\text{Quantity demanded}}}{\dfrac{\text{Change in price}}{\text{price}}}$$

In symbolic terms :

$$ep = \frac{\dfrac{\Delta q}{q}}{\dfrac{\Delta p}{p}} = \frac{\Delta q}{q} = \frac{\Delta p}{p}$$

$$= \frac{\Delta q}{q} \times \frac{\Delta p}{p} = \frac{\Delta q}{\Delta q} \times \frac{p}{p}$$

Where ep stands for price elasticity

q stands for quantity

p stands for price

Δ stands for infinitesimal change

If the law of demand holds good, price elasticity is negative, since change in quantity demanded is in opposite direction to a change in price. When price falls, quantity demanded rises and vice versa. For the sake of clarity, the negative sign is ignored and a numerical value is preferred. For example, if 5 percent change in price leads to 10 percent change in the quantity demanded of a commodity, then the price elasticity is 2. Suppose the price of a commodity is Rs. 20, the quantity sold is 400 and when the price falls to Rs. 15, the quantity sold increases to 600. What would be the price elasticity of demand?

Solution : Here q = Rs.20. $\angle p$ = 5(Rs. 20 – 15)

q = 400 $\angle p$ = 200(600 – 400)

$$eq\frac{\angle q}{\angle p} = \frac{200}{5} \times \frac{20}{400} = 2$$

Price elasticity can also be calculated with the help of a following formula :

$$\text{Price elasticity} = \frac{\text{Percentage change in quantity demanded}}{\text{Percentage change in price.}}$$

If a 5 percent change in price leads to 10 percent change in the quantity demanded, then the price elasticity is 2. This is positive. It gives an incentive for business to increase the sales of the product by lowering the price.

Cases of Elasticity

It is usual to distinguish between five cases of elasticity - (1) Perfectly elastic (Infinite elasticity), (2) Perfectly inelastic or zero elasticity, (3) Relatively elastic, (4) Relatively inelastic, (5) Unit elasticity.

Perfectly elastic

When a small percentage change in price leads to large percentage change, in the quantity demanded, it is called perfectly elastic demand. The shape of the demand curve is a horizontal straight line. The following diagram illustrates the perfectly elastic demand curve.

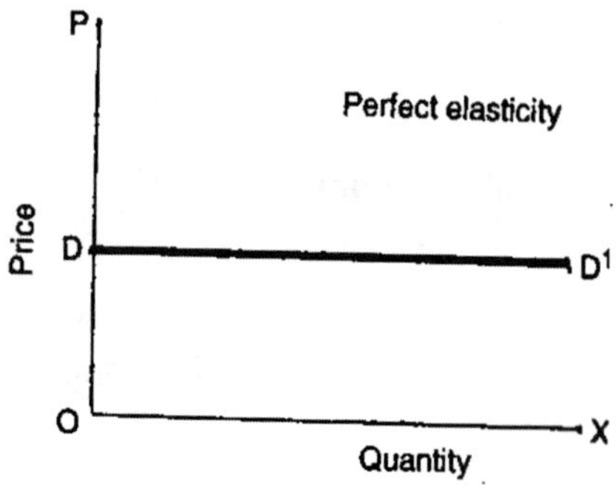

Perfectly Inelastic Demand

Perfectly inelastic demand shows that howsoever much the price may fall or rise, the amount demanded remains the same. It means that demand for the commodity does not show any response to a change in the price. For example, if the price rises from Rs. 5 to Rs. 50, the quantity demanded remains the same. This is called Perfectly Inelastic Demand. Perfectly inelastic demand has zero elasticity. The demand curve for this demand is that of vertical straight line as shown in the following diagram.

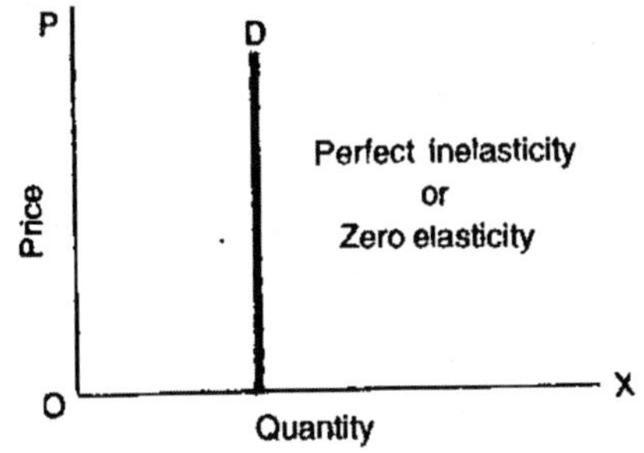

Fairly Elastic Demand

It may be noted that both perfectly elastic demand and perfectly inelastic demand are two extreme limits which are seldom met in real life and therefore can be recognised theoretically. On the other hand, in actual life, we come across elasticity of demand which is some-where between these two extreme limits. It is more, zero or less than infinity. The fairly elastic demand curve is a downward sloping demand curve. The downward sloping is gradual.

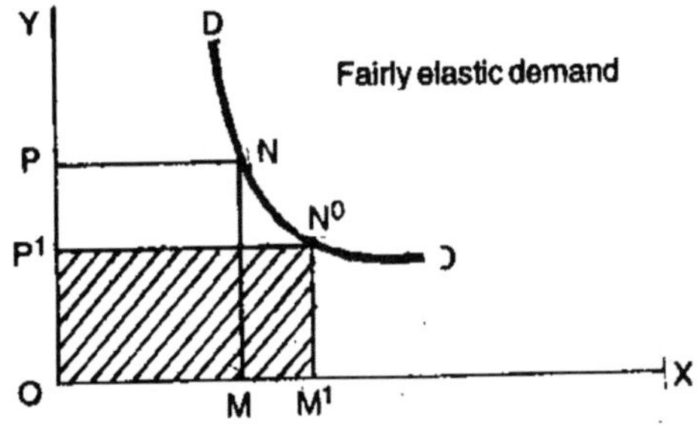

In the above diagram, the price falls from P to P^1 and the quantity demanded rises more than the change in the price to MM^1.

Fairly Inelastic Demand

In the fairly inelastic demand, the quantity demanded changes by a smaller percentage than the change in price. In other words, if the price of

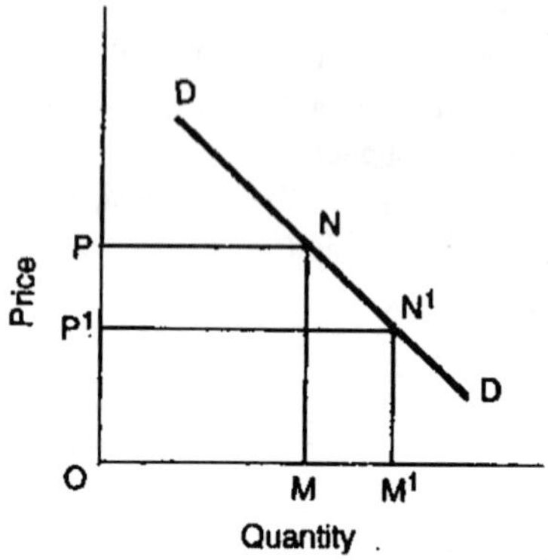

a commodity falls, the demand increases only a small percentage as compared with the fall in price. The numerical value of relatively inelastic demand lies between zero and one. It is also called less than one.

As the price falls from PN to P[1]N[1], the quantity demanded increases from OM to OM[1] which is a small increase when compared with the fall in price. Thus, the demand is inelastic.

Unitary Elastic Demand

Unitary elastic demand is the dividing line between elastic and inelastic demand. In this case, the elasticity of demand is equal to one. It means the response to the change in the quantity demanded is the same as change in the price of a commodiy. If the price of a commodity falls by 10 percent, the quantity demanded also increases by 10 percent. The unitary elastic demand curve is that of a rectangular hyperbola. The following diagram shows the unitary elastic demand curve.

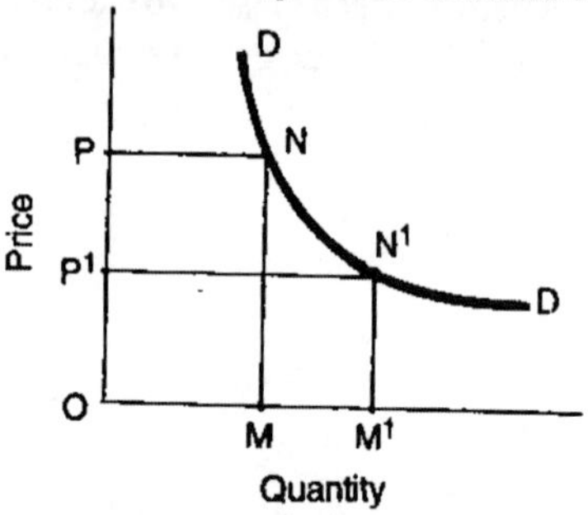

In this diagram, PP[1] equals MM[1]. The area OPNM is equal to OP[1]N[1]M[1]. The total amount spent on the purchase of the commodity at different prices is the same. Thus, the elasticity of demand in this case is unity.

The terms elastic and inelastic are used in relative sense. It means that elasticity is only a matter of degree. Demand for some goods is more elastic, while the demand for some other goods is less elastic. In the case of salt, it is inelastic and in the case of luxuries, the demand is elastic. Some goods of daily requirements such as milk, foodgrains, etc, are unresponsive to change in their prices. Those goods which are indispensable, any rise or fall in price will not induce the customers to buy more or less. Thus, elasticities are different for different commodities.

Measurement of Elasticity

For practical purposes, it is not sufficient to know whether the demand is elastic or inelastic. It is very useful if we find out what exactly it is. For that purpose, it is necessary to measure elasticity. There are three methods of measuring elasticity, which are: (1) Total outlay method, (2) Proportional method and (3) Geometrical method or point elasticity.

Total Outlay Method

According to this method, we compare the total outlay of the purchaser (or total revenue i.e., total value of sales from the point of view of the seller) before and after the variation in price. In this method, it is possible to find out whether elasticity is unity, less than one and more than one.

Unity It is unity, when the total amount spent on a commodity remains the same even though the price has changed. The rise in price is balanced by reduction in purchases and a fall in price results in rise in his purchases.

Greater than One It means that money spent on the purchase of the commodity increases when the price of the commodity falls and vice - versa.

Less than One It means that total amount of money spent increases with every rise in price and decreases with every fall in price.

Let us study the following example :

	Price of the commodity	Quantity demanded	Total Outlay (Revenue)
1.	Rs. 10	5 Kg	50
2.	Rs. 8	8 Kg	64 e>1
3.	Rs. 6	12 Kg	72)
4.	Rs. 4	18 Kg	72) e=1
5.	Rs. 2	32 Kg	64 e<1
6.	Rs. 1	50 Kg	50 e<I

As between I and 2 and 3, the elasticity is greater than unity because with every fall in price, total amount of money spent increases and with every rise in price, the total amount of money spent decreases. As between 3 and 4, the elasticity is unity since the total amount of money spent remains the same, whatever is the price. Between 4 and 5, the elasticity is less than unity, since with every fall in price, the expenditure also decreases.

Thus, elasticity is a warning signal to the businessmen. It tells them that in the case of inelastic demand, reduction in price will reduce his revenue and increase in price will increase the revenue. The effect will be opposite if the demand is elastic.

Proportion method

In this method, the percentage change in the quantity demanded is compared with the change in price. The formula is:

$$\text{Price elasticity} = \frac{\text{Percentage change in quantity demanded}}{\text{Percentage change in the price.}}$$

For example, the original price of a radio is Rs. 500) fall in
New price Rs. 400)price is 20%
Quantity demanded of Radio)
at Rs. 500) - 400) rise in quantity
Quantity demanded of Radio)) demanded is 50%
at the new price of Rs. 400) - 600)

[Price elasticity of demand = $\frac{50\%}{20\%} = 25\%$]

Geometrical Method or Point Elasticity

This method measures elasticity at a given point on a demand curve. Elasticity of demand is different at different points of a demand curve. It is because that it is a relative measure of change. The formula for measuring elasticity at different points is as follows:

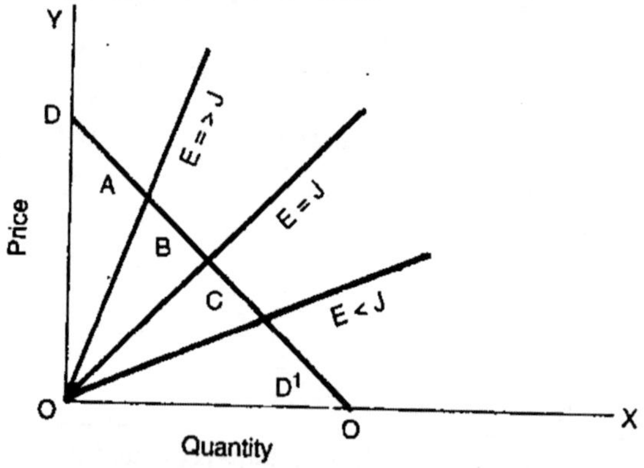

Elasticity is measured in a straight line demand curve as follows: At point A, demand elasticity is D^1A/AD. It is elastic because D^1A is greater than DA. At B, elasticity is equal to one or unity, it is because at this point $D^1B = DB$. At C, elasticity is less than one for at this point $D^1C < CD$.

At the top left, elasticity is infinity and at the between right it is zero. If the demand is a curved line, a tangent has to be drawn at a point and then elasticity is measured.

Factors Determining Price Elasticity of Demand

It is not possible to classify goods according to the nature of their demand and lay down rules to determine whether demand in any particular case is elastic or inelastic. However, some general rules can be formulated in this direction.

Elasticity is always relative. For one person or at any one place, the demand may be elastic, and for another person and at another place, it may be inelastic. The factors governing elasticity of demand are as follows

A. Nature of the commodity There are necessities and conventional necessities for which the demand is inelastic. The demand for luxuries is highly elastic. It must be remembered that the term luxury is a relative term. A luxury to a poor man may be a necessity to a rich person. A thing may be luxury in one country and a necessity in another country. It may also be true that luxuries of yesterday have become necessities of today.

B. Extent of use If a commodity has many uses, the demand is said to be elastic and if a commodity has a specific use, then the demand is said to be inelastic. For example, there is electricity. It has a number of uses like lighting, cooking, ironing, etc. A fall in price increases demand, a rise in price decreases demand and hence demand for these goods is elastic.

C. Substitutes The main cause for the difference in the responsiveness of demand for goods to change in their prices lies in the fact that there are more competing substitutes for the same goods than others. When the price of coffee rises, we may curtail the consumption of coffee and take to tea and vice-versa. In a case like, this a change in price will lead to contraction in demand or expansion in demand.

D. Durability Durable goods have higher elasticity than non-durable goods, because the durable goods satisfy the consumers over a period of time. When the consumption of a commodity can be postponed, the demand is said to be elastic.

E. Proportion Spent on a Commodity If a person spends only a small percentage of his income on a commodity, the demand is said to be inelastic. It is due to the fact that his consumption of that commodity is a small amount, he does not bother about spending some more amount if its price rises.

F. Income Group People with high incomes are not affected by price changes than people with low incomes.

G. Habits and Conventions If the consumption of a commodity has become a matter of habit, it is not much affected by the price changes. Hence the demand is inelastic.

Importance of Studying the Concept of Price Elasticity of Demand

It is an important piece of knowledge for managerial decision making. If the businessmen know the elasticity of demand for their commodities, they can determine the prices accordingly. Here the understanding of the theory of elasticity is very important.

Income Elasticity of Demand

As a result of economic development, the per capita income of the people is increasing every year. In the developed countries, the rate of growth is between 5 and 8 percent per annum. In the underdeveloped countries, it is around 4 percent per annum. Consequently, the demand for goods and services is also rising. If the income of the rich people rises, the demand for luxury goods increases. In the case of common people, the demand for comforts rises. This will result in investment of capital on new industries. This will further result in increase in employment, income and so on. Thus, the demand for goods and services is positively influenced by the level of income, employment and production. What will be the extent of influence of economic development on the sale of particular goods can be known with the help of co-efficient of income elasticity of demanc If the co-efficient is greater than one (unity), sales of the product will increase more than the rate of growth of economic development. The co-efficient of income-elasticity to inferior goods is negative, sales of such products decrease with every increase in economic development.

The knowledge of income elasticity of demand is very much useful in forecasting the influence of possible future changes in economic activity on demand. If the changes in income is long standing, then the demand for superior goods also increases. If the changes in income is all of a sudden, either owing to emergence of war or some inflationary situation in the economy, the demand for goods is very cautious.

What is Income-Elasticity of Demand?

As explained before, income elasticity of demand shows the degree of the responsiveness of quantity demanded of a good to a change in the income of the consumers. To put it more precisely, the income elasticity of demand is defined as the ratio of proportionate change in the purchase of goods to the proportionate change in income.

$$\text{Income elasticity} = \frac{\text{Proportionate change in the purchase of a commodity}}{\text{Proportionate change in income}}$$

Example 1

If the income of a consumer rises from Rs. 1000 to Rs. 1200, his purchase of goods X increases from 10 kg to 12 kg. The income elasticity of demand in this case is :

$$\frac{\frac{2}{10}}{\frac{200}{1000}} = 1. \text{ Income elasticity of demand is } 1$$

Example 2

Increase in the demand for electricity is from 100 units of electricity to 200 units per month with an increase in income from Rs. 3000 to Rs. 4000. Then his income elasticity is :

200 – 100 = 100 units; Rs. 4000 – 3000 = 1000 income.

Increase in the demand for goods is 100. Increase in income is Rs. 1000. The income elasticity;

$$\frac{\frac{100}{200}}{\frac{1000}{3000}} = \frac{100}{200} \times \frac{3000}{1000} = \frac{3}{2} = 1.5\%$$

The income elasticity of demand is 1.5.

There is a useful relationship between income elasticity for goods on the one hand and the proportion of income spent on it. The relationship between the two is described as:

(i) If the proportion of income spent on the goods remains the same as income increases, then the income elasticity of demand for the goods is equal to one. It is Unitary Income Elasticity.

(ii) If the proportion of income spent on goods increases as income increases, then the income elasticity of demand is more than one. It is also called High Income Elasticity.

(iii) If the proportion of income spent on goods decreases as income increases, then the income elasticity for the goods is less than one. It is Low Income Elasticity.

(iv) If a change in income will have no effect on the quantity demanded, then it is negative income elasticity. It is also called zero income elasticity. Goods having negative income elasticity are known as inferior goods. Commodities widely differ in terms of their income elasticities.

Goods like jewellery, ornaments, furniture, automobiles, etc., have high income elasticity of demand, whereas goods like salt, sugar, soap, safety matches, have low income elasticity of demand. In fact, luxuries have a high income elasticity of demand while bare necessities have low income elasticity of demand.

Income Sensitivity of Demand

Modern economists have propounded a concept called income sensitivity of demand. This is almost similar to income elasticity of demand. The difference between these two concepts is only slight. The income elasticity of demand is concerned with changes in physical units purchased as a result of changes in income, while income sensitivity deals with changes in rupee expenditure due to change in income.

The various types of income elasticities are shown in the diagram below :

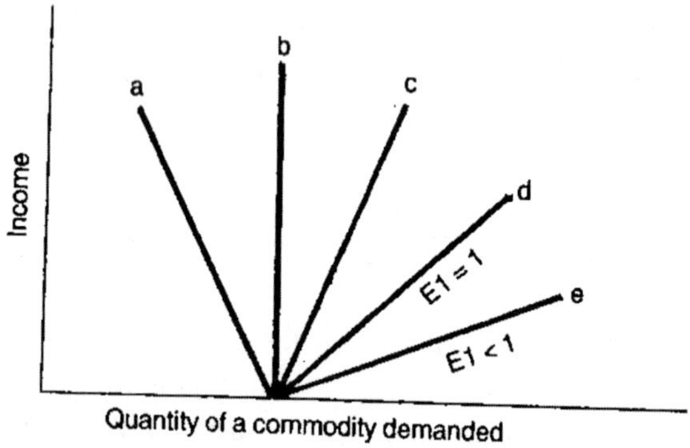

Quantity of a commodity demanded

a = Negative income elasticity
b = Zero income elasticity
c = Income elasticity is less than one,
d = Income elasticity is equal to one,
e = Income elasticity is greater than one.

Cross Elasticity of Demand

Generally, most of the commodities have either substitutes or complements. The demand for a commodity is not only the function of its price but also other things such as income of an individual and price of the related goods such as substitutes and complements. The concept of elasticity of demand can be extended to a situation where two commodities are related to each other. This concept of elasticity is called cross elasticity or elasticity of substitution. Cross elasticity of demand is useful in handling inter-commodity demand relations. Cross elasticity of demand is defined as the ratio of the percentage change in demand for one good to the percentage change in the price of other goods. This tells us how the demand for a good, say coffee depends upon the price of a substitute tea. It may be a complement also. The quantity of bread depends upon the price of butter or jam, because these goods are complements. The formula for cross elasticity of demand is:

$$\text{Cross elasticity of demand for X and Y} = \frac{\text{Proportionate change in demand for commodity X}}{\text{Percentage change in the price of commodity Y}}$$

Let us take up this example: The price of coffee increases from Rs. 60 to Rs. 80 per kg and as a result of this, demand for tea rises from 5 kg. to 10 kg. What is the cross elasticity of tea for coffee?

Solution :

Change in the price of coffee: Rs 80 – 60 = 20

Change in the quantity demand of tea : 10 – 5 = 5

Cross elasticity : $\frac{20}{100} + \frac{5}{100} = \frac{20}{100} \times \frac{100}{5} = 4$

In the above example, coffee and tea are substitutes. Increase in the price of coffee results in increase in the quantity demanded of tea. If the two goods are substitutes, the value of cross elasticity is positive. It is positive when the two goods are good substitutes. If the two goods are perfect substitutes, the cross elasticity is infinity. If the two goods are unrelated (like sugar and salt), then the cross elasticity is zero.

Let us take this example. Torino and Thums-Up are good substitutes. If the price of Thums-Up rises, many of its customers go in for Torino. The cross-elasticity in such a case is positive, because change in the demand for Torino and change in the price of Thums-Up move in the same direction. If the two substitutes are very much closer, the greater is the size of cross elasticity. If the two commodities are poor substitutes (Coffee and Torino) then the cross-elasticity is low.

In the case of complementary goods, if a fall in the price of Y (butter) increases, the demand for bread increases. If the price of one commodity rises, the demand for other commodity falls. In the case of two complementary goods such as sugar and tea, the cross elasticity will be negative. If the price of sugar goes up, its demand also falls and consequently the demand for tea also falls.

In conclusion, it may be stated that cross elasticity of demand for perfect substitutes is highly positive, and for perfectly complementary goods, it is highly negative.

Relationship Between Price Elasticity, Income Elasticity and Cross Elasticity

As already discussed, price effect, that is the effect on the quantity demanded of a commodity due to a change in price depends upon income effect on the one hand and substitution effect on the other. In the same way, the price elasticity of demand depends upon income elasticity on the one hand and cross eleasticity on the other. Thus, price eleasticity is a compromise between income and substitution elasticity of demand. The relationship between these elasticities can be expressed in the form of a formula. The price eleasticity of demand for X goods is given by the formula :

ep = KX. ei + (I - KX) ec

where, ep = stands for price elasticity

ei = stands for income elasticity

ec = stands for cross elasticity

KX = stands for proportion of income spent on goods X.

The first part of the formula KXei represents the influence of income effect on the price elasticity of demand. This shows that the change in quantity demanded of X due to fall in price depends in part upon the magnitude of income effect of the change in price. This income effect of the change in price depends on the one hand upon proportion of income spent on good X (i.e KX) and income elasticity of demand for good X that is (ei) on the other. The proportion of income spent on good X determines what amount of the income spent on goods X will be released as a result of fall in the price of goods X. The income thus released is spent on buying more of good X as well as other goods. Given the income elasticity of demand, the greater the proportion of income spent on good X, and greater the amount of income released for purchasing good X and other goods as a result of fall in the price of good X and consequently greater the increase in the amount demanded of good X. The amount of good X demanded is due to income effect of the price fall depends on the income elasticity of demand for good X. This is because the income elasticity of demand for good X determines how much of income obtained by the fall in the price of X, will be spent on good X, whose price has fallen and how much will be spent on other goods. Proportion of income spent on good X being given, greater the income elasticity of demand for good X, greater the part of income released will be spent on good X. Consequently, there will be a greater increase in the quantity demanded of good X. So, the first part of the formula shows the impact of income effect on the price elasticity of demand.

The quantity demanded of X good does not increase, only because of income effect of the fall in price but also because of substitution effect. When the price of a commodity falls, it becomes a cheaper good and consequently he buys other goods of which the price has not fallen. The second part of the formula (1 – KX) ec shows the influence of substitution effect on the price elasticity of demand for good X. The magnitude of the substitution effect in turn depends in part on the cross elasticity, i.e., to which extent the goods X can be substituted to other goods. The substitution effect also depends upon the amount of other goods which were being purchased before the fall in the price of X good.

From the above analysis, it can be concluded that the price eleasticity of demand is determined by the following four factors: 1) Proportion of income spent on a good, 2) Income elasticity of demand, 3) Elasticity of substitution, 4) Proportion of income spent on other goods.

DEMAND FORECASTING

Meaning and Nature of Demand Forecasting

Forecasting is a prediction about a future event which is most likely to happen under given conditions. Demand forecasting means estimate of expected future demand conditions. Kotler remarked that 'forecasting is like trying to drive a car blindfolded and following directions given by a person who is looking out of the back window'. Looking into the future which is uncertain, is really a difficult task. But it has been so in the experience of mankind. Assuming that future would be bright, every man takes some risks in life and tries to advance further. In the business field, there was lack of forecasting in the past. It was only after the depression in 1930s, that systematic forecasting was realised as a tool of management.

Forecasting is defined as a study with scientific prediction in regard to an event which may have future demand for goods, services either at the micro level or at the macro level. Forecasting deals with the likely shape of future events. It is scientific guesswork.

Forecasting is useful for managerial decision making, effective and efficient planning. It helps to assess the probable demand for goods and services in different periods of time. Demand forecasting translates the demand functions into quantitative guesses. A theoretical demand function seeks to include all the forces that influence sales. If these are to be translated into actuality, some of the demand determinants have to be selected and a formula for forecasting sales has to be evolved. This is the function of demand forecasting. Since the management operated under conditions of uncertainty, a probable estimate of future demand for the products is absolutely essential. This helps in reducing the risk of uncertainty to the absolute minimum. Forecasting is required in all areas of enterprise. Since future is uncertain, no forecast is hundred percent certain. However, it is necessary for every firm to make forecast as correct as possible. Henry Fayol was the first to lay emphasis on forecasting as an important function of business management. A good forecast reduces the scope of uncertainty to the barest minimum.

Types of Forecasting

Short Term Forecasting and Long Term Forecasting

Short Term and Long Term Short term forecasting covers a period up to one year. It relates to policies regarding sales, purchases, pricing and finances. In most of the firms, the information regarding the immediate future is necessary for formulating a suitable production policy. This helps in avoiding both over production and under production. For this purpose, production schedules have to be tuned to expected sales. Short tem is necessary to determine a suitable price policy. It helps the management to reduce cost of production, and controlling inventory. It helps in setting up sales targets and establishing controls and incentives. The sales targets must be set at a reasonable level. It should not be too high or too low. Demand forecasting helps in short term financial forecasting. It can be set up as a programme of cash requirements at different levels of sales. Neglect of demand forecasting will upset financial planning through its repercussions on production scheduling and inventory accumulations.

Most of the demand forecasting is concerned with short term projections for established products. Forecasting for the established products can be made with the information collected from existing markets and past behaviour of sales. Forecast of new products is difficult.

Long Term Forecasting Long term forecasting refers to a period beyond one year. The purposes of long term forecasting are: i) Planning of a new unit or expansion of the existing unit. It requires an analysis of long term demand potential for the products in question. A multi-product firm must know not only the total demand situation, but also the demand for different items. ii) Planning long term financial requirements is necessary for the firm to make necessary arrangements to secure fresh capital for investments. Issuing of new shares at premium, raising debentures, deposits, etc. iii) Planning manpower needs- training and recruitment of personnel to meet the future growth of the firm.

Factors Involved in Demand Forecasting

1. From the viewpoint of span of time, forecasting may be either short term or long term.
2. It is undertaken at different levels,
   (i) International level : International events like hike in petrol prices has worldwide implications.
   (ii) Macro level : It is concerned with the entire economy - the usual measure is GNP
   (iii) Industry level: Industry sales volume is largely a consequence of impersonal economic forces over which a firm has no control. It is prepared by trade associations.
   (iv) Firm level: The firm estimates its sales and relates to industry's sales.

3. Forecasting may be general or specific: A fim may find a general forecast useful to sell its product. Again, sales forecast may be done for specific products for specific areas.
4. Methods and problems of forecasting are different for new products from established products, past trends are known and these guide the future performance.
5. While forecasting, the nature of the commodity should be known. Commodities are either producers' goods or customers' goods. The pattern of demand is different for different types of goods.
6. Nature of competition prevailing in the market and also sociological and psychological aspects have to be considered.

Determinants for Demand Forecasting

Goods which are demanded may be classified into the following categories :

Capital goods,

Durable consumer goods,

Non-durable consumer goods

Demand forecasting for each type of goods is different. That is factors influencing demand for each of these categories are not the same. Factors influencing demand for durable, consumer goods are different from capital -goods.

(i) Capital Goods

Capital goods are defined as goods which are required for further production of goods. They are various types of machineries, equipments, tools, etc. They are various types of machineries, equipments, tools,etc. Capital goods are demanded when there is demand for consumer goods for the production of which capital goods are needed. In other words, the demand for capital goods is derived demand. Further, the demand for capital goods is classified into two types :

Replacement demand,

New demand

Replace of old and obselete machinery arises when the maintenance cost goes high. Repairs of the old machineries involves huge expenditure. In such cases, the management takes a decision to replace old machinery. The replacement involves huge investment as such, it depends upon the profitability of industries. If the market for the products for which old machineries are to be replaced is sluggish and the future is bleak, scrapping of such machines is better than replacement of machineries. When modernisation is contemplated, existing machineries are completely scrapped and new machineries are installed in their places. For example, some factories like textile, cement, sugar are producing with old machineries, consequently the productivity is low and cost of production is high. In such cases, setting up of new factories based on modern technology is more profitable. Demand for capital goods depends upon - (1) their present uses and their capacity utilisation, (2) scrapping rate, (3) the economics of their utilisation and availability of internal finance and bank loans.

The following data are to be collected for establishing the demand for capital goods.

(i) The growth prospects of industries using capital goods,

(ii) The norm of consumption of capital goods per unit of installed capacity. It is assumed that norms of consumption would remain stable. But there might arise a situation of shortages of imported spare parts. For example, spare parts in the case of imported aeroplanes. If locally produced prototype spares can be used as against the shortage of imported parts owing to high cost of import or non-availability of foreign exchange. In such cases, norms of consumption would not remain stable.

(ii) Durable Consumer Goods

Durable consumer goods are those goods which are used continuously for a certain period of time. For example, residential buildings, personal motor cars, refrigerators, washing machines, T.V. sets, furniture, etc. Like capital goods, the demand for durable goods is classified into new demand and replacement demand. Main aspects considered in estimating the demand for durable consumer goods are the following:

1. In the case of durable goods, demand consists of replacement demand (R) and new demand (N). The demand forecast for these two categories has to be made separately. When the consumers find that the existing durable goods such as old T.V. set, refrigerator, automobiles are not serving satisfactorily, they think of replacing the old ones by new ones. When the consumers find latest models of durable goods, they think of selling the old goods and buying new goods. The choice depends on non-economic factors like prestige, social status and economic factors like income or obsolescence. If the price of the new product is very high, then the consumers may think of using the old model with repairs for some more time.

In India, the rate of replacement of old durable goods is very low. If the consumers are very rich, then they are going to buy the new models, selling the old models. Majority of the consumers prefer to use the old model for a long time.

2. Consumer durable goods are generally used by households rather than individuals. It must be noted that for goods which are used by family together, the demand forecast should rely on household figures. A few durable goods like electric shavers are used individually and as such, demand forecast may be made on urban educated population figures.

3. The use of basic consumer durable goods such as electric appliances, automobiles, etc. depend upon the availability of infrastructures like regular supply of electricity, good roads respectively. The existence and growth of infrastructure facilities influence the demand for these durable goods.

4. Many durable goods are used by many members of family, the demand for them depends upon family characteristics, age, sex, distribution of the family, income of the family, etc.

5. In case of durable goods, the demand depends upon the growth of income and psychological factors. The social environment largely influences the demand for them . When once a person starts using a car, he will continue to use for a long time, no matter its servicing cost. In western countries, the demand for automobiles is so high, that a person replaces his car once in four or five years. This is due to enormous increase in the purchasing power of the people. The purchasing power, the number of households and the social status, etc. set up an upper limit to the maximum ownership level of durable goods.

6. The demand for durable goods also depends upon the availability of hire-purchase facility. In western countries, this facility is available in plenty and as such every householder thinks of owning a flat or a house and car, etc., in India, this facility is growing in all metropolitan cities. There are number of hire-purchase companies, specialised in selling durable goods on hire-purchase basis. Some two-wheeler companies themselves are selling on hire-purchase basis. Demand for such durable goods is elastic.

Forecasting the demand for consumer durable goods poses some problems. Most of the costly durable goods are purchased after lengthy deliberation and thinking. They are not purchased instantaneously. It may take several months to take a decision on buying a house. Thus, durable goods are bought sporadically.

(iii) Non-durable Goods

Non-durable goods are those commodities which are used in a single act of consumption. They are food articles, beverages, tobacco, etc. Demand for such goods is influenced by three basic factors such as : A. Disposable income of the people or purchasing power, B. Price of the commodity, C. Size and characteristics of population. The formula used for estimating the demand for non-durable goods is d = f (Y.D.P.) where D is demand, Y is disposable income, D is size of the population and P is the price.

(i) *Purchasing Power of the People*

It depends upon the disposable income of the people of a country. The disposable income is obtained from personal income after making tax and other deductions. In a poor country like India, disposable income is very low and consequently the purchasing power of the people also is very low. Some people prefer to use a concept of discretionary income in place of disposable income. In the case of purchase of food articles, clothing, etc., there cannot be much discretion. Since they are necesities and comforts, everyone will have to buy them. Discretionary income will be an important factor in determining the demand for luxuries. If the disposable income is high, the demand for non-durable goods also will be high.

(ii) *Size of the Population and its Characteristics*

This refers to total population, the different income groups, social status, age-sex composition, urban and rural population, geographical characteristics, level of education, etc. Demand for non-durable consumer goods depends upon all these factors. The demand for various goods can be estimated either for each market segment or for the total market with the help of these characteristics. For example, to determine the demand for toys, it is necessary to note the number of children studying in schools and the income of their parents. In the urban market, the demand for non-durable goods is very high, while it is low in the rural market. In the same way, to determine the demand for detergents and soaps, the size of population, the incomes of the people, the mode of living, etc. have to be taken into consideration. The demand for cloth is a function of price, the income of the people and the size of population. In the forties, fifties and sixties, there was a huge demand for coarse cotton cloth in India. But today, the demand for such cloth has fallen. The demand for blended cloth is increasing. This is mainly due to increase in income of the people and a little bit of education. The demand for fine cotton cloth is also a function of fashion. Thus, many factors influence the demand for non - durable goods.

Objectives of Demand Forecasting

Demand forecasting serves the main purpose of maintaining equilibrium in the economy. Some of the objectives are narrated below:

(i) ***Helping for Continuous Production*** : Demand forecasts help the producers to take up production planning so that the gap between demand and supply of goods is eliminated.

(ii) ***Regular Supply of Commodities*** : Demand forecasting induces the producers to maintain sufficient inventory of products, so that when supply falls and demand increases, the product may be released in the market to fill up the gap.

(iii) ***Formulation of Price Policy*** : Demand forcast helps the management to formulate appropriate price policies, so that the prices do not fluctuate over a period of time.

(iv) ***To Formulate Effective Sales Performance*** : One of the objectives of demand forecasting is to formulate effective sales performance. Since demand forecasting is made regionwise, movement of products may be arranged suitably. It helps the management to determine sales targets accordingly.

(v) ***Arrangement of Finance*** : Finance is indispensable for procuring materials and labour for production. On the basis of demand forecast, the management can prepare the budget for institutional finance.

(vi) ***To Determine the Production Capacity*** : The demand forecasting enables the companies to decide about the production capacity . If the demand forecast indicates that the demand for the product is elastic, then the Board Of Management can plan for a large sized plant. By studying the demand pattern for the products, the organisation can plan for a suitable plant and desired output.

(vii) ***Labour Requirement*** : Production of product requires skilled and trained labour force. If the demand forecasting indicates favourable trend, then the management can take up measures to train the labour force. This can ensure better labour supply and there will be no hindrance in the production process.

Thus, overall success of an enterprise mainly depends upon the quality and reliability of demand forecasting.

METHODS OF DEMAND FORECASTING

It should be noted that there is no easy method or simple formula for predicting the future demand. But demand forecasting is essential and hence some techniques have been tried in estimating the future demand. There are various techniques in forecasting demand, but too much emphasis on each technique is not desirable. The critical problem is to choose the most efficient technique subject to certain limitations. There are dangers in adopting any single technique and as such care must be taken in using the technique. Mathematical and statistical techniques are employed in forecasting future demand. Though statistical and mathematical techniques are essential in classifying relationships and providing techniques of analysis, they are not substitutes for judgement. Second danger is that sound judgement is no doubt an essential requirement but it needs to be supplemented by information and analysis. Thus, efficient forecast must depend on both sound judgement and rigorous analysis.

There are two approaches generally followed in demand forecasting. Firstly, to collect information regarding the intentions of the consumers by means of market research, survey and economic intelligence. Secondly, to use past trends and taking them as a guide and by extrapolating past trends to estimate future demand. The first approach is followed to estimate short run forecasting while the second approach is resorted to long run forecasting. The following chart indicates the different methods of demand forecasting.

Methods of Demand Forecasting

Demand forecasting methods are classified into 1. Survey methods, 2. Statistical methods. Survey methods are classified into i. Survey of buyers' intentions, ii. Survey of expert opinions. Statistical methods are classified into i. Naive forecasting, ii. Barometric method, iii. Simultaneous equations, iv. Econometric method, v. Input-output analysis.

Statistical methods use past behaviour of sales as a guide and by extrapolating past statistical relationships and predict the future demand. The demand for established products can be forecast either by survey methods or statistical methods, but for new products, survey method is the only source.

Survey Methods

Forecasts are done both for established products and new products. Demand forecasting for the established products can be done in a routine manner with information drawn from the existing markets and past behaviour of sales.

Forecasts for new products are necessarily custom built jobs that involve more ingenuity and expense. Since the product has not been sold before, it is difficult to get any clue for demand forecasting. Therefore, forecasting for new products needs to be done by survey methods alone.

Forecasting of established products is based on personal judgement and experience while others are based on statistical methods. Both methods are frequently used to cross check each other with a view to make forecasting as accurate as possible.

METHODS OF FORECASTING

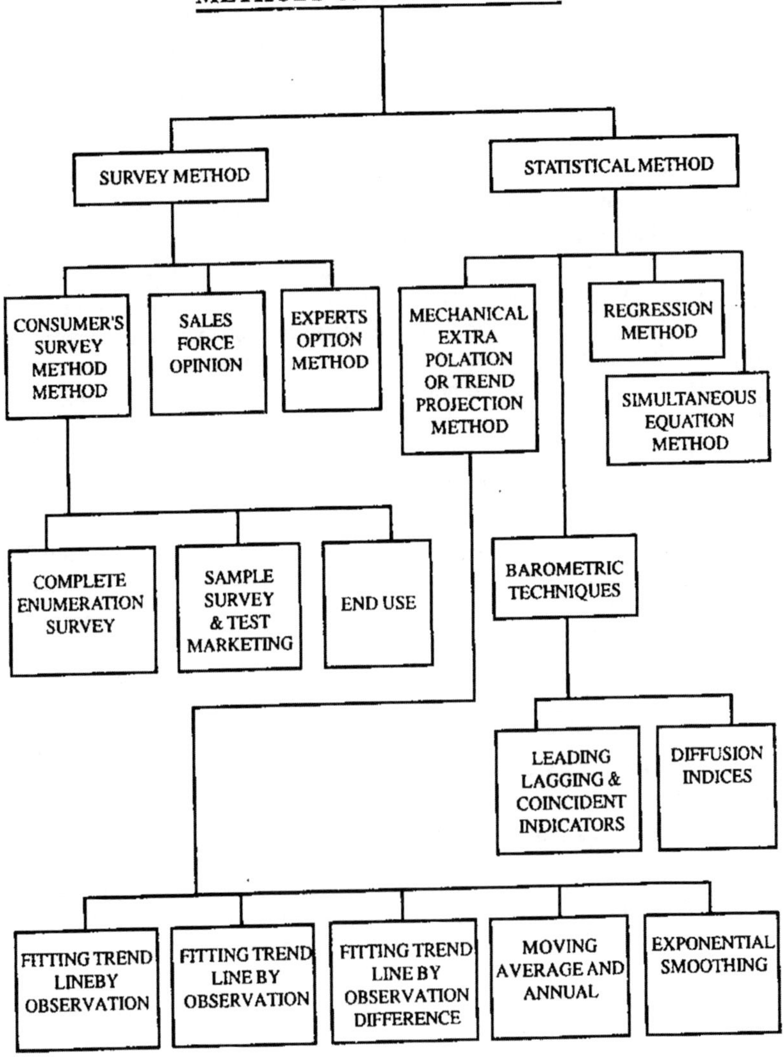

Survey of Buyer's Intentions

This is the least sophisticated method and the most direct method of estimating sales in the near future. In this method, customers are directly contacted in order to find out their intentions to buy commodities in the near future. This method is known as *opinion survey* method. This method is useful to estimate the demand for raw-materials used by industrial concerns, who are buying them in bulk. When the products are consumer goods, it is very difficult to gather the intentions of household consumers. For, it is impracticable to contact each and every consumer to know the intentions of buying the products in the coming months. Therefore, much is learnt by sampling or by concentrating on the few who purchase large quantities in the market. When the information is collected in this manner, and a forecast is estimated by adding the probable demand of the consumers' interviewers for this purpose. Though this method is very simple, it is expensive, for a good number of interviewers have to be appointed to undertake this laborious task. Yet, it is not free from limitations. Consumers' inconsistency in buying intentions as well as their inability to foresee what choice they will make when faced with multiple alternatives in the market is an important aspect. And also there is no assurance that their intentions do not change during the period of a year. It is stated that one year period is an extremely long span in consumer planning. Depending upon the product and on the price expectations, a sudden change in prices may either shock the consumers into a short buyer's strike or be completely ignored by them in their passion for the product.

Therefore, though this method is direct and simple, it suffers from several shortcomings in forecasting, in that, according to Joel Dean, consumers' plans may be trigger-sensitive to short run economic changes while consumers' plans are fragile, capricious and expensive to collect.

Survey of Opinions of Experts

There are people who are experts in the field of selling goods like wholesalers and retailers. They will be in a position to tell what consumers would buy. Many companies get their basic forecasts directly from their salesmen who have the most intimate 'feel' of the market. The wholesalers and retailers by their experience are in a position to 'feel' about the probable sales in the coming year. In this kind of forecast, the total is built up by adding individual salesman's projections, then scaled down for errors of optimism by pooling the collective wisdom of top executives in second guessing and consolidating results. These people have been dealing in the products for a long period and are therefore in a position to predict the likely sales in the future period on the basis of experience. This work is simple and calculation also is very easy. This method may be used in place of opinion method. But there is one limitation in this method too. It is because the basis of forecast by the experts is difficult to indentify for it may spring largely from hints and impulse under the pressure of enquiry. It is purely subjective for different experts may give different kinds of forecast or they may be biased for some reason. Despite this limitation, some companies use this method of forecasting for their products.

Controlled Experiments

Under this method, different determinants of demand are varied (price, advertising, packaging, etc.) and price-quantity relationships are established at different points of time in the same market or different markets. Only one determinant is varied and others are kept constant or controlled. In America, Parker Pen Co. used this method to find out the effect of price rise on the demand for Quick Ink. This method is relatively new. It is difficult to decide which variable is to be varied and what variables should be kept constant.

Forecasting Demand for New Products

Joel Dean observes that methods of forecasting demand for new products are quite different from those for established products. For new products which are new to the economy and new to the company, an intensive study of the economic and competitive characteristics of products provide a guide to projections of demand. Forecasting techniques have to be tailored to the particular product. Possible approaches of forecasting demand for new products are as follows:

(i) ***Evolutionary Approach*** Project the demand for the new product as an outgrowth and evolution of the existing old product. For example, it may be assumed that colour T.V. picks up where black and white T.V. sets are off. This approach is useful only when the new product is very close to the old product. Scooter is an improvement of motor cycle. Mopeds are the improvement to the bicycles. The demand can be very much a projection of potential demand of the existing product.

(ii) ***Substitute Approach*** According to this approach, the new product is to be considered as a substitute for the old product. For example, the new Foto Setter substitutes photographic composition for the established type-setting equipment (Linotype) or linoleum as a substitute for carpets or polythene bags as substitutes for cloth bags or ball pens for fountain pens. Since most of the new products are substitutes for old products and an improved one, the demand will have to be studied very scientifically.

(iii) ***Growth Curve Approach*** The rate of growth and the ultimate level of demand for new products can be estimated on the basis of the pattern

of growth of the old products. For example, analyse the growth curves of the all household appliances and establish an empirical law of market development applicable to a new appliance.

(iv) ***Opinion Polling Approach*** Estimate the demand by direct inquiry of the ultimate purchasers, then blow up the sample to full scale. Sending an engineer with drawings and specifications for new industrial products to a sample company is an example. Opinion polling is widely used to explore the demand for new products.

(v) ***Sales Experience Approach*** The new product is offered for sale in a sample market and then demand may be estimated for a fully developed market. The sample market has to be identified first. If, Bombay or Calcutta is selected, and the results are applied to small towns, it becomes a failure. Therefore, selection of a sample has to be carefully done from middle sized cities to large cities.

(vi) ***Vicarious Approach*** The consumers' reactions are indirectly studied in this approach. Specialised dealers are contacted because they have an intimate 'feel' of the customers. Dealers' opinions are very much solicited regarding the demand for new products. This approach is easy but difficult to quantify. Bias on the part of the dealers cannot be ruled out completely. Care must be taken against undue enthusiasm of some dealers and undue pessimism of some others.

These methods are not usually exclusive. It would be desirable to combine all and then an estimate may be arrived at. The evolutionary approach is useful only when the new product is very close to the existing product. Its demand can be projected on the basis of the demand pattern of the old product.

Most of the new products are substitutes, though not exactly. For example, air travel is a substitute for land transport. Many a time, an upper limit of substitution is framed but what is important is the penetration of the new product and how this would replace the old product (ball pen).

Criteria of a Good Forecasting Method

Thus, there are a good many ways to make a guess about future. They show contrasts in cost, flexibility, and the necessary skills and sophistication. In order to make demand forecast realistic, the following criteria has to be remembered:

(i) ***Accuracy :*** It is necessary to check the accuracy of past forecasts against present performance and of present forecast against the future performances.

(ii) ***Plausibility :*** It means belief. The executives who use the forecasting results must be willing to believe in the market. Elaborate mathematical procedures become less desirable if the management does understand what the forecaster is doing.

(iii) ***Durability*** : Whenever a forecast is made, it should hold good for a certain period of time. It depends upon reasonableness and simplicity of the function fitted.

(vi) ***Availability*** : The technique employed should produce quick results and the data required by the management must be easily available.

(v) ***Economy*** : The cost of forecasting must be within limits.

Statistical Methods

Demand forecasting also uses statistical methods. In this method, some statistical and mathematical techniques are used to predict the future demand. This method is useful for long run forecasting for the existing products. There are several ways of using statistical and mathematical data. They are:

(i) Trend projection method,

(ii) Method of moving averages,

(iii) Barometric method,

(iv) Simultaneous equation method.

Trend Projection Method

This method is based on analysis of past sales patterns. A firm which has been in existence for quite a long time will have accumulated considerable data regarding sales for a number of years. Such data is arranged chronologically with regular intervals of time. This type of data is called *Time Series*. The time series shows effective demand for the product during the period of past ten or fifteen years. On the basis of the data, a graph can be drawn and this is called a *sales curve*. The sales curve shows fluctuations and turning points in demand. If the turning points are few and their interval is widely spread over, firm forecasting becomes possible. Frequency of turning point indicates uncertain demand conditions. When a turning point occurs, the trend projection breaks down. If the turning points are few and spaced at long intervals, accurate forecast is possible. The real challenge is to point out the turning points.

Time series refer to the data over a period of time, during which time fluctuation may occur. Therefore, the time series has four types of components, namely,

(1) Secular trends, (2) Seasonal variations, (3) Cyclical variations, (4) Random variations.

- Secular trend refers to the general tendency of the data and it is known as long period or secular trend. This can be upward or downward, depending upon the behaviour.
- Seasonal variations refer to changes which occur during a climatic season or a festival season. It may be that of festival season like Deepavali or Dussherra etc. Normally, these changes which are repetitive in character are related to a 12 month period.
- Cyclical variations refer to the changes arising out of booms and depressions.
- Random variations refer to changes which occur unnoticed like famines, floods, earthquake, etc. These cannot be predicted.

The real problem in forecasting is to separate and measure each of these four factors. When a forecast is made, the seasonal, cyclical and random factors are eliminated from the data and only the secular trend is used. The trend in time series can be estimated by using any one of the following methods :

(i) the least square method,

(ii) the free hand method,

(iii) the moving average method,

(iv) the method of semi-averages.

Illustration : In the time-series or trend projection analysis, past data of sales are taken to determine the nature of existing trend and then this trend is extrapolated into the future and thus a forecast is made.

Suppose a producer of toilet soap decides to forecast the next year's sales of his product using this method. The data for the last five years is as follows :

Sales of X Company

	Sales in Rs.	Lakhs
1986	...	45
1987	...	52
1988	...	48
1989	...	55
1990	...	60

This data is plotted on a map which is shown in the following diagram:

In the graph, it can be seen that sales have fallen in 1988 and then have increased. It shows that sales are fluctuating. But during the whole period, the sales trend is upward. The line so drawn is called *trend line.*

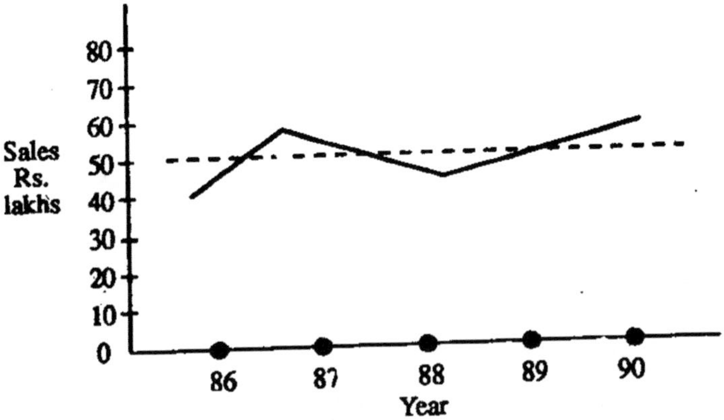

The trend line is filled by developing an equation giving the nature and magnitude of the trend. The common technique used in constructing the line of best fits is by the method of least squares. The trend is assumed to be linear. The equation for the straight line trend is : Y = a + bx, where a is the intercept and b shows the impact of the independent variable. Sales are dependent on variable Y. Since sales vary with time, the time periods will be the independent variable X. The Y intercept and the slope of the line are found by making appropriate substitutions in the following normal equations :

$$\Sigma Y = na + b\Sigma X \quad \text{------(i)}$$

$$EXY = a\Sigma x + b\Sigma x^2 \quad \text{-----(ii)}$$

In the table below, we find the magnitudes of required quantities from the original data given above.

Year	Sales Rs. in lakhs	Y	X^2	XY
1986	45	1	1	45
1987	52	2	4	104
1988	48	3	9	144
1989	55	4	16	220
1990	60	5	25	300
n = 5	ΣY260	ΣX = 15	ΣX^2=55	ΣXY= 813

Substituting the above values in the two normal equations, we get the following:

$$260 = 5a + 15b \quad -3\}$$

Solving equations 3 & 4 we get b = – 3.3

$$813 = 15a + 55b \quad -4\}$$
$$260 = 5a + 15\,(3.3)$$
$$260 = 5a + 49.5$$
$$a = 42.1$$

Therefore, the equation for the line of best fit is equal to :

$Y = 42.1 + 3.3X$

Using this equation, we can find the trend values for the previous years and estimates of the sales for 1991. The trend values and estimates are as follows:

$$Y \quad 1986 = 42.1 + 3.3\,(1) = 45.4$$
$$Y \quad 1987 = 42.1 + 3.3\,(2) = 48.7$$
$$Y \quad 1988 = 42.1 + 3.3\,(3) = 52.0$$
$$Y \quad 1988 = 42.1 + 3.3\,(4) = 44.3$$
$$Y \quad 1990 = 42.1 + 3.3\,(5) = 58.6$$
$$Y \quad 1991 = 42.1 + 3.3\,(6) = 61.9$$

Based on the trend projection equation illustrated above, the forecast sales for the year 1991 is Rs. 61.9

The trend projection method is very popular in business circles on account of simplicity and lesser cost. The basic idea in this method is that past data serves as the guide for future sales. But this method is inadequate for prediction whenever there are turning points in the trend itself. Moreover, while irregular factors such as storms and strikes can be averaged out and contained into the equation, it is desirable to know how valuable such an exercise could be.

Method of Moving Averages

A moving average is an average of some fixed or pre-determined number of observations which moves through the series by dropping the top item of the previous over aged group and adding the next item below in each successive average. This method is based on past data and also designed to compensate for regular cyclical or seasonal variations, it is also the moving average combined with the annual difference method. This method is used for short run forecasting. Data are averaged for the whole cycle and this average is rolled forward for the new data.

The calculations depends upon whether the period should be odd or even.

In the case of odd periods like (5, 7, 9), the average of the observations is calculated for a given period and the calculated value is written in front of central value of the period, say 5 years. The average of the values of five years is calculated and recorded against the third year. In the case of five yearly moving averages, the first two years and the last two years of the data will not have any average value.

If the period of observation is even, say four years, then the average of the four yearly observations is written between second and third year values. After this, centering is done by finding the average of paired values. Let us take up the following illustration:

The following are the annual sales of dresses during the period of 1981-1991. We have to find out the trend of the sales using (1) 3 yearly moving averages, (2) 4 yearly moving averages and forecast the value for 1993.

Year	Sales in Rs. Lakhs.
1981	12
1982	15
1983	14
1984	16
1985	.18
1986	17
1987	19
1988	20
1989	22
1990	25
1991	24

Demand Analysis

Solution : 3 yearly period:

Year	Sales	3 yearly moving total	3 yearly moving average trend values
1981	12	(–)	–
1982	15	41	41/3 = 13.7
1983	14	45	45/3 = 15
1984	16	48	48/3 = 16
1985	18	51	51/3 = 17
1986	17	54	54/3 = 18
1987	19	56	56/3 = 18.7
1988	20	61	61/3 = 20.2
1989	22	67	67/3 = 22.3
1990	25	71	71/3 = 23.7
1991	24	–	–

e.g. The value of 1981 + value of 1982 + 1983

12 + 15 + 14 = 41 – written

at the capital period 1982 of the years 1981, 82 & 83.

Four yearly Moving Averages

Year	Sales	4 yearly moving totals	Moving total of pairs of yearly totals	4 yearly moving averages
1981	12			
1982	15			
1983	14	57		
1984	16	63	120	120/8 = 15
1985	18	65	128	128/8 = 16
1986	17	70	135	135/8 = 16.9
1987	19	74	144	144/8 = 18
1988	20	78	152	152/8 = 19
1989	22	86	164	164/8 = 20.5
1990	25	91	177	177/8 = 22.1
1991	24			

57 = the value of 1981 + value of 1982 + value of 1983, value of 1984

= 12 + 15 + 14 + 16

= 57 written between 1982 and 1983

120 = 57 + 63, 128 = 16 + 65 ... written in the centre of 1982, 1983, 1984 i.e., 1983, 1983, 1984, 1985 i.e. 1985 and so on. 120 is the total of 8 years, so average is calculated by dividing 120 from 8.

Forecast for the year 1993

The trend values from the previous tables can be plotted on graph which is as shown below :

Trend line for 3 yearly and 4 yearly moving averages is the same.

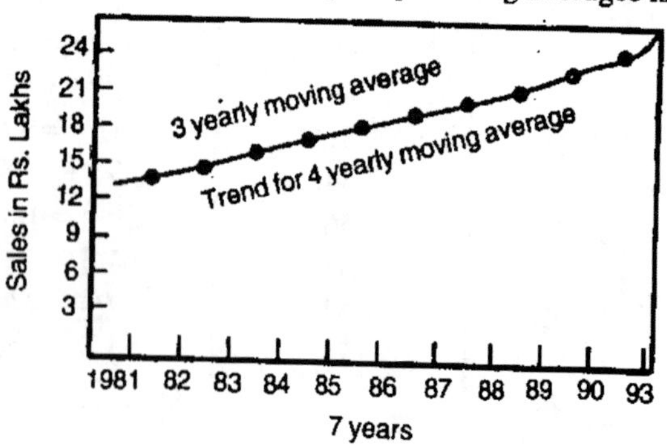

ADVANTAGES OF THIS METHODS

This method is simple and can be applied easily. Secondly, it is based on mathematical calculations and finally this is more accurate.

DISADVANTAGES OF THIS METHODS

The disadvantage of moving average method is that it gives equal weightage to the data related to the different periods in the past. It cannot be applied if some observations are missing.

Regression method

The sales of any commodity does not depend on time only. It may be associated with competitors, advertising, one's own advertising, change in population, income and size of the family, environmental factors, etc. The nature of relationship between these factors can be used and future sales can be forecast. Regression analysis denotes methods by which the relationship between quantity demanded and one or more independent variables (income price of the commodity, prices of related commodities, advertisement expenses, etc.) can be estimated. It includes measurement of errors that are inherent in the estimation process. Simple regression is used when the quantity demanded is estimated as a function of single independent variable. Multiple regression analysis can be used to estimate demand as a function of two or more independent variables.

Simple Linear Regression

In case of linear trend in the dependent variable, a straight line to the data can be fit in, whose general form would be : Sales = a + b price.

The straight line regression equation can be fit in either graphically or least square method. In the graphical method, the sets of data of two variables (sales and income) on a graph are plotted and a scatter diagram can be obtained.

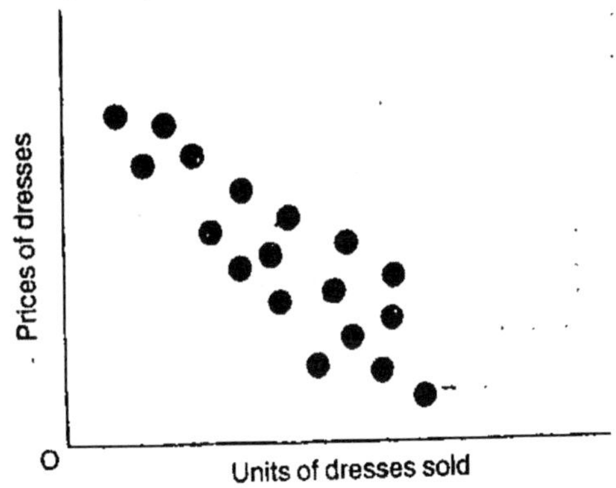

The regression line can be approximated by sketching it free hand in such a manner that the line passes through the middle of the scatter.

In the least square method of estimating the regression line, S = a + bP, the value of the constants, a and b can be with the help of a following formula:

$$b = \frac{n\,\varepsilon\, S_1\, P_1 - \varepsilon\, S^1\, \varepsilon P^1}{n\varepsilon P^2{}_i - (EP_i)^2} \quad \text{and} \quad a = \frac{\varepsilon Si - b\varepsilon P_i}{n}$$

Example

Fit a linear regression line to the following data and estimate the demand at price Rs. 30.

Year	1981	82	83	84	85	86	87	88	89	90	91	92
Price Pi	15	15	12	26	18	12	8	38	26	19	29	22
Sales Si in 1000 Units	52	46	38	37	37	37	34	25	22	22	20	14

Solution

Find the values of a and b and then the following table is constituted:

P_i	S_i	P_J^2	S_1^2	S_1P_1
15	52	225	2704	780
15	46	225	2116	690
12	38	144	1444	456
26	37	676	1369	962
18	37	324	1369	666
12	37	144	1369	444
8	34	64	1156	272
38	25	1444	625	950
26	22	676	484	572
19	22	361	484	418
29	20	841	400	580
22	14	484	196	308
$\Sigma P_i = 240$	$\Sigma S_i = 384$	$\Sigma P_i^2 = 5708$,	$\Sigma S_i^2 = 13716$	$\Sigma S_iP_i = 7098$

Then we will have

$$b = \frac{n\Sigma S_i P_i - \Sigma S_i P^i}{\Sigma S_i P^2 - \left(\Sigma P_i^2\right)} = \frac{12(7098)-(240)(384)}{12(5708)-(240)^2}$$

$$= \frac{-6984}{10,896} = 0.641$$

$$a = \frac{\Sigma S_i - b\Sigma Pi}{n} = [384 - (240)(-0.641)^{1/2}] = 44.82$$

∴ The equation of the regression line is as

$$S = 44.82 - 0.641 \text{ P}$$

By assigning value 30 to P in the equation, the corresponding sales level is :

S (when P is Rs. 30) = 44.82 – 0641 × 30 = 25.29 thousand units

Barometric Method

Barometric method is an improvement over trend projection method. in the trend projection method, the future is some sort of an extension of the past, while in the barometric method, events of the present are used to predict the future demand. This is done by using certain economic and statistical indicators. The barometric techniques use time series to predict variables. The barometric techniques using time series, which when combined in certain ways, provide direction of change in the economy or in industries. These are called *barometers* of a market change.

This method may also be called "Economic Indicatare" method. The economic indicators will help in estimating the demand for product at a future date. There are three types in this,

Leading indicators

Co-incident indicatars.

Diffusion indicators.

Leading indicators

There are leading indicators which serve as useful guide for forecasting the demand for some products. The sales of baby milk can be forecast with the help of birth of children in the past five years, There is a correlation between the demand for baby milk and the birth rate of children. If the indicator is known, the sales forecast may be made on that basis.

Coincident indicators

There are certain indicators which coincide with the rise or fall of general economic activity. The coinciding indicators are the gross national product index of industrial production, retail sales and labour force in the economy.

DIFFUSION INDICES

These indices help the forecasters in relying on the leading indicators used. These indices move up and down behind some other series.

The following indicators are used in assessing the future demand for certain products : -

Indicator	Demand for the product
Construction contracts	Demand for building materials
Increased prices of agricultural commodities	Demand for agricultural inputs
A rise in disposable income	Demand for consumer goods
Automobile registration	Demand for petrol

In the barometric method, it is necessary to find out the existence of any relation between the indicator and the demand for the product. After establishing the relationship through the method of least squares, we have to derive the regression equation.

If the relationship is linear, the equation will be Y = a + bx. Once the equation is derived, the demand for the product can be estimated.

The demand forecasting can be computed by adopting the Simultaneous Equation Method.

Example :

A refrigerator manufacturing company observes that there is a relationship between the consumer's disposable personal income index and purchase of refrigerators by them.

The following data is available to the firm:

Year	Consumer DPI Index (x)	Refrigerator sold (y)
1994	100	100
1995	120	140
1996	150	150
1997	160	170
1998	220	200

From this data, compute the possible demand for the year 1999, if the index would be 250.

Solution :

Regression equation of y on x

y = a + bx

Adopting simultaneous equations, find out the value of "a" and "b"

$$\Sigma y = na + b\Sigma x \qquad \text{------(i)}$$

$$\Sigma xy = a\Sigma x + b\Sigma x^2 \qquad \text{-----(ii)}$$

COMPUTATION OF VALUES

Year	DP 9 Index (x)	Sales of Refrigerator	Square of DP II (x^2)	Product of DP II & Sales (xy)
1994	100	100	10,000	10,000
1995	120	140	14,400	16,800
1996	150	150	22,500	22,500
1997	160	170	25,600	27,200
1998	220	200	48,400	44,000
n=5	$\Sigma r = 750$	$\Sigma y = 760$	$\Sigma r^2 = 1,20,900$	$\Sigma ry = 1,20,500$

By attributing values to the above equations

$$760 = 5a + 750b \qquad \text{-----(iii)}$$

$$120, 500 = 750a + 120, 900b \qquad \text{-----(iv)}$$

To bring equation (iii) to common base multiply it by 150

$$114000 = 750a + 112500b \qquad \text{-----(v)}$$

$$120500 = 750a + 120900b \qquad \text{-----(vi)}$$

$$-6500 = -8400b$$

$\therefore$ $b = 6500 + 8400 = 0.77$

Substituting the value of b in equation (iii)

$$760 = 5a + 750(0.77)$$

$$760 = 5a + 577.5$$

$$5a = -760 + 577.5$$

$$5a = 182.5$$

$$a = 182.5 \div 5$$

$$= 36.5$$

If the index would be 250 for 1999 the number of refrigerators sold would be : $(y = a + bx)$

$$y\ 1999 = 36.5 + 0.77(250)$$

$$= 36.5 + 192.5 = 229 \text{ numbers}$$

Some other methods of demand forecasting :

1) Market research method.

2) Exponential smoothing method.
3) Simulation method.

Simultaneous Equation Method

In this method, all variables are considered simultaneously, for every variable influences other variables. It is a system of n equations with n unknowns. The advantage of this method is that an estimate of future demand for the product can be made with pre-determined variables.

Market Research method

In all big industrial enterprises, there are market research cells. This cell is entrusted with collecting required information for sales forecasting. Or, there are independent market research Organisation which can collect data for the customer industries. They conduct field surveys to collect information directly from the users of commodities. The collected information is then analysed and with the help of the data, the sales department make future estimates of demand for the product.

Exponential Smoothing Method

This is an improvement version of moving average method of forecasting. In this method, the past data is not used very much. All irregularities in the demand pattern are screened out. This method allows for trend and takes it into consideration the short term fluctuations in the detennination of the forecast. In this method, new demand forecast is made from latest actual demand plus old estimate. The formula used in this method is

$$F_t = (aD_t + 1-a)\,F_t + 1$$

Where F_t is the forecast at time t, D_t is the actual demand at time t, F_t–I is the forecast at time (t – 1) a is the smoothing coefficient.

It is necessary to determine the value of smoothing coefficient 'a'. The size of 'a' reaction of response to real changes in demand. The value of a lies between 0 and t. It is also observed that larger a's do not necessarily contribute to better forecasts. A high value of 'a' gives more weight to current values than to past ones.

Simulation Method

Every day life experiences cannot be mathematically explained. Sometimes the model may become complicated and its solution will become difficult. In such a situation, simulation method will be helpful.

The simulation method is associated with the name of Monte-Carlo. Pioneers in this field are Von Neumann, Ulam and Fermi. The simulation method is used to solve the problem by trial and error approach. It is defined as a device for studying an artificial stochastic model of a physical or, mathematical process. This method combines probability and sampling methods to solve complicated problem. This method is useful in a situation where practical experience cannot be used as a guide.

"General simulation method is based on the selection of random numbers from random number tables and these numbers are considered to be probabilities of desired characteristic under study drawn from present population."

In this method, some preliminary survey is conducted to study the past behaviour of the system. Then an appropriate model is formulated with the help of sample observation. This model is used to determine the probability distribution of the characteristics under study. The probability distribution can be easily changed into cumulative distribution functions. Random numbers are chosen from the random tables and are then used to find the sequence values of the variable interest. Then some mathematical functions is filled to obtain the values.

Some of the Difficulties in Forecasting of Consumer Durables

The demand for consumer durables has certain peculiarities. Each durable product requires special study and distinct technique is to be adopted. Consumer durables fall into two categories, one is the new demand and the other is the replacement demand. Forecasting for these two categories has to be made separately. Some of the peculiarities found in forecasting consumer durables are as follows:

(i) Changes in the size and characteristics of population

Demand for consumer goods is related to the demographic characteristics like changes in size, growth rate, age-sex composition of population, etc. For example, the demand for tinned milk and toys depends upon the population of children. In fact, durable goods like T.V., washing machines, etc. depends upon household mcome.

(ii) Saturation limit of the market

There are durable goods which are going to reach saturation point. They are cars and electrical appliance, furniture, etc. Once the. people have these commodities, they are not going to buy the new one.

(iii) Existing stock of the goods

The size and age of the consumer durables determine the time of replacement. Longer the stock, greater is the replacement, shorter the life of the goods, earlier will be the replacement.

The replacement demand for consumer durables is conditioned by psychology, income and social status of the consumer. Most of the consumer durables are status symbols. It is only the rich people who want to maintain their social status. Naturally, when they see new modes with better service, they think of replacing the old ones. It is believed that higher the disposable income, higher is the demand for durable goods. There is one incentive which induces high income groups to buy a durable goods, that is credit facilities available. Wherever instalment credit system is prevailing, demand for some consumer goods also rises.

Thus, the forecaster of consumer durables uses different techniques to forecast the future sales. The forecaster uses barometer method in order to study the effect on demand of changes in size and characteristics of population, of income level of the consumers, etc. He takes up consumer's survey plan in order to study the consumer attitudes towards replacement of the old stocks. Once these difficulties are known, these changes can be incorporated in the model.

Constraints of the Firm

Before any firm can arrive at a decision it has to keep in mind the restrictions that it has to contend with. These restrictions can arise in two ways. Sometimes they may come from within the organisation ie. they are internal to the firm. For eample, a firm which has very capital at its disposal need not explore all alternative possibilities of goods and services that it can produce. Knowing that it has limited capital, it may explore only a few possibilities and decide to produce one of the goods. Here, capital is the constraint which has to be kept in mind before arriving at the decision of what to produce.

Conversely, sometimes restrictions may be imposed on the firm's decision-making, by external factors such as inavailability of sufficient quantity of raw materials, or restrictions imposed by laws and regulations etc. Some of the important external restrictions are discussed below:

(i) Restrictions relating to Output

In case of most of the commodities, the quantity that has to be produced by the firms is determined by an external authority. This authority has the liberty to specify how much has to be produced and this can act as a restriction to the producing firm.

Again, the licensing authority can specify the rules relating to the quality of the commodity and the firm is expected to abide by it. This can also act as a constraint to the producing firm. For example the firm producing of baby foods may be expected to meet certain nutritional requirements specified by the competent authority.

(ii) Restrictions relating to resources

Quantity of resources available to a firm may be fixed or limited. Keeping the availability of resources, the firm will have to take the appropriate decision. Especially in a developing country like India, scarcity of resources acts as a major obstruction to the firm's production levels.

(iii) Restrictions imposed by law

The government may impose certain restrictions on the firm's activities. It may define specify the level of wages and bonus, or the measures to be taken to maintain the health and safety of employees. Restrictions may also take the form of taxes, subsidies, quotas, differential rates of interest on loans etc. Before the firm can arrive at any decision it has to consider all these legally imposed restrictions.

(iv) Restrictions imposed by environmental factors

All firms have to operate within the framework of a given economic, social and political environment. These environments may vary from country to country. The decision-making firm, therefore, needs to have a clear knowledge of these environment both within the domestic economy and also outside it, because today no economy is a closed economy.

The decision maker must have a thorough knowledge about all aspects relating to objectives and policies of the government such as plan objectives, industrial policies, fiscal and monetary policies, foreign trade policy etc. He is also expected to have a fair idea in all the relevant macro-economic trends such as national income, money supply, levels of poverty and unemployment etc. It is necessary for him to keep track of the changing social and political environment in the country.

It is in these matters that the services of economists and analysts can be of great use to the producers. There are specialists who are in constant touch with the changes that are occuring in the economy and it is their responsibility to keep the top level management, well-informed about the forthcoming changes.

(iv) Decision Process

The goal of managerial economics is to solve practical problems of business. This requires decision-making at the level of the firm. Decision making is the process of selecting the appropriate action from among various alternative actions. Decisions have far-reaching effects on the firm and are often easy to make. The following steps should be followed to arrive at right decisions:

(a) To establish objectives.
(b) To express the decision-problem.
(c) To identify alternatives.
(d) To assess alternatives.
(e) To select the best possible alternative.
(f) To implement the decision.
(g) To monitor the performance.

At the outset, it is necessary to be clear about the objectives of a firm. In today's complex world, there are many alternatives available to a firm and also several constraints facing them. In order to have a clear understanding of these, a thorough examination of the environement opportunities and constraints is necessary. An evaluation of alternatives involves collection of all relevant data and their analysis through appropriate techniques. Once the above four steps are completed, it is simple to choose an alternative on the basis of the objective. However implementation of the decision taken requires resources, an explanation to those who are affected by it and the ability to face the consequences. After implementing the decision, its performance must be monitored in comparison with expectations, so that errors are minimised in the future.

Ours is a dynamic economy and decisions have to be made within a time constraint. Things change over time and an undue delay in decision-making may turn opportunities into risks.

Questions

1. What is meant by demand. Explain the factors which influence demand.
2. Examine the role of price, income and price of the related goods in affecting demand.
3. What is the significance of demand analysis to the managerial economist.
4. Explain the law of demand. What do you mean by shifts in demand curve.
5. Explain the concept of elasticity of demand. What factors are influencing in making the demand for a product elastic or inelastic.
6. "If the demand is elastic, it will pay a businessman to charge a low price. If the demand is inelastic, he would be better off with a high price". Discuss.
7. Explain the concept of cross elasticity of demand. How would you measure such elasticity.
8. Distinguish between the following :
   a) Producers goods and consumers goods
   b) Durable goods and perishable goods.
   c) Superior goods and inferior goods.

d) Complementary goods and substitutes.

e) Company demand and industry demand

9. Explain the factors which are involved in demand forecasting.

10. Discuss the various methods of demand forecasting of established and new products.

Short Answer Questions

1. Distinguish between incremental revenue and marginal revenue.
2. Distinguish between demand schedule and demand function.
3. Distinguish between price elasticity and income elasticity.
4. Distinguish between substitution effect and income effect of a change in price.
5. What is the utility of demand forecasfing.
6. How is the demand for new products estimated.
7. Explain briefly different methods of demand forecasting.
8. State the general approach to demand forecasting.

❖✻❖✻❖

CHAPTER 4

LINEAR PROGRAMMING

INTRODUCTION

Linear Programming is a new branch of mathematics developed for solving constrained optimization problems. This new technique was developed during 1950s. The problems of constrained optimization arose because of the limited resources available to maximise or minimise a certain objective. The main objective of linear programming is to find the permissible allotment of resources so as to yield maximum profit, turnover etc. and to minimise the production cost, labour cost etc.

Linear Programming

Definition

Linear Programming is a mathematical technique developed for determining the optimal use or allocation of available limited resources to obtain the desired objectives.

The desired objective is expressed as a linear function of individual allocation (in terms of basic variables of the type $2x + 3y = 5$) and the limitations or restrictions imposed on the use of resources are expressed as linear inequalities involving the decison variables (of the type $2x - y \leq 1$; $x + 2y \leq 3$; $x \geq 0$; $y \geq 0$). These restrictions are called *Constraints.*

Mathematical Formulation of Linear Programming Problem

Given a linear programming problem, it is very important to recognise the objective function to form the linear inequalities, involving the limited resources, subject to the given constraints. The method of formulation is explained in the following examples.

Example 1

A boy wants to buy some clothes. A pair of trousers cost Rs.150/- and shirt Rs. 90/-. The boy wants to buy at least two trousers and three shirts, but he is not allowed to spend more than Rs. 1000/- on clothes. How many trousers and shirts should he buy so that he buys a maximum number of clothes.

In the above example, let x and y be the number of trousers and shirts respectively purchased by the boy. Then the total cost of the purchase will be $150x + 90y$. Since the boy wants at least 2 trousers and 3 shirts, we have $x \geq 2$ and $y \geq 3$. Further, he is not allowed to spend more than Rs. 1000/ on clothes.

This can be put in the form

$$150x + 90y \leq 1000$$

Here we have to maximise the function $p = x + y$ subject to constraints.

$$150x + 90y \leq 1000$$

$$x \geq 2 \text{ and } y \geq 3.$$

Example 2

A manufacturer produces two types of products M and N. The product M gives per unit profit of Rs. 8/- while the product N gives Rs. 10/-. Both the products pass through two machines, machine1 and machine 2. The processing of one unit of product M takes 2 hours of machine 1 and three hours of machine 2 time. The processing of one unit of product N takes three hours of machine 1 and two hours of machine 2 time. The total machine time per week available with machine 1 is ninety hours and with machine 2 is one hundred and twenty hours. Find out the product mix giving the maximum profit.

Objective : Maximise the weekly profit by the products M and N.

Constraints : Machine I time - 90 hours per week.
Machine 2 time - 120 hours per week.

Let 'x' be the number of units of product M and 'y' be number of units of product N. If p is the total profit of both the products, then the weekly profit of both the machines is given by

$$p = 8x + 10y$$

Constraints : $2x + 3y \leq 90$ (Machine time of Machine I per week)
$3x + 2y \leq 120$ (Machine time of Machine 2 per week)

and $x \geq 0$ and $y \geq 0$

(Because number of units produced cannot be less than zero)

Example 3

A multivitamin tablet has to be manufactured by using a mixture of two products 'x' and 'y'. The quantity of each vitamin available per gram in 'x' and 'y', the minimum requirements and the cost of manufacture are given in the following table :

	No. of units of each vitamin content in one gram of product			Cost
	V_1	V_2	V_3	
Product x	6	2	4	20P
Product y	2	2	12	16p
Min.requirement of each vitamin	12	8	24	

Find the least expensive combination which provides the minimum requirements of the three vitamins.

Let 'a' and 'b' be the number of units of products 'x' and 'y' respectively in the mixture. Then the total cost of the manufacture is 20a + 16b.

i.e., ***Objective Function*** $P = 20a + 16b$.

Constraints : Since the mixture has to contain at least 12 units of vitamin 1.

We have $6a + 2b \geq 12$

Similarly, other constraints are

$$2a + 2b \geq 8$$

and $$4a + 12b \geq 24$$

Hence, the formulation of linear programming for the above problem is as follows :

Minimise : $P = 20a + 16b$

Constraints : $6a + 2b \geq 12$

$2a + 2b \geq 8$

$4a + 12b \geq 24$

Solution of Linear Programming Problems

Graphical Method

We observe from the formulation of simple linear programming problem, as explained in earlier pages, that the objective function is a linear function of two variables. Also, the available limited resources known as *constraints* are expressed as linear inequalities involving the decision variables. In the graphical method, we consider the given constraints as linear equations (of two variables) to draw straight lines in the OX and OY plane and then identify the common region represented by the inequalities under non-negativity restriction $x \geq 0$; $y \geq 0$. The point of intersection of these lines with the coordinate axes and their own intersection are called the *corner points*. The region bounded by the lines joining the corner points in the first quadrant is known as *feasible* region. The corner points of this feasible region, optimizes (maximise or minimise) the objective function. The feasible region, will be bounded region in the case of maximisation and unbounded in the case of minimisation.

Outlines of Graphical Method are as follows :

Identify the decision variables.

Formulate the objective function.

Consider each inequality constraints as equations.

Since each equation is linear, it represents a straight line. Draw the straight lines to represent the given equation.

Identify the corner points, and hence the feasible region.

Determine the set of ordered pairs (x, y) which satisfy the constraints and optimizes the objective function.

The method of solving linear programming problem by graphical method is illustrated in the following examples.

Example 1 ***Maximize :*** $P = 4x + 3y$

Subject to the constraints : $2x + y \leq 10$

$$x + y \leq 6$$

$$x \geq 0 \; ; \; y \geq 0$$

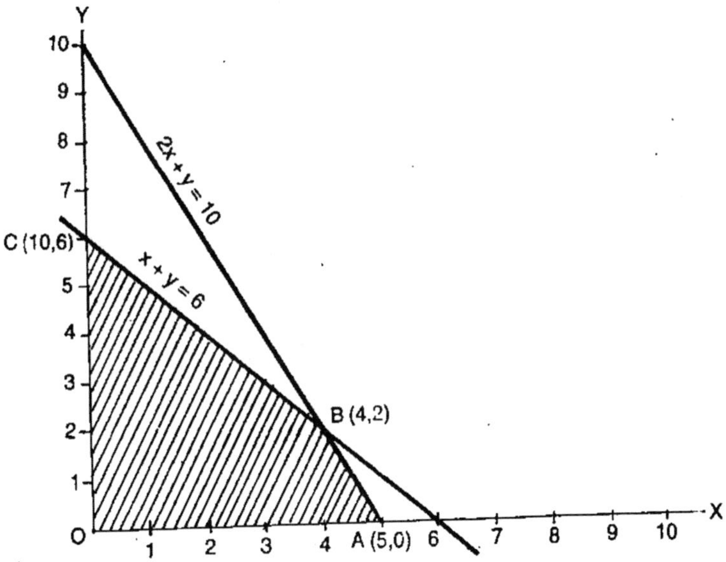

Solution

Let OX and OY be the co-ordinate axes. The non negativity condition that $x \geq 0$; $y \geq 0$ implies that the feasible region of permissible values of the variables x and y lies in the first quadrant. Draw the line $2x + y = 10$ as shown in the figure 1.

Putting $x = 0$, we get $y = 10$

Putting $y = 0$, we get $x = 5$

Hence, (0, 10) and (5,0) are the points on the line $2x + y = 10$.

Similarly, draw the line $x + y = 6$

Putting $x = 0$; $y = 6$

Putting $y = 0$; $x = 6$

Hence (0, 6) and (6, 0) are the points on the line $x + y = 6$.

The two lines intersect at (4, 2)

Thus, the feasible region is the shaded area of the polygon OABC, whose vertices are O(0, 0), A (5, O), B(4, 2) and C (0, 6).

Substituting these values of (x, y) in the equation $P = 4x + 3y$, we get

$P_A = 4(5) + 3(0) = 20$

$P_B = 4(4) + 3(2) = 22$

$P_C = 4(0) + 3(6) = 18$.

Clearly, the maximum valve of P is 22 at $x = 4$ and $y = 2$.

Example 2 A farmer is going to grow rice and wheat. He estimates that rice needs four men per hectare and wheat needs six men. He has 26 men available. Rice costs Rs. 240/- per hectare, wheat Rs. 160/- per hectare. He is prepared to spend upto Rs. 960/-. Find the maximum area of land in which he can grow.

Solution

Let x be the area of land required for rice. Let y be the area of land required for wheat (in hectares).

Crop	*Requirement* *Man Power*	*Cost*
Rice	4	Rs. 240
Wheat	6	Rs. 160
Max man power available		Rs. 26
Max cost		Rs. 960

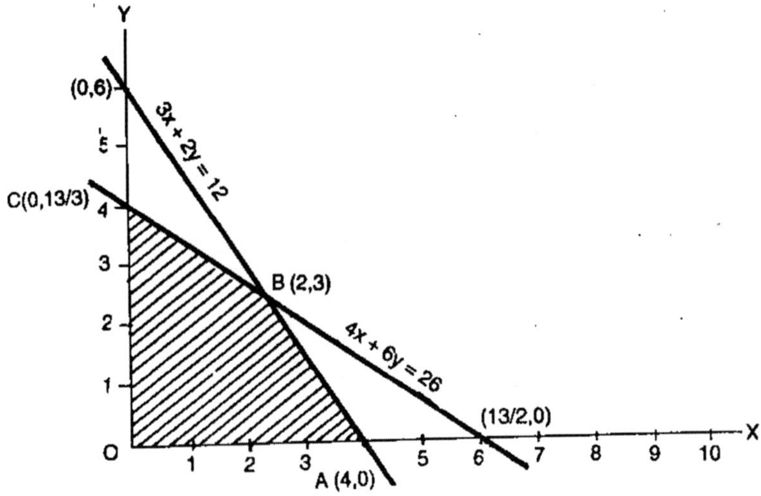

Mathematical Formulation

Constraints : $4x + 6y = 26$

$240x + 160y = 960$

or $3x + 2y = 12$

Objective function : $P = x + y.$

We have to

Maximise : $P = x + y$

Constraints : $2x + 6y = 26$

$3x + 2y = 12$

$x \geq O; y \geq O.$

Let OX and OY be the co-ordinate axes.

Consider $4x + 6y = 26$

Putting $x = 0, y = 13/3$

Putting $y = 0, x = 13/2$

Hence, (0, 13/3) and (13/2, 0) are the points on the line $4x + 6y = 26$.

Similarly, consider $3x + 2y = 12$.

Putting $x = 0, y = 6$

Putting $y = 0, x = 4$

Hence (0, 6) and (4, 0) are the points on the line $3x + 2y = 12$.

From the figure, we observe that the two lines intersect at (2, 3). Thus, the feasible region is the area OABC, with the corner points O(0, 0). A(4, 0), B (2, 3) and C(0, 13/3)

Substituting these values in P = x + y

We have $P_A = 4 + 0 = 4$

$P_B = 2 + 3 = 5$

$P_C = 0 + 13/3 = 1313$

Clearly, the maximum value of P is 5 at B(2, 3). Hence, the maximum area of land he can crop is 5 hectares.

Example 3 ***Minimise P*** = 4x + 2y

Constraints : x + 2y ≥ 2

3x + y ≥ 3

4x + 3y ≥ 6

x ≥ 0 ; y ≥ 0.

Solution

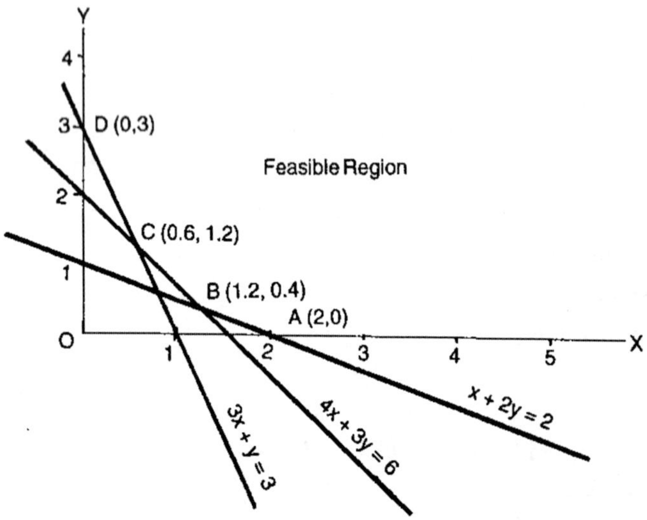

Consider the coordinate axes OX and OY.

Consider x + 2y = 2

Putting x = 0, we have y = 1

Putting y = 0, we have x = 2

Hence, (0, 1) and (2, 0) are the points on the line x + 2y = 2. Draw the line x + 2y = 2 as shown in the Figure 3.

Now Consider $3x + y = 3$

Putting $x = 0$, we have $y = 3$

Putting $y = 0$ we have $x = 1$

Therefore, (0, 3) and (1, 0) are the points on the line $3x + y = 3$. Draw the line $3x + y = 3$ as shown in figure 3.

Finally, consider $4x + 3y = 6$

Putting $x = 0$, we get $y = 2$

Putting $y = 0$, we get $x = 3/2$

Hence, (0, 2) and (3/2, 0) are the points on the line $4x + 3y = 6$ Draw the line $4x + 3y = 6$ as shown in the fig.3 From the fig.3, we observe that the feasible region (shaded area) is an unbounded region with corner points A(2, 0), B(1.2, 0.4), C (0.6, 1.2) and D(0, 3)

Substituting these values of x and y in $P = 4x + 2y$, we have

$P_A = 4(2) + 2(0) = 8$

$P_B = 4(1.2) + 2(0.4) = 4.8 + 0.8 = 5.6$

$P_C = 4(0.6) + 2(1.2) = 2.4 + 2.4 = 4.8$

$P_D = 4(0) + 2(3) = 6$

From the above, we infer that P_{min}. is at the point C (0.6,1.2)

Hence, minimum value of the objective function $P = 4x + 2y$ is 4.8 at $x = 0.6$ and $y = 1.2$.

Example 4 A factory manufactures two types of electronic machines, A and B, and earns a profit of Rs. 20/- per unit of A and Rs. 30/- per unit of B. Each unit A requires three motors and two transformers and each unit of B requires two motors and four transformers. The total supply of the components per month is restricted to 210 motors and 300 transformers. How many of each machine should be manufactured per month so as to maximise the profit?

Solution

	Components	
Machine Type	**Motors**	**Transformers**
A	3	2
B	2	4
Max. available Components	210	300

Let x and y be numbers of type A machine and type B machine manufactured per month.

The objective function is given by

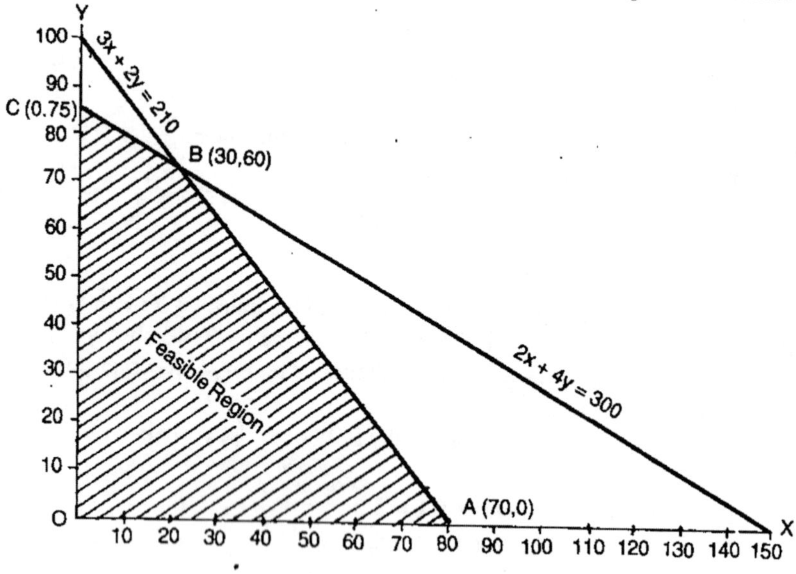

$P = 20x + 30y$ Subject to constraints

$3x + 2y \leq 210$

$2x + 4y \leq 300$

$x \geq 0; y \geq 0$

Consider the coordinate axes OX and OY. $x \geq 0$; $y \geq 0$ implies that the feasible region lines in the first quadrant

Consider $3x + 2y = 210$

Putting $x = 0$; $y = 105$

Putting $y = 0$; $x = 70$

Hence, (0,105) and (70,0) are the points on the line $3x + 2y = 210$ Draw the line $3x + 2y = 210$ as shown in the Figure 4.

Now consider $2x + 4y = 300$

or $x + 2y = 150$

Putting $x = 0$, we have $y = 75$

Putting $y = 0$, we have $x = 150$

Hence, (0,75) and (I 50,0) are the points on the line $x + 2y = 150$

The two lines $3x + 2y = 210$ and $x + 2y = 150$ intersect at (30, 60) Hence, from the fig.4, we observe that OABC is the feasible region. The corner points are A (70, 0), B(30, 60) and C (0, 75).

Substituting these values of x and y in the object function

$P = 20x + 30y$

we have $P_A = 20(70) + 30(0) = 1400$

$P_B = 20(30) + 30(60) = 600 + 1800 = 2400$

$P_C = 20(0) + 30(5) = 2250$

Hence, the maximum value of P is 2400 at B (30,60)

Hence, to maximise the profit, the factory should manufacture 30 units of type A and 60 units of type B machines.

The Simplex Method

With the help of the graphical method, it was possible for us to solve simple linear programming problems. But if the linear programming problem is a little complicated involving more than two variables in the constraints, then it is possible to solve such problems using Simple Method. This method is also known as 'Simplex Algorithm Method'. The simplex algorithm was developed by George B. Dantzig, in the year 1947. The method of solving a linear programming problem by the simplex method is explained below, taking an example to maximise the object function subject to 'less than or equal to' constraints. The same method with modification can be applied to minimisation problems having equality constraints and 'greater than or equal to' constraints.

Slack Variables

We cannot use the Simplex Method unless all the constraints are stated as equations. The given inequalities are converted into equations by the device of adding what are known as *slack variables*. A slack variable represents unused machine time (as in case of machine time constraints), or unemployed capacity (as in the case of warehouse capacity) etc.

We add the slack variable, to the left hand side of the inequalities, while we replace the 'less than or equal to' sign by 'equality' sign.

The Simplex Method of solving an LP problem is explained in the following example.

Maximise : $P = 300x + 200y$ subject to

Constraints : $5x + 2y \leq 180$

$3x + 3y \leq 135$

$x \geq 0 \,;\, y \geq 0$

The given constraints can be re-written as

$5x + 2y \leq 180$

$x + y \leq 45$

$x \geq 0 \,;\, y \geq 0$

Let S_1 and S_2 be the slack variables. The two inequalities can be converted into equalities by adding the slack variables S_1 and S_2 to the left hand side of the inequalities. Then the resulting equations will be given as

$$5x + 2y + S_1 = 180$$
$$x + y + S_2 = 45 \qquad \text{----- (1)}$$
$$x \geq 0, y \geq 0$$

We shall minimise $P = 300x - 200y$ subject constraints given in (1)

The initial Simplex Tableau is set up as follows

Initial Simple Tableau :

	x	y	S_1	S_2	
S_1	5	2	1	0	180
S_2	1	1	0	1	45
.	300	200	0	0	P = 0

The entries in the first row and the second row are the co-efficients of the variables of (1) and the entry in the last row are called the *indicators*.

As we proceed with the Simplex Computation - the value of P will appear at the right hand bottom corner of the table where P = 0 is written.

Putting x = 0 and y = 0, we get P = 0. The other variables S_1 and S_2 which are not zero are called *basic* variables.

Step 1

We observe from the Initial Simplex Tableau that indicators are negative in sign. We observe that the solution obtained is not the optimum solution and that we can improve the solution.

Since both the coefficients are negative in P, we can decrease the value of P, by making either of the coefficient positive. In the place of a basic variable, we can put either x or y. Since –3000 is less than –200, we choose to put x in the place of S_1.

We try the following alternatives :

1. Putting y = 0, $S_2 = 0$, we get x = 45 and $S_1 = 45$, which is negative. Therefore, the solution is not a feasible solution.
2. Putting y = 0 and $S_1 = 0$, we get x = 36 and $S_2 = 9$
   Thus, this is a feasible solution.

From the above, we find a simple rule to replace S_1. The rule is : Find the ratios of the numbers in the last column to the coefficient of x, i.e, $\frac{180}{5}$ and $\frac{45}{1}$. Choose the least of these i.e., $\frac{180}{5}$ .which corresponds to S_1.

The column headed by x in this problem is called *pivotal* column. In general, the column which contains the smallest indicator is the pivotal column. The row containing S_1 is the pivotal row. The entry at the intersection of the pivotal row and pivotal column is called the *pivot*. Here, in this problem, 5 is the pivot. We shall make the pivot unity and the other number in this column zero, by applying suitable row transformation.

In this example, we apply

1) $1/5 R_1$
2) $R_2 - R_1$
3) $R_3 + 300R_1$

With this, we can write down the first simplex tableau.

	x	y	S_1	S_2	
x	1	2/5	1/5	0	36
S_2	0	3/5	-1/5	1	9
	0	-80	60	0	P = 10800

Step 2

From the first simplex table, we observe that there is a negative indicator – 80 in the third row. Hence the solution obtained above is not the optimum solution. The column containing – 80 is now the pivotal column. Now calculate the ratio $\frac{36}{2/5}$ and $\frac{9}{3/5}$ which gives 90 and 15 respectively. The second one being the least, the second row is the pivotal row and the pivot is 3/5. Now we have to replace S_2 by y in the next simplex tableau.

Now we shall make the pivot unity and the other elements in the column are made zero, by the following row transformation.

1. $5/3 R_2$
2. $R_1 - 2/5 R_2$
3. $R3 + 80 R_2$

With the help of these row transformations, we can write down the second simplex tableau.

Second Survey Tableau

	x	y	S_1	S_2	
x	1	0	1/3	-2/3	30
y	0	1	-1/3	5/3	15
	0	0	100/3	400/3	P = 12000

We observe from the second simplex tableau that there are no negative indicators in the third row. Hence the solution obtained is the optimum solution. The second simplex tableau in this case is called the *canonical* form of (1)

The elements in the last column of the second simplex tableau gives the solution of linear programming problem. Hence the solution of the LP problem is

$x = 30$; $y = 15$ and $P_{max} = 12000$

The method of solving linear programming problem may be summed up in the following steps:

Step 1

Express the constraints as equations by introducing slack variables. Write down the initial simplex tableau, the entries being the coefficients of x, y, s_1, and S_2 of constraint equations and the entries in the last row are the coefficients of x and y in p with their signs changed. Take $P = 0$.

Step 2

Observe the indicators. If there is no negative indicator, then the current solution $P = 0$ is the optimum solution. If there are negative indicators in the third row, choose the least among them. The column containing the least is the pivotal column.

Step 3

Calculate the ratios of the elements in the last column to the elements of the pivotal column. The least of the ratios is the pivot, and the row containing this is the pivotal row.

Step 4

By elementary row transformations, convert the pivot to unity and make the other entries in the pivotal column zero.

Step 5

Replace the variable corresponding pivotal row, determined in Step 3 by the variable in the pivotal column. Now we get the new set of basic variables. With this, write down the First Simple Tableau.

Step 6

Examine the indicators again. If there are negative indicators, repeat steps 2 to 5 and construct second simplex tableau, third simplex tableau, etc. If there are no negative indicators, then the process stops and the maximum value of p has been attained.

Duality

Every linear programming problem is associated with an intimately related linear programming problem called its 'dual'. The original problem is called the 'primal'. By working either of the problems, 'primal' or its 'dual' one can obtain the desired answer. The dual has the same optimum solution as the primal but is obtained by an alternative method. If the original linear programming problem called the primal is a maximizing problem, its dual will be a minimizing problem. The dual is formed by rearranging the coefficients of the object function and constraints.

Constructing the Dual Problem

We shall take a simple maximizing problem (primal) to form its dual.

Original problem (primal problem)

Maximize: $Z = 5a + 6b$

subject to $2a + 3b \leq 90$

$3a + 2b \leq 120$

$a \geq 0; b \geq 0$

Dual Problem

Minimize: $Z_1 = 90a_1 + 120b_1$

$2a_1 + 3b_1 \geq 5$

subject to $3a_1 + 2b_1 \geq 6$

$a_1 \geq 0; b_1 \geq 0$

To write the dual linear programming problem, we follow the following steps :

The dual will also have an objective function. Let the objective function be Z_1 instead of Z.

Let a_1 and b_1 be the new set of variables which appear in the dual.

90 and 120 as appearing in the right hand side of the constraints are made coefficients of the variables a_1 and b_1 in the objective function of the dual. Since the dual problem is to be the opposite of the primal problem, we shall minimize this objective function instead of maximizing it.

Thus, the objective function of the dual problem is :

$$\text{Minimize} : Z_1 = 90\, a_1 + 120\, b_1$$

Interchange the coefficients in the rows of the constraints with the coefficients in the columns.

Reverse all the inequalities in the constraints.

Thus, the dual of the given primal is given by :

Minimize : $Z_1 = 90a_1 + 120b_1$.

Subject to $2a_1 + 3b_1 \geq 5$

$3a_1 + 2b_1 \geq 6$

$a_1 \geq 0, b_1 \geq 0$

Properties of Duality

The dual of the dual is the primal

The optimum value of the primal, if it exists, is equal to the optimu value of the dual.

Example 1

Primal : Minimise : $P = 2a_1 + 9a_2 + 5a_3$, subject to constraints

$a_1 + a_2 - a_3 \geq 1$

$-2a_1 + a_3 \geq 2$

$a_1 \geq 0; a_2 \geq 0; a_3 \geq 0$

Dual: Maximize : $P_1 = b_1 + 2b_2$

Subject to constraints

$$b_1 - 2b_2 \leq 2$$
$$b_1 \geq 9$$
$$-b_1 + b_2 \leq 5$$
$$b_1 \geq 0; b_2 \geq 0$$

The above primal and dual problems have the same optimum solution.

Example 2

Primal : Maximize : $Z = 30x + 23y$

Subject to:

$$x + 0.6y \leq 28$$
$$9x + 2y \leq 400$$
$$0.8x + 0.7y \leq 20$$
$$x \geq 0; \; y \geq 0$$

Dual problem :

Minimize : $C = 28a + 400b + 20c$

Subject to: $a + 9b + 0.8c \geq 30$

$0.6a + 2b + 0.7c \geq 23$

and $a \geq 0; b \geq 0; c \geq 0.$

EXERCISE

1. (i) Maximize: $Z = 3x + 4y$

Subject to constraints

$$x + y \le 450$$
$$2x + y \le 600$$
$$x \ge 0 ; y \ge 0$$

Ans : $x = 0$, $y = 450$, $Z_{max} = 1800$

(ii) Maximize: $P = 3x + 2y$

Subject to constraints

$$2x - y \le 1$$
$$x + 2y \le 3$$
$$x \ge 0; \ y \ge 0$$

Ans : $x = 1 ; y = 1$, $P_{max} : 5$

2. (i) Minimize: $P = 20x + 16y$

Subject to constraints

$$6x + 2y \ge 12$$
$$2x + 2y \ge 8$$
$$4x + 12y \ge 24$$
$$x \ge 0; \ y \ge 0$$

Ans : $P_{min} = 68$ at $(1, 3)$

(ii) Minimize: $Z = 40x + 50y$

Subject to constraints

$$8x + 12y \ge 32$$
$$10x + 6y \ge 22$$
$$x \ge 0; \ y \ge 0$$

Ans : $x = 1, \ y = 2$

3. A manufacturer produces two types of products A and B which must be processed through two types of machines. The product A requires two hours of machine 1 time and 1 hour of machine 2 time. The product A earns a profit of Rs.4/- per unit and the product B earns a profit of Rs. 3/-per unit. The total machine time available is 30 hours on machine 1 and 24 hours on machine 2. How many of each type of products should be manufactured so as to maximise the profit ?

Ans : Type A = 12 units . Type B = 6 units

4. A factory manufactures two types of products X and Y, using the ftm machines A, B and C. The following table gives the time required and time available on each machines. The product X earns a profit of

Rs. 50/-and product Y earns a profit of Rs. 30/-. How many of each type should be manufactured so as to maximise the profit.

Machine	*Time in Hours.*		*Max. time available*
	X	*Y*	
A	6	8	380 hrs.
B	8	4	300 hrs.
C	12	4	404 hrs.

Ans : Product X : 22; Product Y : 3 1; P_{max} = Rs. 2030

5. A dealer is going to buy some readymade shirts and trousers. He plans to buy a total of 100 units. The cost of each shirt and trouser is Rs. 80/- and Rs. 240/- respectively. He is prepared to spend Rs. 20800/-. The profit on shirt is Rs. 32/- and trouser is Rs. 64/-. Find the maximum profit he can make. Ans : Rs. 5760/-

6. A dietician has to prepare a mixture of two foods X and Y that provides at least 600 grams of proteins and 800 grams of carbohydrates. Each unit of X contains 20 gms. of protein and 30 gms. of carbohydrates and costs 40 paise. Each unit of Y contains 25 gms of proteins and 20 gms of carbohydrates and costs 60 paise. Find the minimum cost mixture of X and Y which provides the specified requirements.

Ans: 30 and 0, (C_{min}= Rs. 12)

7. The number of units of vitamin A and B per kg of two breakfast cereals M and N are shown in the following table :

	Vitamin A	*Vitamin B*
M	16	8
N	18	4

The minimum daily intake required is 60 units of A and 40 units of B. What is the least total weight of breakfast cereal one must eat to have enough of these vitamins. Ans : 7Kg.

8. A drug manufacturer wants to make a vitamin tablet containing vitamins A, B and C using two types of natural resources x and y. Each tablet has to contain at least 10 units of vitamin A, 42 of B and 14 units of C. Further one gram of x contains 2 units of vitamin A, 15 units of B and 2 units of C. One gram of Y contains 3 units at A, 6 units of B and 7 units of C. If the cost of the source 'x' is 30 paise and that of 'y' is 20 paise per gram, how many units of x and y must be used so as to make the cost minimum.

Ans : x = 2; y = 2; P_{min} = Re 1.

❖✻❖✻❖

CHAPTER 5

PRODUCTION ANALYSIS

Introduction

Organising production of goods and services is an important managerial function. After ascertaining the nature of demand for goods and services, manufacturers arrange for producing them. Business managers keep their objective of maximum profits while undertaking production of goods. While undertaking production, the business managers are involved in incurring expenditure in order to buy raw-material, fuel and power, pay wages to employees, etc. These expenditures are costs. After producing the products, they offer them for sale where they get revenue. The difference between the costs and revenues is the profit for the firm. The managers are required to keep the total cost of production within manageable limits. To do this, the managers try to produce optimum level of output and use the least cost combination of factors of production. Since the cost of production is an important determining factor in production, the managers try to find out a level of product in which the cost is minimum.

The purpose of understanding the costs is two fold one is which helps to determine the price of the product manufactured in the factory. It provides a basis of decision making regarding what price is to be fixed for the product. It also provides him an understanding whether to continue to produce the old product or to produce a new product. Cost analysis helps the managers to arrive at a correct decision. Secondly, this analysis helps him to control costs. They always attempt to keep the cost of production at the lowest level possible.

Production and cost analysis together determine the supply of the product to the market. Production is calculated in physical terms, while the costs are determined in financial terms. Production analysis shows the relationship between physical inputs of the factors of production and the output of the product and studies the least cost combination of factor inputs and returns to scale, while costs analysis deals with various types of costs and their role in decision making.

Meaning of Production

Production in economic terms is generally understood as the transformation of inputs into outputs. The inputs are what the firm buys namely productive resources and outputs are (goods and services produced) which it sells. Production is not the creation of matter, but it is the creation of value. It means that it is the transformation of raw product into consumable product. Apart from physical transformation of matter, it includes services like buying and selling, transporting and financing. In our study, the term *production* is used to mean the production of products for which we require the services of various factors of production. The factors of production are generally known as land resources, labour, capital and entrepreneurship. These factors of production are termed as *inputs*. The firm buys inputs and sells outputs. Inputs are those things that firms buy to produce goods. Outputs are those produced goods. The theory of production centres round the concept of production function.

Production Function

Production function is defined as the functional relationship between physical inputs(factors of production) and physical outputs (i.e., the quantity of goods produced). As Stigler puts it, 'the production function is the name given to the relationship between the rates of input of productive services and the rate of output of the product. It is the economist's summary of technical knowledge.'

Thus, the production function expresses the technological relationship between the quantity of output and the quantities of inputs used in production. More precisely, it can be stated that how maximum output is produced from a given input in the existing state technology. Like demand, production refers to a period of time. Accordingly, it refers to a flow of inputs resulting in a flow of outputs over a period of time leaving prices aside.

Production function depends on (i) quantities of resources (raw-materials, labourers, capital, machinery, etc.). (ii) state of technology, (iii) possible processes, (iv) size of the firms, (v) nature of firm's organization and (vi) relative prices of inputs and the manner in which the inputs are combined. As these change, the production function also changes. Output can be increased by increasing the quantities of inputs used in production. Production function depicts the whole set of choices open to the producer. The adoption of new technology will also change the combination of inputs. These will materialise in the long period.

Since production function is the job of the technologist, he has to specify what quantity of inputs are to be used in order to produce a given output, A production function is expressed as under:-

$O = f(a, b, c, d......)$,

where O stands for output, a to d stand for inputs such as land, labour, capital and organisation and f stands for function.

The equation shows that a given quantity of output depends upon the quantities of inputs.

Every management has to make a choice of the production function depending not only on industrial knowledge and the prices of various factors of production, but also on its own capacity to manage. The management has to select the various inputs and knit them together in economical combinations. These two choices are interlinked. The overriding consideration is to select a combination which gives him the minimum average cost and the maximum aggregate profit.

The Nature of Production Functions

The production function is purely technological - i.e., the knowledge of engineering is essential. That is why the production function is executed by engineers or production managers. This aspect of production function has nothing to do with the price.

Production function is a continuous function. The output is the result of joint use of the factor inputs. If the quantity of one factor is changed, keeping the other factors constant, then output also changes. Production function is determined by the state of technology used. For example, labour productivity depends upon the high quality of labour used in production, which depends upon their technical education and training. Again, the productivity of machine depends on technical advances embodied in them. It is on the basis of technical knowledge that labour, machinery and other inputs are combined. A change in technology means a shift to another production function. It will alter the cost of production. Improvement in technology will result in large output from a given combination of factors of production. Further, it is assumed that firms utilize their inputs at maximum levels of efficiency.

Type of Production Function

Production function may take several forms. One is the relation where quantities of inputs used are fixed. In this case of fixed proportions of production function, the factors of inputs are used in fixed proportion. For example, a fixed number of workers are employed to produce a given unit of output. This is the second type of production function, where the proportion of factor inputs are varied. The behaviour of production, when all factors are varied, is the subject matter of law of returns.

In order to produce a given amount of output, several factors of inputs have to be used. Suppose to produce 200 units of output, 10 workers are required, this amount of labour is fixed. If the management wants to increase the output to 400 units, then 20 workers will be employed. In this state of technology, there is no scope for substituting labour for other factors. This is the case of *Fixed Proportion Production Function* in which the proportions of labour and capital used are fixed. The fixed proportion production function can be shown in the following diagram.

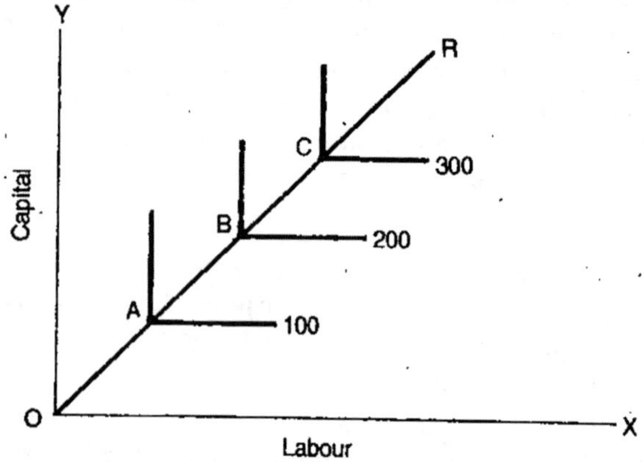

In this diagram, OR represents the fixed capital labour ratio and two units of capital and three units of labour produce 100 units of output. In order to produce 200 units of output, the factor units have to be doubled. In other words, four units of capital and six units of labour are required. A - B - C are isoquant curves. An *isoquant* is defined as the curve representing different combination of inputs which will yield a certain amount of output. In the above diagram, the isoquant is right angled. If one input is substituted for another input to produce the same amount of output, then the isoquant curve moves from upwards to the downwards as shown in the following diagram.

In order to produce 100 units of output, either OY^1 and OX^1 or OX^3 or OY^3 combinations of inputs can be used. If the quantities of one input is decreased, the quantities of other inputs have to be increased, to produce a given output.

The production function differs between short period and long period. In the short period, one or more inputs are fixed. In order to produce more units of output, the management has to increase the variable factor. For example, machinery is fixed and labour input is variable. In this case, the quantity of machinery cannot be increased in the short period. Then the only possibility is to increase labour inputs. This is called variable proportion of production function. Diagram 2 refers to variable proportion of production

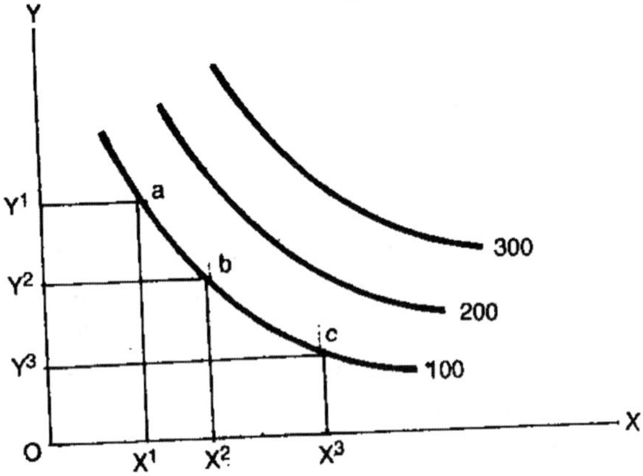

function. In this case, the ratio in which the factor inputs are used is not fixed but it is variable.

In the long period, all factor inputs can be varied. In the long period, the management can choose between increasing production through the use of more labour or through plant expansion, depending upon which the combination of labour and plant size is more efficient in producing a given output.

Cobb-Douglas Production Function

Economists have examined several production functions and have used statistical analysis to measure the relation between changes in physical inputs and outputs. One such statistical production function is Cobb-Douglas Production function. In its original form, this concept was applied to the whole of manufacturing in U.S.A. In Cobb-Douglas production function, the output is goods produced by the manufacturing industries. The inputs are labour and capital. The Cobb-Douglas formula says that labour contributes about 75 percent increase in manufacturing production while capital contributes only 25 percent. The formula is as follows:

$O = KL^{a} C (1 - a)$

Where O is output, L is the quantity of labour,

C is the quantity of capital employed, K and

a(a < 1) are positive constants.

a and 1 – a measure percentage response of output to percentage change in labour and capital respectively.

The production function shows 1 per cent in labour, the capital remaining constant, is associated with 0.75 per cent change in output.

Similarly, one per cent change in capital, labour remaining constant, is associated with a 0.25 percent change in output. Returns to scale is associated with a 0.25 percent change in output. Returns to scale are constant. That is, if factors of production are increased, each by 10 per cent, then the output also increase by 10 per cent.

ISO Cost Curves

The production function so far discussed is concerned with physical or technological aspects. It does not tell us about optimal combination of inputs. Further, the management has to incur expenditure in buying inputs.

The management has to buy many kinds of labour, raw-material, machinery etc. In order to buy them, the manager is expected to know the prices of the inputs. In other words, the manager has to know what it costs to produce a given output. He wants to minimize the cost of any output he produces. He is required to draw ISO cost curves. An ISO cost curve is a curve or line representing equal cost. An ISO cost line is so called because, it shows all combinations of inputs having equal total cost. The ISO cost lines are straight lines which means that the firm has no control over the prices of the inputs and the prices are the same irrespective of the units of inputs bought by the firm. Let us study the following diagram:

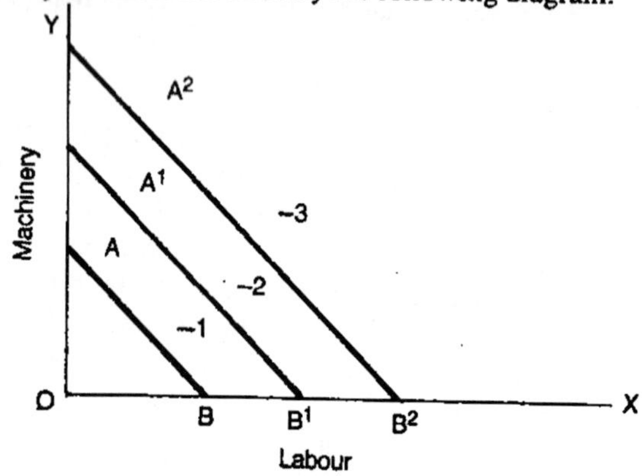

The prices of factor inputs are given. Say, the price of factor X is Rs. 4 and that of factor Y is Rs. 5. With outlay of Rs. 200, we can buy 50 units of X or 40 units of Y. The straight line AB is the ISO cost line. If the outlay increases, then the ISO cost line moves upward. The ISO cost line will change if the prices of factors change. Outlay will be remaining the same.

Let us suppose that the prices of inputs such as labour and machinery are fixed. One ISO cost curve represents the quantities of labour and machinery, which may be obtained at a fixed amount. For example ISO cost curve 1 shows that quantities of X and Y inputs can be bought by Rs.200. ISO cost curve 2 shows that quantities of X and Y can be bought by Rs.400 and so on.

Cost Minimisation

The firm wants to produce any amount of output at the least cost. This is obtained by the point of tangency of the isoquant to an ISO cost line. In other words, minimum costs mean that isoquants are tangents to ISO cost lines.

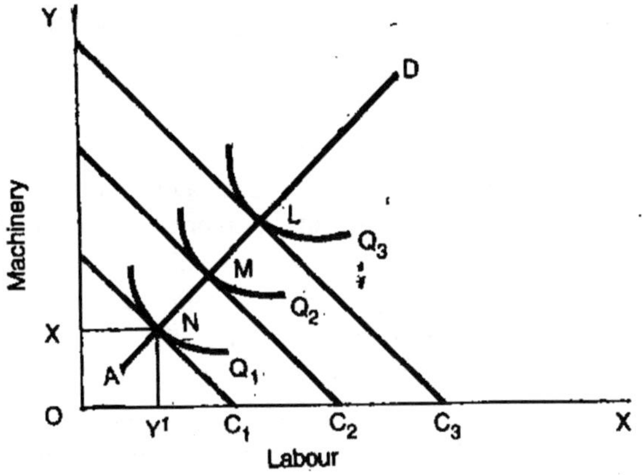

In the above diagram, the maximum output is obtained at a point of tangency between isoquant and ISO cost lines. N,M,L are the points of tangency. The firm expands output along the line D. At the point of N output, the firm buys OX^1 and OY^1 inputs. This is the optional combination of inputs. At this point, the marginal rate of substitution between inputs is equal to the ratio between the prices of the inputs. The minimum cost is represented by the point of tangency between the isoquant and ISO cost line.

Managerial Uses of Production Function

The production functions developed in economic theory is a micro-economic concept. But the production function developed by Cobb-Douglas is a macro-economic concept. Anyway, production function is concerned with explaining how maximum quantity of output can be produced from the minimum quantities of inputs. Further, it clearly states how much of inputs are required to produce a given quantity of output. The knowledge of production function though technological, has immense managerial use. Though the combining of inputs in the production function is purely technological, its direction is to be secured from management. The production function analysis mentions how some factor inputs have to be kept constant and some others are varied in order to produce a given amount of output. But there are certain indivisible inputs like machinery, technical skill, etc. which have to be used to the maximum extent. Therefore, the variable factors must be made suitable to the indivisible fixed factors. As such, the knowledge of the characteristics of various inputs is necessary in order to give managerial direction for their uses.

The knowledge of production function is very much necessary to managers whenever they want to maximise production from given inputs. In this regard, they use the isoquant and ISO cost curve concepts in order to choose the optimum combination of factor inputs. The ISO cost line plays a crucial role in determining the combinations of factor inputs in the production of a chosen commodity.

The producer like a consumer has to function in equilibrium. It is the responsibility of the management to produce a given quantity of output at the minimum cost. The management, in order to do so, has to equate the marginal rate of technical substitution with the price ratio of the two inputs. Its practical usefulness can be explained with the help of an example: Supposing the price of one input rises while the other input remaining constant, then he substitutes one with the other. How this can be done is known by drawing an ISO cost line and thereby equating this with the minimum cost. It buys the inputs and uses them in a certain proportion. The production function analysis suggests that the optimal ratio of factor inputs is obtained at a point where the ISO cost line is tangent to isoquant curve. The position of tangency between these two curves is the point of least cost combination of inputs. In this analysis, it is assumed that the prices of inputs remain unchanged. Supposing the price of one input rises, while the other is unchanged, then the firm substitutes the input, the price of which has risen to the input for which the price has not risen. In such cases, he would recast the ISO cost curve and change the combination of inputs. Managements can use this analysis for increasing the output from their expenditure on inputs.

The production function is not just theoretical, but very much practical. The production function is now being used in decision making. This analysis helps us to solve two important issues, namely, i. how to obtain maximum and output from a given set of inputs and ii. how to obtain a given output from the minimum aggregation of inputs. But in some complex situations where several inputs are to be used to produce a large quantity of output, then mathematical equations are being used. With the development of linear programming, complex problems have been solved to a great extent.

Very recently, Earl Heady and his associates developed a device called *Pork Costulator* to solve complex problems which arise in production function. They developed this device to determine the most profitable ration for feeding hogs under different price conditions. With the application of computers, the complex problems in production function are being solved to the satisfaction of the manager.

Multiple products

A firm or an organisation which produces a single-product may find it difficult to cater to the needs of the consumers which keeps changing over time. A firm producing multiple products, on one hand, has a better chance of satisfying consumers' needs. Firms, therefore, prefer to diversify and produce a variety of products.

A firm producing multiple products can produce similar products or it may produce entirely distinct and different products. A talcum powder manufacturing firm can produce baby foods or detergent powders.

Opportunities for Multiple Products

Opportunities for producing multiple-products may arise due to several reasons, such as :

(a) to make better use of the existing marketing facilities.

(b) to cater to customers' demands.

(c) to consolidate on the reputation already enjoyed by the firm.

(d) to improve the sales of existing products of the firm.

(e) to utilize the technological development in the production process in a better manner.

(f) to identify new markets.

(g) to achieve full utilisation of installed capacity.

Thus, to increase its competitive strength and earn more profits, a company aims at adding new products to its product line. Only when there is excess capacity, firms think of diversifying their product line by adding new products. Excess capacity can be interpreted as the type of idleness which can be exploited profitably by manufacturing some more products. This excess capacity may be the result of over-optimism, seasonal variations, cyclical fluctuations, secular shifts in the markets, research etc.

Policy on Adding New Products

Before adding a new product, it is necessary for the firm to compare the incremental costs with incremental returns. Only when the net returns from adding a new product is greater than net return from other alternative investments, the firm can think of producing the new product.

In addition to this, the decision-makers, before adding a new product must first identify potential product additions. They must further evaluate the proposals and select the right ones. Most important of all, they must introduce the new product in a manner profitable to the company.

The several stages involved in introducing a new product are discussed below:

(i) Generation of ideas

The first step in the development of a new product is getting an idea. Ideas may be generated from various sources both internal and external. From within the organisation, ideas may be put forward by the executives, managers, technical personnel, research personnel, or even the company's sales force who are in close contact with the market. From external sources, ideas may come through competitors, customers, etc.

(ii) Examining the ideas

It is improbable for any firm to accept all ideas that have been generated. Moreover, no firm can afford to pursue many product ideas at the same time. Careful evaluation and selection of the most economically viable product ideas is a must for the firm. In addition to this, the firm must take into consideration, availability of raw materials, technical know-how, finance, market potential and profitability before accepting a new product idea.

(iii) Product concept and Analysis

A product concept refers to the clear presentation of the product which the firm is offering to its customers. This requires giving information about the specific needs of consumers which the firm aims to satisfy, the way in which it is to be satisfied, the benefits which the consumers are going to receive and the price the consumers are expected to pay etc.

The product concept must also be evaluated in terms of utilisation of existing capacity, profit expectations etc. Further, some important considerations relating to future sales, investment, costs etc have to be thoroughly analysed.

(iv) Development of the Product

This is the stage where the abstract idea of developing a product, takes concrete shape. It is in this stage that the management takes the final decision regarding developing the new product on commercial basis. Once the firm decides to implement the idea, the process building the product and releasing it for testing is carried out.

(v) Testing of the Product

This is a very crucial and important stage, where the acceptability of the product is tested. In the first place, testing the concept is done by evaluating the reactions and responses of the consumers. For this, the product must be made available in its finished form including packaging, price range etc. Secondly, testing of the product is done by assessing the acceptability of its form, size, shape, colour etc. This enables the firm to identify the consumers' tastes and preferences. Lastly, testing the market is undertaken by releasing the product in selected markets to determine how successful it is. This helps the firm in modifying the product, devising better advertising campaigns and dealing with competition more effectively.

(vi) Commercialise the Product

This stage involves introducing the product to a wider market and this can be done either in a phased manner or simultaneously. It is always advantageous for the firm to launch the new products in different phases in different regions. This ensures that there is no difficulty in meeting the demand of the consumers.

Policy on dropping old Products

Firms sometimes may have to face situations where it becomes necessary for them to drop certain products or a product from their product line. Such situations may arise due to the following reasons :

(i) A fall in the effectiveness of the product may force the firm to delete the product.

(ii) The entry of a substitute product which is superior to the existing product may force it out of the market.

(iii) Reduction in sales trend may slowly eliminate the product.

(iv) A downward trend in prices and profits may result in the removal of the product.

The decision-maker must therefore assume the responsibility of selecting the products for elimination after carefully examining the entire product line, analysing the results and considering the opportunities for future profit possibilities before deleting a product.

The most important reason for product deletion is a falling trend in profits. It is necessary to find out the reason for declining profits before a decision to discontinue the product is arrived at.

The Law of Variable Proportions

The law of variable proportion occupies an important place in managerial economics, for it examines the production function with one variable input, keeping the quantities of other inputs fixed. It refers to input output relation when the output is increased by increasing the quantity of one input. When the quantities of one input is varied, keeping the other inputs constant, the proportion between the fixed factor and the variable factor is altered. When the combination of inputs are thus altered, the resulting output also changes. The effect of output of variations in factor proportions is called the *law of variable proportions*. The law examines the production function with one factor input variable, while other factor inputs remain unchanged. The law of variable proportions is defined as follows, 'As the quantity of one input is increased, keeping the quantity of other inputs fixed, the output increase in the beginning and afterwards decreases.' Alfred Marshal defined it as ' An increase in labour and capital applied in the cultivation of land causes in general a less than proportionate increase in the amount of produce raised unless it happens to coincide with a improvement in the arts of agriculture.'

Samuelson defined it as 'An increase in some inputs relative to other fixed inputs will, in a given state of technology, cause output to increase; but after a point, the extra output resulting from the same additions of extra inputs will become less and less'.

Assumptions of the Law of Variable Proportions

The law of variable proportion refers to the behaviour of the output as the quantity of one factor is increased, keeping the quantity of other factors fixed and further, it states that the marginal product and the average product will eventually decline. The law of variable proportions as stated above holds goods under the following conditions:

(i) The state of technology of production remains unchanged. If there is an improvement in the technology of production, the marginal and average product may increase instead of diminishing.

(ii) Some inputs are kept fixed during the process of production. It is only in this way that factor proportions are altered to know its effect on output. The law does not apply if all factor inputs are proportionately varied.

(iii) The law is based on the possibility of varying the proportions in which various factors can be combined to produce a product. This law does not apply to cases where the factor inputs have to be used in fixed proportions to yield a product.

The production function can be expressed in the form of a schedule. In the following illustration, the amount of capital equipment employed is fixed and only the labour input is varied.

No. of Workers	(x) Output (O)	Average Product O + Y	Marginal product $\Delta O + \Delta Y$
1	8	8	-
2	17	8.5	9
3	27	9	10
4	36	9	9
5	43	8.6	7
6	48	8	5
7	48	8	5
8	48	6	–2

From the total output, average and marginal output can be derived. Marginal product is the addition to total product which can be produced by addition of more units of the variable input. Average output is the ratio of total output to the amount of the variable input. The behaviour of the total average and marginal output is shown in the diagram below.

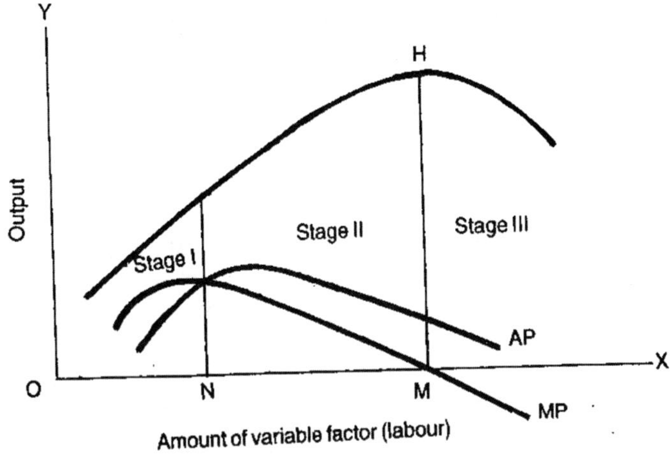

The behaviour of total product, average product and marginal product curves is shown in the above diagram.

In the stage I, total product increases at an increasing rate. Two men produce more than twice as much as one man. In this stage, both marginal product (MP) and average product (AP) are rising. Because MP is greater than AP, MP pulls up the average product. The boundary line of the I stage is reached when average product and marginal product are equal. This takes place at the point N in the diagram. The first stage is known as the stage of increasing returns, because the average product of the variable factor is increasing throughout this period. It may be seen that the marginal product also is rising but later, it starts declining.

In the stage II, the total product continues to increase, but at a diminishing rate. When the marginal product is zero, the total product is the maximum. In this stage, both AP and MP are declining. MP being below the average product, pulls the average product down. At the end of the second stage at the point M, the marginal product to the variable factor inputs becomes zero, while the total point reaches the highest point. This stage is called the stage of diminishing returns as both the average and marginal products of the variable factor continuously fall.

In the III stage, total product declines and therefore the total product curve slopes downward. As a result, the marginal product is negative and the MP curve goes below OX axis. The average product decreases still further. It shows that the variable factor is too much to mixed factor. This stage is called the stage of negative returns.

It may be noted that stage I and III are completely symmetrical. In the I stage, fixed factor is too much relative to the variable factor. In this stage marginal product of the fixed factor is negative. On the other hand, in the III stage, variable factor is too much relative to the fixed factor. Therefore, marginal product of the variable factor is negative.

The Stage of Operation : The question is which stage of operation is rational to production. A rational producer will not choose to produce in the III stage. At the end of II stage at the point M, the marginal product to the variable factor is zero, the producer will be maximising the total product and thus will be making the maximum use of the variable factor. In the I stage, the producer will not be making maximum use of fixed factor and he will not be utilising fully the opportunities of increasing production by increasing the quantity of variable product, whose average product continues to rise throughout the I stage. Thus, a rational producer will not stop in the stage I, but will expand further. At the point N, the marginal product to the variable factor is the maximum and at the end point N of the stage I, he will be making maximum use of the fixed factor. So long as the average product, marginal product and total product are rising, the entrepreneur will not stop producing. Therefore, he goes to stage II, where both marginal product and the average product of the variable factor are diminishing. The stage II represents the range of rational production decisions.

Returns to Scale

The laws of production describe the technically possible ways of increasing the level of production. These show how the output can be increased by changing the quantities of factor inputs. In the short run, only one factor can be altered, keeping the other factor unchanged. It is because, in the short period, fixed factors like machinery, cannot be altered. It is possible to alter the fixed factor in the long period. The laws of returns to scale refer to long run analysis of production.

The laws of returns to scale are entirely different from the laws of variable proportion. In the laws or returns to scale, all productive factors or inputs are increased or decreased in the same proportion. In returns to scale, we analyse the effect of doubling or trebling, quadrupling and so on of all inputs on the output of the product. The study of changes in the output as a consequence of changes in the scale, forms the subject matter of 'Returns to Scale'.

The Three Phases of Returns to Scale

Producers who have not studied economic analysis think that output can be doubled by doubling all the inputs or treble the output by trebling all the productive inputs. But actually, this is not so. In other words, actually the output or returns do not increase/decrease strictly according to the change in the scale.

If the increase in output is proportional to increase in the quantities of input, returns to scale are said to be constant. It means that a doubling of inputs causes a doubling of output. If the increase in output is more than proportional, returns to scale are increasing and if the increase in output is less than proportional, returns to scale are increasing and if the increase in output is less than proportional, returns to scale are diminishing.

Let us take up an illustration :

Returns to Scale

[Out put in Quintals]

Sl. No.	Scale of inputs	Total Product	Marginal Product or returns
1.	1 Worker + 3 acres of land	2	2
2.	2 Workers + 6 acres of land	5	3 Stage I, increasing
3.	3 Workers + 9 acres of land	9	4 returns
4.	4 Workers + 12 acres	14	5
5.	5 Workers + 15 acres	19	5 Stage II Constant
6.	6 Workers + 18 acres	24	
7.	7 Workers + 21 acres	28	5 Returns
8.	8 Workers + 24 acres	31	4 Stage III
9.	9 Workers + 27 acres	33	3 Diminishing
			2 Returns

In the table, it can be seen that as all the factor inputs are together increased to the same extent, the marginal product or return increases first up to a point, then constant for some further increase in the scale and ultimately starts declining. At the scale of 1 workers + 30 acres of land, the total product is 2 quintals. To increase the output, the scale is doubled, the total increases to more than double (5 quintals instead of 2 quintals). When the output is trebled, the total output increases to 9 quintals, the increase this time being 4 quintals instead of 3 quintals. In other words, the return to scale is increasing. If the scale of production is further increased, the marginal product remains constant up to a certain point and beyond it, it starts diminishing. This is illustrated in the following diagram.

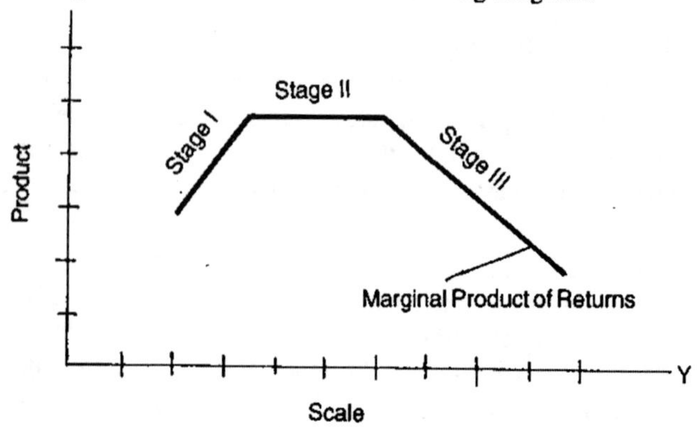

Increasing Returns to Scale

Increasing returns to scale means that output increases in a great proportion than the increase in inputs. If, for example, all inputs are increased by 25 per cent, the output increases by 40 per cent, then the increasing returns to scale is prevailing. When the firm is expanding, increasing returns to scale are obtained in the beginning. One chief reason for this increase is the effect of technical and managerial indivisibility. Indivisibility means that equipment is available only in minimum sizes and the firm has to start producing from the minimum size of equipment. In the beginning, the firm will not be in a position to use the equipment to its optimum capacity. In other words, the equipments are under-utilised in the beginning. When the scale of operations are increased, they are put into maximum use and hence the output or return increases more than proportionately.

Another cause for increasing lies in dimensional relations. Prof. Baumol gives an interesting example. A wooden box 3 ft. cube contains 9 times greater wood than the wooden box of 1 ft. cube, i.e., 3 ft cube wooden box is 27 times greater than that of 1 ft. cube. In the same way, if the diameter of a pipe is doubled, the flow through it is more than double.

Lastly, increasing returns to scale comes from higher degree of specialisation.

Constant Returns to Scale

If the scale of inputs are increased in a given proportion and the output increases in the same proportion, returns to scale are said to be constant, i.e., doubling of all inputs, doubles the output. In mathematics, the case of constant returns to scale is called linear and homogeneous production function or homogeneous production function of the first degree. In some industries, expansion of output produces no net economics or diseconomies and the cost of production remains the same. Such industries are said to be governed by the law of constant returns.

Diminishing Returns to Scale

When the output increases in a smaller proportion than the increase in all inputs, decreasing returns to scale are said to prevail. When a firm goes on expanding by increasing all its inputs, then eventually diminishing returns to scale occurs. Economists give different causes for diminishing returns. Some economists view that the entrepreneur is one fixed factor, while all other inputs are variable factors. But the entrepreneur factor cannot be increased. On this view, they say that the law of diminishing returns is the special case of the law of variable proportions. In this case, they say that we get diminishing returns beyond a point, because varying quantities of all other inputs are combined with the entrepreneur as a fixed factor. Other economists do not subscribe to this view, but they say that diminishing returns to scale occur because of increasing difficulties of management, coordination and control. When the firm becomes gigantic, it is difficult to manage it with the same efficiency as before.

Importance of the of Diminishing Returns

Prof. Cairnness observed that in the absence of diminishing returns, the science of political economy would be as completely revolutionised as if human nature itself were altered. Such is the importance of the law of diminishing returns. Whenever some factors of production are fixed and cannot be varied and other factors are varied, then the techniques of production remaining the same, diminishing returns are bound to follow sooner or later. There is no escape.

The validity of the law of diminishing returns is not merely based on theoretical reasoning, but it has been supported by empirical evidence. It has been remarked that if there is no possibility of diminishing return, then it is possible to grow sufficient food grains in a flower pot by simply increasing the doses of labour and capital. But experience has shown that it is not so.

Prof. Lipsey remarked, *'Indeed were the hypothesis of diminishing returns incorrect, there would be no fear that the present population explosion will bring with it a food crisis'.* It is because that the law of diminishing returns is bound to operate, enlightened thinkers are trying to prevent the occurrence of the law. With the application of science and technology, it is possible to keep the operation of diminishing returns in check.

Economies and Diseconomies of Scale

Scale of production means the size of the plant which has an important bearing on cost of production. It is the manufacturers' experience that larger the scale of production, lower is the average cost of production. That is why entrepreneurs are tempted to enlarge the sale of production so that they may earn maximum profit. These economies are broadly classified into internal economies and external economies.

Economies and Diseconomies of Scale

In the scale of production, all factor inputs are increased simultaneously. The proportion of factor inputs is increased in the same manner to get higher output.

When a firm decides to produce the product on a large scale, it has to increase all inputs. The large scale production refers to the production of a commodity on a big scale, i.e., by enlarging the size of the plant and using higher quantities of law materials, labour etc. Large scale production covers many advantages. Some of the advantages are:

(i) Efficient Use of Capital Equipment

In the large scale production, the producer instals most modern machinery and enlarge the scope of division of labour. Consequently, output increases and costs become minimum.

(ii) Economy in Management

In a big organisation, there is plenty of scope for division of labour. Specialised labour produces a larger output, keeping in mind the quality of the product. It is only in large scale business, that every person can be put on the job which he can perform most efficiently. The management can be better utilised in the large scale production. The entrepreneur is able to translate his ideas into practice in a large scale organisation. He can direct the organisation functioning most efficiently.

(iii) Economies of Buying and Selling

A big organisation can arrange for the purchase of raw materials and spares on favourable terms. Bulk purchase of raw-materials is always economical. While selling goods, it can attract customers by offering a greater variety of concessions and by ensuring prompt supply. A lower rate of profit results in larger sales and higher net profits in a larger scale business.

(iv) Economies on Overhead Charges

The expenses on administration and distribution are very much controlled in a big business. Interest, pay bill and other overhead charges are the same whether production is undertaken either in the medium scale or big scale. The same amount of expenditure is being distributed over a large output and as such becomes lower per unit of output.

(v) Research and Development

A large organisation can set apart a certain sum of money for research and development from the total gross profit, which will not be a burden to the organisation. It is well known that in the long run, these expenses more than repay. Successful research may lead to simplification or productive processes which may bring large profit to the firm.

(vi) Advertisement and Salesmanship

A big concern can spend sufficient money on advertisement and salesmanship. Ultimately, they bear fruit. A big business can challenge the competitors by means of maintaining frequent advertisement and capture the market of the rivals.

Diseconomies of Large Scale Production

Though there are a good number of advantages in the iarge scale production, it is not free from some diseconomies. Some of the weaknesses of the large scale production are:

(a) Over - worked Management

When a business grows very big, management becomes impersonal and consequently tells on the efficiency and honesty of the employees. Owing to delegation of responsibilities to the different cadres in the organisation, supervision becomes formal and laxity enters the field which causes higher expenditure. The management becomes overworked. Lack of personal contact and increase in impersonal relationship between top level officers and the lower level employees results in clashes and conflicts. This is positively harmful to the business.

(b) Over - production

There is every possibility in big business that production may exceed the requirements, resulting in over production. It is very difficult to dispose off a large output profitably.

Inspite of these weakness, large scale production offer several economies in production. The advantages outweigh the disadvantages. The scale of production is to be enlarged till the firm reaches the optimum size. At this scale of production, the total profit is the maximum and the average cost is the minimum. If the size of the firm goes beyond the optimum size, diminishing returns steps in and marginal cost will be more than marginal revenue. Differences in efficiency between firms will show themselves not in differences in marginal costs, but differences in output. The more efficient firm will produce larger output than inefficient firms.

(c) Internal Economics and External Economies

The possibility of large scale production is due to the emergence of internal and external economies. If the cost of production falls with every expansion of output, this is due to availability of internal economies. If firms enjoy many advantages from the growth of the industry, such measures are called external economies.

Internal Economies Internal economies are defined as those economies in production, those reduction in production costs, which accrue to the firm itself when it expands its output or enlarges its scale of production. The internal economies arise within a firm as a result of its own expansion independent of the size of and expansion of the industry. The internal economies arise when a firm increases the scale of production. From the managerial economies point of view, internal economies are more important as they can be effected by managerial decision of an individual firm to change its size or to increases of scale of production.

Internal Economies are of Several Types

(i) Technical economies

Technical economies pertain not to the size of the firm but to the size of the factory. A firm may own and operate several factories at different places. The size of the factory depends upon the nature of the industry. If it is agriculture or diary, large plants can be duplicated in several establishments. In such industries, the size of the establishment is small. But in the case of mining, manufacturing of steel, automobiles, etc., the size of the factory is invariably big. It is because, it is economical to have such a large size.

Prof. Cairncross classifies technical economies into three types, (a) economies of superior techniques, (b) economies of increased dimension, (c) economies of linking process.

Economics of superior techniques arise when the firm uses machines representing superior techniques, for example, N.C. Machines. When large machines with superior technology are used, the firm can make use of the economies of increased dimension. For example, double decker bus is more economical than a single decker. What it means is that without using additional man power and other inputs, big sized machines can be operated and a larger quantity of output can be produced. A large plant can enjoy the economies of linking process. For example, the sugar factory having its own cane farm. Paper making and pulp making may be combined in the factory itself. Such linking saves transport costs.

There is another technical economy derived from a big factory which is that of using by-products. For example, molasses is used to manufacture liquor in a sugar factory. In large factories, it is possible to derive considerable technical internal economies.

(ii) Managerial Economies

Managerial economies refer to the advantages that a firm derives from efficient management. These economies arise from the creation of functional department and thereby several functions may be entrusted to these departments. For example, Personnel Department looks after recruitment, training and welfare, etc. This is possible only for a big firm. The management expenses can be reduced by means of rationalisation of administration. In a big firm, it is possible to make the fullest use of the services of the experts. Delegations of responsibility to subordinate officers will increase efficiency.

(iii) Commercial Economies

Commercial economies arise from the purchase of raw-materials and sale of manufactured product. Large businesses have bargaining advantages in the purchase of raw material and are given preferential treatment by the suppliers. They are able to get concessions from transport organisations. A large firm can employ experts in the field of keeping and selling of inputs and outputs respectively. A big firm can effectively undertake sales promotion and bear that expenditure. Since the mangnitude of sales is high, it can spend a huge amount on advertisement. A firm having small means, cannot be like a big firm in the matter of aggressive sales.

(iv) Financial Economies

These economies arise from the fact that a firm has borrowing capacity from the financial institutions on favourable terms. It can raise money needed either for renovation or expansion of the factory through public deposits and floating of right and convertible debentures at a premium. This cannot be done by a small producer.

(v) Risk Bearing Economies

A big firm can absorb certain risks by means of diversifying production, diversifying the market and also diversifying the process of production.

Diversification imparts strength and stability and makes the firm less vulnerable to changes in commercial fortunes. For example, if a company produces a number of products, it can spread risks easily. Many firms are diversifying their operations, consequently, they are in a position to cover the loss which may occur from any item.

The firms can eliminate risks by diversifying the market. Instead of depending on local market, it can sell goods in far off places and thereby prevent the risk of incurring losses.

(vi) Economies of Vertical Integration

A big firm can enjoy cost advantages by integrating number of stages of production. This is called vertical integration. This integration has the advantages of flow of goods through various stages of production processes which is more readily controlled. Regular supply of raw materials and steady outlets for these raw materials make the production planning more certain and less subject to erratic and unpredictable changes. Vertical integration helps the firm to control costs. Transport may be reduced by means of transportation planning and direction.

(vii) Real and Pecuniary Economics

Real economies arise from physical reduction in quantity of output. There may be economies in production, marketing, decentralisation in decision making and mechanisation, etc. Pecuniary economies arise from lower rates of advertising and lower transport costs.

External Economies

External economies are those economies which accrue to each member firm as a result of expansion of the industry as a whole. Expansion of industry may lead to the availability of new and cheaper raw materials, tools and machinery and to the discovery and diffusion of a superior technical knowledge. As a result of the expansion of the industry, improved tools and implements may be made available at reduced prices. Raw materials also may be available at reasonable prices, because, as the industry grows, a number of subsidiary firms may be established to provide new raw materials and tools.

As the industry expands, technical journals may be started by the industry association and thereby supply technical information to the firms.

As industry expands with the establishment of new firms, the external economies help the firms to produce goods at lower costs. The large scale firm reaps internal economies while the large scale industry brings to the firms external economies.

External economies may arise due to localisation and specialisation. Concentration of firms producing similar products in one place or in one region bring several benefits to all firms, such as availability of skilled workers, provision of better transport and credit facilities, stimulation of improvement benefits from subsidiaries, etc. If the firms are scattered all over the country, these benefits do not arise to firms. These are the advantages of localisation. For example, sugar industry in eastern Uttar Pradesh, Bihar, Maharastra, jute industry in West Bengal, cotton textile industry in Gujarat, Maharastra, etc. According to Prof. S.E. Thomas, external economies are those benefits which arise from the localisation of industries and are at the disposal of all firms in the same industry.

Economies of specialisation arise when firms are concentrated in industrial regions. If some firms are developing as a result of specialisation, this induces other firms to follow the established firms. When an industrial area is developed, a huge number of factories are established and in course of time, they act as complements to each other. For example, since the Second Five Year plan, a cluster of industrial estates and ancillary industrial estates have been developed all over the country in order to derive benefits from external economies. The main industry purchasing components from ancillary industries, has become very common these days. Similarly, when an industry grows, many service institutions may be established for providing various services. For example, banks, chartered accounting firms, legal firms and consultancy organisations may come up and offer specialised service to the firm at reasonable prices.

Economies of Information

These economies refer to the benefits which all firms engaged in an industry derive from the publication of trade journals and technical magazines. This may encourage the setting up of a research laboratory in a region which will benefit all the firms belonging to the industry. Textile Research Laboratory at Ahmedabad is an example. The research findings are shared by all the firms of the textile industry. All these external economies are in essence advantageous to the firms.

Relation between Internal and External Economies

It is rather difficult to distinguish between internal and external economies. When a number of firms combine into one, external economies become internal economies. Whether particular economies are internal or external, depends upon what operations it is possible to combine. Internal economies are the result of expansion of an individual firm, while external economies are the result of expansion of an industry of which individual firms are members.

It is worthy to remember that as commercial and technical education spreads, the field of internal economies are narrowed down and that of external economies are widened.

Diseconomies

Diseconomies arise when with the expansion of the firm, the costs of production rise. In other words, when the average cost of production rises with every expansion of the size of the firm, diseconomies is said to have arisen. This may arise due to employment of inefficient factor inputs. When a firm expands beyond proper limits, it becomes difficult for the manager to manage this expansion. This is an example of internal diseconomy.

In the same way the expansion of an industry may result in diseconomies, which may be called external diseconomies. The result is that the individual firms in the industry are faced with diseconomies.

It is a fact that when an industry expands in an industrial centre, there may arise keen competition for factor inputs such as labour and raw materials. As a consequence, prices of raw materials and other inputs rise. All the firms are forced to pay higher prices for the inputs. In course of time, specialised labour may not be available and capital may be scarce and costly. As a result of all these, the cost of production goes up.

The main point for examination is that the additional factors of production are necessary for the maintenance of tempo of production, but they are less efficient and are obtained at higher prices. It is in this manner that diseconomies arise as the industry expands.

Size of the Unit

Size here refers to the size of the business unit. An entrepreneur has to first decide the size of the business unit, he wants to establish. Size of the unit means the scale of operation of the firm that is adopted at the time of the promotion. Size actually determines the profitability and quality of operation of the enterprise. Two vital aspects connected with the problem of size are "Laws of Returns" and the principle of "Division of Labour". Because of these two factors, economists were more worried about the concept of 'Optimum Firm'. Several factors determine the size of the business unit. Every size - big or small - should reach the optimum production by utilising the inputs to the full capacity. Even before determining the size, let us examine the factors influencing the size of the business unit.

Factors Influencing Size

Following are the factors which influence the size of business unit.

(i) Capital outlay.

(ii) Workers employed.

(iii) Size of output.

(iv) Output value.

(v) Management Structure.

(vi) Raw material consumption.

(i) ***Capital outlay.*** One of the factors which determine the size of the unit is the total capital employed in the business. Although the total outlay is not properly disclosed by financial statements (certain financial resources are concealed), it is one of the factors which determines the size of the business unit. There are capital intensive units where more capital is employed. Normally, the size of such unit is considered as a big one. These are managed under the form of Joint Stock companies. If the capital outlay is small, they are managed by small forms like partnership firm and sole trading concerns. Thus, volume of capital determines the size of the business unit.

(ii) ***Workers Employed.*** This is one of the indicators of the size of the business unit. Prior to introduction of mechanisation in business units, labour employed in the unit was considered for determining the size. With the introduction of information technology in business operations, labour force is reduced even in big business houses. However, human factor cannot be ignored in an enterprise. It is one of the parameters considered to determine the size of the business unit.

(iii) ***Output size.*** Another factor which determines the size is the volume of output. Large volume of output can be produced by adopting economics in operation in big units. Smaller units cannot enjoy the economics of large-scale operations. The output of a firm also determines the size . If a unit produces more units or on a large-scale, it is considered as a big unit. Lesser output unit will be considered as a small unit. The size of the plant also determines the size.

(iv) ***Output value.*** Value of output is another indicator of the size of the business unit. But it is not a good factor to determine the size, when conditions in the economy are abnormal. For example, in an inflationary period, the value of output will be high. But in real terms, it may be less. Only under stable economic conditions, this factor can be considered for determining the size of the unit.

(v) ***Management Structure.*** Peter Drucker, considered to be the father of modern management thought, opines that "management structure is the ideal criteria or indicator of the size. The complexity of management structure is a more reliable indicator." More the levels of management, bigger will be the size of the unit. But this indicator cannot measure the size statistically.

(vi) Raw Material Consumption. This aspect is also considered in determining the size. The units which are self-sufficient and the output of these units are uniform or having little difference, the volume of consumption of raw material in these units can be taken as a parameter to determine the size of the unit.

These factors can be considered to measure the size of the business unit. However in real business situations, there is a blending of the factors like (i) Labour employed (ii) Capital employed and (iii) Volume of output to measure the size of the business unit.

Economics of Size and Capacity utilization

Economics of size refers to the type and degree of economy a firm would enjoy due to the size of operation it possesses. In the previous paragraphs, the various types of economics a large firm would enjoy have been discussed. Diseconomics has also been briefly explained. In the whole analysis, it is observed that large firms have a definite edge over small and medium sized firms in availing benefits of operation and thereby reduce cost of labour/management per unit of output. Inspite of these economies that a large firm enjoys, they fail at times in their operations. On the other hand, many small firms with no or less economics in operation also exist side by side and get a firm footing in business operations and they gradually diversify and grow into big units.

Small firms survive, create large employment opportunities, can bring about balanced and diversified economic development, can ensure equitable distribution of wealth and power. They exist on a big scale because of the following reasons:

(i) Widely fluctuating demand.

(ii) Standardisation of components by ancillary firms.

(iii) Shorter gestation period.

(iv) Promotion by government by providing facilities like industrial estates, venture capital, soft loans etc.

(v) Small units have a greater support with employees and they are motivated by employers. As the units are small, personal care will be taken by the employers.

(vi) Manufacturing process will be simple.

(vii) Changing taste, fashion and preferences of consumers.

Whether it is big or small, enterprises operate with understanding and they are complimentary to each other. The only aspect under full consideration in all these units of varying nature is that how they utilise the full capacity of production. Capacity utilisation is a task stage. Hence in the process of getting optimum output which will be the best in the existing conditions, managers cannot ignore the cost of production. Increasing cost will reduce the revenue. Therefore, the firms should not produce anything beyond optimum level. Optimum level is the maximum size indicating the most profitable combination of resources.

E.A.G.Robinson states that "By the optimum firm, we must mean a firm operating that scale at which in existing conditions of techniques and organising ability, it has the lowest average cost of production per unit, when all these costs which must be covered in the long run are included." The following figure indicates the optimum capacity of a firm:

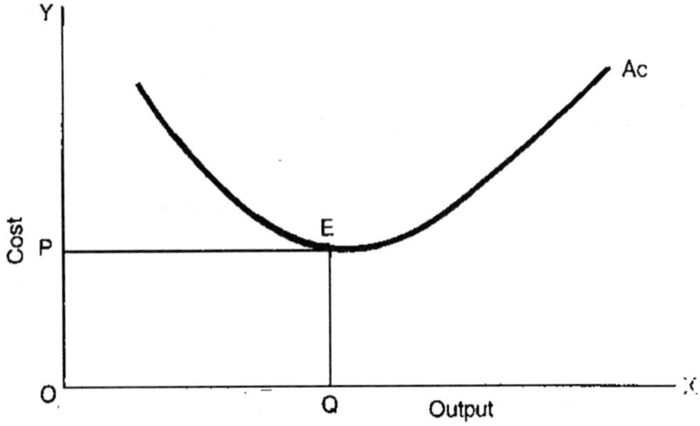

In this diagram, it may be observed that firm produces OQ output to reach the optimum level. At point E, Average cost is lowest and beyond this point, the production cost raises before the managers and the promoters have to co-ordinate activities to achieve full production. Even at the time of promoting the enterprise, the promoters have to think of a viable business unit and plan accordingly. Thinking and establishing an Optimum unit is a dynamic concept and it changes in accordance with the change in technology. When once an unit is established, it has to work to the full capacity. Reaching full capacity of production needs good co-ordination of various factor services like managerial, market, financial and technical forces. Then only the firm can produce to the optimum.

The firm becomes optimum when further growth is not possible under the existing conditions of technology and managerial ability. When the firms are promoted, they have to think of a size below which it is not profitable to operate. After establishing the firm, they start growing and a point will reach where cost will be equal to revenue. Since the law of diminishing returns is bound to occur at a later stage, the cost will be more than revenue at this. Therefore, the firm produces only optimum output and if it has to raise the production beyond this level, it has to change or increase the production facilities like installing a new plant, appointing more labour etc.

The conditions of optimum level are :

(i) All resources or factor services employed in production process have equi-marginal returns;

(ii) There will be rational allocation of resources and the inputs will be best combined to secure maximum output;

(iii) The size of production should yield maximum profit to the firm.

If all these conditions are fulfilled, the firm is said to be working at an optimum level and has fully utilised the capacity.

Capacity utilisation is governed by the factors or forces like (i) Technical forces (ii) Managerial forces (iii) Marketing forces (iv) Financial forces and (v) Forces of Risks and Fluctuations.

However, capacity utilisation can be achieved by conscious planning. But there should be a healthy market condition which provides constant demand for the product and firms playing in the market should maintain healthy competition.

Questions

1. Define production function. Explain the isoquant and ISO cost curves.
2. Explain the nature and managerial use of production function.
3. What is the production function. Explain various types of production function.
4. What are the laws of variable proportions. Explain the three laws of production.
5. Explain the concept of 'Returns to Scale'.
6. Discuss the advantages and disadvantages of large scale production.
7. Distinguish between internal and external economies.

Short Answer Questions

1. Explain the three stages of production.
2. What are isoquant curves.
3. Distinguish between isoquants and ISO cost curves.
4. Distinguish between return to a factor and returns to scale.
5. Explain economies of scale.
6. What are managerial uses of production function.
7. Distinguish between returns to scale and returns to proportion.

❖✻❖✻❖

CHAPTER

6 COST ANALYSIS

INTRODUCTION

In the earlier chapter, the different concepts of demand, demand analysis, demand determinants and demand forecasting have been discussed elaborately. In the present chapter, Cost Analysis has been dealt with in the same way as demand analysis has been earlier considered. The knowledge of various cost concepts are very useful to managerial economists. There is a lot of difference between the approach of an accountant and that of an economist. The managerial economist does not consider the accounting aspect, but considers the costs. Many policy decisions are framed in terms of profitability calculations which are estimates of changes in the amount of future expenses and future revenues. The only expenses and revenues that need to be included in such calculations are those that will differ. The unchanged quantities cancel out in the comparison.

Meaning of Costs

The term *'Cost'* means different things to different persons. For business executives, the use of cost figures is very important in the determination of profit. For the managerial economist, cost analysis has a specific purpose, namely to solve managerial problems. This calls for an economic analysis of the data about which costs are appropriate for different decisions.

The managers use the cost data for future planning and to choose an appropriate production pattern form among alternative plans. As Joel Dean says, 'It should be recognized at the onset, the only costs that matter for business decision are future costs, actual costs, i.e., current or historical costs'. In estimating profits, the manager is required to compare costs with revenue. While information regarding the future demand for a product is difficult to obtain, but it is not so with regard to information about costs.

Cost is the expense incurred in producing a commodity. The cost of production of a product is the most important force governing the supply of a product. The cost of producing a unit of product is determined by the price of factor inputs used in the production of a product. If the prices of the factor inputs are high, the cost of production also will be high. While determining the profit, the cost is compared with revenue. The revenue depends upon the price of the product in the market. The business manager cannot control the price prevailing in the market, but he can control the cost by restricting the output.

Cost Concept

It is necessary for the proper understanding of cost analysis, to know various cost concepts that are often employed. When an entrepreneur decides to produce a commodity, he has to pay prices for inputs, which he uses in production. When he employs labourers, he pays wages to them and pays money when he buys raw-material, fuel and power, rent for the factory building and so on. All these are included in the cost of production. The kind of cost concept used in a particular situation depends upon the business decisions that the management makes. An accountant will take into account only the payments and charges made by the manager to the suppliers of various productive inputs. But the managerial economist views the cost in a somewhat different form. The cost estimates made by conventional financial accounting are not appropriate for all managerial uses. Further, different business problems call for different kinds of costs. Therefore, it is necessary to have a complete understanding of different cost concepts for clear business thinking. One way of getting clear-cut distinctions among different notions of cost is to up the several alternative bases of classifying costs and show the relevant set of each for different kinds of problems. The very purpose of defining and distinguishing concepts of cost is to scout the fallacy that cost estimates produced by conventional financial accounting are appropriate for all managerial uses. Actually, they serve only the purpose of financial accounting. There is another purpose, namely different business problems call for different kinds of costs.

Cost concepts differ because of differences in view point. Different combinations of cost ingredients are important for various kinds of management problems. Disparities occur from deletions, from additions, from recombination of elements, from price level adjustments and from the introduction of measurements which do not appear anywhere in the accounting records. Different cost concepts explained in our study are

Actual cost and opportunity costs

Past vs. future costs

Short run vs. long run costs

Variable and constant costs or fixed costs

Incremental costs vs. sunk costs.

Traceable and common costs (direct and indirect cost)
Replacement vs. historical costs
Past and future costs.

Actual Cost and Opportunity Cost

Actual costs are those that involve financial expenditure incurred for acquiring inputs for producing a commodity. These expenditures are recorded in the books of accounts of the firm. The expenditure are wages paid, payment made for the purchase of raw materials, machinery, etc. These costs are called *actual costs* or outlay costs. Opportunity cost is not the actual expenditure, but it is the revenue earned by employing that good or service in some other alternative uses. Opportunity cost is the cost of producing any commodity which is the next best alternative good that is sacrificed. Opportunity cost may also be called *alternative* cost. For example, the inputs which are used for manufacturing a car may also be used in the production of a military equipment. Therefore, the opportunity cost of the production of a car is the output of the military equipment foregone or sacrificed, which could have been produced with the same amount of inputs, that have gone into making a car. Let us take another example. A farmer who is producing paddy can also produce sugarcane with the same factors. Therefore, the opportunity cost of one quintal of paddy is the amount of sugarcane given up.

Two points must be noted in the definition of opportunity cost. Firstly, the opportunity cost of any commodity is only the next best alternative foregone. Secondly, the next best alternative commodity could be produced with the same value of the factors, which are more or less the same.

In managerial decision making, opportunity cost concept is very important. The economic significance of opportunity cost is as follows:

It helps in determining relative prices of factor inputs at different places. For example, there are 100 building sites in a remote village and one building site in the heart of a city like Mumbai, Calcutta, etc. That one building site in the heart of Mumbai is equal to100 sites in a far off village. The opportunity cost of one site in the heart of the city is 100 sites of the villages which are foregone. In other words, opportunity cost is the imputed cost.

Joel Dean says that in business problems, the message of opportunity cost is that it is dangerous to confine cost knowledge to what the firm is doing. What the firm is not doing is frequently the critical cost consideration which is perilous but easy to ignore. Imputed costs are the costs which are not actually incurred but would have been incurred in the absence of employment of self-owned factors. In the case of a factory, where the owner is the manager, the cost of managerial function is ignored.

It helps in determining the remuneration to service. For example, a mechanical engineer is drawing a salary of Rs.10,000 in a steel factory.

It helps the manager to decide what he should produce in the factory. He can produce electric motors and telephone equipment. The opportunity cost of one electric motor is 20 telephones. The market price of one electric motor is Rs.5,000 and the price of telephone is Rs.200. Then it is profitable to produce electric motors.

Importance of the Concept of Opportunity Cost

When the company, with its limited resources, wants to make a choice between another layer of advertising in the established markets or some basic changes in the product line, it has to examine the opportunity costs of these two proposals. The profit that could be otherwise earned in these alternatives is the opportunity cost of using the funds. If the prospective earning from the expansion is less than the alternative earnings, there is a real loss. But the alternative earnings or opportunity costs can only be determined by comparing projected cash outlay costs and revenues which are thus the basic data for decision.

Incremental cost and Sunk cost

Incremental costs are the added costs of a change in the level of production or the nature of activity. It may be, adding a new product, or changing distribution channel, or adding new machinery, etc. It appears to be similar to marginal cost, but it is not marginal cost. Marginal cost refers to the cost on the added unit of output.

Sunk costs are costs which cannot be altered in any way. Sunk costs are costs which have already been incurred. For example, cost incurred in constructing a factory. When the factory building is constructed, cost has already been incurred. The building has to be used for which originally envisaged. It cannot be altered when operations are increased or decreased. Investment on machinery is an example of sunk cost.

The distinction between the sunk cost and the incremental cost is very important in evaluating the alternatives. Incremental cost will be different in the case of different alternatives. Hence, incremental cost is relevant to the management in decision making. Sunk costs will remain the same irrespective of the alternative selected. The only costs that matter for the decision are the added costs. Each alternative marketing programme has its own set of incremental costs for equipment, delivery men, executive time and so forth. These are outlays that are relevant to the decision on the kind of selling job to undertake, as well as to the prior decision whether market expansion is preferable to increased advertising or new products. To the extent the existing operations are unaffected, different programmes have the same kinds of sunk costs. Incremental costs change.

Past and Future Costs

Past costs are actual costs incurred in the past. These costs are mentioned in the financial accounts. Future costs are those costs which are to be incurred in the near future. This is only a forecast. Future costs matter for managerial decisions because, the management can evaluate the desirability of that expenditure. Since the past costs are costs that have already been incurred, there is no scope for managerial decision. If the management finds out that the past costs are excessive, it cannot do anything to rectify it now. In the case of future costs, if the management considers them very high, it can either reduce them or postpone the use of them.

For price policy, it is the future cost than the past cost that is needed. To the extent that costs are relevant at all, it is expectations that govern policy decisions and that should also guide the determination of specific prices. Though the future is uncertain, it is necessary to make explicit forecasts of future costs.

Short Run Vs Long Run Costs

Short run costs are those associated with variation in the utilization of fixed plant or other facilities, whereas long run costs encompass changes in the size and kind of plant. Short run cost is relevant when a firm has to decide whether or not to produce more or less with the given plant and equipment. If the firm decides to expand the capacity of the plant, it must examine the long run cost. Long run cost is useful in making investment decisions.

Replacement and Historical Cost

Historical cost is the actual cost incurred at the time of the purchase of machinery while replacement cost is the cost which will have to be incurred if machinery is purchased in place of the old machinery. The two costs differ because of the differences in prices during that period. For example, a machine purchased in 1985 for Rs.5 lakhs was Rs. 7 lakhs in 1990. For this, it may be concluded that replacement cost was higher than historical cost. During the period of substantial price changes, historical cost is a poor indicator of actual cost.

Classification of Cost Distinctions

There are some cost distinctions as variable costs, constant costs, incremental costs, sunk costs and accounting costs. Some other cost restrictions such as opportunity cost, outlay costs, etc. are economic costs. The various cost distinctions are classified as follows:

Dictomy		Basis of distinction
Opportunity	Outlay cost	Nature of the sacrifice -Economic Concept
Past cost	Future costs	Degree of anticipation. -Computation.
Short run costs	Long run costs	Degree of adaptation to present output.
Variable costs	Constant costs	Degree of variation with output rate.
Increment costs	Sunk costs	Relation to added activity.
Replacement cost	Historical cost	Timing of valuation.
Marginal costs	Incremental costs	Economic concept.

Cost - Output Relationship

Costs play a key role in determining theoretically optimum level of production. The accepted economic doctrine has been that marginal costs rise continuously as output increases above a given level. The average cost has a U shaped relation to output.

In the cost output relationship analysis, several cost concepts are studied. They are fixed cost, variable cost, total cost and the marginal cost. The cost - output relationship in different periods is very important for various kinds of managerial problems such as expense control, profit prediction, pricing, promotion etc.

Fixed and Variable Costs

There are some inputs which can be readily adjusted to the changes in the level of the output. Thus, a firm can readily employ labour and raw-material inputs without any delay if it wants to expand the output. Thus, labour, raw materials are the inputs which can be readily varied which change the quantity of the output. Such factors are called *variable* factors.

On the other hand, there are factors such as capital equipment, factory buildings, and top management cannot be readily varied, with the change in output. It requires more time to make variations in them. It takes time to expand the factory building. Similarly, it takes more time to manufacture the machinery. These factors are called *fixed* factors.

The distinctions between fixed and variable costs is not a watertight one. It is very difficult to decide which is fixed and which is variable at a situation. Again, it may be noted that the variability of costs is in relation to output and not to the time factor though in the long run, all costs tend to be variable. What is fixed at one level of output may vary at another level output.

In between the fixed and variable costs, there are semi-variable costs which vary but not at the same rate by which production increases or decreases. For example, a salesman may get a monthly salary as well as commission. Monthly salary is treated as fixed while commission is treated as variable cost, for it varies with the output.

The distinction between fixed and variable costs is important in forecasting the effect of short run changes in the volume upon costs and profits.

(i) Short Run and Long Run Costs

Traditional theory distinguishes between short run and long run. *Short run* is defined as a period in which the firm can vary its output by varying only the amount of variable factors such as labour and raw-materials. In the short run, the quantities of fixed factors like capital equipment, buildings, top management cannot be varied. In other words, in the short run, the firm cannot build a new plant or abandon an old plant. If the firm wants to increase production, it can do so only by increasing labour and raw material inputs. It has to overwork the existing capital equipment. It cannot increase output in the short run by enlarging the size of the existing plant or building a new plant of a large size. Thus, short run is a period of time in which only quantities of the variable factors can be increased while fixed factors remain constant.

Long run is defined as a period in which quantities of all factors can be increased. It means that the firm can increase the quantities of both fixed and variable factors in order to increase the output. In the long run, capital equipment can be increased or the size of which can be changed or a new plant may be set up. In the long run, there are no fixed costs, but all costs are variable.

Short run becomes relevant when a firm has to decide whether or not to produce more in the immediate future. In this case, there is no need for setting up of a new plant. The firm manages with the given plant itself. Long run costs become relevant when the firm has to decide whether to set up a new plant. Long run costs help the businessman in running the best scale of plant or best size of the firm for his purposes.

(ii) Short Run Fixed Cost and Variable Cost

The cost of production may be analysed from another point of view. Some costs vary more or less proportionately with the output while others are fixed and do not vary with the output. The former is called *prime* costs while the latter is called *supplementary* costs. The supplemented fixed costs are incurred even though production has been stopped temporarily. For example, rent of the factory building, interests on capital invested on machinery, salary to the essential staff, etc. The prime costs on the other hand are variable costs. Variable costs vary with the output. They are incurred only when the factory is at work. Total cost is obtained by adding total fixed cost and total variable cost.

Short run cost curves are shown in the following diagram :

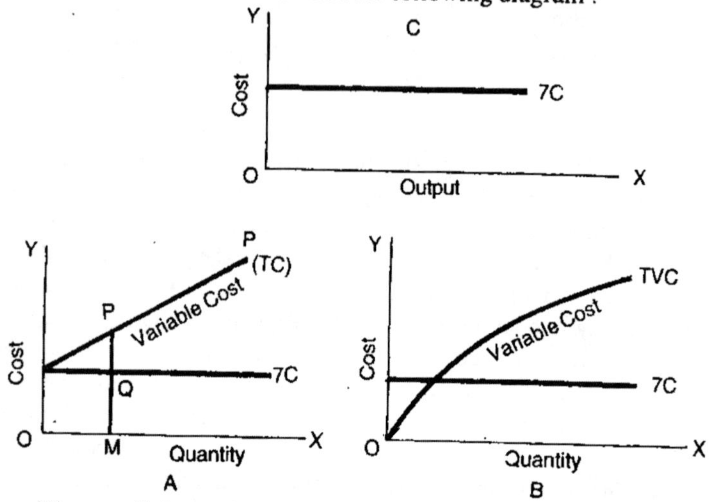

Diagram C shows the fixed cost curve. This is a straight line parallel to OX axis. This means that the total fixed cost remains constant whatever the level of output. Diagram B shows the total variable cost curve. TVC curve rises upward showing thereby, as the output is increased, the total variable cost (TVC) also rises. TVC starts from the origin which shows when the output is zero, the total variable cost also is zero. Diagram A shows the total cost curve, which is the aggregation of diagram C and B. TC indicates total fixed cost and total variable cost. For zero output, the fixed cost is OS and there is no variable cost. For OM output, the fixed cost is MQ = OS, while the variable cost is PQ and the total cost is MP. For zero output, the total cost is OS. As output rises, the total cost curve also rises. SS is shown as the total cost curve.

Average Fixed Cost and Average Variable Cost

Average fixed cost is the total fixed costs divided by the number of units of output produced. Graphically, total fixed cost is shown by a straight line parallel to OX axis. As output rises, the average fixed cost also decreases. AFC falls steadily as output rises. AFC curve slopes downwards throughout the length. For example, a firm starts with a fixed cost of Rs.50,000. When the output includes 100 units, AFC will be Rs.500. When the output rises to 200 units, the AFC will be Rs.250. When the output rises to 400 units, the AFC will be Rs.125. Since the total fixed cost is a constant quantity, the average fixed cost will steadily fall as output rises.

Average variable cost is the total variable cost divided by the number of units of output produced. The average variable cost is the variable cost per unit of output. The average variable cost will generally fall as output rises from zero to normal capacity output due to increasing returns. But, beyond the normal capacity output, the average cost will rise steeply because of the operation of dimishing returns. The average fixed cost and average variable cost curves are shown below :

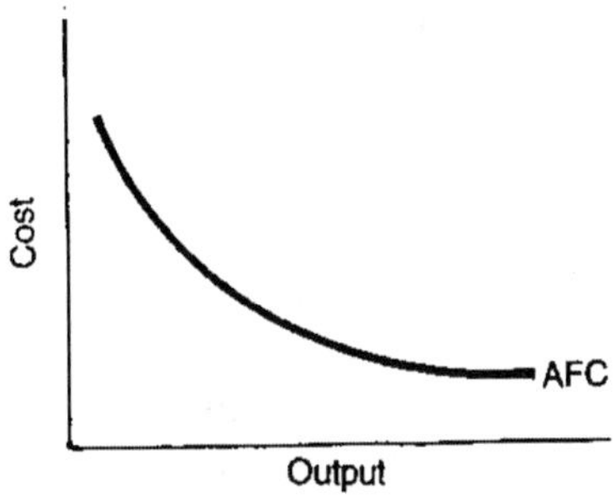

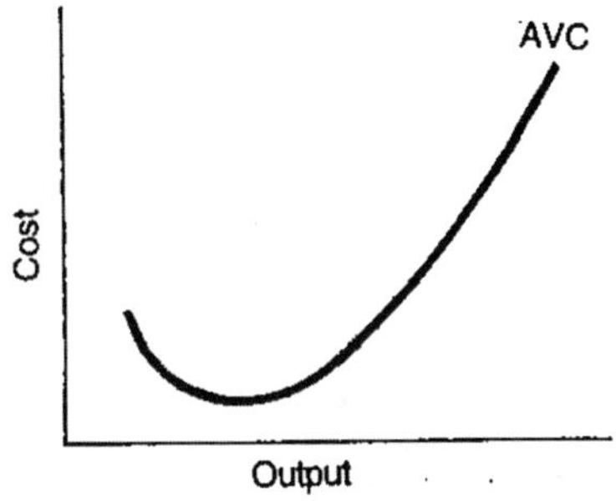

Average Total Cost and Marginal Cost

The average total cost or what is called average cost is, total cost divided by the number of units of the product. Average total cost is obtained by adding average fixed cost and average variable cost. This can be proved as follows :

$$ATC = \frac{TC}{Q} \quad \text{Since } TC = TVC + TFC.$$

$$\text{Therefore, } ATC = \frac{TVC + TFC}{q}$$

$$= \frac{TVC}{q} + \frac{TFC}{q} = AVC + AFC$$

Average cost is also known as *unit cost,* since it is the cost per unit of output.

It follows from the above that the behaviour of ATC depends upon the behaviour of AFC and AVC curves. In the beginning, both the AVC and AFC curves fall. Then, the ATC curve also falls sharply in the beginning. When AVC curve begins rising, though AFC curve is falling, the ATC curve begins to rise. Afterwards, ATC rises steeply. Therefore, ATC curve falls first, reaches the minimum and rises afterwards. The ATC curve is thus U shaped. The U shape of both AVC and AFC relfects the law of variable proportions.

Marginal Cost

The concept of marginal cost is very important in economic analysis. Marginal cost is the addition to the total cost caused by producing one more unit of the output. In other words, marginal cost is the addition to the total cost of producing n units instead of n - 1 units (i.e., one less) where n is any given number. In symbolic language, it is stated as MC - TCn – 1TCn – 1

Suppose the production of 100 units of a product costs Rs.2,000. If the increase in production to 101 units raises the total cost to Rs.2,025, then the marginal cost of 101th unit of output is Rs.25 (2025 - 2000 = 25). Marginal cost is derived from the total costs of two successive units. Marginal cost of any product closely follows the average cost of the product. When the average cost is falling, marginal cost is below it. When the average cost is rising, marginal cost rises above it more sharply than the average variable cost. The following diagram shows the average cost and marginal cost curves.

Marginal cost is independent of the fixed cost. Since fixed cost does not change with output, it then follows the average variable cost. It should be noted that the marginal cost of production is intimately related to the marginal product of the variable factor. Marginal cost varies inversely with the marginal product of the variable factor. The shape of the marginal cost is determined by the law of variable proportion, i.e., the behaviour of the marginal product of the variable factor.

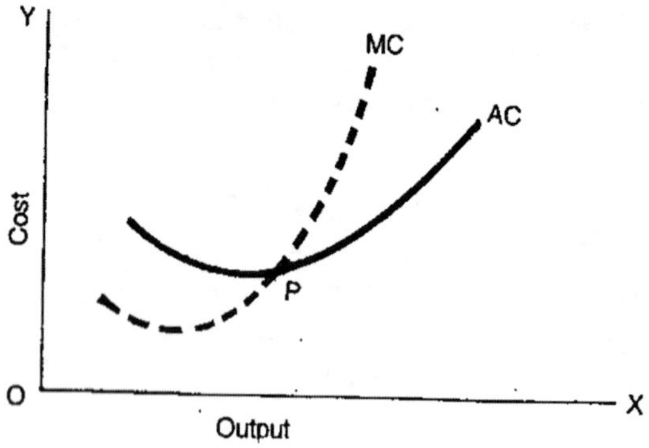

Marginal cost concept, when taken with marginal revenue concept, helps the management in rational decision taking.

Diagrammatic Illustration

The cost-output relationships can be explained through the illustration of the following diagram :

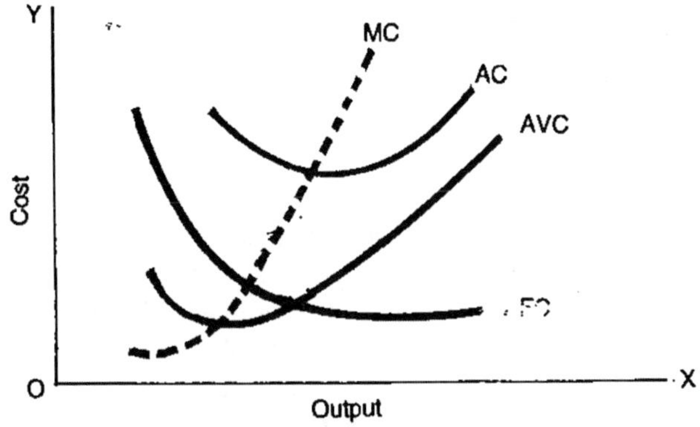

The AFC curve shows the average fixed cost. The total fixed cost is constant for any amount of output, while the average fixed cost falls as output rises. The shape of the AFC is a rectangular hyperbola. The average variable cost curve (AVC) first slopes downwards and then rises slowly as output rises. The ATC curve shows the average total cost. Since ATC is the sum total of average fixed cost and the average variable cost, it is related to downward sloping of ATC and upward rising of the AVC. The MC curve shows that the marginal cost curve intersects both AVC and ATC curves at their lowest points. If marginal cost is less than average cost, it pulls average cost down. If MC is greater than AC, it will push up AC. If MC is equal to AC, equilibrium is restored. Therefore, MC will intersect AC at its lowest point.

Long Run Cost Output Relationship

The *long run* is defined as a period of time during which the firm can vary all its inputs. In the short run, some inputs are fixed, while in the long run, none of the factors are fixed. All are varied in order to increase the output. The long run production function has no fixed factors and the firm has no fixed costs in the long run. It is conventional to regard the size or scale of plant as a typical fixed input. The term *plant* refers to input size of the plant which is fixed and it cannot be increased or decreased. That means, one cannot change the size of the capital equipment in the short period if one wants to increase or decrease the output. On the other hand, long run is a period of time sufficiently long to permit the changes in plant, that is, in capital equipment, machinery, land, etc. In the short run, the firm is tied with a given plant, but in the long run, the firm moves from one plant to another. If the firm wants to increase the output, it can make a large plant. The long run cost of production is the least possible cost of combination of producing any given level of output when all inputs are variable including of course the size of the plant.

The long run average cost is the long run total cost divided by the level of output. The long run average cost curve depicts the least possible average cost for producing all possible level of output. To derive the long run average cost curve, we have to take three short run average cost curves as shown in the following diagram. The three short run average cost curves are also called *plant curves,* and the three short run average cost curves show three different scales of production or three different sizes of plants. In the short run, the firm is operating on any short run average cost curves given the size of output. For each of these scales, there is an optimum output. The producer would like to produce the optimum output, because his average cost is the least cost at that point. If the demand for the product increases, he wants to produce more by increasing the variable inputs. But, in the long run, the firm can choose among the three possible sizes of plant as depicted by short run average cost curves. In the long run, the firm will examine which size of the plant or short run average curve is profitable to produce the given output at the minimum possible cost.

In the above diagram, there are three possible short run average cost curves depicting three different sizes of plant or scale of production.

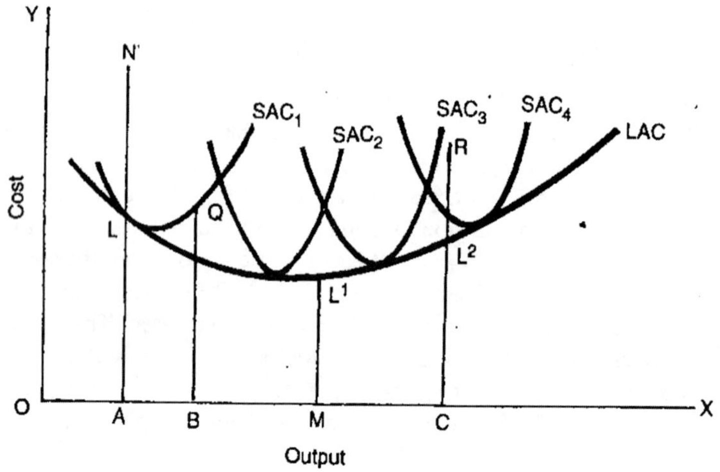

In the above diagram, SAC_1, SAC_2, SAC_3 are short run average cost curves or three different plant sizes. The firm is producing under short term average cost curve SAC^1. The firm is producing OB output at lower cost. If it produces OA output, the average cost (AL) is lower than OB output. If it produces the same output in SAC^2 curve, it costs AN. Since AL is smaller than AN, the firm will produce with SAC^1 curve. Similarly, all other output levels up to OB can be produced with the smaller plant size of SAC^1 rather than SAC^2. In the long run, the firm will be producing OB output in the SAC^1 size of the plant. It will be seen that if more output could be produced in SAC_2, the average cost will be lower than SAC_1. If the output OM is produced, the average cost will be OL^1, which is taken to be the lowest in the SAC_2 plant size. If the firm wants to increase output up to OC, it incurs CR cost which is higher than the cost of SAC_3 size. If it produces OC output, at SAC_3 plant size, the average cost CL^2 is lower than CR on the SAC_2 size. Therefore, for output larger than OC, the firm will employ a plant size corresponding to the short run average cost curve SAC_2. If the tangents of all the short run cost curves are added, a long run average cost is derived. This will be the LAC. It is also U shaped and it will be flatter than the short run average cost curves. The longer the period to which the curve relates, the less pronounced will be the U shape of LAC curve. Economists generally call this curve as envelope since it envelopes all the short run average cost curves. It is also called the *planning curve* of the firm.

The tendency for the long run average cost to fall as the firm expands its scale of operations is a reflection of cost economies available with the increase in size, while the ultimate rise in the long run cost curve is largely due to the setting up of the diseconomies of scale.

It is to be noted that the long run average cost curve (LAC) is not tangent to the minimum points of the short run average cost curves. When the long run average cost curve is declining that is for the output less than OM, it is tangent to the falling portion of the short run average cost curve. This means that if there is any output smaller than OM, it will not pay to operate the plant at the minimum average cost. If the output is produced at the lowest point of the short run cost curve, it means the average cost is higher in the short run than in the long run. If the firm expands the size to SAC_2, then the LAC is tangent to its lowest point.

When the long run average cost is rising, it will be tangent to the rising portion of the short run average cost curve (SAC_3). This implies that the output larger than OM is produced more cheaply by constructing a plant with a given optimal capacity and operating it to produce larger than its capacity, i.e., using it to produce at more than its minimum unit cost of production.

Usefulness of Long Run Average Cost curve

Long run average cost curve often called *'the planning curve'*. It is because it helps a firm to plan to produce any output by choosing a plant on the long run average cost curve. The long run average cost curve reveals to the firm how large a plant should be for producing a certain output at the least cost. Thus, while making decisions regarding the choice of a plant, the firm has to look at its long run average cost curve enveloping a family of plant curves (short run cost curves). The long run average cost curve thus helps the firm to select the best size of the plant.

Optimum Plant-Optimum Output-Optimum Firm

Optimum scale (plant) is the lowest scale of enterprise. It is not necessarily the most profitable scale. In many cases, the market may not be big enough to absorb the entire output produced at the optimum scale. In such cases, a firm is required to operate at lower costs per unit with a small plant than will a larger plant using only partial capacity. There are instances where firms to attain dominance, may over expand beyond the optimum scale disregarding profit. Sometimes, out of the fear of the government action, the firm may not expand to reach the optimum point. In the interest of the economy, it is useful for the firm not to expand beyond the optimum size.

The plant is said to be of optimum size, when it operates at the point of its minimum average cost of production. It is the plant, the minimum point of its whose short run average cost curve coincides with the minimum point of the long run average cost curve. In the above diagram, SA_2 is operated at its minimum cost of production for producing OM output. This plant size is being used to its full capacity to produce optimum output. Any size of the plant other than SAC_2 will be producing at higher average cost.

In the diagram, OM is the output. It is optimum because it is the least cost output. If the output is smaller or bigger than OM, the cost of production is more than what it is at OM output.

The firm is said to be optimum when it produces optimum output, i.e., the least cost output with the optimum plant. The optimum firm can also be defined as the firm which produces at the minimum point of the long run average cost curve. The optimum size of the firm varies a great deal in different industries. In agriculture, and extractive industries like mining, optimum size is relatively small. That is, the minimum point of the long run average cost curve is reached at a comparatively small output. On the other hand, optimum size of the firm in steel industry, automobile industry, other heavy industries and public utilities, is relatively very large, i.e., a minimum point of their long run average cost curve is reached at a relatively very large output.

Cost Estimation

There are three methods of estimating production. They are Statistical method, Engineering method and Accounting method.

In the Statistical method of cost estimation, statistical techniques are used. The objective is to find a functional relationship between changes in costs and the factors upon which the costs depend such as output, rates, sales quantity, etc. Statistical method has the advantage of isolating fixed cost elements from the total cost.

The Engineering method of cost estimation depends upon the knowledge of physical relationships. Usually, the engineering estimate is built up in terms of physical units, such as man-hours, and quantity of materials.

The Accounting method is based on historical data found in the account books of the firm. Its objective is to find the relationship between output levels and cost for similar cases to that for which the present estimate is needed. In this method, costs are classified into fixed, variable and semi-variable cost. Fixed costs are those which the accounts show to be the same in the monthly total regardless of the output rate. Variable costs are those which the accounts show to vary in direct proportion to the level of output. Semi-variable costs are neither perfectly variable nor absolutely fixed in relation to output. They change in the same direction as volume but not in direct proportion thereto. For example, electricity bills often include both a fixed charge and a charge based on consumption.

The advantage of accounting method is that it is very simple. It must be noted that the future may not be like the past records of the firm. Therefore, this method is used in cost estimation.

Cost Awareness

The long run prosperity of the firm depends upon the ability of the firm to earn sustained profits. The profits depend upon the selling price of the product and the cost of production of the product. Very often, the firm is not in a position to dictate the price of the product to the market. But, it has all the possibility of controlling the cost. The firm is required to aim at doing at the minimum cost. If the firm wants to produce a certain amount of output during a given period, control must be exerted to ensure that the given output is produced at the minimum cost. This aspect of management is called *cost awareness*. Cost awareness by management is a search for a better and efficient way of completing the production of the product. It means bringing down the cost of production as much as possible.

There are two ways of minimising cost

(1) Reduction in specific expenses, (2) Efficient use of the money spent. Cost control involves keeping the costs down than bringing the cost down. There is more profit in cost control when the business is good than when business is bad.

Cost control helps a firm to improve its profitability and competitiveness. In the absence of control, despite large and increasing business, profits are bound to be reduced. A big sale will not indicate big profit. An increase in sales may create a false sense of prosperity while behind the scene increasing costs will eat up profits. Therefore, cost management is indispensable for stability of a firm.

Tools of cost management. A control of any type depends upon comparing actual performance with some pre-determined criterion. The two criteria which are in use today are: (1) Standard cost and (2) Budgets.

(i) Standard Costs: The techniques of standard costing has been developed to establish standards of performance for producing goods and services. These standards serve as a goal for attainment and basis of comparison with actual cost. The standard cost is a pre-determined cost which determines what each product or service should cost under given situations. Standard costing starts with an estimate of what a product ought to cost during a future period, given reasonably efficient working. Once the standard costs have been worked out, then actual costs for the products have to be compared with them. If there is any adverse difference, cost control could be enforced. Standard costing makes it possible to isolate the causes which have contributed to high costs.

Standard cost need not be ideal cost or the best cost under ideal conditions, but a cost could be reached if it were operated efficiently. Standard cost is not rigid but can be revised from time to time.

Standard costs provide a yardstick against what actual costs may be measured. Since standard cost is calculated under efficient operating situations, it is a good yardstick for measuring efficiency. If the standard cost is below the actual cost, there is a need for immediate investigation. Standard costs provide a valuable aid to management in determining pricing policies.

(ii) Budgets: A budget is a pre-determined statement of management policy during a given period which provides a standard for comparison with the results actually achieved. Budgetary Control is a system of controlling costs which includes the preparation of budgets, coordinating the departments and establishing responsibilities and comparing actual performance with the budgeted one.

Estimated cost of future operations is used as standard against which actual costs are compared. Estimated future costs are determined from the past experience. Estimated costs are better than historical costs for it takes into consideration future development. In a business of rapidly changing situations, estimated costs are feasible for cost control purposes. Intangible operations such as research and development, public relations, morale building etc., are not subject to control by any other standard except estimated cost.

Cost control even with budgets and standard cost remains unconvincing because they are not cent percent accurate. If the standards are set, they have to be adhered strictly. But normally, such adherence is not to be seen anywhere. However, a realistic standard has to be set up and managers must be encouraged to achieve them.

For decision taking purposes, cost information is necessary. If the cost information is given in an arbitrary way, then this misleads the managers. Therefore, realistic cost information is to be supplied to the managers to take timely action. (A detailed study follows)

Cost Benefit Analysis

Cost-benefit analysis is a method for assessing the desirability of projects when it is necessary to take both a long and a wide view of the repercussions of a particular programme expenditure or policy change. Cost benefit analysis is being used in government undertakings in order to study the economic consequence of a project. It seeks to measure all economic imports of the project, direct as well as the side effects.

As in the case of collective goods like defence, public health measures, educational facilities, it is not possible to use market price to evaluate their benefits. These are not quantifiable and hence cannot be valued in any market sense.

Rate of Discount

There is the question of ascertaining the present value of the future costs and benefits. This is called *discounting* process. The rate of discount is very important, because a higher rate may completely switch investment priorities. Baumol has preferred the opportunity cost criterion for estimating social discount rate. This approach is based on the fact that resources invested in one sector might be withdrawn from that sector and invested elsewhere, which yields a higher return. For example, if the resource can earn 10 percent in one sector, it should not be transferred to another sector unless it earns more than 10 percent.

RELEVANT CONSTRAINTS

The constraints are classified as physical, legal, distributional and budgetary constraints. The most common physical constraint is the production function which relates to physical inputs and outputs of a project. This directly enters into the calculation of costs and benefits. If the supply of one input is inelastic, regulated pricing is to be made. There are administrative and distributional constraints such as constraints in the income distribution, etc. It is not possible to make the gainers compensates the losers. The budgetary constraint is that the project should be completed within the budget allotment.

The main purpose of the cost-benefit analysis is to select the project for investment or lay down the investment criteria. Where no projects are inter-dependent or mutually exclusive and where there are no constriants, the projects which maximise the present value of total benefits less total costs are to be selected.

In those projects where the present value of the benefits exceed the present value of costs, they are supposed to be good projects. Further, in those projects where the rate of return exceeds the chosen rate of discount, they are considered to be good.

Cost Effectiveness

It is not possible to apply cost benefit analysis in those governmental activities like defence, environmental protection, income distribution, etc. Cost effectiveness analysis may be used as an alternative strategy. Cost benefit analysis asks the question: What is the money value of programme costs and benefits and do the benefits exceed the costs to justify undertaking the programme? Cost effectiveness asks the question: Given that some pre-specified objective is to be reached, what are the costs of various alternative means for reaching that objective?

Cost effectiveness analysis is similar to cost benefit analysis. But the former is used in defence programmes while the latter is used in the civilian sector.

There are many programmes where the output is abstract and hence difficult to evaluate in money terms. One such programme is pollution control. It is not difficult to measure the pollutions being emitted in big factories and by motor vehicles, but it is difficult to evaluate the social benefit derivable from various levels of discharge reduction.

In evaluating the programme, the most important task to do is to find out whether the goal has been achieved. If the goal is achieved from the cost incurred for running the project, then it is considered as beneficial.

While selecting projects for investments out of a number of technically feasible alternatives, the most important consideration is to weigh their costs and benefits and to select those which maximise the differences between costs and benefits. The costs include capital cost, cost of raw-material, rent, salaries, wages, etc. and benefits refer to returns obtained from the sale proceeds of the output. The aim is to maximise the present value of all benefits less that of all costs.

The purpose of cost-benefit analysis is to indicate whether a particular industrial project is worth starting. If there are alternative projects for investment, a correct choice is to be made for this purpose. The cost benefit analysis is thus useful.

The alternative projects differ in type and also require a number of labourers, raw-materials and their quantity and capital equipment, the period required for completion and also the resultant revenue from such investments. The differences affect costs and benefits of these projects. A selection of a project requires valuation of costs and benefits.

The general principles of cost benefit analysis involve the following issues. They are:

(i) What costs and benefits are to be considered.

(ii) The ways of evaluating the costs benefits of the projects.

(iii) The rate of interest to be charged for the gestation period.

(iv) The constraints that are to be faced.

In this connection, it is necessary to distinguish between social costs-social returns and private costs-private returns. *Social cost* means the opportunity cost. Social costs and benefits are different from accounting costs and returns. *'The costs and the benefits of a project are the time streams of consumption foregone and provided by that project.'* It is necessary to find out the opportunity cost of various alternative investment opportunities when benefits of a project are reinvested. Some of the funds used for the project would otherwise have been invested or it has been rendered impossible to invest these funds in some other mutually exclusive investment projects, because the cost has been used here in the sense of opportunity cost.

Costs and Benefits

In this cost-benefit analysis, generally direct and supplementary costs and benefits are to be considered. When an investment is made, there will be production of a commodity and the investing firm gets the revenue. Apart from it, society also derives benefit. For example, when an investment is made on road building, apart from the total tax revenue the organisation gets; which is the primary benefit, others like road side restaurants, gas refuelling stations generate individual incomes. These are *secondary* benefits. The total benefit is to be imputed. The benefit which causes in the form of changes in land value and rents to land-lords also count in the calculation of benefit.

Valuation of Costs and Benefits

In the valuation of costs and benefits, if they are expressed in money terms, we have to make adjustments to the expected prices of future inputs and outputs in order to make allowance for the anticipated changes in the relative prices of the concerned items, but not for the expected in the general price level. The expected changes in the level of output are also to be noted. Some corrections will be needed for the distortions resulting from the market imperfections.

Social costs of materials, machinery and equipment should be calculated like labour. In the case of a material like sand, stones, the only social cost of labour is the use of labour for collecting and digging, etc. In the case of imported machinery, social cost is higher than the private accounting cost.

Cost Control and Cost Reduction

The business organisations aim at producing the product at the minimum cost. This is necessary in order to achieve the goal of profit maximisation. The success of financial management is judged by the action of the executive in controlling cost. Modern business is not only highly complex but also competitive. The business organisations are incurring a large number of costs, all of which go to the production cost. If the cost of production is increasing, the firm has to sell the product at a higher price. It is then that the competitive capacity of the firm comes into existence. If the firm fails to take note of cost control, its very survival is threatened.

What is Cost Control ?

Cost control is referred as a programme, but it is not something that the executive sets out to achieve apart from his other activities. In fact, it is a programme of effective management. Cost control does not mean mechanical cost reduction. It means better management of material purchases, effective organisation of factors of production, etc. Cost control aims at keeping the cost of production at a manageable limit.

Cost control is defined as the regulation by the executive action of the costs operating in an undertaking. Cost control means a search for better and more economical ways of completing each operation. In other words, it is a device of reduction in the percentage of costs and in turn increase in the percentage of profits. By controlling costs, the competitve strength of the firm increases. It also means how a firm is making the best use of every rupee spent in producing a commodity. If the costs are unmanagable, the profits of the firm decline and in course of time, it is called an *inefficient* firm.

Cost control is a function of better management. What it means is the better operation of the units. By so doing, unnecessary costs are avoided and the unit is run under optimum level. Thus, cost control is an integral part of the operations of the firm.

Aspects of Cost Control

Cost control is exercised through many techniques such as Standard Costing, Budgetary Control, Inventory Control, Quality Control, Performance Evaluation, etc. Cost control has to be brought in the following manner:

(a) Initially, a plan of action in the form of determining production targets, upholding the quality of the produce etc.

(b) The plan of action is to be communicated to concerned persons.

(c) After the plan is into action, the evaluation of performance has to be undertaken. It is here that costs are compared at different levels of production.

(d) Comparison has to be made with the predetermined tragets and actual performance. Deficiencies are noted and discussion is started to overcome deficiencies.

(e) Corrective action and remedial measures are followed and the goal is realised.

Effective cost control is possible only when it is exercised by the executives who spend money on resources like material and labour. Since it is a management action, it should be borne in mind what exactly is cost control. It means keeping the costs down rather than bringing the costs downwards. This aspect of cost control has been earlier mentioned in the book. It is further stated that the amount of effort put into cost control tends to increase when the business is bad and decrease when the business is good. There is more profit in cost control when business is good. Therefore, the management must be alert as regards expenditure when the business is good.

Advantages of Cost Control

Cost control has several advantages :

(a) It improves the performance of the firm by means of getting good profit and ensuring competitiveness.

(b) In the absence of cost control, even though the firm is increasing the sales, the profitability may be drastically reduced.

(c) Cost control is indispensable in achieving great productivity.

(d) Cost control enables the firm to restrain cost escalation and maintain the price of its product stable and reasonable.

(e) If the price of the product is stable and reasonable, it can maintain higher sales and thus the employment of work force.

Cost reduction and Cost Control

Cost control does not mean cost reduction. It is cost management. Cost reduction refers to bringing down the cost of production. In a competitive situation, bringing down the price poses severe problems. If the price goes below the average cost, the firm is sure to incur loss. Therefore, in order to maximise profit, certain costs will have to be lowered. Cost reduction is possible only when the firm makes the optimum utilisation of resources. It is again possible by incorporating internal and external economies. That means by economising the cost of manufacture, administration, selling and distribution, average cost reduction may be achieved. It is in this respect, that cost reduction holds good. Thus, cost reduction is stated as the real and permanent reduction in unit costs of goods manufactured or services rendered without impairing their suitability for the intended use.

Cost control is not cost reduction. It is an efficient tool of management. Cost control and cost reduction aim at the same thing, though in application, their scope is different. Cost control aims at achieving the target of sales. While costs reduction aims at bringing down the average costs, cost control involves setting the standards. The firm is expected to adhere to the standards. Any deviation from the established standards is not preferred. While cost reduction has nothing to do with standards, cost control makes an emphasis on past and present. While cost reduction considers the present and future only, cost control are applied to things which have standards. Cost reduction is applied to all departments of business. Cost control is a preventive function while cost reduction is a corrective function.

Techniques of Cost Control

There are two distinct but inter-related techniques of cost control. They are: (1) Budgetary Control and (2) Standard Costing.

Budgetary Control

A *budget* is defined as a financial statement prepared to achieve an objective of cost control. It is a comprehensive statement which includes separate statements for different work centres of a firm. A budget is both a device for planning and coordination as well as for control. Budget control is a system which uses budgets as a means of planning and controlling. It involves constant evaluation of results with the original budget objectives.

Budget control involves planning, coordination and control. Planning is a device in which future action is very well defined. In planning, details are given as regarding production schedules, material requirement, labour force requirement, inventory management, and sales targets. Then comes coordination of all executive action. It is concerned with establishing coordination between production department, materials department and sales department. This coordination is done through budget control. Thirdly, there is an operational performance which controls action, is resorted to ensure that objectives are achieved. Budgetary control makes the control effective by comparing actual performance with that of budgetary goods and the gap is filled up by suitable administrative action.

Advantages of Budgetary Control

Budgetary control provides a norm in which actual performance can be compared with the budgetary details. It provides a clean enunciation of objectives and policies and with the help of budget control, these policies are scrutinised. It provides for sufficient funds for the execution of activities. Budget control enables the management to safeguard the finances of the company by means of effective utilisation of allotted funds. Since budget represents the company's overall functions, it helps in promoting coordination between different departments. Budget control directs the spending departments to be accountable for every rupee spent. Since detailed expenditure items are given in the budget, the persons responsible for expenditure are given greater responsibility which in turn helps them to work efficiently. Budget control indirectly performs the function of internal audit and thereby ensures continuous appraisal of performances.

Essentials of Budgetary Control

The traditional accounting system gives a picture of expenditure made in the past. Under the system of budget control, the accounting system is required to peep into the future also. That is why the system of budget is adopted. The budget is a plan for the future and as such it is a base for cost control in the long run. The management may take up several cost reduction measures, in the course of day to day functioning, but without budgetary control, there can be no long range processes. It is now felt that though budgetary controls require time and money, it is effective in bringing about cost improvement.

In order to get the best results from budgetary control, it is necessary that there must be cooperation among the top executives of the firm. It is equally necessary that highly placed executives should prepare the budget estimates. As far as possible, any deviation from the budget is minimum and resorted only when there is the sign of unfavourable performance. It is very important that periodic reports should be prepared to compare the actual performance with the targets.

Fixed and Flexible Budgets

Cost budgets form the kingpin of the expected level of economic activity of any company. Other budgets are prepared on the basis of (1) selling and distribution costs, detailed and planned marketing personnel, advertising and transport costs, (2) administration costs, personnel department costs, accounting department costs, (3) production costs which include material costs, labour costs and factory overhead costs.

Cost budget also indicates detailed expenditure on plant and machinery. All these budgets influence the company's cash position and to trace out these efforts, a cash budget may also be prepared for the whole organisation.

All major departments are required to prepare their budgets and these are aggregated to the Company's Master Budget.

A budget may be flexible or fixed. A fixed budget is prepared for a specific output level and it has no concern with the changes in the level of activity of the firm. Fixed budgets are called *short period* budgets in which there is no possibility of change in the output pattern.

A Flexible budgets are also called *variable* budgets. In the flexible budget, provision is made for change in the production level of the firm. Flexible budget is adaptable to change in operating conditions. It provides a flexible standard of comparing the costs of an actual volume of activity with the cost that should be or should have been. The variance can then be analysed and necessary action taken in the matter. Flexible budget is thus more realistic and useful.

Flexible budgets are necessary to have an effective cost control. It is possible to compare the performance of a manager about his actual achievement with that of anticipated achievement. In a system of flexible budgets, a series of fixed budgets are prepared for each manufacturing budget centre, so that within limits, whatever the level of output achieved, it is possible to compare the achievement with an appropriate budget. In the flexible budget, all items of anticipated expenditure are classified into fixed, variable and semi-variable groups. In the fixed cost group, costs remain the same for all levels of activity. In the variable and semi-variable group, the costs vary. Let us take an example.

XYZ BISCUIT COMPANY

	Standard Hours of direct labour		
	25,000	30,000	35,000
	Rs.	Rs.	Rs.
Labour cost at Rs.5 per hour	1,25,000	1,50,000	1,65,000
Other variable cost	25,000	30,000	35,000
Semi-variable costs	10,000	12,250	13,000
Fixed cost	1,00,000	1,00,000	1,00,000
	2,60,000	2,92,250	3,13,000

In the above table, there are three budgets, one each for 25,000; 30,000 and 35,000 standard hours of work. In practice, there might be many cost items in the budget.

Limitations

In the budgets, the future expenditure is shown and as such there remains a certain amount of uncertainty regarding reality. In the budget estimates generally, accuracy is not possible because there is no guarantee that material prices remain constant throughout the period of the budget.

Whenever there are changes, the budgetary programme also is to be changed to fit into changed circumstances. It takes a long time to develop a reasonably good system of budgetary control.

Its success depends upon operational efficiency. The executives must be trained suitably to use the budgetary tools effectively. Further, budgeting also to be reviewed as a tool of management. Its effectiveness depends largely on the dedication and coordination of top management.

Performance Budgeting

To make budgetary control effective and realistic, its dimension is extended. One such dimension is *performance budgeting*. In the performance budget, each item of expenditure is related to a specific performance. Each executive in charge of an expenditure is required to be responsible for effectiveness of an expenditure. The conventional budget is not effective because the concerned department does not like expenditure with performance. The performance aspect is side-tracked in all government or public sector industries department. It is therefore necessary to have performance budgeting. To make performance budgeting successful, it is necessary to establish a programme of target performance for each centre. It should be followed by the evaluation of performance.

Zero Base Budgeting

The USA was the first country to introduce Zero Base budgeting in 1969. In the conventional budget, the previous years figures are extrapolated to become the basis of next year's budget. In zero-base budgeting, it is assumed that the budget for the next year is zero and starts the demand for the project. The burden of execution shifts on each manager and he has to justify the demand for money. Such an analysis indicates which activities are important and which are not important. Unimportant activities are eliminated or made productive and profitable. Thus, zero base budgeting helps in choosing those activities which are essential and important.

In the case of manufacturing industries, costs cannot be zero and as such the executives in charge of production are asked to state the basic requirements of their departments, while over and above that, the requirements are reviewed and justified. However, zero based budgeting may be adopted in areas where discretionay costs are incurred such as marketing and administration.

Standard Costing

Standard costing is defined as the preparation and use of standard costs, their comparison with actual costs, and the measurement and analysis of variances to their causes and points of incidence. Standard costs are the costs that should be obtained under efficient operations. They are pre-determined costs and represent targets that are considered important for cost control. Standard costing starts with an estimate of what a product ought to cost during a future period given reasonable efficiency. Standard costs are established by bringing together information collected from various sources within the company. For example, material costs are compiled from the product specifications indicating quantities of materials used in producing a given unit of commodity.

In the standard costing, the first requisite is to establish standards of performance for producing goods and services. For example, the actual cost of producing a commodity is Rs.180 while the standard material input of a unit of the commodity is Rs.200, then the variance of Rs.20 measures the performance. This shows that actual performance is better than standard performance. This comparison of actual costs with standard cost will help in fixing responsibility for non-standard performance and will focus attention on areas in which cost improvement should be sought by showing the source of loss and inefficiency.

Advantage of Standard Costing

(i) Standard costing will help in establishing a yardstick with which the efficiency of performance is measured that helps to exercise control.

(ii) It suggests how the goal is to be achieved by providing incentives and motivation.

(iii) Standard costs provide the management the basic information to fix the selling price, transfer pricing, etc.

(iv) It helps in fixing responsibility and suggests delegation of authority.

(v) It provides means for cost reduction. It helps in achieving optimum utilisation of plant capacity.

Limitations

Even though this method confirms several benefits, there are difficulties in formulating standard costs and apply it in practice.

Secondly standards many a times becomes rigid, outdated, loose, inaccurate and unrealisable and as such they become unhelpful in application.

Thirdly, if standards set are higher than reasonable, they act as discouraging factors.

Fourthly, when there are random factors, it is difficult to explain variance properly. However, for cost control, the authorities must concentrate on significant variances from the standard. If effective action is to be taken, the case and responsibility of a variance, as well as its amount must be established.

Basis of Setting Standards Costs

The standard costs are to be established by collecting all information pertaining to material cost, labour cost, production cost, overhead cost and so on. The main basis of setting standard costs are technical and engineering aspects. A major issue in standard costing is the determination of tightness of standards, which may range from a desire for engineering perfection to very slack practices. The other basis of setting standards are: (1) time of use, (2) performance level, (3) price level and (4) output level.

Normal standards

The *normal* standards represent the maximum level of efficiency i.e., using minimum resources to complete the goal without any loss of time. Since the objective of setting standards is to motivate individuals towards achievement, it is very difficult to use ideal standards. Hence, a certain amount of waste is permitted and the ideal standard is so modified that it may be possible for application.

Basic Standards

Basic standards are those standards which are at their initial level. Since the basic standards emphasise the past instead of the future, its effectiveness is very little in situations of change in production methods, range of products and prices.

However, it is necessary to arrive at a standard cost taking into consideration material costs, labour costs, other production costs and overhead costs. After preparing the standard costs for the products, actual costs can be obtained from the finance department and comparison can be made. Adverse difference or variances arise due to (a) excess use of material, (b) higher material prices, (c) lower labour efficiency, (d) greater expenditure on overhead items, etc., and in such cases reappriasal of standard costs has to be made. It should be noted that deviation should not go beyond tolerance limits. The standard must not be very tight and at the same time it should not be very loose. Therefore, it is necessary to establish currently attainable standard costs. Standard costing helps to isolate the causes which have contributed to higher costs and identifies the person responsible for such a thing.

Variance Analysis

There are four broad kinds of variance, namely,

(i) Material cost variance,
(ii) Labour cost variance,
(iii) Sales variance and
(iv) Overhead variance.

Material cost variance is the difference between the standard cost of materials and actual cost of materials. Material cost variance arises due to change in prices of the materials used in the production of a commodity. Material cost variance may arise due to price changes, usage of materials and mixing of materials and finally the yield.

Labour cost variance is the difference between standard wages and actual wages paid. If the wages rise, variation rises. There is also labour efficiency variance due to the operating efficiency of labour.

Sales variance is the difference between specified standard cost of sales and actual sales cost. In the same way, as that of material variance, sales variable arises due to sales mix, quantity of the product sold and price variance.

Overhead variance is the difference between the standard cost of overhead absorbed and the actual overhead cost. If the overhead expenditure rises, efficiency changes, and variations arise.

Illustration

Standard Price	Material A	Rs.5 per kg.
	Material B	Rs.10 per kg.
Standard mix	A – 75%	
	B – 25%	

Standard yield weight of the final product to the weight of the materials used, 80%.

Actual usage	5000 kg. of A costing Rs.25,000
	2500 kg. of B costing Rs. 25,000
Actual output	7200 kg. of product
Budgeted output	8000 kg.

Solution

Standard yield 6000 kg. of final product.

Standard Mix A = 75% of 75000 kg

= 5625 kg. at Rs.5 = Rs.28125

B = 7500 + 25%

= 1875 kg at Rs.10 = Rs. 18750

Rs.46875

Less loss 20% of 7500 kg.

1500 kg.

Standard output 6000 kg.

Standard cost for actual output

$$\frac{7200 \text{ kg} \times \text{Rs. } 468751}{6000 \text{ kg.}} = \text{Rs.}5620$$

Actual cost

A 5000 kg at Rs.5

= 25000

B 2500 kg at Rs.10

= 25000

Rs.50000

Less : Loss

7500 kg

$$\frac{300}{7200} = 5000 \qquad \text{Rs.}50000$$

Variance analysis

(a) *Material variance = Actual cost -Standard cost*

5000 - 56250 = 6250 (Favourable variance.)

(b) *Price variance*

Material A 25000 – 23800 = 1200 (Unfavourable variance)

Material B 25000 – 26000 = 1000 (Favourable variance)

(c) *Mix variance*

Material A 28125 – 23800 = 4325 (Favourable variance)

Material B 25750 – 26000 = 7250 (Unfavourable variance)

(d) *Yield variance :* $\frac{\text{Rs.}46875}{6000\text{kg.}} \times 7200\text{ kg} - 6000\text{ kg}$

= 9375 Favourable variance.

Ratio Analysis

Ratio analysis is used to exercise cost control. Ratio is a statistical yardstick which measures the relationship between two figures. The ratios may be expressed as a rate i.e. costs per unit of sales as a percent (cost of sales as a percentage of salęs or as a quotient, sales as a certain number of time the inventory). Since the use of absolute figures mislead, ratios are used commonly in the operation analysis.

Ratio can be used for comparing the performance of the firm over time. In the ratio analysis, an acceptable ratio is determined first and then it is compared with actual performance and then corrective measures can be resorted to. The most significant aspect in this analysis is that the management can take a greater interest in relative as opposed to absolute figures. Ratio analysis is mainly used as an external standard i.e., for comparing performance with the other organisations in the industry.

Ratio analysis is used as an instrument of cost control. It is used in two ways:

(i) Ratios can be used to compare the performance of a business firm between two periods. Such a comparison helps it to identify areas which require its immediate attention.

(ii) Then standard ratios are used to compare actual ratios. Standard ratios are averages of the results achieved by several firms in the same line of business.

With the help of these comparisons, the management can analyse the causes for differences and then take necessary action to control increase in costs. Some of the commonly used ratios are:

(i) Net profit and sales,
(ii) Gross profit and sales,
(iii) Net profit and sales,
(iv) Sales and total assets,
(v) Production costs and of sales,
(vi) Selling costs and cost of sales,
(vii) Administration costs and cost of sales,
(viii) Sales and inventory or inventory turnover,
(ix) Material costs and production costs,
(x) Labour costs and production costs,
(xi) Overheads and production costs.

Some Other Techniques of Cost Control

There are two other tools used in control. They are *value analysis* and *method study*.

Value Analysis

Value analysis is a technique which studies cost in relation to product design. Normally, a study of the utility of the machine or an equipment is made before making its purchase. This study would reveal whether the machine or the material would serve the purpose for which it is purchased. Either, there are other designs available at lower costs or is it possible to obtain an alternative at lesser cost. Can scrap be used by changing the design or the type of raw materials or is there any product design which is cheaper, or is there any less expensive process design? Thus, value analysis helps the management to establish the appropriate costs and determine the alternatives which are effective in performance.

The objectives of value analysis are to identify the areas of alternative processes of production design of the product, which is available at reduced costs. It is a process of reducing costs of production without sacrificing the required standard of performance. The emphasis is on the identification of the required function and then on the way in which the function is performed at a lower cost.

Value analysis is closely related to value engineering. It is very useful in industries where production is done on a large scale and in such cases even a fraction of savings in cost would help the firm significantly. Some of the areas where savings are gained through value analysis are:

(i) Discarding tailored products where standard components can do.

(ii) Dispensing of facilities not required by the customer.

(iii) Use of newly developed materials in place of traditional materials.

(iv) To examine the use of alternatives which are available at a lower price, for example, plastic cabinets as against wooden cabinets in the case of TVs, radios, etc. In the same way, decision can be taken on effective alternatives easily available at reduced prices.

Method Study

It is a systematic study of work data and critical evaluation of the existing and proposed ways of undertaking the work. This technique is known as *work study* and organisation method.

Work study helps to investigate all factors which enable the management to get the work done efficiently and economically. The primary object of work study is to analyse all factors which effect the performance of a task, to develop and install work methods which make optimum use of human and material resources available and to establish suitable standards by which the performance of the work can be measured.

Method study is the creative aspect of work study. It suggests improved methods of doing existing jobs or efficient methods of doing new jobs in order to achieve the optimum use of human and material resources. It also involves standardisation through which cost reduction of capital equipments can be brought about.

Area of Cost Control

Cost control can be effected in the following main areas:

(1) Materials, (2) Labour, (3) Overheads, (4) Sales

Materials

There are many ways of reducing material costs. If purchasing of materials is done properly, the firm can get various types of discounts. As such, the sources where materials are available will have to be identified. Along with that, the cost of freight also has to be examined. For example, iron ore may be available at cheaper prices in some places but to transport coal and other materials, costs much. Consequently, the advantage of lower iron prices is not available to the firm. While buying the product, it is necessary to examine carefully whether there are any alternatives to the product. It is very necessary to have a suitable product design so that the firm can derive the benefit of reduction in material usage. It is indispensable to concentrate on items where saving potential is the highest.

At the same time, alternative processes of production have to be examined, namely, whether it is advantageous to buy a component or to produce it in one's own factory. In many cases, buying the components from outside is cheaper than producing in one's own factory. Suppliers deliver them at low cost. Many automobile firms purchase components from outside.

Better utilisation of materials will result in preventing wastes. The use of standard parts and components and utilisation of waste and by-products may lead to a significant reduction in costs.

There are many areas in which materials cost can be reduced. They are inventory management, improved production planning, elimination of slow-moving stocks and the improved flow of parts and materials.

Labour

Labour costs also contribute to high reduction costs. Reducing wages in any factory is not a solution to reduce labour costs. It is only through proper utilisation of labour that saving in this field can be achieved. It is by increasing labour productivity, improving the working conditions and by means of proper training, that production of optimum output becomes possible. Labour productivity is a function of motivation, working conditions and coordination. Therefore, the firm should have a benevolent labour policy. A proper recruitment and training policy, incentive and penalty system, reducing absenteeism and coordination among different sections of the firm, improved methods of production, proper scheduling of work and materials and efforts to boost labour morale will go towards increasing labour productivity.

Overheads

Overhead costs are fixed costs which are incurred at the commencement of production. Factory overheads may be better utilised by the proper selection of equipment and effective utilisation of space and equipment. Proper maintenance of equipments will reduce costs to a considerable extent. Lighting costs can be reduced by fluorescent lighting. Faulty designs result in excessive use of power and materials. It is stated that in India, there is no economy in the use of power. It is also stated that fuel wastages in the Indian industry is as high as 25 percent. This can be reduced by means of effective planning and implementation. Transport costs may be reduced by means of better utilisation of time and space. Proper training of sales personnel and by good designing of sales programme, extra selling costs can be reduced. There is enormous wastage in advertisements too. There is considerable scope in reducing the wastages in advertisements. There are strategic ways of reducing wasteful expenditure which should be considered.

Sales

Sales is another area which needs monitoring of costs. In appointing sales personnel, only persons talented in sales are to be recruited and suitable training is to be given in effective selling of goods and services. Sales costs can be controlled by rearranging market segments on the basis of demand. Advertising also has to be done accordingly. Sales campaign must be planned properly and thereby wastage in advertisement can be brought down.

All these are areas where there is plenty of scope for the reduction in costs.

Cost Reduction in Practice

Cost reduction is more practical than theoretical. It is purely a management function. The most important thing to remember is to see that the output is produced according to its full production capacity. If the production capacity is under-utilised, then the cost per unit is bound to be high. There are many ways in which cost reduction can be accomplished. Cost reduction is a continuous process extending to all departments of a company. Every responsible executive must take up this matter seriously. Cost reduction requires cooperation of all spending departments. With better office automation, administrative expenses can be controlled.

The most important aspect in cost reduction is that the top management must be sincere in cost reduction programme. If the expenditure on directors is not controlled and any attempt to control costs at the lower levels fails, the very objective of cost control gets defeated. Therefore, every individual from the managing director to supervisor and to the labourer should recognise the need for cost reduction. There is a need for a committee to suggest cost reduction in areas where it is possible. The committee also should examine the practical difficulties in executing this assignment. Cost reduction does not mean stoppage of any activity, but it is better management of the activity. Cost reduction does not mean mere money cost reduction but also the reduction in real costs.

A programme of cost reduction should consist of the following :

(i) Cost centres must be identified and grouped department wise.

(ii) All the cost centres must be subject to the scheme of value analysis and they must see whether the performance is of optimum efficiency.

(iii) Suitable corrective measures and techniques are to be followed.

(iv) Employees should be convinced about the need for cost reduction.

(v) It should be a continous programme in which the management should have sustained interest.

Factors Inhibiting Cost Control Programme

Cost control programme is not seriously viewed in India, especially in government departments and public sector industries. Costs of raw materials and other intermediate products are very high. Transport costs also are very high. When the public sector enterprises producing goods and services are incurring losses, the losses are covered by increasing their prices. As a consequence, cost of raw materials, steel and other intermediate goods rise higher than international prices. Though overheads have been provided fully, due to under-utilisation of production capacity, overhead costs per unit of output are very high. Huge working capital is locked up in inventories and as a result of this, cost reduction has become an utopia in India.

Indian Industries want to live in protected markets. They, to a certain extent, hesitate to face competition from other countries. They are not cost-conscious. With the promulgation of the new economic policy, namely liberalisation and free competition, the Indian industries are now strategically working towards paying great attention to cost consciousness.

Cost of Multiple products

For a single - product firm, it is easy to determine the cost of production per unit. But for a multi - product firm, the problems that arise become difficult to deal with for instance, if a firm produces three commodities X, Y and Z, then the cost of raw materials and cost of labour employed on each of these products can be easily calculated. This is the variable cost. But the total cost of production includes no only variable costs, but also fixed costs. For example the electricity bill for a big firm producing three different kinds of products cannot be easily distributed. When a decision has been taken by the management, the conventional full costs are of no relevance because the fixed costs may have been distributed arbitrarily.

Some costs are traceable to individual products while other costs are common to several products, for example, the cost of a factory building is common to all the products produced by the firm. The problem of product costing arises in identifying parts of common costs with particular products.

Some of the common costs are not affected and need not be allocated, as they are irrelevant for any decision involving such major changes of the cost structure, implying that special cost studies are needed to determine the incremental costs but the occasions for such decisions are quite rare. Problems that are closely related to variations in output are more frequent. For these decisions, variable costs are most important and demand special attention to the allocation of variable common costs.

Joint Products and Alternative Products

When an increase in the output of one product leads to an increase in the products, they are called joint products. In principle, two joint cost situations can be distinguished. First, when the proportions of the end product can be altered; second, when these proportions are fixed. The case of fixed proportions, presumably, cannot exist in the long - run, due to changes in technology etc. Even in the short run, it may be assumed that in all cases of joint products, it is possible to vary the proportions in some degree so that there is no instance of the absolutely invariable proportion of end products.

For joint products of both fixed and variable proportion, cost problems relate more commonly to the incremental effect of an increase in output levels, in order to meet new demands for one of the joint products. Such an increase results in higher output of all the products and may therefore cause a reduction in prices of joint products in order to get rid of them. Thus, the added revenue from one joint product must cover not only the marginal cost of the whole products package, but also loss of revenue resulting from lowered prices of the other joint products as well.

When an increase in the output of one product is accompanied by a reduction in the output of other products, it is a case of what may be called *alternative* products. The existence of alternative products is generally the direct result of incomplete adaption. The cost of an alternative product can always be computed in turns of the foregone profits from the other product. This is nothing but opportunity cost. So, for decision making, opportunity cost analysis is useful in respect of alternative products.

Cost and Profit Forecasting

Profit forecasting forms the basics for planning cash and capital expenditures, pricing policy etc.

Three approaches to profit forecasting may be distinguished :

(i) Spot projections,

(ii) Break - even Analysis,

(iii) Environmental Analysis.

These aspects are discussed elsewhere in this book.

Questions

1. Discuss briefly different cost concepts relevant to managerial decision making.
2. Define short-term and long-term costs. What are the practical uses of distinguishing between them.
3. Distinguish between :
   a) Past costs and future costs.
   b) Direct costs and indirect costs.
   c) Incremental costs and sunk costs.
   d) Fixed costs and variable costs.
4. Explain the 'Opportunity Cost Principle'.
5. Explain Cost-Output Relationship in the short run.
6. Explain the relationships between Average, Fixed and Output, Average Variable Cost and Output and Average Total Cost and Output in the short run. How are short run cost curves derived.
7. State the features of the long period cost curve of a firm.
8. The long run average cost curve though 'U' shaped will be flatter and less pronounced than the short run average cost curves. Explain it with the help of a diagram.
9. 'While marginal cost is essentially incremental cost, incremental cost is not so'. Explain.

CHAPTER 7

SUPPLY ANALYSIS

Supply means the amount of a commodity offered for sale at a given price or at different prices. Supply refers to a schedule of quantities of commodities that will be offered for sale at different prices. Mayers has defined "Supply as a schedule of amount of a commodity that would be offered for sale at all possible prices, at any one instant of time or during any one period of time, for example a day, a week and so on in which the conditions of supply remain the same".

Supply is different from the stock of a commodity. *Stock* is the total volume of a commodity brought into market for sale. Supply means the quantity which is actually brought to the market for sale. If the price of a product in the market is high, larger quantities are offered for sale from their stock. If the price is low, only small quantities are offered for sale, while the remaining is kept in the godown. In short, stock is potential supply.

Law of Supply

Supply is the function of price. The law of supply states that other things remaining the same, as the price of a commodity rises, its supply is extended and as the price falls, its supply is contracted. The quantity offered for sale directly varies with price - higher the price, larger is the supply and vice-versa.

Supply schedule represents the relation between prices and the quantities that the producers are willing to manufacture and sell. The following is the supply schedule of Firms A,B, & C.

Supply Schedule of Firms A, B and C

Price	Commodity is identical			Aggregate of A,B,and C
	A Firm	**B Firm**	**C Firm**	
Rs.2	zero	zero	zero	zero
Rs.4	300	400	50	450
Rs.6	400	200	150	750
Rs.8	500	400	300	1200
Rs.10	600	500	400	1500
Rs.12	700	600	500	1800
Rs.14	900	800	750	2450

It can be seen from the above schedule, if the price is Rs.2, no firm is willing to produce and sell. As the price rises, the quantity offered for sale by the firms also increase.

SUPPLY CURVE

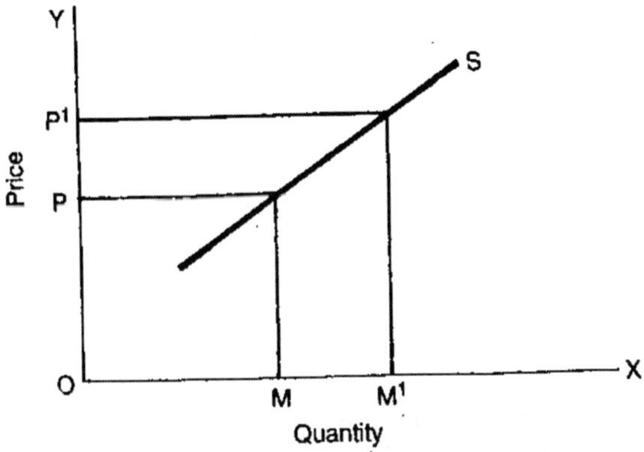

At OP price, quantity offered for sale is OM. Prices rise from OP to OP1 and the quantity offered for sale also increases to MM1. Supply curves slope left to right upwards. If the price falls too much, supply may dry up *altogether*. The price below which the producer refuses to sell is called the *reserve price*. The causes for upward sloping supply curve are as follows:

(i) An increase in price implies higher profits leading the producers to produce more and offer increasing quantities for sale. **(ii)** This may cause incentive to new producers entering into the industry and setting up firms and produce more or the existing firms may instal new plants and produce more. All these factors result in higher quantity of products for sale.

Changes in Supply

Supply is said to increase when at the same price, more is offered for sale or the same quantity is offered at a lower price. The supply is said to decrease, when, at the same price, less is offered for sale or the same quantity is offered at a higher price. This is shown in the following diagram.

Increase in decrease in supply: SS is the supply curve, at OP price OM is offered. At the same price, less is offered (OM^1) or more is offered (OM^2). S^1S^1 shows decrease in supply, S^2S^2 shows increase in supply. In the case of increase and decrease in supply, new supply curves come into being. In the case of extension and contracting supply, the same supply curve prevails.

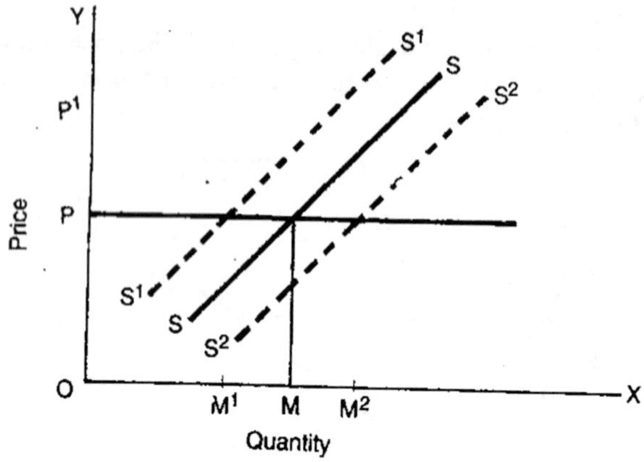

Causes for change in supply

The increase and decrease in supply may take place on account of several factors.

If the costs of production of the product rise, supply of the product also decreases. On the other hand, if the cost of production falls on account of application of a new technology, with the discovery of a new resource, the supply of the product rises.

In the case of agricultural commodities, good rainfall, application of improved seeds, fertilisers and new methods of production will cause increase in supply. If the rains fail, supply of the commodities falls.

Introduction of new technique of production will cause an increase in supply. The cost of production also will be lower in such cases. Political disturbances like war and other disturbances (man - made and natural) create scarcity for products and hence supply is reduced. Supply may be decreased by cartel agreements among the producers.

Finally, the supply of the commodity depends upon the prices of the product. Higher the price, higher is the supply and vice-versa.

The Supply Function

The supply function is determined mathematically as follows:

$Q_x = F(P_x : P_y : P_i.T.\ MT.)$

The quantity supplied of X varies with the price of that good (X), the prices of other goods (Y), the prices of factor inputs (P_i), technology (T), and time periods (MT).

Thus, the supply of commodities is very much influenced apart from price, by factors like availability of raw materials and other inputs at reasonable prices, technology, favourable political environment, etc.

According to Prof. Hirschman, the economic inter-dependence governs the supply of goods. He says that with dependent relationship in supply, it can be of two types - one is horizontal and the other is vertical. There is horizontal relationship between goods when they are used at the same stage of production. In this case, the two goods compete with each for the buyer's choice. Consequently, there is a unique pecuniary linkage relationship between the two that is essentially a demand cross elasticity relationship.

In the case of vertical relationship, one good is an input to another. A good has forward linkage relationship when it is used as an input for another, the good produced has a backward linkage relationship. In this case, there is functional relationship between the price of one good and the supply of another.

When the relationship is horizontal, it is almost an inverse relationship. If the price of one good rises, the demand for another good also rises. The coefficient cross elasticity is negative.

In the case of forward vertical relationship, an increase in the price of the final product will induce a rise in the price of the factor input.

Thus, the supply of a product depends apart from the price, on other factors like technology etc.

Elasticity of Supply

Elasticity of supply explains the response to any change in the price of the commodity. It is a measure of the case with which an industry can be expanded and of the behaviour of the marginal costs. If slight increase in price is followed by an increase in supply followed by the entry of new firms having minimum average, cost is equal to price and the marginal cost does not rise, then the supply is said to be perfectly elastic. In case the increased output can be obtained only by an infinite increase in price and no new firms enter into the industry, the supply will be inelastic. In between these two extremes, there will be a different degree of elasticity.

Prof. Boulding gives a beautiful simile to explain the elasticity of supply. The relation between the price and the quantity supplied is rather like the relation between a whistle and a dog - the louder the whistle, the faster comes the dog - raise the price, the quantity supplied increases. If the dog is responsive - in economic terminology elastic-quite a small sound in the whistle will send him bounding along. If the dog is unresponsive or inelastic, we may have to whistle very loudly before he comes along at all.

Measurement of Elasticity

If the supply curve is a vertical straight line, the supply is absolutely inelastic and a horizontal straight line an infinitely elastic supply. In between the two extremes, there will be varying degree of elasticity. A straight supply curve drawn through the origin has a unit elasticity. The following formula is a general measure of elasticity of supply.

Price elasticity of supply

$$= \frac{\text{Proportionate change in the quantity supplied}}{\text{Proportionate changes in price}}$$

The following diagrams explain three cases of elasticity.

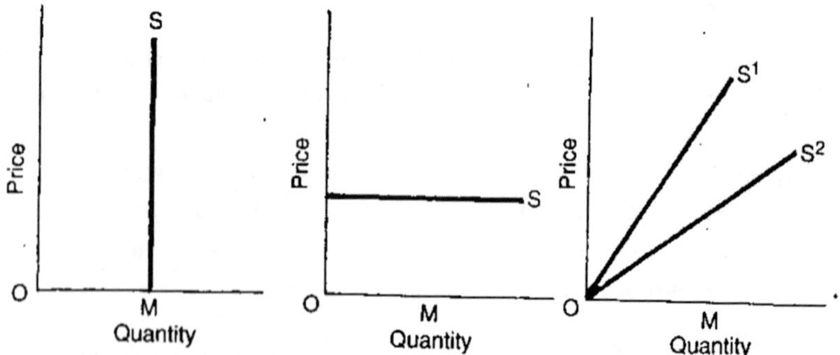

Absolutely inelastic Perfectly elastic Unitary elastic

Factors Influencing the Elasticity of Supply

In the short period, the supply of a commodity is inelastic but in the long period, it is elastic.

In the case of agricultural commodities, supply is inelastic but in the case of industrial goods, it is elastic.

The factors influencing supply are the following :

(a) Generally, the firms aim at producing the goods to the maximum extent. If the cost of production rises, they are not sure that they can sell the entire output at higher prices. At higher prices, the demand for the products are elastic. Therefore, the producers have to take risk and produce the commodity. If they are not prepared to take risk, the production will suffer. If they expect that the price of that product would rise in future, they would withhold the supply and vice-versa.

(b) The supply of a commodity depends upon the prices of that commodity. Higher the price, higher is the profit from the sale of the commodity, as such the supply also would rise.

(c) The supply of a commodity depends upon the prices of all other commodities. An increase in the price of other commodities will make the production of that commodity, whose price does not rise, this would be less attractive and as such, the supply of that commodity falls, when the prices of other commodities rise.

(d) The supply of a commodity depends upon the prices of factors of production and their availability. If the prices of raw-materials, cost of transport of minerals from the mines to the production centres rises, then the production of a final commodity is very much affected.

(e) Technology is the catalytic agent in increasing output. It reduces the cost of production and at the same time, contributes to an increase in output. Technology is changing fast on account of inventions and discoveries. Modern technology has revolutionised the process of production. Consequently, host of new goods are coming into the market almost every month. Thus, technology's contribution is tremendous in increasing output and reducing the cost of production. This will be possible only through strategic planning.

CHAPTER 8 MARKET STRUCTURES

The Role of Time Element in Price Determination

Market Structures

The determination of prices of the products is an important managerial function. Price affects profits through its effect both on revenue and cost. Total profit is the difference between total revenue and total cost. Total revenue is the sale proceeds of the firm at a single price or at different prices. The quantity sold varies with the price and the total revenue depends upon the total volume of the output produced. If the producer sets a high price for the product, he cannot sell more of it and as such his profit also is reduced. If the producer sets a low price, he can sell more of it, but he cannot make much profit. Therefore, pricing occupies an important place in economic analysis. However, all firms are not able to set prices for their products. There are some firms which are price takers while others are price makers, depending upon the market situations they face.

The knowledge of market structure which a firm is to operate is useful in understanding the nature and extent of manouevreability which the firm has in deciding about the price and the quantity of the products.

The Market

Market structures are different. Market forms are based on the degree of competition prevailing in the market. Broadly, the market forms are classified into two types, (a) Perfectly competitive market. (b) Imperfectly competitive market. Before we begin to study the characterstic of market structure, let us understand what we mean by market.

Market in economics means, a meeting place of buyers and sellers directly or indirectly. Cournot, a French Economist, defines market as "Economists understand by the term market not any particular market place in which things are bought and sold, but the whole of any region in which buyers and sellers are in such a free intercourse with each other that the prices of the same goods tend to equality easily and quickly."

In the words of Jevons, "The word market has been generalised so as to mean any body of persons who are in intimate business relations and carry on extensive transactions in any commodity."

Stonier and Hague have explaind the term market as "any organisation whereby buyers and sellers of goods are kept in close watch with each other........There is no need for a market to be in a single building.........The only essential for a market is that all buyers and sellers should be in constant touch with each other either because they are in the same building or because they are able to talk to each other by telephone at a moment's notice."

Benham explains the term market as "any area which buyers and sellers of a commodity are in close touch with each other either directly or indirectly that the price obtainable in one part of the market affects the prices paid in other part. 'Ely observes', market "as the general field within which the forces determing the price of particular product operate."

If we study the above definitions, we find that a market comprises of the following components:

(a) ***Consumers*** : The buyers of the product are called consumers. The buyers of a product are identified by means of income, need, etc. If there are high income groups and they are concerned with trade and commerce or higher government administration, they need luxuries like motor cars, VCRs etc.

(b) ***Sellers*** : There should be manufacturers of a product in the market. There must be industries manufacturing motor cars in a country. They form sellers in the market.

(c) ***A Commodity*** : A market means the buying and selling of a commodity. If there is no commodity, the market will not exist. Each commodity has a separate market, in the sense that every commodity has a separate set of buyers and sellers.

(d) ***A Price*** : If the commodity is to be bought and sold, there must be a price for the product. The exchange of the product between buyers and sellers occur at a particular place.

Thus all the four components form a market.

Classification of the Market

Market is classified on the basis of an area, such as local market, regional markets, national markets and international markets.

On the basis of the nature of transactions, the market is classified into spot market and future market. Where goods are physically exhanged on the spot, the markets are called *spot markets*. In the case of transactions involving agreements of future exchange of goods, such markets are known as *future markets*.

Market is classified into wholesale market and retail market on the basis of the volume of business.

Market is classified on the basis of time as very short period market, long period market and very long period market or the secular market.

On the basis of status of sellers, the market is classified into primary,secondary and terminal markets. The primary market consists of manufacturers who produce and sell the product to the wholesalers. The wholesalers who sell the product to retailers comprise of the secondary market. The business involving the retailer who sells it to the ultimate consumers are called *terminal markets.*

Market is further classified into regulated market and unregulated market. If the government stipulates certain conditions and regulations for the sale and purchase of product - then that market is called *regulated markets*. These are absent in unregulated markets.

Market is further classified on the basis of competiton as perfectly competitive market, monopoly market, monpolistic competitive market, oligopoly market, monopoly market, monopolistic competitive market, oligopoly market, etc. If there is no competiton for the product, then such a market is called *monopoly* market. In a competitive market, several producers are manufacturing the product. The product is homogeneous. There are large number of buyers and sellers in the market. Such a market is called perfectly competitive market.

In the table below, market forms are classified on the basis of number of firms producing the product and the nature of products produced by them.

Classification of Market Forms

Form of market structure	Number of firms	Nature of product	Price elasticity of demand for an individual firm	Degree of control over price
1. Perfect Competition	Large number of firms	Homogeneous Product firms	Infinite	None
2. Imperfect competition				
a) Monopolistic competition	-do-	Differential products-but (close substitutions)	Large	Some
b) Monopoly	One	Unique product with out close substitute		
c) Pure Oligopoly Oligopoly with-our product differentiation	Few firms	Homogeneous product	Small	Some
d) Differentiated oligopoly	-do-	Differential product (close substitutes)	Small	Some

Perfect Competition

Perfect competition comes into existence when there are a large number of firms producing homogeneous products. The maximum output that a firm produces is so small when compared to the industry output, that a firm cannot affect the price by varying output. With a large number of firms and homogeneous products, no individual firm is in a position to influence the price. The demand curve of firms under perfect competition is horizontal straight line. That is the price elasticity of demand for a single firm is infinite. Joan Robinson says, 'Perfect competition prevails when the demand for the output for each producer is perfectly elastic. This entails first that the number of firms is large, so that the output of any one seller in negligibly small proportion of the total output of the commodity and second that the buyers are all alike in respect of their choice between rival sellers, so that the market is perfect.'

Imperfect Competition

Since perfect competition is very rare, what actually prevails is imperfect competition. In imperfect competition, the number of firms exercising control is large since the product is differentiated. Imperfect competition has several sub-categories. One such category is monopolistic competition. Prof. E.H. Chamberlin defines monopolistic competition as a market form characterised by a large number of firms with product differentiation. Demand curve facing the firms in monopolistic competition is highly elastic indicating that the firm enjoys control over the price.

Oligopoly

The second category of imperfect competition is oligopoly. There are two types of oligopoly - one without product differentiation and this is called pure oligopoly. Under this category, there exists competition among the few firms producing homogeneous product. Since the number of firms is few, each of them exercises some control over the price. The demand curve facing the firms under oligopoly is downward sloping.

Monopoly

Monopoly is a market form in which a single producer produces a single product which has no close substitute. This is an extreme case of imperfect competition. Since a monopoly firm wields a solid control over the supply of the product, which can have only remote substitutes, the expansion and contraction of output will affect the price. Contraction of output will raise its price while expansion of output will lower it. Therefore, the demand curve facing the monopoly is downward sloping but has steep slope. For monopoly, sometimes, the words absolute monopoly or pure monopoly, complete monopoly are used. But such a pure monopoly or absolute monopoly does not exist in the real world.

Duopoly

Duopoly is another type of imperfect market situation where there are only two sellers producing identical products or differenciated products. When there is product differenciation, each seller has his own set of cleints and is not affected by his rival. But when the two sellers are dealing with identical products, both will be aware of each other's price and output policies. Suppose they have a good relationship and understanding, it is possible for them to avoid competition and enjoy monopoly in determining price and output

Monopsony

Monopsony refers to exclusive control over a particular product or service by one buyer in the market. In other words, monopsony is buyer's monopoly. The monopsonist as the only buyer, enjoys control over purchases so as to obtain the lowest possible price.

Oligopsony

Oligopsony is the equivalent of oligopoly on the buyer's side. Simply speaking, there is the existence of only a few buyers in the market. It refers or service by a small number of buyers (oligopsonists).

Forms of Non-Price competition

Any attempt made by sellers to win more customers through means other lowering the price, is called as *non-price competition*. The seller may try to compete by resorting to product differentiation, advertising, packaging, special services, future payment plans etc.

In non-price competition, the seller keeps the prices stable and tries to improve their market positions through other means. They make an attempt to chalk out other means. They make an attempt to shift the demand curve to the right by differentiating the product through some other promotional activities.

Suppose a producer can sell 40,000 shirts a year at Rs.250 per shirt on the basis of price competition alone, he can increase the sales to 50,000 shirts if he sells them at Rs.220 per shirt. However, the producer is interested in boosting sales without reducing the price. He resorts to a novel advertising strategy (a form of non-price competition) which persuades customers to buy at the original price of Rs.250 only.

In figure 1, change on shift in demand curve from DD to D'D' due to non-price competition has been represented graphically.

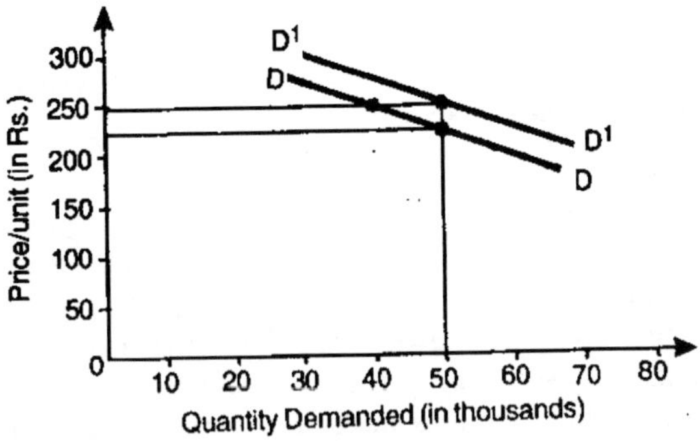

In the case of price-competition, there is the danger of the customer preferring the brand only as long as its price is lowered. Customer loyalty is very weak if price is the only feature differentiating the products. When it is resorted to for a long time, it may have dangerous effects on profits. However, with non-price competition, companies have more control over their sales. The best approach in non-price competition is to build a strong brand name for the company's product either by developing a unique, distinctive product or by creating a new promotional programme.

Perfect Competition

Pure or perfect competition is said to exist when there are a larger number of buyers and sellers found in the market and the product sold is homogeneous. In perfect competition, in addition to the above two conditions of pure competition, there are some other conditions to be fulfilled. They are (1) free entry and exit of firms, (2) perfect mobility of factors of production, (3) perfect knowledge of the market and (4) a uniform price.

Large Number of Buyers and Sellers

The first condition of pure competition is, there should be a large number of buyers and sellers operating in the market. The quantity bought or sold by the buyer or the seller respectively is so small that no single seller or buyer can influence the market price. The output of a single firm is only a small portion of the total output and the demand of the single buyer is only a small portion of the total demand. Hence, the market price has to be taken as given and unalterable by every purchaser and seller. Thus, no individual buyer can influence the market price by varying his own demand and no single firm is in a position to affect the market price by varying its own output. In perfect competition, the individual seller is only a price taker and not a price maker. If he charges a slightly higher price than the ruling price, no one will buy from him. If he sells at a lower price than the market price, every one will buy from him. If he sells at a lower price than the market price, every one will come to buy from him, but his stock is so limited that he cannot meet the rush of demand. Thereby, he increases prices to the level of market price. This leads to the perfectly elastic demand curve of the perfectly competitive firm.

Homogeneous Product

The product produced and sold by producers is homogeneous. It is standardised and purely identical. It means that the products of various firms are indistinguishable from each other. They are perfect substitutes for one another. In the case of homogeneous products, the quality is the same and identical in size and everything that there is, leaves nothing to distinguish one from the other. In these circumstances, if the firm raises its price, it will lose all the customers. It can sell as much as it likes at the prevailing price. The firm enjoys complete freedom to operate in the potential market.

Free Entry or Exit

This is another essential characterstic of perfect competition. The firms under perfect competition enjoy full freedom either to start a strategic business venture or close their business. In this situation, all firms are earning normal profit. If the profit is more than normal profit, new firms will enter into production and extra profit earned by old firms will be shared by new firms. If on the other hand, profit is less, some firms will stop producing this product and consequently the profits of the remaining firms will rise. If there are restrictions on the entry of firms, some existing firms will earn super-normal profit. Only when there are no restrictions on entry or exit, the firms will earn only normal profits.

Perfect Knowledge of the Market

Another condition for the existence of perfect competitions is that both buyers and sellers are fully aware of the prices that are being offered and accepted. In perfect competition, all buyers are expected to know the market price of the product and as such, the seller cannot charge more than the market price. When the producers and customers have full knowledge of the prevailing price, nobody will offer more and none will accept less and the same price will rule throughout the market. The producers can sell at that price as much as they like and the buyers also can buy as much as they like.

Perfect Mobility of Factors of Production

The factors of production move from one place to another without any restriction. If the demand for factors of production increases more than the supply, then the additional factors move into the industry. Mobility of factors of production is very essential to enable the firms and the industry to achieve an equilibrium position.

Thus, perfect competition is marked by a large number of buyers and sellers all engaged in the purchase and sale of homogeneous commodity with perfect knowledge of market prices and quantitites. Perfect competition is thus an extreme case and is not found in the real world. Actual competition departs from the ideal of perfection. Perfect competition is a mere concept and a standard by which to measure the varying degrees of imperfect competition.

Pure Vs Perfect Competition

It is necessary to make a distinction between Pure and Perfect competition. For a market to be considered pure competitions, three essential conditions have to be fulfilled. Firstly, there must be a relatively large number of buyers and sellers. Secondly, the product must be homogenous. Thirdly, there must be no restrictions either for entry or for exit of firms.

On the other hand, for a market to be called perfect, some more additional conditions have to be fulfilled *viz* (a) the buyers and sellers must have perfect knowledge of existing market conditions (b) the factors of production must be perfectly mobile between industries (c) the government should adopt the policy of laissez-faire (d) we must assume that there are no transportation costs.

Perfect competition is a myth and is non-existent in the practical world. On the other hand, pure competition tries to prove the ideal of perfect competition without actually accomplishing it.

Price Determination under Perfect Competition

One main objective of a firm under perfect competition is to maximise its profit. The most important question which the management of the firm has to decide is how to determine output in such a way as to maximise its profit. In perfect competition, the firm is a price taker. That is, he has to accept a price which is determined by the force of demand and supply. The price for the product is fixed at a point where demand is equal to supply. This is shown in the adjacent diagram.

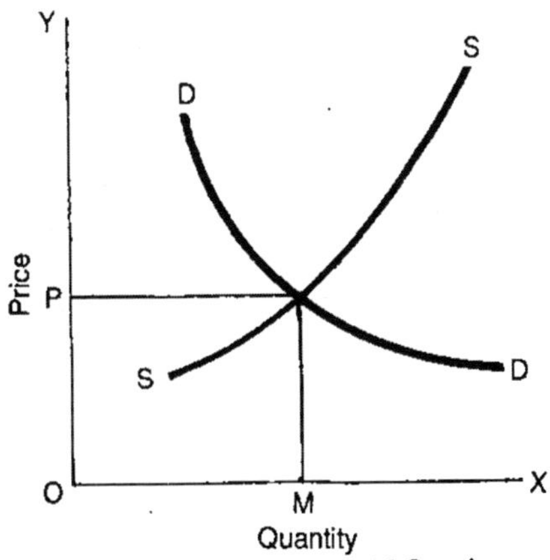

Interaction of Demand & Supply

Price per metre	Quantity demand	Quantity supplied Million metres	Pressure on price Million metres
Rs.50	10	25	Falling
Rs.40	15	23	Falling
Rs.30	20	20	Netural
Rs.20	25	15	Rising
Rs.10	30	10	Rising

DD is the demand curve and SS is the supply curve. A look at the diagram shows at higher price, demand is low, but supply is high. At lower price, demand is high and supply is low. At OP price, demand and supply are equal. As shown in the Table, at Rs.30, demand and supply are equal.

From the above discussion, it is clear that the equilibrium between demand and supply or market equilibrium determines the price. Price comes to stay at the level where demand and supply are equal.

INTERACTION OF DEMAND AND SUPPLY

Response to a change in demand and to a change in supply may be due to change in price or change in quantity. If the demand is highly elastic, consumers will respond to price changes. As a result, most of the adjustments to change in supply will take place. If the demand is inelastic, adjustment will take place in price. Sellers also are responsive to changes in price. If price falls, supply is restricted, if price rises, supply also rises. Let us study the following case.

Price rises on account of an increase in demand while supply remains the same

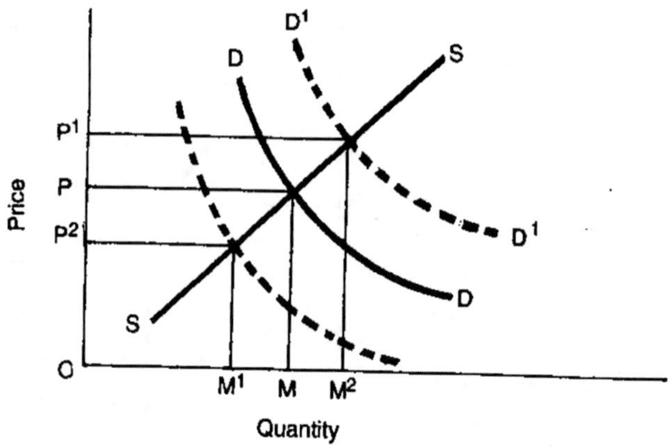

Increase in demand results in shift in the demand curve, upward to the right from DD to D^1D^1, whereas the supply remains the same. As a result, price goes up from OP to OP^1. Quantity supplied goes up from OM to OM^1. If demand falls, supply remains the same, price falls from OP to OP^2. Quantity supplied also falls from OM to OM^2. This is shown in the following diagram. In other words, when demand changes and supply remains the same, equilibrium position also changes.

In following diagram, the demand remains the same, but supply changes. To begin with, the SS supply curve interacts with DD demand curve at the price OP. If supply increases from SS to S^1S^1, the equilibrium price falls from OP to OP^1. Price falls when supply increases from OM to OM^1. When supply decreases from OM to M^2, price rises to OP^2. Decrease in the supply is shown as S^2S^2. The equilibrium price becomes OP^2. Thus, changes either in demand or supply will change the equilibrium price.

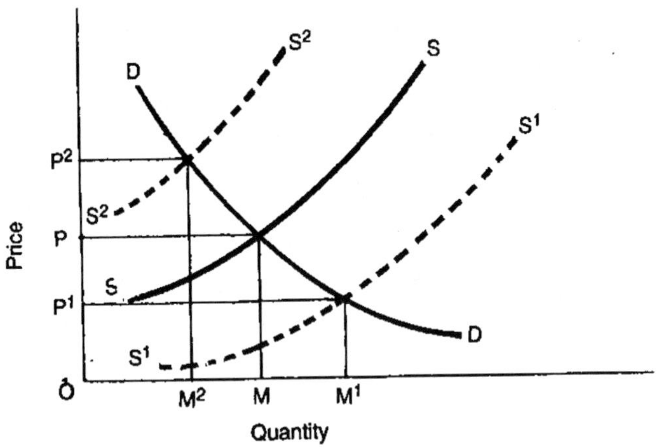

Conclusion

When the demand curve shifts, supply remaining the same, price changes. The rise or fall depends upon the elasticity of supply curve. If the supply curve is elastic, the demand curve being inelastic, price will be less. If the supply curve is steep, price will rise.

Given the shifts in supply curve, the price will rise or fall if the demand curve is elastic. If both demand and supply are inelastic, the price will rise more or fall more. If both demand and supply increase, sales are bound to increase, but price may rise or may not rise. An increase in demand with a simultaneous decrease in supply will raise price and increase in sales if the new demand price for the old equilibrium amount is higher than its new supply price. Similarly, price will rise and sales will diminish, if the new supply price for the old amount is higher than its new demand price.

Limitations of Demand and Supply in Determining Price

The above analysis shows how price is determined by the interaction of demand and supply. Demand and supply are not independent identities. They in turn are governed by a host of other factors. It is stated that 'supply and demand' is only a superficial formula. Prof. Samuelson has remarked that, *'Supply and Demand are not ultimate explanations of price. They are simply useful catch-all categories for analysing and describing the multitude of forces causes and factors impinging on price. Rather than being final answers supply and demand simply represent initial questions. Our work is not over but just begun.'*

The role of cost of production in determining the price cannot be ignored. A change in the cost of production will change the supply curve, and will thus change the equilibrium price. In the same way, market demand may change because of change in the incomes of the people, resulting in an increase in the number of consumers owing to increase in population.

Thus, the factors like cost of production and income of the consumer and the size of the population influence in determining the price. But all of them work through either supply or demand.

The Role of Time in Determining the Price

Supply of any commodity is the result of production. Production of any commodity whether agricultural or industrial, takes considerable amount of time. To decide what to produce and how to produce takes considerable planning and formulation of policies of implementation. This aspect was not examined thoroughly by economists earlier to Alfred Marshall. Marshall suggested three periods of time, i.e. market period, short period and long period.

Market Period

Marshall defined market period to be so short a period in which supply of a product is fixed or limited to existing stock. In other words, supply curve in the market period is absolutely inelastic. Graphically, it is a vertical straight line. The supply remains fixed for whatever the price may be. Market period supply curve differs between perishable goods and non-perishable goods. In the case of perishable goods like fish, flowers and vegetables and other agricultural commodities, which is also limited by the quantity available and other agricultural commodities, the supply is limited by the quantity available in a day and which cannot be kept back for the next period. In such cases, a sudden shift in demand will result in the increase in price. In the case of non-perishable goods, the supply curve cannot be a vertical straight line, but it is inelastic for the supply may be slightly increased by bringing from the stock. The stock is so limited and as such, the price is bound to rise in the market period if there is a sudden spurt in demand.

Short Period

Marshall defines short period as a period long enough for the supplies of the commodity which can be altered by increases or decreases in the current output. But not enough for the fixed equipment to be changed to produce a larger or a smaller one. In other words, short run average curve remains the same. It means that the size of the plant remains unchanged in the short period. Thus, short period is a period sufficient only to make a limited output adjustment with the existing equipment by expanding output along the short run marginal cost curves. The output in the short period is greater than the market period output. Here, the supply curve would be a sloping line moving upward from left to right, thereby indicating that as price goes up, supply also goes up.

The determination of short period price is again at the point of intersection between the short period supply curve and the new demand curve. Under the stimulus of demand, the producers will increase the production by making intensive use of fixed factors and increasing some variable inputs. The short period equilibrium price is lower than the market period equilibrium price.

Long Period

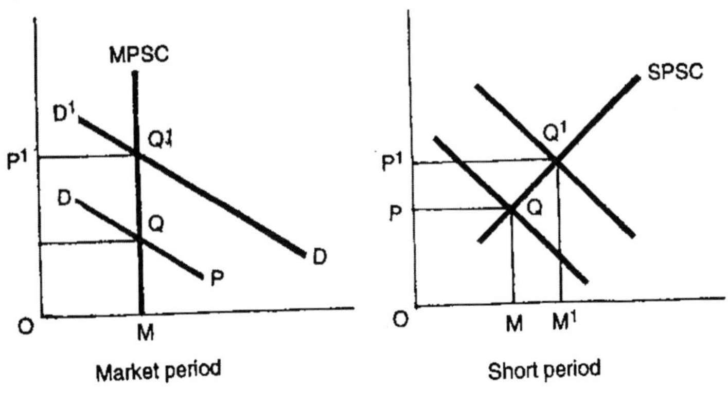

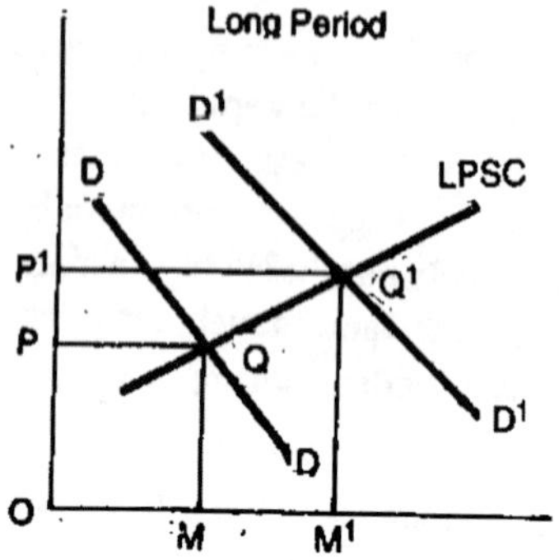

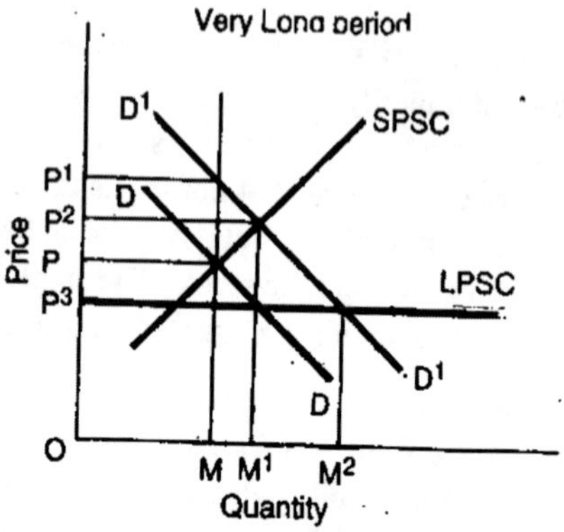

Long period is defined as a period in which there is plenty of time for the firms to change the size of their plants or build new plants. New firms may also start producing this commodity by installing more modern plants. As a result of expansion of the firms, the output rises considerably. The long period supply curve will be more elastic and the supply curve will lie flat. The long period equilibrium price is determined at a point of intersection between long period supply curve and the new demand curve. In the long period, a larger output is supplied and sold at lower prices. Thus, in the long run, larger supplies of the product will be forthcoming at reduced prices.

Questions

1. Discuss the meaning and characterstics of a market.
2. Discuss the criteria on the basis of which the market is classified.
3. What is the role of demand and supply in determining the period.
4. Explain how price is determined under different periods of time.
5. What is the role of supply in the market period.
6. Distinguish between short period price and the long period price.
7. Write a comprehensive note on different types of markets.

CHAPTER

9 REVENUE ANALYSIS

CONCEPTS OF AVERAGE REVENUE AND MARGINAL REVENUE

INTRODUCTION

The demand analysis was studied in the previous chapter from the view point of the consumer. But the producer or seller of a commodity is very much concerned with the demand for goods, because revenue obtained by him from selling the product depends mainly on the demand for that product. The producer or seller is, therefore, very much interested in knowing what sort of demand curve is facing him. The demand curve of the buyers for the product is the average revenue curve from the standpoint of view of sellers, since the price paid by the buyers is revenue for the sellers.

AVERAGE REVENUE

Price paid by the consumer for the product forms revenue or income to the seller. The whole income received by the seller from selling various units of the commodity either at the same or at different prices is called *total revenue*. For example, if a seller sells 100 units of a product at Rs.15 then Rs.1500 is the total revenue. On the other hand, *'average revenue'* is revenue earned by per unit of the product sold. It is found by dividing total revenue by the number of units of the product sold. If different units are sold at different prices, then the average revenue is also different. Average revenue equals prices at which the units of the product are available at the same price, then average revenue would be the same thing as price. If he sells different units of product at different prices, then the average revenue will not be equal to price. For example, a seller sells two units of product at Rs.10, then the average revenue is 20/2=Rs.10. Here average revenue is equal to price. Now, suppose, he sells two units at different prices to the consumer, i.e., for one consumer at Rs.12 and for another consumer at Rs.10. His total revenue is Rs.22 and the average revenue is Rs.11. Thus, in this case, when different units are sold at different prices, average revenue will not be equal to prices charged for the product. But, in real life, sellers sell different units of a product at the same price in the market and hence average revenue equals price. Thus in economics, the words average revenue and price occur synonymously except when the monopolist discriminates the prices. Since buyer's demand curve represents graphically the quantities demanded or purchased at various prices of the product, it also shows the average revenue curve at which various amounts of the goods are sold by the seller. This is because price paid by the buyer is revenue from the seller's point of view. Hence, average revenue curve of the firm is the same thing as the demand curve for the consumers.

Marginal Revenue

Marginal revenue is the net revenue earned by selling an additional unit of the product. In other words, marginal revenue is the addition, made to the total revenue by selling one more unit of the commodity. Expressing it in algebraic terminology, marginal revenue is the addition made to the total revenue by selling *n* units of a product instead of *n-1* where *n* is any given number. For example, if a producer sells 10 units of a product at Rs.15, then the total revenue is Rs.150. If he increases the sales by 11 units, suppose the price falls of Rs.14.50, then the total revenue is Rs.159.50 for 11 units. This means that the 11th units of the product sold added Rs.9.50 to the total revenue. Hence Rs.9.50 is the marginal revenue.

Total revenue for 10 units (Rs.15) = 150

Total revenue for 11 units (Rs.14.5) – 159.50

Marginal revenue = 159.50 – 150 = 9.50

From the above example, it can be inferred that marginal revenue is less than the price at which the additional unit is sold.

Marginal revenue can be found either by taking out differences between total revenue, before and after selling the additional units or it can be obtained by subtracting the loss in revenue on previous units due to the fall in the price at which the additional unit sold.

It follows from the above that, when the price falls as additional units are sold, marginal revenue is less than the price. When the price remains the same, as additional unit is sold, as under perfect competition, marginal revenue is the same as average revenue.

Relationship between Average Revenue and Marginal Revenue

The concepts of total revenue, average revenue and marginal revenue are explained in the following table:

TABLE

Total, Average and Marginal Revenue Schedules

No. of units of a product sold	Price or Average Revenue	Total Revenue Av.Revenue x Quantity sold	Marginal revenue Addition made to the total revenue
1	20	20	20
2	18	36	16
3	16	48	12
4	14	56	8
5	12	60	4
6	10	60	0
7	8	56	–4

The above table shows that when average revenue is falling, marginal revenue is less than the average revenue. Marginal Revenue is positive so long as total revenue is increasing. Marginal Revenue becomes negative when total revenue declines.

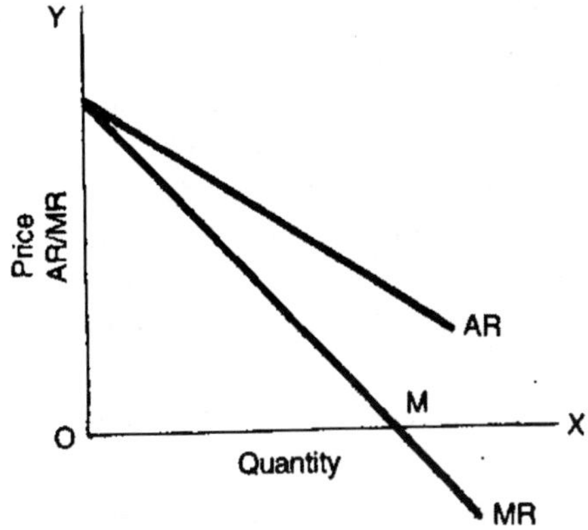

In all forms of imperfect competition, i.e., monopolistic competition, oligopoly, monopoly, the average revenue curve facing the individual firm slopes downwards. This is because, the firm lowers the prices of the product if it wants to increase their sales. In the adjacent diagram, this aspect is explained.

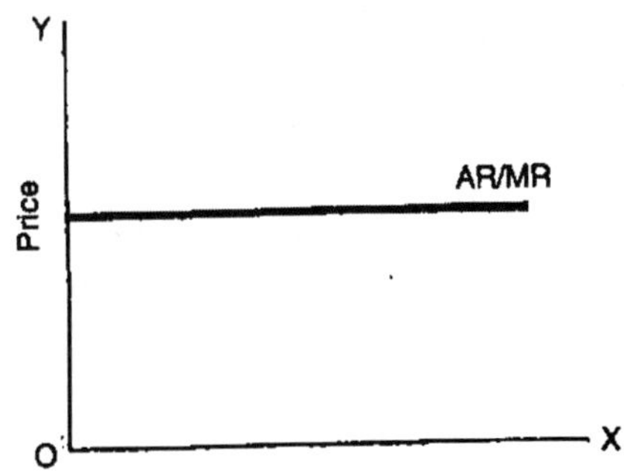

Under perfect competition, the price or the average revenue remains the same throughout sale of the output. Hence, marginal revenue will be equal to average revenue.

The average revenue and the marginal revenue of the firm is a horizontal straight line under perfect competition. This is because the firm under perfect competition cannot influence the price. He has to sell the product at the ruling market price. As such, the marginal revenue and average revenue curves merge with one another.

Incremental Revenue and Marginal Revenue

Incremental revenue is the difference between the existing total revenue and new total revenue. Incremental revenue is the change in total revenue, irrespective of change in sales, whereas marginal revenue is the change in total revenue per unit of change in sales.

Incremental revenue is not confined to the effects of price change. It rather measures the effect of any kind of managerial decision on total revenue.

Elasticity of Demand, Average Revenue and Marginal Revenue

The concept of elasticity of demand is very much useful in determining the prices of products in different market conditions. Elasticity of demand can be measured in a straight line demand curve at any point. The point method helps to measure the elasticity of demand at any point on the demand curve. Let us study this aspect with the help of the adjacent diagram.

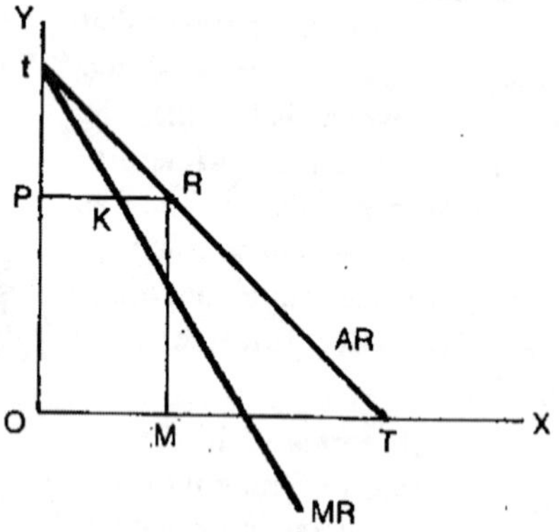

In this diagram AR and MR are average revenue and marginal revenue curves respectively. The elasticity of demand at point R on the demand curve tT is $\frac{RT}{Rt}$.

In the triangles, PtR and MTR,

$\angle tPR = \angle RMT$ (Right angles)

$\angle tPR = \angle RTM$ (Corresponding angles)

$\angle PtR = \angle MRT$ (being the third angle)

Therefore, triangles PtR and MTR are equiangular.

Hence $$\frac{RT}{Rt} = \frac{RM}{tP}$$

In the triangles of PtK and KRQ,

$$PK = RK$$

$$\angle PKt = \angle RKQ \quad \text{(Vertically opposite)}$$

$$\angle tPK = \angle KRQ \quad \text{(Right angles)}$$

Therefore, triangles PtK and KRQ are equal in all respects.

Hence $\quad Pt = RQ$

From 1 and 2, we get,

$$\text{Elasticity at } R = \frac{RT}{Rt} = \frac{RM}{tP} = \frac{RM}{RQ}$$

Now it is obvious from the above diagram that :

$$\frac{RM}{RQ} = \frac{RM}{RM - RQ}$$

$$\text{Hence, elasticity at } R = \frac{RM}{RM - QM}$$

For OM output, RM is average revenue, OM is marginal revenue.

$$\text{Elasticity at } R = \frac{AR}{AR - MR}$$

Elasticity at the point R is half average revenue.

Prof. Joan Robinson's formula for measuring the relationship between marginal revenue, average revenue and price elasticity of demand is as follows:

At any output :

$$\text{Average revenue} = \text{Marginal revenue} \times \frac{e}{e-1}$$

$$\text{Marginal revenue} = \text{Average revenue} \times \frac{e-1}{e}$$

Where e is the price elasticity of demand.

The relationship between them can be summed up as follows :

(i) When price elasticity of demand is greater than one, the marginal revenue is positive and total revenue rises as price falls.

(ii) When the price elasticity of demand is unity, the marginal revenue is zero and a change in the price will not change the total revenue.

(iii) When the price elasticity of demand is less than one, the marginal revenue is negative and the total falls as price falls.

Questions

1. What is marginal revenue.
2. Distinguish between incremental revenue and marginal revenue.
3. Draw average and marginal revenue curves both in perfect competition and monopoly.
4. Explain how elasticity of demand is useful in determining the price.
5. Explain the relationship between average and marginal revenue.

❖✻❖✻❖

CHAPTER

10

EQUILIBRIUM OF A FIRM UNDER PERFECT COMPETITION

Under perfect competition, a large number of firms are producing and selling homogeneous commodities to a large number of buyers. The firms which are producing the commodity under perfect competition enjoy perfect freedom either to start producing or stop producing. Under perfect competition, no buyers have a preference to buy from a particular seller and no seller has a preference to sell the products to a particular buyer.

CONDITIONS OF EQUILIBRIUM

Under perfect competition, price for the individual firm is given. The firm cannot influence the price by its own action. The firm works under the assumption that it can sell as much as it likes at the prevailing price. The demand curve facing the firm under perfect competition is a horizontal straight line. It shows perfect elasticity of demand.

The firm, under perfect competition, aims at maximising profit. The most important question is how to determine the output in such a way as to obtain maximum possible net revenue. At the same time, the firm has to attain equilibrium. Equilibrium is a state of business in which the firm is earning maximum money profits. When a firm attains equilibrium, it has no tendency either to expand or contract its output. Since his aim is to earn maximum net revenue from a level of output, he goes on producing the output when his total revenue is equal to total cost. Total revenue is the amount realised by output, the expenditure incurred is the total cost. It includes the total fixed cost and the variable cost. An increase in output means an increase in revenue and cost. A firm is in equilibrium when it does not change the amount of output produced. The output that maximises net revenue of a firm is the best profit output of a firm.

Total Revenue and Total Cost

The equality between total revenue and total cost at a point of output is called the *equilibrium output*. In the following diagram, the equilibrium position of the firm is illustrated.

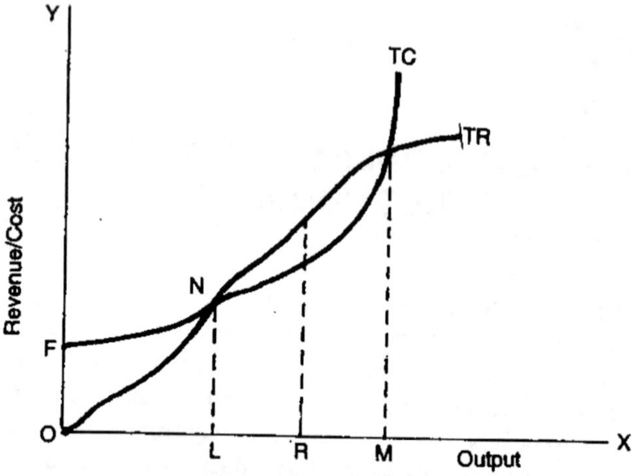

Equilibrium of a firm - Total cost and total revenue

In the above diagram, TC represents total cost and TR represents total revenue. Total cost curve starts at the height of OF. This is because that even if the firm produces nothing, it has to bear a certain cost of production due to fixed factors. These are the *fixed costs*. At the output less than OL, the cost is higher than the revenue and hence the firm incurs losses. At OL, the total revenue is equal to total cost but the firm is neither getting profits nor incurring losses. This point N at the output OL is called *break even* point. At the output larger than OM, the total costs are higher than total revenue and hence the firm is incurring losses. The point M is the break-even point. Between OL and OM will lie the optimum point of maximum profit.

The maximum profit will be where revenue cost spread is the largest or where the vertical distance between the total revenue and total cost curve is the greatest. The maximum profit is determined where the tangents to the total revenue and total cost curve are parallel as shown in the above diagram. At OR output, the firm attains equilibrium.

Though this method of finding out the maximum profit is reasonable, yet it suffers from some difficulties. This method uses total revenue and total costs concepts, and to find out the total revenue, it is necessary to sell all the units of output. At the same time, when some cost has been incurred, all the inputs must have been used full and nothing should remain in stock. Such a situation is difficult to come across in any industry and therefore another way of finding equilibrium has been used. This is called *marginal revenue* and *cost equality*.

Marginal Revenue and Marginal Cost

Marginal revenue and marginal cost concepts are readily available for the management to examine whether the firm is moving on the desirable path. The marginal revenue and the average revenue curves are one and the same under perfect competition. The firm under perfect competition cannot influence the price by its individual action. As a result of this, the demand curve or the average revenue curve of the firm is a horizontal straight line (perfectly elastic) at the prevailing price level. Since additional output is sold at the same price, marginal revenue coincides with average revenue curve. Marginal cost is U shaped like the average cost curve. In order to decide about the equilibrium level of output, the firm will compare marginal cost with marginal revenue. It will be in equilibrium when the marginal cost is equal to marginal revenue at the level of output. At this level of output, marginal cost curve cuts marginal revenue curve from below. At this level, it will be maximising profits. Since the marginal revenue is the same as price or average revenue, the firm will be in equilibrium when the marginal cost is equal to price. The level of output where marginal cost and marginal revenue are equal is the point of maximum profit. The following diagram shows how a firm attains equilibrium and gears up earning maximum profits.

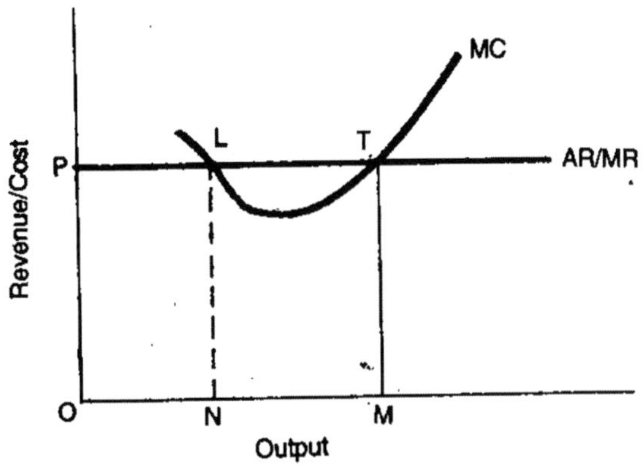

The firm attains equilibrium at a point where marginal cost is equal to marginal revenue. In the diagram, the MR and AR show the marginal revenue curve and the average revenue curve. MC is the marginal cost curve. MC cuts at two points L and T. At both these places, the marginal revenue is equal to marginal cost. But the equilibrium output is OM but not ON. At ON output, the firm's marginal cost is equal to marginal revenue but it is not the equilibrium point, for at this level, the marginal cost curve cuts the marginal revenue curve from above. At the same time, any increase in output after ON is more profitable for marginal cost is lower than marginal revenue. But beyond the level of output OM, the marginal cost is greater than the price. Hence OM is the equilibrium output and the company is making maximum profits. Thus, there are two conditions which must be followed if the firms want to attain equilibrium under perfect competition.

(i) MC = MR = Price

(ii) MC must cut MR from below and MC must be rising after the point of equilibrium.

If these conditions are fulfilled, the firm is said to have attained equilibrium. But, it is not possible to know whether the firm is making profit or not from this analysis. To make the analysis complete, one more aspect is to be added. That is, the average cost concept. As already known, average cost curve is a U shaped curve. After drawing the average cost curve, it must be compared with the average revenue curve. If the average cost equals average revenue, the firm is making normal profit while attaining equilibrium. It may also be possible where average cost is lower than average revenue. If that is the situation, then the firm is making super-normal profit. In the following diagram, the profit aspect is shown:

In the following figure, there are three diagrams:

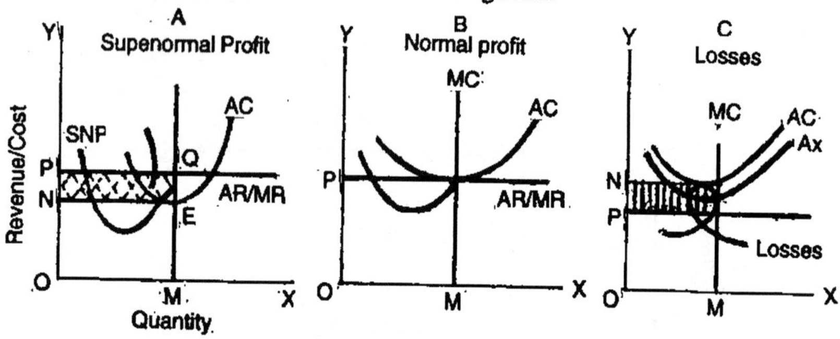

In the diagram `A,' the average cost curve is drawn along with average revenue, marginal cost and marginal revenue. The MR cuts MR/Price at the Q. OM is the equilibrium output. The firm sells the product OM at the price OP. It costs ON or ME to produce this output. The average cost is lower than the price. Hence, the firm is making supernormal profit. The shaded portion in the diagram is the supernormal profit. NEQP indicates supernormal profit. Because the normal profit is included in the average cost, NEQP indicates supernormal profit. In the diagram `B', the firm is making normal profit and in the diagram `C', the firm is shown making losses.

Short sun and long run equilibrium

Short run as already defined a period in which output can be increased by the existing plant. Each short run average cost curve indicates the plant size. If the firm produces more with the existing size of the plant, the average cost rises. In perfect competition, there are a large number of firms producing the output. Since all firms are not alike, cost differs. But the firms have to accept the price given by the interaction of demand and supply. And as such, profit earning also differs. What happens in perfect competition is that when the firms are making supernormal profits (AR is greater than A), some more firms enter into the industry to share the supernormal profits earned by some firms. On the other hand, it may be that circumstances are so unfavourable that some firms would record losses. With the entry of some firms, more output is produced. This causes the price to fall. If the price is equal to average cost, the firms earn only normal profit. If the price is lower than the average cost, then the firms experience losses. The loss making firms leave the industry, which means they stop producing the output. As a result of these changes, the industry will not be in equilibrium. In the short run, the industry will be in disequilibrium which is due to the fact that supernormal profit-making firms attract new firms to the industry and loss making firms leave the industry and those firms making supernormal profit will now be making only normal profit. The output is changing and the price also is changing.

The industry will be in equilibrium only in the long period. In the long period, there will be no entry or exit of firms. All firms are attaining equilibrium and earning only normal profit, which is shown in the following diagram:

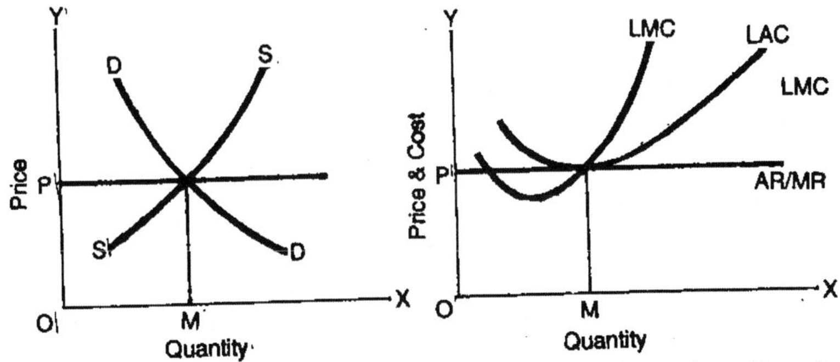

The long period is a period of time which is long enough to allow the firms to buy all the inputs including plant and machinery. In the long run, all costs will be variable. In the long run, no firm will be making supernormal profit. In fact, all firms are making only normal profit. In the long run, the average cost will be equal to price. If the price exceeds average cost, there arises supernormal profit, which is an incentive for some more firms to enter into the industry and increase the output. When supply rises, prices fall to the equilibrium level. In the long run, all firms will have identical costs and price will be equal to average cost.

The industry will be in equilibrium when the following conditions are fulfilled. There should be equality between long period demand and supply of the industry's product. All firms in the industry must be in equilibrium and all firms are making normal profit equating A and AR. There should be no incentive for new firms to enter the industry and old firms to leave the industry. In other words, all firms function in equilibrium.

Normal Profit

The concept of normal profit is important in describing the equilibrium of the industry. Normal profit is a fixed amount (independent of the level of output) which the firms must earn if they are to remain in the industry. Normal profit is included in the average cost itself. As normal profit is considered as a fixed amount, when output rises, normal profits, must cover at least the average total cost. If, on the other hand, some firms in the industry are running below normal (i.e., when they are having loss) profit, they will leave the industry and search for normal profits elsewhere. Then the number of firms in the industry will diminish and consequently output will also decrease. With a decrease in supply, price rises to the equilibrium level. In conclusion, it can be said that equilibrium of the industry or full equilibrium, as it is sometimes called, would be attained when the number of firms in the industry are in equilibrium (i.e., no movement into or out of the industry) and also all the individual firms are in equilibrium. At this point, all the firms are equating average cost, average revenue and marginal cost and marginal revenue with one another.

Industry Equilibrium

It is necessary here to distinguish between short run equilibrium and long run equilibrium of an industry. For a firm to attain equilibrium in the short run, marginal cost must be equal to marginal revenue. If this condition is fulfilled, it is sufficient. There is no criteria that all firms must earn normal profits. For the industry to attain equilibrium in the long run, all firms are producing output at the minimum point of the average cost curves. When all firms are having identical cost curves, all would be making either normal profits or supernormal profits. In the long run, the industry will be in equilibrium when all firms are in equilibrium. But, it is very rare to come across all firms attaining equilibrium and also the industry as a whole attaining equilibrium. It is more likely that the long run adjustment in the number of firms takes place before the industry comes to be in equilibrium.

Conclusion

When industry expands in the long run, several adjustments take place such as number of firms may increase, the existing firms may expand by adopting new technology, etc. It is possible also that firms derive benefits of internal and external economies. Consequently, costs may decline. The firms will be in a position to sell the output at a lower price. The price will settle at a point where marginal revenue is equal to marginal cost. All firms are selling at that price and thus achieve equilibrium.

Questions

1. What is equilibrium of a firm. Under what conditions is a firm is in equilibrium under perfect competition.
2. Distinguish between the equilibrium of a firm and industry under perfect competition.
3. Distinguish between short run and long run equilibrium.
4. Why is short run equilibrium called unstable equilibrium.
5. Why is long run equilibrium stable equilibrium.

❖✻❖✻❖

CHAPTER 11

PRICING UNDER MONOPOLY AND MONOPOLISTIC COMPETITIONS

Pricing and Output under Monopoly

Monopoly is another important market structure which extensively prevails in the capitalist economies of the world. It is found in India also with slight variations. In fact, the monopoly form of business is found in public utility services. We shall study the output and price determination under monopoly.

Meaning

Monopoly is defined as that market form in which a single producer controls the whole supply of a single commodity which has no close substitute. Three points should be noted in regard to this definition. Firstly, there must be a single producer, a seller or a product. This single producer may be a joint stock company or a proprietary firm. If there are many producers producing a product, either perfect competition or monopolistic competition will prevail depending on whether the product is homogeneous or heterogeneous. If there are a few producers, this will be oligopoly. If there is to be monopoly, there must be one firm producing the commodity. This firm itself becomes the industry in the essence of monopoly. In monopoly, there is no distinction between firm and industry.

A second condition which is essential for a firm to be called a monopoly is that there must be only one commodity produced by the firm for which there is no substitute. This means that there is no rival for the monopoly firm. Monopoly implies absence of competition as such. If the product produced by a firm has close substitutes, it cannot be called a monopoly. The second condition of monopoly can be expressed in terms of gross elasticity of demand. The gross elasticity of demand for the monopoly product and the product of another producer is zero.

Thirdly, there are strong barriers for the firms to enter into the industry. It means other firms for one reason or other are prohibited from entering the monopoly industry. The barriers may be economic or else institutional and artificial in nature.

The above conditions ensure that monopolist can set any price for his product and can follow an independent price policy. Since the monopolist is producing a commodity for which there is not even distant substitute, he can dictate price, as well as the quantity of the product sold in the market. Though he has got absolute power to determine price and the output, he cannot do both. He can do one of these things only - either he can fix the price and, leave the amount sold in the market or he can fix the quantity of output produced and leave the price to be determined by demand. Joel Dean has called a monopolised product '*a product of lasting distinctiveness*'. Such a product has no acceptable substitutes and its distinctiveness lasts for several years.

Causes of Monopoly

Monopoly is formed by domineering producers by means of engulfing the small firms through cut-throat competition. A producer may possess certain raw materials, patent rights and the secret methods of production or specialised skill might give a monopoly power. Wherever a huge amount of money is required for investment, which for the other it might not be possible, then such a company becomes a monopoly naturally. The public utility services like water supply and electricity are state monopolies everywhere. In some industries, economies of scale are so particularly pronounced that competition is impracticable, inconvenient or simply unworkable. Such industries are called *natural monopolies*. The public utilities are given exclusive rights by the governments to run as monopolies.

Output and Price Determination under Monopoly

Monopolists are price makers and not price takers as under perfect competition.

The AR curve for the monopolist is a downward sloping curve. If the monopolist reduces the price of his product, he can sell more. If he raises the prices, naturally the demand for his product decreases. When he decreases the price to sell additional units of his product, then the price for his total output goes down. Since his output affects the price at which he can sell, price is not a given factor for him, as it is for the firm producing under perfect competition.

A monopolist like the firm under perfect competition wants to maximise the profit. At the same time, he has to attain equilibrium. In order to maximise the profits, he has to raise the price. If he raises the price, he cannot sell more. Therefore, in determining the price, the monopolist has to look into the market forces. The question is how the monopolist is going to determine price and the output of the product. It again depends upon the demand and the cost consideration.

As said earlier, the demand curve or Average Revenue curve is a downward sloping curve. The marginal revenue curve falls bêlow average revenue curve. The cost curves do not undergo any change in imperfect competition. They are the same everywhere where output is produced. The average cost is U shaped and the marginal curve cuts the average revenue curve at its minimum point.

Attaining Equilibrium

Equating marginal and average revenue curve is an important condition for the monopoly firm to attain equilibrium. It is only by equating these two concepts, that the monopoly firm maximises its total money profits. Therefore, the firm will produce upto a point and charges a price which brings him maximum money profits. In other words, the firm will be in equilibrium at the price-output level at which its profits are maximum. The firm will go on producing so long as marginal revenue is equal to cost. It does so because, as long as marginal revenue exceeds marginal cost, the firm will be increasing its total profits. At the point where the marginal revenue is equal to marginal cost, the profit are maximised and here the firm stops producing further. If the production is continued after this point, the firm experiences loss for every additional unit produced.

In the following diagram, the price-output determination by the monopoly firm is shown. AR is the demand curve. MR is the marginal revenue curve. A and MC are average cost and marginal cost curves respectively. The MC and MR are equal at the point Q. The firm produces OM output and sells the OM output at OP price. For this output, OL is the average cost and since the AR is higher than OL, the firm is earning monopoly profits as shown in the shaded area.

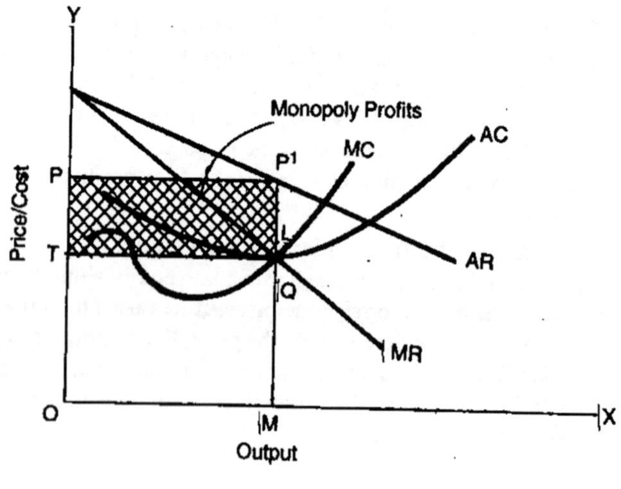

MONOPOLY AND ELASTICITY OF DEMAND

One important point about the equilibrium of the monopolist is that the equilibrium of the monopolist will lie at that level of output where the elasticity of demand for his product is greater than one. It means that the monopolist will never be in equilibrium at a point on the demand curve or average revenue curve at which elasticity of demand is less than one. If he wants to fix the output, where the elasticity of his average revenue curve is less than one, he can not equate marginal cost with marginal revenue. Therefore, no sensible monopolist will produce on that portion of the demand curve which gives him negative marginal revenue.

Monopolist's sole consideration is to maximise his profit. He is not interested in the production for social welfare. Therefore, it is the total profit that guides the monopolist in the price and output determination.

Long run consideration

For the monopolist, long run considerations also influence in determining price and output.

A monopolist wants to make monopoly profit even in long run too. The price determined by him depends upon the elasticity of demand. If the demand for his product is elastic, the monopoly power becomes weak. It happens when he finds a competitor for his product. The more inelastic the demand, the stronger is the position of the monopolist.

In the long run, the monopolist changes the size of the plant in response to a change in demand. In the long run too, he has to equate marginal revenue with marginal cost. In the long run too, he is maximising profit by producing the equilibrium output.

MONOPOLY AND COMPETITION COMPARED

Under perfect competition, price is determined by the intersection of demand and supply and the individual producer has no control over the price. Whereas under monopoly, the producer has control over the price. Under perfect competition, the demand curve or the average revenue curve is perfectly elastic and is a horizontal straight line parallel to the horizontal axis. Under perfect competition at the equilibrium level, marginal revenue curve is a downward sloping cure and the marginal revenue is less than average revenue at all levels of output. In the equilibrium position, average revenue is greater than marginal revenue under monopoly.

The monopolist will always sell the product at a price higher than average cost and marginal cost. But, under perfect competition, the price is higher than average cost only in the short period but both are equal in the long period. Under perfect competition, a firm is attaining equilibrium at the lowest point of the average cost curve. But under monopoly, the firm is attaining equilibrium at the highest point on the left side of the average cost curve. The chief reason, if the monopolist stops producing at the lowest point of the average cost curve, implies that he cannot equate marginal revenue and marginal cost and attain an equilibrium.

Under perfect competition, there may be supernormal profits in the short run but they will be competed away in the long run. In monopoly however, supernormal profit persists even in the long run. In monopoly, the price is higher and output is less than in perfect condition and conditions of cost and demand remain unchanged. Competitive industry implies more efficient utilisation of resources and provides the consumers a product at a lower price while the monopoly restricting the output sells it at a higher price ignoring the interest of the consumers. It is a common saying that monopoly means the exploitation. Therefore, the governments consider it necessary to curb the tendency of monopolistic growth. Generally, the governments restrict the prices of the monopoly products and also levy excise duties on them. In case the monopoly becomes harmful, the government may take over such monopoly firms and run them in the interest of the public as public utility concerns.

Joan Robinson viewed that perfect competition would bring about all economies, which monopoly could introduce. She observed that cost curve will not shift downward, as a result of the establishment of a monopoly in place of large number of firms working under perfect competition. Thus, according to her, monopoly price is higher and monopoly output always is smaller than perfect competition.

There is another significant difference that is monopoly can discriminate prices for the same product, while firms under perfect competition cannot do. By discriminating price, monopolist increase his profits.

Discriminating Monopoly

Monopoly firms have the sole objective of earning maximum profits. They may charge uniform price for their products to all the consumers or they may charge different prices for their product to different consumers. Charging different prices to different consumers of their product is called *price discrimination.* Price discrimination refers to the practice of a seller selling the same product at different prices to different buyers. Joan Robinson defines price discrimination as charging different prices for the same product or same price for differential products. Product may be differentiated by time, appearance or place, so that the purchasers are not able to shift to the low price commodity. The concept of price discrimination may be broadened to include the sale of various varieties of the same product at different prices. When a seller sells different varieties of the same product at different prices, such an act of the seller implies this discrimination. For example, a bookseller selling the same edition of a book in an ordinary cover at Rs.25 and with deluxe cover at Rs.50, then he is said to be discriminating prices-those who want deluxe cover pay Rs.50 and others pay Rs.25 for the ordinary cover of the same book.

Types of Price Discrimination

Three types of price discrimination have been analysed. They are: (a) personal discrimination (b) local discrimination and (c) discrimination according to use or trade. Price discrimination becomes personal when a seller charges different prices for different customers. This depends upon the ability of the buyers to pay. This type of price discrimination is not made openly but in a disguised manner. For example, a publisher may sell a book as a deluxe edition at a high price. It will cater to rich consumers. He may sell the ordinary editions to middle class consumers. This principle is also followed by public utility concerns. Passengers travelling in air-conditioned carriages pay more than the cost of providing extra facilities.

Then there is local discrimination where different prices are charged from different localities or places. Prices in fashionable shops are higher than ordinary shops. Only rich persons go to fashionable shops and buy the same product at a higher price. Dumping is an example of local discrimination. The monopolist charges higher prices in the home market and a lower price in the foreign market.

Lastly, there is price discrimination according to use. Different prices are charged for a commodity according to the uses to which the commodity is put. For example, electricity is sold to agriculturists at lower prices and to households in cities at higher prices. Many a time, the producers make product discrimination by means of special labels and charge different prices for the same product packed in different covers.

The types of price discrimination practised by monopolists are summarised in the table below :

Types	Basis of discrimination	Examples
Personal	Income of the buyers	Doctor's fees.
Group	Age	Children are charged at half price in transport organisations.
	Status of buyers	Higher discount to bulk buyers.
Product	Quality of the product	Higher rate to deluxe models.
	Labels on products	Lower price to unbranded.
	Producers	
	Sizes of products	Relatively lower prices to economy sizes.
	Season	Lower prices in slack season and higher price in busy season.

Degree of Price Discrimination

Prof. A.C. Pigon has distinguished between the three types of price discrimination.

Price discrimination of the first degree is also known as *perfect price discrimination,* where the buyers are fully exploited. Under this, monopolist charges the maximum that each buyers is willing to pay, rather than go without the goods.

Price discrimination of the second degree would occur if a monopolist was able to classify buyers into different groups and from each group, a different price is charged which is the lowest demand price for that group. This is explained below with a diagram.

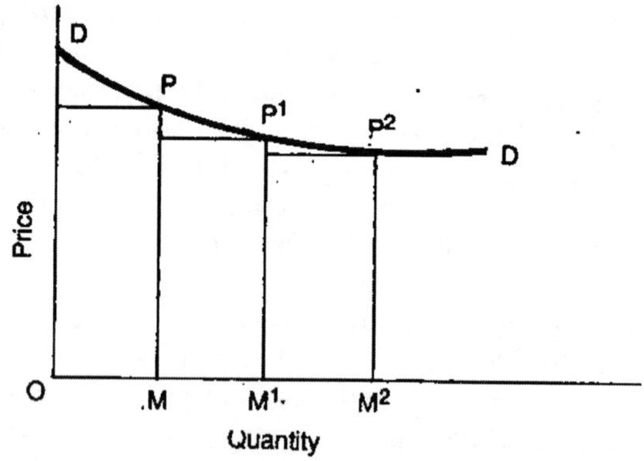

DD is the market demand curve. M^{th} unit of a product has a demand price MP and earlier units have a demand price (greater MP) as indicated in the slope of demand curve. All OM units of output are sold at MP price. On M^{th} unit of output, buyers do not enjoy consumer surplus but buyers of earlier units enjoy consumer surplus. Similarly, for M^1th unit, the demand price is M^1P^1. For units between M and M^1. demand price is greater M^1P^1, but all units from M to M^1 and M^1P^1 price prevails soon. In this way, price discrimination of the second degree is made.

Price discrimination of the third degree occurs when the monopolist divides the buyers into different groups and then charges different prices to different groups. The price charged in a sub-market need not be the lowest demand price of that sub-market or group. The price charged in each sub-market depends upon the output sold in the sub-market. Price discrimination of the third degree is most common. A common example of such price discrimination is found in the practice of a manufacturer who sells his goods at a higher price at home and at a lower price abroad. Another example may be mentioned here. Where the electricity company sells electric power at a higher price to households, it charges lower prices to industrial users. Price discrimination of the third degree is more commonly found in the real world.

When is price discrimination possible

Monopolists practice price discrimination provided that it is profitable. If price discrimination is to be practised, the monopolist has to fulfil the following conditions:

The sub-markets so classified by the monopolist must maintain a separate identity. It should not be possible to transfer any unit of a commodity from one market to another market. The classification of a sub-market is based upon the elasticity of demand for the product. Price discrimination is possible only if the elasticity of demand in one submarket is different from another market. Supposing he classifies his buyers into two markets, a market with an elastic demand and a market with an inelastic demand, he sells at a lower price in the former market and at a higher price in the latter. If the buyers in the elastic market were to sell the product in the inelastic market to make the advantage of higher prices, the monopolist will not stand to gain anything from price discrimination.

Secondly, it should not be possible for the buyers in the dearer market to transfer themselves into cheaper markets to buy the product at cheaper price. For example, if a doctor is charging a smaller price from poor patients than from the rich patients, then his price discrimination would fail if the rich patients assume themselves to be poor.

Price discrimination is possible under the following circumstances:

(i) The nature of the product or services should be such that there is no possibility of transfer of product from one market to another.

(ii) Discrimination occurs when the markets are separated by large distance or tariff barriers, so that it is expensive to transfer goods from one market to another market.

(iii) In some cases, there may be legal sanction for price discrimination. For example, travelling in railways in different classes. A person with a second class ticket is forbidden to travel in the first class.

(iv) Price discrimination may become possible due to the preference or prejudices of buyers. A commodity is generally converted into different varieties by providing different packings, different names or labels etc., in order to convince the buyers that certain varieties are superior to others. Different prices are charged for different varieties though they only differ in name or label. In this way, the producers are usually able to break-up their market and sell the so called superior varieties to the rich people at higher prices and the so called ordinary varieties to the poor people at lower prices. This is a clear case of price discrimination based on the preferences or prejudices of various buyers of the product. Joan Robinson puts this aspect of price discrimination in a very clear manner: *"Various brands of a certain article under names and labels which induce rich and snobbish buyers to divide themselves from poor buyers and this way the market is split up and the monopolist can sell what is substantially the same thing at several prices. In posh localities, the prices of the same goods are different from congested and ugly localities".*

Price discrimination is being practised all over the world by producers. As said earlier, price discrimination is found only under imperfect competition, especially in monopoly and not in perfect competition.

Is price discrimination profitable

Monopolists practice price discrimination with a view to make monopoly profits. If it is to be profitable, the elasticity of demand in one market must be different from the elasticity of demand in a different market. If different elasticities of demand are there in two markets, the monopolist can discriminate prices and make profits. If the demand curves in the two market, are iso-elastic, at every price, elasticity of demand is the same. Then, it will not pay the monopolist to charge different prices. If the elasticity of demand is the same in the two markets, marginal revenue in the two markets at every price of the product will also be same. If marginal revenues at every price of the product are same in the two markets, it will not be profitable for the monopolist to transfer any amount of goods from one market to another market and thus charge different prices of the product in the two markets.

Let us study how a discriminating monopolist is going to attain equilibrium and earn profit through monopoly.

Equilibrium under price Discrimination

Under simple monopoly, the firm charges uniform price for the whole output. But under price discrimination, different prices are charged for the same product. In order to do price discrimination, the monopolist has to divide his total market into two sub-markets on the basis of differences in elasticities of demand.

In order to reach an equilibrium, the discriminating monopolist has to take two decisions :– (i) How much total output he should produce and (ii) How should he distribute the total output between the two markets and what prices he should charge in these two markets.

The following diagram presents the technique adopted by the discriminating monopolist in order to attain equilibrium.

In order to determine equilibrium, the discriminating monopolist has to equate marginal revenue with marginal cost. Since he has to sell the output in two markets at different prices, he has separate demand and marginal revenue curves. He has to add the marginal revenues in two markets and then compare this to the marginal cost of the total output. The third diagram shows the equality between marginal revenue and the marginal cost. AMR is the aggregate marginal revenue. The AMR curve cuts the marginal cost curve at E (Diagram iii) and the total output produced is OM. This output is to be distributed to the two markets.

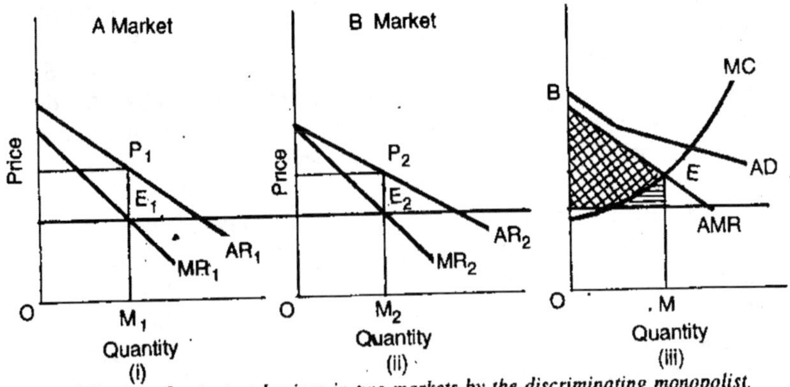

Fixation of output and prices in two markets by the discriminating monopolist.

The monopolist will distribute OM output in the two markets in such a way that marginal revenues are equal. Marginal revenues in the two markets must be equal if the profits are to be maximised. If the marginal revenue is high in one market and low in another market, it will pay him to transfer some amount from a market where marginal revenue is less to the market where it is more. Therefore, marginal revenues must be the same in the two markets. Then, it will be unprofitable for him to shift any amount from one market to another.

In order to attáin equilibrium, it is essential, that not only the marginal revenues must be same but also they should be equal to the marginal cost of the whole output. As shown in the diagram (iii), at the equilibrium output OM, marginal cost is ME. Now the output OM is to be distributed in the two markets in such a way that marginal revenue in them should be equal to marginal cost of the whole output.

It is now clear that in diagram (i), OM_1 output is to be sold in A market, because marginal revenue M_1E_1 at the OM_1 output is equal to marginal cost ME. Similarly OM^2 output is sold in B market, since marginal revenue M_2E_2 is equal to marginal cost ME of the whole output. Thus, the discriminating monopolist produces OM output and sells OM_1 output in Market A at M_1P_1 price and OM_2 output in market B at M_2P_2 price. The total output is now equal to $OM_1 + OM_2$. As shown in the diagram, he sells at a higher price in the A market and at a lower price in the B market and finally makes profits as shown in the shaded area in the diagram (iii).

Is price discrimination justified

It is rather difficult to say whether price discrimination is beneficial from the social point of view. Sometimes, price discrimination may be beneficial to society. Discrimination in consultation practiced by the physicians and surgeons is considered beneficial to poor patients who are charged low fees. This extends the basic medical services to them. It is not economically objectionable to make the rich pay more for the same service. The rich people have greater ability to pay and the society does not stand to lose if money is transferred from rich people to the monopolist. Another example may be given to justify the policy of price discrimination. If there is a uniform fare for rail travel, the railways cannot provide the service and make some profit. It has been observed by many that if railway authorities are not permitted to charge higher fare from the rich people who travel in upper classes, then it may not be profitable for the authorities to run the railways on a single uniform fare from the two economic strata of the society.

From the social welfare point of view too, since discriminating monopoly produces more output than a simple monopoly, it is desirable. Under price discrimination, when price is raised for the rich and is lowered for the poor, it has a redistributive effect, the poor are benefitted at the expense of the rich. From the point of view of reducing inequalities of personal real income, price discrimination is justified. If the price discrimination increases the production of the output and more is provided for the poor, then it is desirable. In those cases in which discrimination will decrease the output, it is undesirable on both counts.

Joan Robinson has observed from the point of view of society as a whole, that it is impossible to say whether price discrimination is desirable or not. From one point of view, price discrimination may be held superior to simple monopoly when there is increase in output. If price discrimination results in maldistribution of resources between different uses, it is not desirable.

MONOPOLISTIC COMPETITION

We have already seen how price and output are determined under perfect competition and monopoly. But pure or perfect competition and perfect monopoly are rarely found in the real world. In the real world, we do not find commodities which are perfect substitutes. What we find in the real world is that commodities have close substitutes. Therefore, firms which are producing close substitutes come under imperfect competition. Monopolistic competition is another form of imperfect competition.

Theory of monopolistic competition was propounded by Prof. E.H. Chamberlin while the theory of imperfect competition was developed by Prof. Joan Robinson. Though the theory of imperfect competition propounded by the latter is similar in various ways, it differs in some important respects. The nutshell of these theories is that pure or perfect competition and pure monopoly are the two opposite limiting cases, lying in between in a market structure where there is imperfection in competitive elements.

Meaning and nature of monopolistic competition

Monopolistic competition refers to a market situation in which there are either many producers producing goods which are close substitutes to one another or the product is differentiated.

Chamberlin's concept of monopolistic competition is a strategic blending of monopoly and competition. The distinguishing feature of monopolism produced by various producers are not homogeneous but different, though they are closely related to each other. When there is differentiation between the products produced by many producers, the monopoly element comes in. These monopolies are competing with each other. Since each producer is a monopolist and yet has competitors, a market situation comes into existence which is described as *monopolistic* competition.

It is thus clear that products produced by firms in monopolistic competition are not identical as in perfect competition, but they are close substitutes. The important distinguishing features of monopolistic competition are (i) existence of large number of firms, (ii) differentiated products and (iii) products are close substitutes.

Product differentiation is an important characteristic of monopolistic competition. The product of various sellers are fairly (but not the same) similar and serve as a close substitute to each other. Product differentiation means that the products are different in some ways, but not altogether so. The producers differentiate the product in such a way that each one has a monopoly of his own product. Many examples of monopolistic competition can be given from the Indian market scene. Many firms in India produce tooth paste, brush, soap, etc., and the product of each one is different from its rivals in one way or the other. Different toothpastes like Colgate, Binaca, Forhans, Koynos, McClean soaps like Lux, Hamam, Rexona, Breeze, etc., tooth, brushes like Colgate, Binaca, Dr. Wests', Wisdon, etc are strategic examples of monopoly. Thus, monopolistic competition corresponds more to the real world than pure competition or monopoly.

Product differentiation is made in several ways. Firstly, differentiation is made in the product itself. It may be a patent, trademark, package, use of wrapper, differentiation in quality, design, colour or style of the product, of attractive packets, etc. Secondly, differentiation is made with regard to conditions of sale. This means that a product is differentiated if the services rendered in the process of selling the product by one seller is not identical with those of other firms. Product is differentiated through fair dealing, market courtesy and efficiency. Thus, in the case of differentiated products, we find the existence of the characteristics of both monopoly and pure competition.

Many Firms

Under monopolistic competition, there are many firms producing the products. It may not be thousand firms but about sixty to seventy firms. Since there are many firms, what an individual firm produces is only a small proportion of the total output, so that each has a limited control over the price of the product. Since there are many firms, there is no possibility of collision of firms to restrict the output. And also, there is a feeling of mutual inter - dependence and as such, each firm determines the price and the output.

Independent Price Policy

Firms under monopolistic competition follow an independent price policy. The firms are producing differentiated products which are close substitutes and as such, each one determines the price taking into consideration his cost of production and demand. If a firm were to lower the price of product, there is no assurance that it can sell more. In such cases, the rival firms would not take retaliation. In monopolistic competition, the competition between the sellers is not on the price basis. It is based on the quality of the product, the package, the service attached to it and so on. The buyers are willing to pay for their favourite product more than the price of the rival products.

Price - Output Determination

Firms under monopolistic competition are producing products which are similar but not identical and hence the price of the differentiated products are also different. Firms under monopolistic competition have restricted market in the sense, that the sales are limited depending upon the price, the nature of the product and the advertising campaign it makes. The objective of the firm is to achieve equilibrium and to maximise its profit. Since there are many rivals in the market competing for a potential selling base of their products, the firms have to make adjustments in price, output and advertisement outlay. Equilibrium under monopolistic competition involves individual equilibrium (equilibrium of a firm) and group equilibrium of all firms put together.

Equilibrium of a Firm under Monopolistic Competition

Individual equilibrium refers to the equilibrium of the individual firm. Every firm is required to attain equilibrium if it wants to continue in business. Equilibrium of a firm requires equality of marginal revenue with marginal cost. Marginal rèvenue of a firm closely follows the average revenue of the firm. Average revenue curve or the demand curve for the product of an individual firm is shown downward sloping. Since various firms under monopolistic competition produce products which are close substitutes of each other, the position and the elasticity of the demand curve depends upon the availability of competing substitutes and their prices. Therefore, equilibrium adjustment of an individual firm cannot be attained in isolation from the group of which a firm is only a part.

The demand curve of the firm under monopolistic competition is more elastic since there are several substitutes available in the market. Even though the firm under monopolistic competition has monopolistic control over its product, but its control is restricted with the availability of close substitutes and if it sets too high a price for his product, many customers will shift to the rival products.

The individual equilibrium in the short run is graphically shown below :

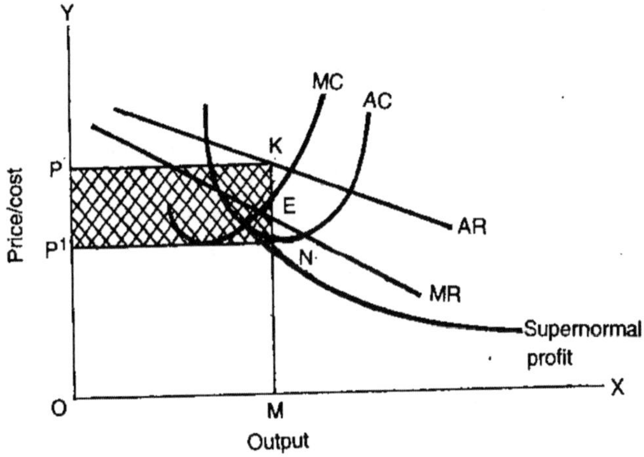

AR is the demand curve for the product of an individual firm, the nature and prices of substitutes are assumed as given MR, the marginal revenue curve follows the average revenue curve. AC and MC are the average cost and marginal cost curves respectively. MR and MC intersect each other at E and OM is the output produced. OP or MK is the price because K is a point on the average revenue curve. The firm is making a supernormal profit equivalent to the area known in the diagram P¹PKN. KN is the supernormal profit per unit of output. Since the demand and cost are very favourable, the firm is earning supernormal profit and also attaining equilibrium.

If the demand and cost conditions are less favourable, then a monopolistically competitive firm experiences losses. This is shown in the following diagram:

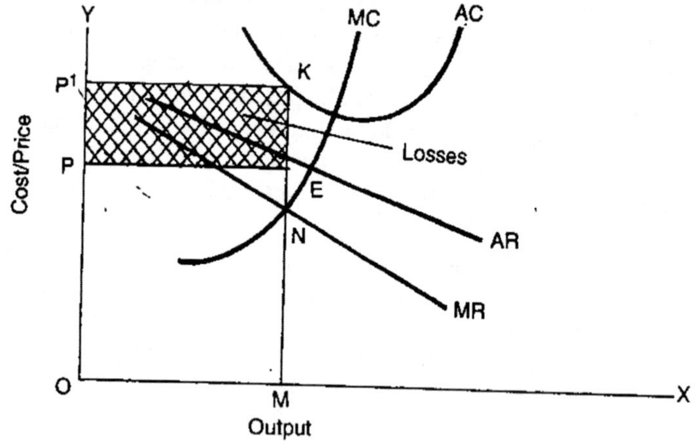

The firm is in equilibrium equating marginal revenue with MC. But average cost is greater than average revenue OE. Price OP is less than the cost MK per unit of output. The loss is shown as the area KEP_1. In such circumstances, there is no alternative for the firm except to make the best of the bargain.

Thus, a firm is in equilibrium but may be earning supernormal profit or making loss depending upon the position of the demand curve relative to the position of the cost curve. It is also possible for a firm making normal profit in the short run if the demand curve happens to be tangent to the average cost curve.

When once a firm fixes the price, it will not deviate from the price anymore. If it varies its price upwards, the loss due to fall in the quantity demanded will be more than made up by the higher price. If it cuts down the price, the gain due to increase in sales will be less than the loss due to the lower price. Hence, the price will remain stable.

Group Equilibrium

Group equilibrium means price - output adjustment of a number of firms, whose products are close substitutes. The industry in monopolistic competition, consists of a number of firms producing differentiated products. In other words, the firms are producing heterogeneous products. Hence, the firms producing heterogeneous products cannot be added to form the market demand and supply schedules. Hence, Prof. Chamberlin uses the concept of *'product group'* for the industry. In modern parlance, though the firms are producing heterogeneous products, they are brought under the concept of industry. For example, though there are six or seven car manufacturers in the country, though each is different from the other, they are all clubbed to be called the *motor car industry.* But the costs and revenue structures vary between firms. In Prof. Chamberlin's analysis, the product group includes products which are closely related, i,e., they are technological and economic substitutes. Technological substitutes are products which can technically cover the same want and economic substitutes refer to products which cover the same want and have similar prices. The 'group' is defined as *'the demand for each single product which is highly elastic and that it shifts appreciably when the price of other products in the group changes'*, i,e., products forming the group or industry should have high costs and price elasticities. Product differentiation enables each firm to charge a different price.

Each firm in the group is a monopoly. Yet, there is competition among those firms which are producing closely related products. The price-output determination of one firm will affect the decision of other firms. There is not much qualitative difference between the products of the firms. Yet, there is price and cost difference between the firms. The demand curves and cost curves vary between firms. As a result, there are differences in prices, including output and profits of the various firms in the group.

In order to develop the theory of 'group equilibrium' Prof. Chamberlin makes certain assumptions. Firstly, he makes uniformity assumption. It means that the demand and cost curves of all the products in the group are uniform. The differentiation in quality between the product is very much reduced. He assumes that consumers' preferences are evenly distributed among different varieties and differences among them are not such as to give rise to differences in costs.

Prof. Chamberlin has introduced another assumption, namely symmetry assumption. It means that the number of firms under monopolistic competition are large enough to ensure that individual decision regarding price and output adjustment has little influence on the rivals. This means that there is no possibility of retaliation.

Keeping the above assumption in mind, the *'concept of group 'equilibrium'* is illustrated in the diagram shown.

The diagram A represents short run equilibrium and diagram B represents long run equilibrium. In the short run, the firms earn supernormal profits. In the long run, all firms make only normal profits. The situation is similar to one prevailing under perfect competition. But there is a great difference. Under perfect competition, the demand curve is a horizontal straight line. The firms attain equilibrium at the lowest point of the average cost curve. While in monopolistic competition, the demand curve is downward sloping and it is in tangent to long run average cost curve at the higher slope of the long run with average cost curve at its left side. It indicates that equilibrium occurs at a smaller output than perfect competition.

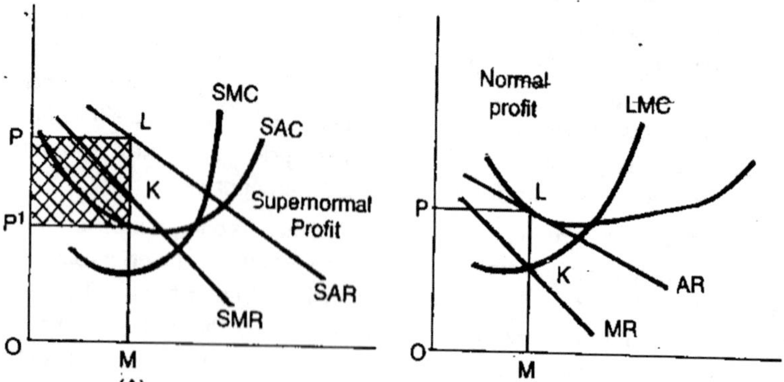

(A) Short run equilibrium

(B) Long run equilibrium

Selling Costs

The firms under monopolistic competition manufacture and sell closely related products in the potential market. As such, the firms are required to incur expenses in order to advertise in papers and other media. The expenses incurred for advertisements and other selling mediums are called selling costs. Prof. Chamberlin defines selling costs as 'costs incurred in order to alter the position or shape of the demand curve for a product'. As examples, he mentions, advertising of all varieties, salesmen's salaries and the expenses of sales department, margins granted to dealers in order to increase their efforts in favour of particular goods, window displays, demonstrations of new goods, etc. Thus, selling costs represent the costs on all those selling activities which are directed to persuade the buyers to change their preferences, so as to raise the demand for a given article.

Selling costs are distinguished from production costs. Production costs are those costs which include the cost of raw - materials, cost of manufacture and labour used in production. Cost of production includes all expenses connected with the manufacture of a commodity, its transportation to the market etc, while the selling costs include all expenses incurred in order to secure a demand for the product. Chamberlin distinguishes the two costs as follows:

Production costs adopt commodity to the demand, while selling costs adopt demand to the commodity. This is to say that production costs create utilities which will satisfy demand, while selling costs create and shift the demand itself.

Need for Selling Costs

The temptation for incurring selling costs arises on account of the fact that people have imperfect knowledge and that there is possibility of altering the desires of the people through advertisements. Advertisements are directed to spread the information regarding the quality, the price and other features of the product. Advertising increases a seller's market and changes the location of the demand curve for the product. Advertising about price offer makes the sales curve more elastic while that about quantity, shifts the sales curve to the right.

Varying Returns to Selling Costs

Advertisement is intended to secure an increase in demand for the product. When a firm takes sales promotion campaign through advertisements, it may find its sales have increased. This creates retaliation psychology among the other rival firms. Consequently, all firms under monopolistic competition incur selling costs. The main point is that the producers, by spending money and efforts on advertisements, can alter the demand curve for a product. Persuasive advertisement usually results in increase in sales, by attracting the attention of a large number of prospective buyers. The aim is to increase the sales of one firm at the expense of the other.

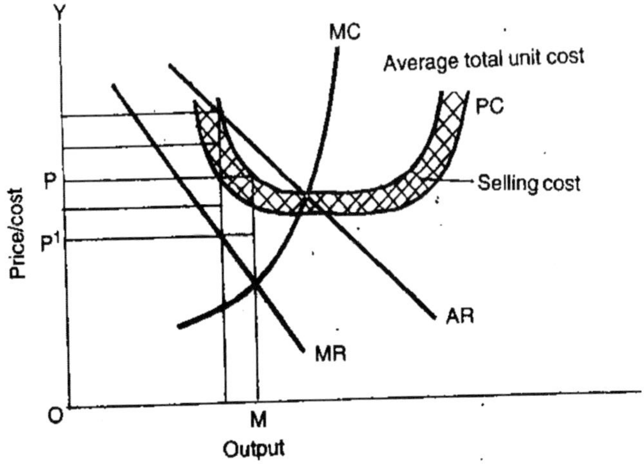

At first, selling costs may not yield increasing returns because of the built up habits of the consumers. As advertisements are prolonged, it becomes easier to attack more customers. A point is reached where additional or increased advertisements would not increase the sales. That is after the optimum is reached, any additional expenditure on advertisements would result in diminishing returns.

Selling cost is considered as a variable cost required to dispose the output at the same price. When the selling costs are added to the production cost, then the cost curve moves up. The diagram illustrates the effect of selling cost of price.

Before the advertisement, the average price for OM output is OP[1] while after the advertisement, the price rises to OP. If the advertisement expenditure shifts the demand curve, the firm by increasing sales makes more profit. In the above diagram, PC is the production cost. ATUC is the average total unit cost after incurring of selling cost. If the firm sells the OM product at the same price, as was done before the incurring of selling cost, the profit is reduced. If the firm incurs selling cost, its average cost is bound to rise. As a result of selling costs, if the demand curve shifts, then it can sell more. When the firm is selling more, its sales expenses rise and consequently its total average cost also rises. The firm considers whether it is making maximum profit by selling more at a higher price. If the profits rise, its sales expenses also rise. This cannot go on for ever. The firm has to stop producing more when the marginal revenue equals marginal cost. Beyond this, further expenditure on advertisements will reduce profit, since it will add more to the cost than to revenue. Thus, for a firm under monopolistic competition, corresponding to different levels of selling costs, there are a series of average revenue curves and average cost curves. The producer has to select that set of cost and revenue curves where the profits are maximum. The following diagram illustrates this:

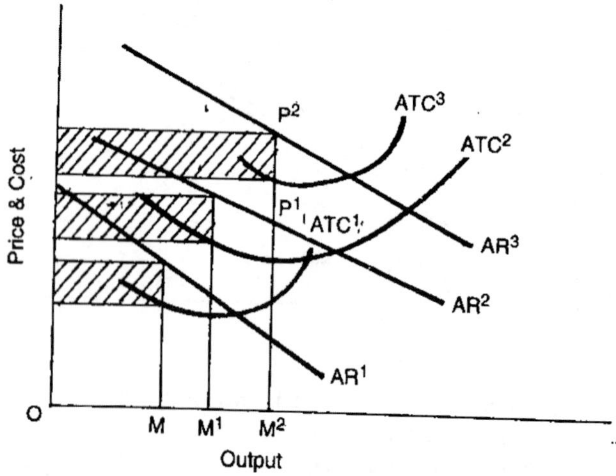

In this diagram, AR_1 is the average revenue curve before the advertisement. ATC is the average cost curve. OP is the price. OM is the equilibrium output. Suppose the firm incurs selling expenditure of about Rs.1 lakh, the average cost curve is ATC_2. As a result of this sales expenses, the firm sells more output, i.e., MM^1. The price rise to P^1. This again is *profit maximising position.* Here the output is larger and the price is higher than the original equilibrium price. But the most important point to note is that the firm does not bother about the price or the volume of the output. It is only concerned with maximising profit. Since the profits have increased, the firm wants to increase the selling expenses. As a result of this, price rises to AR_3. The ATC also rises to ATC_3. In this price and cost, the total profits of the firm are slightly reduced. Beyond this, any increase in advertisement is not profitable. Therefore, while considering the problem of selling cost, the managerial economist is required to consider whether it is bringing maximum profit or not. However, management has a social responsibility towards minimising the undesirable implications of advertising.

Wastes In Monopolistic Competition

Under monopolistic competition, output is slightly less and prices are higher than perfect competition. According to Prof. Chamberlin and Joan Robinson, firms under monopolistic competition or imperfect competition produce less than socially optimum or ideal output. In other words, the firms do not produce that level of output at which the long run average cost is the minimum. This will happen when the firms operate at a point on the falling portion of the long run average cost curve. A firm under monopolistic competition will attain equilibrium when the demand curve is tangent to the falling position of the long run average cost curve. If the firm produces at the minimum level of the long run average cost curve, it cannot attain equilibrium. Since the demand curve is a sloping curve, the equilibrium is attained at a falling portion of the long run average cost curve. It means to say that the productive resources of the company are not fully utilised. This gives the measure of excess of capacity which lies unutilised under imperfect competition. This is also called *waste.*

Under monopolistic competition, the consumers can buy any product which satisfies them, since there are many close substitutes. The firms engage in high pressure salesmanship, which directly influence the buyers to have preference of a product over another product.

All these have resulted in the restriction of output and higher prices for the products. The consumers have to pay a price higher than the marginal cost. This excess of price causes additional burden on the consumers. It is not the total amount of profit that pinches, but selling too high a price is the greatest evil of imperfect or monopolistic competition.

Expenditure on competitive advertisements is considered as a waste of financial resource. If competition is perfect, there is homogeneous product and as such there is no need for advertisement. Since competition is imperfect, the expenses on advertisements are unavoidable. Every firm in the group is required to set apart a certain percentage of revenue for this expenditure. Under imperfect competition, much larger reduction in price will be necessary to prevent consumers from shifting their preferences to other products. They spend money on advertisements to persuade the consumers to buy the product which has been concentrated upon by the advertising firm. Such expenditure is a waste from the point of view of social welfare of the community.

Another similar waste is expenditure on cross transport. A firm in South India is selling the product in North India. At the same, the same commodity is being sold by a firm located in North India. This state of affairs is due to the absence of perfect competition. Since the firm in South India makes advertisement of its product in the whole of India, a sort of preference is created in the minds of the buyers in North India. Then the product will have to be transported to other regions. The firm considers it worthwhile spending money on advertisements and transport rather than reducing the price sufficiently to attack the neighbouring consumers with irrational preference.

Wastes in imperfect competition arises from the non-utilisation of opportunities for specialisation by each firm. Under perfect competition, the firms specialise for which they are best suited. Consequently, they enjoy various economies in operation. While under monopolistic competition, since each firm has to spend a considerable sum of money on advertisements, they do not resort to improvements of the product.

Thus, under imperfect competition, firms incur losses. Valuable resources of the country are wasted and consumers are considered to be victim of very high prices.

Questions

1. Define monopoly. State the factors which give rise to monopoly.
2. Explain the difference between perfect competition and monopoly.
3. Is monopoly price higher than competitive price. Explain.
4. Could long run profits ever exist in a monopoly.
5. What do you mean by degrees of monopoly. Explain them.
6. How does a monopolist fix the price and output. Explain with diagrams.
7. What is Price Discrimination. What are different types of price discrimination?

8. What is discriminating monopoly. Under what conditions is price discrimination possible and profitable.
9. Illustrate how price discrimination is done by a monopolist.
10. Illustrate how price discrimination is done under world market and home markets.
11. What is meant by Monopolistic Competition.
12. Distinguish between price discrimination and product differentiation.
13. Explain what do you mean by non-price competition.
14. What is meant by monopolistic competition. Is product differentiation an outcome of monopolistic competition.
15. Explain how a firm attains equilibrium under monopolistic competition.
16. What are selling costs. How do selling costs influence in shifting the average revenue curve of a firm under monopolistic completion.
17. Price is higher and scale of output is smaller under monopolistic competition than under perfect competition. Explain.
18. Discuss the main features of monopolistic competition.
19. Distinguish between production cost and selling cost.
20. Distinguish between industry equilibrium and group equilibrium.

❖✻❖✻❖

CHAPTER

12

OLIGOPOLY

Meaning

Oligopoly is an important form of imperfect competition. Oligopoly is said to prevail when there are few firms or sellers in the market, producing or selling a product. In other words, when there are four or five firms producing and selling a product, oligopoly comes into existence. Oligopoly is defined as competition among the few. When there are only two firms producing the product in the market, duopoly prevails. When there are a few firms but not more than eight or ten, then oligopoly comes to prevail. In this market form, a large portion of output is produced by a small number of large firms.

Firms under oligopoly are classified into pure oligopoly and differentiated oligopoly. In pure oligopoly, the product produced by firms is homogeneous while in differentiated oligopoly, the products produced by the firms are close substitutes. But in the present day world, only differentiated oligopoly is found.

Characteristics

In oligopoly, sellers are few in number. The firms are interdependent. It means the competition among them is less important than firms under monopolistic competition. If a firm were to reduce its price, it affects the prices and the output production of rivals. Therefore, every seller can exert influence on the price and output of rivals. Every seller is so influential that his rivals cannot ignore the adverse effects on their price and output policies. It is therefore necessary for the oligopolistic firm to consider not only the entire demand for the product and also the likely effect of other firms in their price and output policies.

Importance of Advertisement and Selling Costs:

The firms are so few that each wants to sell as much as possible. In order to do so, they incur enormous expenditure on advertisements and other modes of selling campaign. They resort to aggressive and defensive marketing weapons to gain a greater share in the market and to prevent a fall in the price of the product. Baumol in his book *'Economic Theory and Operations Analysis'* says that it is only in oligopoly that advertising comes fully into its own. Under perfect competition and monopoly, advertising is not required. Under monopolistic competition, advertising plays an important role because of product differentiation. But in oligopoly it is a matter of life and death, if a firm fails to keep up with the advertising budget of its competitors, it may find that its customers are drifting away to a new product. True competition is found only in oligopoly which involves corporate struggle, a rival against rival.

Indeterminates of Demand Curve

The demand curve facing the oligopolist is indeterminate. The demand curve shows what amounts of the product a firm can sell at different prices. Under perfect competition, the demand curve is given as definite. He knows the price and the amount of output that he can sell. Since the firm under perfect competition is producing an identical product, it is incapable of influencing the prices by its own individual action. Even the demand curve of the monopolist is definite. He knows at what price he can sell the amount of a product. Under monopolistic competition too, the demand curve is somewhat definite and is given by the buyer's preference for its product.

But under oligopoly, the situation is different and the firms are interdependent. Under oligopoly, a firm cannot change its price assuming that rivals do not take any retaliatory action. As a result of this, the demand curve facing the oligopoly firm loses its definiteness.

There is one particular shape of demand under oligopoly that is called Kinky Demand Curve. There is a kink in the demand curve. The kink is always at the ruling price. Assuming a ruling price as given, a rise in price on the part of a given oligopoly firm will not invite retaliation from the rivals. It means that rivals will not resort to increase in their prices to neutralize the effects of price increase by the first producer. Since he has increased the price, he is sure to lose his customers. So, the upper part of the curve is more elastic while the downward part of the curve is less elastic. This is because, a price cut will invite retaliation from the rivals, they also cut the prices with a view to protect their own sales. The result will be, if a firm lowers its price, it can increase the sales. The demand curve of a firm under oligopoly is shown in the diagram clearly.

MR is the marginal revenue curve. Since it follows AR, there is discontinuity in the marginal revenue curve below the point corresponding to the kink. The marginal cost cuts the marginal revenue curve between the points T & S. Hence the equilibrium output and price do not undergo any change. The firm will be in equilibrium. This is one of the ways of pricing a product under oligopoly.

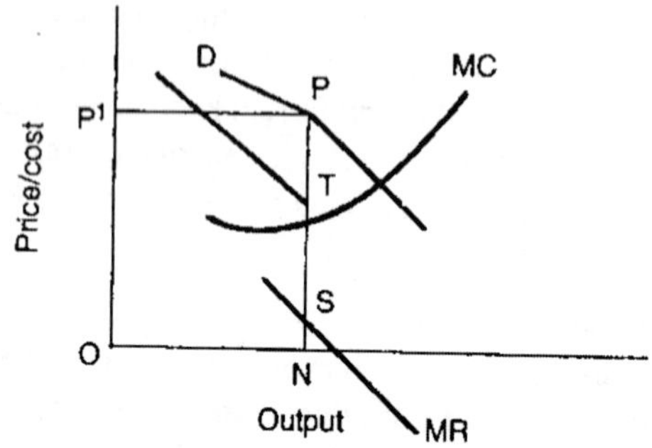

Objective of Firms Under Oligopoly

It is natural for a firm to achieve profit maximisation. This objective has been refuted by several economists. According to Prof. Rothschild, oligopolists aim at maximizing their security of achieving reasonable amount of stable profits over a long period of time. On the other hand, Prof. Baumol thinks that it is sales maximisation as a objective of an oligopoly firm. Some other economists say that it is maximizing the utility function. Prof. R.L. Morris thinks that firms try to maximise their growth rate. Thus, there is lot of controversy about the most probable objective of the oligopolists. This controversy has led to the indeterminancy in the price and output policies. Indeterminancy means the non-availability of a single solution to the problem of price and output determination. If an acceptable solution is to be offered, then the concept of inter-dependence is to be ignored. If this is assumed, then we can have a determinate demand curve. With this, the standard analysis of the theory of the firm can be applied to provide a determinate solution to the price and the output problem of oligopoly. Economists have accepted the *Cournot model* of an oligopoly firm. In this model, the assumption of interdependence is ignored. Here, the demand curve is downward sloping curve of a monopolist. It is assumed that the firm would fix the price for the output on the belief that other firms keep their price and output unchanged. But critics point out that ignoring interdependence is a mistaken approach.

Price Leadership

The price determination under oligopoly is not an easy talk. The practical solution is that of the formation of a collusion, formal or tacit and thereby work out an agreed pattern of price and output determination. The firms under oligopoly collectively come to an agreement on price and output. A variant approach is that firms or low cost firms exist as their leader. This firm may be a dominant firm or a low cost firm and other firms follow their leader in the fixation of price and output.

Generally, there is a tacit agreement among the oligopolists. Under tacit agreement, wihtout any face to face contact, consultation or discussion, they come to have some understandings between themselves and pursue a uniform policy with regard to the price and output. An example to tacit agreement is found in price leadership. There is no formal agreement found for such types of leadership, but informally, the firms follow the instructions of the leader. Exeprience is that this type of price leadership does not violate anti - trust laws. Sometimes, price leadership emerges from a formal agreement among the oligopoly firms.

Types of Price Leadership

There are several types of price leadership. The main types of price leadership are as follows:

a) Price leadership of a dominant firm

Under this, one of the few firms in the industry, which produces a large portion of the product is selected as the leader. This is a dominant firm which wields a great influence in the market. It sets the price and makes other firms to accept this price. The other firms being small are hence not capable of exercising any influence on the price. The dominant firm estimates its own demand for the product and fixes a price which maximises its own profits. The other firms which are small, having no individual influence on the price, follow the dominant firm and accept the price set by the dominant firm and adjust their outputs accordingly.

b) Barometric Price Leadership

Under this type of price leadership, an old experienced, largest or most respected firm assumes the role of a custodian and thus protects the interests of all. This firm, instead of promoting its own interest, acts as a custodian of all firms. It assesses the market conditions with regard to demand for the product, costs of production, competition from the related products etc. and fixes the price which is suitable to all firms in the industry, since the interest of all firms is suitable to all firms in the industry. All firms are protected by the dominant firm and all firms follow the leader willingly.

c) Exploitative or Aggressive Price Leadership

In this case, one big firm comes to establish its leadership and follows aggressive price policies and thus compel other firms to follow this leader and accept the price fixed by it. If a firm shows any independence, it is threatened with dire consequences and hence it is also forced to accept the price.

Price and output determination under price leadership

Economists have developed various models concerning price and output determination under price leadership, taking different assumptions about the behaviour of the price leader and his followers. Let us take up a simple case here to show price - output determination under dominant price leadership on the following assumptions:

(a) There are only two firms A and B. The firm A has lower cost of production than B.

(b) The product produced by the two firms is homogeneous so that the consumers have no preference between them.

(c) Both A and B firms have equal share in the market. In other words, they are facing the same demand curve which will be half of the total market demand curve.

The following diagram illustrates the price output determination subject to the assumptions stated above:

Price-output determination under price-leadership

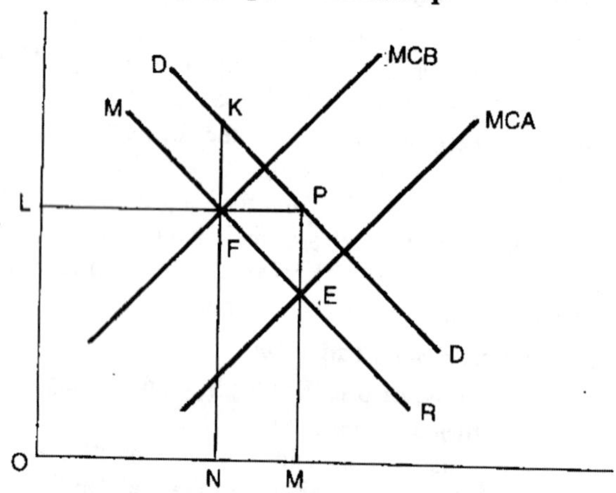

In the above diagram, DD is the demand curve facing each firm which is half of the total market demand curve for the product. MR is the marginal revenue curve of each firm. MC(a) and MC(b) are the marginal cost curves of A and B firms respectively. Firm A will be maximizing its profits by selling OM output MP price. Since at OM, its marginal cost is equal to marginal revenue. For firm B, the profits will be maximum when it sells ON output at NK price, because at this output, its marginal cost is equal to the marginal revenue. It will be seen from the above diagram that profit maximizing price MP of A firm is lower than the profit maximizing price NK of B firm. Since the two firms are producing homogeneous products, they cannot charge two different prices. They have to sell the product at a uniform price because the product is homogeneous. Because the profit maximizing price MP of firm A is lower than the profit maximizing price NK of firm B, firm A will dictate its price to firm B. In case the firm B refuses to fall in line, it can be ousted by firm A which is charging a low price. Thus, firm A will be the price leader and firm B will be the price follower.

It can also be seen that although the firm B is compelled to sell at the price MP, the firm B will produce OM output like firm A. It is because at price MP, it can sell OM output like firm A, since the demand curve DD facing each firm is the same. Thus, both firms will charge the same price and sell the same amount of output, while in the case of firm A, the price leader will be maximizing its profit by selling OM output at MP price. But at this price and output, the firm B will not be maximising its profit. It is because that firm B by selling OM output at MP price will be smaller than firm A, because its costs are higher.

When the products of the price leader and his followers are differentiated, then the price charged by them will be different, but the prices charged by the followers will be only slightly different either way from that of the price leader and they will conform to a definite pattern of differentials.

Difficulties of Price Leadership

In the real world, price leadership does not operate smoothly, because it involves some practical difficulties:

(a) One such difficulty is that the price leader cannot assess correctly the reactions of his followers. If his estimate about the reactions of the rivals to price changes proves to be incorrect, then not only the success of his price policy, but also his leadership in the market will be jeopardized.

(b) When a price leader fixes a higher price than the followers would prefer, there is a strong tendency on the part of the followers to make hidden price cuts in order to increase their share in the market, without openly challenging the price leader. The manufacturers use a good number of devices which amount to secret price cutting such as rebates, favourable credit terms, `money - back'guarantees, after-delivery free services, sale on the payment of price in easy instalments with low rates of interest, etc. Price leaders are generally fed up with the increasing number of concessions granted by their rivals and they make an open price cut to prevent further fall in their share of the market. In such circumstances, price leadership becomes infructuous.

Oligopoly and Non-Price Competition

The price leader has to face another difficulty, when he finds that the rival firms are indulging in non-price competition. Non-price competition is a device used by rival firms to capture a higher share of the market. This device is viewed with far more equanimity than price cutting and is frequently quite unrestrained.

The devices used under non-price competition are advertising, personal selling, product improvement, better quality packing and appearance, easier credit items, improvement of the quality of the product and so on. While charging the same price, the rivals try to increase their share of the market by resorting to non-price competition. As a result of non-price competition, the price leader has also to adopt similar devices to prevent the fall in its sales or has to make an outright cut in price in order to achieve his objective. In view of these facts, the price leader may not be able to maintain his leadership.

There is a great limitation on the price leader to fix a high price. It is because, if he fixes a high price, it will induce the rivals to make secret price cuts, which will adversely affect the price leader. Moreover, a higher price fixed by the price leader will attract new competitors into the industry which may not accept his price leadership. Lastly, differences in costs also pose a problem. If the cost of production of the price leader is higher on account of which he fixes a high price and the rival producers with lower costs of production, they will have no problem in under cutting the price. On the other hand, if the price leader has lower costs than the rivals, then he will set a low price which will antagonise his rivals who will try to break his price leadership.

Collusive Oligopoly

There is another development witnessed in oligopolic industries and that is of collusion. Under this situation, the oligopolists arrive at a tacit or formal agreement on a common policy to be followed by them. These firms may reach an agreement after indulging in price-war. Otherwise, cut-throat competition is harmful to all of them. Alternatively, they may show foresight and enter into collusion with each other believing that they can promote their interests best if they pull together to survive in the market.

When the various oligopolists of an industry enter into a formal agreement, they are said to form a *Cartel*. Originally, the term cartel was used for the agreement in which there existed a common sales agency which alone undertook the selling operations of all firms which were party to the agreement. Nowdays, all types of formal agreements reached by oligopolists are known as cartels. Since these cartels restrain competition among the member firms, their formations have been made illegal in some countries by the government passing laws against them. For example, the formation of a cartel is illegal in United States of America. However, inspite of the illegality of cartels, they are still formed in USA through secret devices.

There is an extreme form of collusion in which the firms entering into an agreement, surrender completely their right of price-output determination to a central agency, so as to secure maximum joint profits for them. Formation of such a formal collusion is called *perfect cartel*. Under this perfect cartel type of collusive oligopoly, the price and output are determined for the whole industry as well as for each member firm by the central agency. The total profits are distributed among the member firms in agreed proportions which may not be necessarily in proportion to the output quota assigned to each firm. The total cost is sought to be minimised by asking the firms of the cartel to produce such separate outputs as to make their output costs equal.

But the formation of perfect cartels is not very common in the real world, even when their formation is not illegal. In the actual collusion, the agreement is only on the price which is generally the joint profit maximizing price and member firms are free to produce and sell the outputs which will maximise their individual profits given the fixed agreed price. Each firm in this case will earn profits depending on the output produced and sold by it. If a firm produces and sells a small output, its profit also is small.

Effects of Oligopoly

The economic effects of oligopoly are briefly described as follows :

(i) ***Small output and higher prices :*** Under oligopoly, the total output is restricted while the prices are high.

(ii) ***The prices exceed the average costs :*** Owing to restrictions on the entry of new firms, the prices are fixed and such prices are higher than costs. The consumers have to pay more than what is necessary to restrain the resources in the industry. The resources of the economy cannot move into the making of products desired by the consumers from those where they are desired less. In other words, the productive capacity of the economy is under-utilised in oligopoly.

(iii) ***Lower efficiency :*** There is no tendency for the firms under oligopoly to build plants of optimum scale and consequently they cannot attain maximum potential economic efficiency. This is because the production of the output is dependent on the quota fixed by the industry.

(iv) ***Selling costs :*** The firms under oligopoly have to spend a considerable sum of money on advertisements. The firms engage in aggressive and extensive sales promtoion effort by means of advertisement and by changing the design of the product and by improving the quality of the product.

(v) ***Welfare effect :*** Under oligopoly, since output does not generally correspond to the minimum long run average cost, more units of resources per unit of output are used than it is necessary. And also the price is higher than average and marginal cost. Huge sums of money are spent on sales

promotion and hence from the welfare point of view, oligopoly fares very badly. The oligopolists push non-price-competiton beyond socially desirable limits.

Empirical Evidence Regarding Oligopolistic Behaviour

On the basis of empirical evidence, the following conlcusions have been made regarding the behaviour of oligopoly business:

(i) When the pricing decisions are centralised in the case of stores with branches spread all over the country, the prices are set by the central office and the branches are to face competition from rivals, then price cuts are resorted to by branch managers only for a short duration. Stores managers felt that they would retaliate if they thought that the price cut was permanent. In Australia, the stores announce weekly specials, making price cuts lasting not more than a week and this is too temporary to call for retaliatory price changes by competitors.

At times, the oligopolist may fail to obtain proper information regarding the possible reactions of the competitors, since many firms would like to keep their decisions very secret.

Safeguarding Competition and Anti-Trust Laws

In several countries, the governments have enacted legislations to prevent the formation of monopolies and oligopolies. The objective of those governments in curbing the formation of monopolies is to encourage the spirit of competition. The U.S. Attorney General's Committee on Anti-Trust laws mentions that where there is workable competition, rival sellers whether existing competitors or new or potential entrants into the field, would keep this power in check by offering or threatening to offer effective inducements, so long as the profits to be anticipated in the industry are sufficiently attractive in comparison with those in other employment when all risks and other deterents are taken into account.

Many economists have upheld the economic benefits of competition on the following grounds :

(i) Firms do not make agreements as to prices, output, investment or the allocation of markets.

(ii) A very wide and ever-increasing range of goods and services are offered to the consumers at reasonable price and competition is what increases the alternatives for the consumer and monopoly is what narrows the choice.

(iii) Increasingly close substitutes for most products tend to make their appearance in competition. The closer the substitutes for most products, the less important it is whether there is one producer or more than one for each of the substitutable products.

(iv) The consumer is exercising actively and positively the function of directing the production towards those suppliers who make the best offer. The best offer would be decided in terms of price, quality and service in the mixture preferred by the consumer.

Though there are several advantages in competition, obstructions to it have been found since times immemorial. Many producers by means of forming combinations and conspiracies have been making competition unfair and unworkable. Competitive functions of the trade industry are undermined through various concerted acts of minimum prices to be charged on resale, exclusive dealings, exclusive areas to be served, typing up arrangements etc . Such practices are required to be curbed by means of enactment and enforcement of anti-monopoly and trade restrictive acts.

The governments in a good number of countries have enacted a number of legislations to declare the monopoly formation as illegal. Some of the importent legislations enacted in several countries are worth examination. The Monopolies and Trade Restrictive Practices (Industry and Control Act) 1948 was the first legislation enacted in England to deal with the problems of monopoly and restrictive practices. In the USA, the government enacted several Anti-Trust laws between 1885 and 1891 to declare the formation of monopolies anti-national. One such famous legislation is the Sherman Act which declares illegal every contract, combination in the form of Trust or otherwise or conspiracies in the restraint of trade and commerce. The Federal Trade Commission Act of 1914 prohibits unfair methods of competition in commerce.

In Australia also, the government enacted a comprehensive legislation in 197 to prohibit the monopolisation and restraint of trade and commerce.

In India also, Monopolies and Restrictive Trade Practice Act (MRTP Act) was enacted in 1969 to prevent the concentration of economic power in the hands of few persons. The Government of India constituted a Commission to implement the MRTP Act.

QUESTIONS

1. What are the striking features of a oligopoly market.
2. Diagrammatically show price determination under oligopoly.
3. Explain price rigidity under oligopoly.
4. What is price leadership. Explain the conditions necessary for price leadership and advantages of price leadership.

5. Industrial structure of India is characterised by oligopoly. Comment.
6. What is a Kinked Demand Curve.
7. "If the firms under oligopoly collide, they earn only normal profit, if they collude, they earn supernormalprofit" Comment.
8. Write short notes on :
   (a) Barometric price leadership.
   (b) Collusive price leadership.
   (c) Need for anti-trust laws.
   (d) Aggressive price leadership.

❖✻❖✻❖

CHAPTER

13

PRICING METHODS, POLICIES AND PRACTICES

INTRODUCTION

Managerial decision making involves two important things, one is the formulation of rational price policy and secondly, the setting up of prices which are remunerative to the producers. All businessmen have a fundamental objective in business, i.e., to make maximum profits not only at a particular point of time but also during the whole period of existence. It is possible only when the producers set a price for the product which is greater than the cost. The businessmen use the pricing device for the purpose of maximising profits. At what price the product is to be sold depends upon a number of factors. Many problems come in the way of determining a price for the product. The price theory points out that the equilibrium price is determined at a point where marginal revenue is equal to the marginal cost. Some economists like Hall and Hitch of the Oxford University, rejected the assumption of profit maximisation as unrealistic and inapplicable to actual business conditions. Business firms do not determine price and output at the point of equality between MR and MC. Besides, businessmen are reluctant to charge a high price for the product, because this might result in bringing more producers into the industry. In other words, in real life, the firms want to prevent the entry of rivals and therefore they prefer to charge a high price which would bring supernormal profit. Often firms with a view to get a higher share in the market charge a right price.

Two factors which influence in determining prices are classified into internal and external factors. Internal factors are costs and the management policy. The external factors are the elasticity of supply and demand, the goodwill of the company, the extent of competitions in the market, the purchasing power of the buyers and the government policy towards prices.

The following considerations are involved in formulating the pricing policy:

Kind of Market Structure

Pricing policy is to be set in the light of the competitive situations in the market. We have to know whether the firm is facing perfect competition or imperfect competition. In perfect competition, the producers or sellers have no control over the price. It is because that they have to sell the homogeneous product at a price determined by the market demand and supply. They have no pricing discretion. Pricing policy has special significance only under imperfect competition. Under the present competitive market situation, the producers are forced to sell the best product at a reasonable price. Joel Deal says that the following market conditions influence in determining the price.

(a) The number, relative size and product line of competitors, (b) the likelihood of potential competition, (c) the stage of consumer's acceptance of the product, (d) the degree of product differentiation adopted by firms in the market, (e) the richness of the mixture of service, advertisement and sales propaganda and the reputation of the firm and the qualitative improvement in the product bundle.

Goal of Profit and Sales

Pricing should normally aim at stimulating profitable combination sales. Sometimes, the firms seek profit maximisation and at some other times maximisation of sales. In any case, the sales should bring more profit to the firm.

Long Range Welfare of the Firm

Pricing should take care of the long run welfare of the company and at the same time should discourage entry of new firms into the industry considering the market essence of the existing firms.

Flexibility

The prices determined should be flexible enough to meet the changes in the demand pattern and the market situation. Prices should also be flexible to take care of cyclical variations. If a firm is selling its product in a highly competitive market, it will have little scope for pricing discretion.

Government Policy

It is also possible that the Government may prevent the firms in forming combinations to set a high price. Very often, the government prefers to control the prices of essential commodities with a view to prevent the exploitation of the consumers. The entry of the government into the pricing process, in the alliance with farmers and trade unions, tend to inject politics into price determination.

Objectives of Pricing Policy

Pricing is a very difficult process. There is no infallible formula in determining a right place for a product. Every pricing situation is unique and therefore, the management has to use discretionary powers in determining a just price. In fact, pricing is a matter of judgement. The judgement should be based on sound principles in order to be effective. Pricing is not an end in itself. It is a means to an end. Therefore, while determining a price, the following objectives have to be borne in mind:

Survival

In these days of severe competition and business uncertainties, the firm must set a price which would safeguard the welfare of the firm. A firm is always interested in its survival. For the sake of its continued existence, it must tolerate all kinds of obstacles and challenges from rivals.

Rate of Growth and Sales Maximisation

A firm has to set a price which assures maximum sales of the product. Only then, it can achieve growth. As Kotler says that the firms should set prices which would increase the sales of the product's line, rather than yield a profit on one product.

Market Share

The firm wants to secure a large share in the market by means of following a suitable price policy. It wants to acquire a dominating leadership position in the market.

Preventing Competition

By adopting a suitable price policy, the firm wants to restrict the entry of rivals. It would try to fix up a price which would avoid competitors.

Making Money

Some firms want to use their special position in the industry by selling the product at premium and thus making quick profit as much as possible.

Price-profit Stabilisation

The firms are interested in keeping their prices stable within a certain period of time irrespective of changes in demand and costs, so that they may get the expected profit.

Phillip Kotler has mentioned the following objectives in his book 'Marketing Management'.

(i) ***Market Penetration*** Here the firm sets a low price to stimulate the demand and capture the market.

(ii) ***Market Skimming*** In the beginning, the firm charges a high price to take advantage of some buyers who are willing to pay that price and

afterwards charge a low price to enable the less fortunate buyers to buy the product.

(iii) Early Cash Recovery Some firms set a price which will create a mad rush for the product and recover cash early. They may also set a low price as a caution against uncertainty of the future.

(iv) Satisfaction In order to achieve a satisfactory rate of return, the firms set a price which will result in higher sales.

However, the survival of the firm is the main objective in pricing. At the same time, the firms bear in mind the following objectives while pricing the product :

(i) to fulfil a good rate of return on investment,

(ii) to seek anticipated rate of growth,

(iii) to improve the market share,

(iv) to stabilise prices and profit margin.

Factors Involved in Pricing Policy

The pricing of the products involves consideration of the following factors :

(a) Costs, (b) demand and psychology of consumers, (c) competition, (d) profit, (e) government policy.

Cost Factor in Pricing

Cost data occupy an important place in the price setting processes. There are different types of costs incurred in the production and marketing of the product. There are production costs, promotional expenses like advertising or personal selling as well as taxation, etc. They may necessitate an upward fixing of price. The prices of petrol and gas are rising due to a rise in the cost of raw materials such as crude, transportation, refining etc. If the costs rise, the price of the product also rises. For setting prices, apart from costs, there are other things which cannot be turned down. They are the demand and competition. Costs are of two types: fixed costs and the variable costs. In the short period, i.e., the period in which a firm wants to establish itself, the firm may not cover the fixed costs but it must cover the variable costs. But in the long run, all costs must be covered. If the entire costs are not covered, the producer stops production. Consequently, the supply is reduced which in turn may lead to higher prices.

Regarding the role of cost in pricing, Nickerson has observed that costs may be regarded only as an indicator of demand and price. He further says that the cost at any given time represents a resistance point to the lowering of price. Again, costs determine the profit margins at various levels of output. Cost calculations may also help in determining whether the product whose price is determined by its demand is to be included in the product line or not. 'What costs determine is not the price, but whether the production can be profitably produced or not' is very important. If the price in the short run is lower than the cost, then the question arises, whether this price covers the variable cost. If it runs, the firm cannot sell at a price lower than the cost. Product pricing decision should therefore be made with a view to maximise the company's profits in the long run.

Demand Factor in Pricing

In the pricing of a product, demand occupies a very important place. In fact, demand is more important for effective sales. The elasticity of demand is to be recognised in determining the price of the product. If the demand for the product is inelastic, the firm can fix a high price. On the other hand, if the demand is elastic, it has to fix a lower price.

Demand for the product depends upon the behaviour of the consumers. There are consumers who buy a product provided its quality is high. In fact, product quality, product image, customer service and promotion activity influence many consumers more than the price. Supposing the consumers want to buy durable goods such as television set, refrigerator, car etc., they go in for quality than price. If the price of the product is too low, the product is regarded as of poor quality and hence the demand may not rise. Manufacturers of durable goods always set a high price, even though the sales are affected. If the price is too high, it may also affect the demand for the product. They wait for the arrival of a rival product with a competitive price. Therefore, the demand for a product is so sensitive to price changes. With an increase in personal income, the consumers become quality conscious. This may also lead to an increase in the demand for durable goods. People of high incomes buy products even though their prices are high. In the affluent societies, price is the indicator of quality. Advertisement and sales promotion also contribute very much in increasing the demand for advertised products. It is because, the consumers think that the advertised products are of good quality. To conclude, income of the consumers, the standard of living and the price factor influence the demand for various products in the society. In determining the price, the income elasticity and the price elasticity will have to be taken into consideration.

Competition Factor

The market situation plays an effective role in pricing. In perfect competition, the individual producers have no discretion in pricing. They have to accept the price fixed by demand and supply. In monopoly, the producer fixes a high price for his product. In other market situations like oligopoly and monopolistic competition, the individual producers take the prices of the rival products in determining their price.

Profits

In setting the price for products, the manufacturers consider primarily the profit aspect. Each producer has his aim of profit maximisation. Usually, the pricing policy is based on the goal of obtaining a reasonable profit.

Most of the businessmen want to hold the price at constant level. They do not desire frequent price fluctuations.

The price rigidity is the practice of many producers. Rigidity does not mean inflexibility. It means that prices are stable over a given period, say a year.

Government Policy

In the capitalist societies, the government generally does not interfere in the economic decisions of the economy. It is only in planned economies and socialist states that the government's interference is very much. In a mixed economy like India, the government resorts to price control. The firms have to adopt the government's price policies. Within the maximum parameters fixed by the government, the individual firms have to determine the price. In the case of agricultural commodities, the government announces the support prices. In the case of essential commodities and services, the government determines the prices. All others have to accept this price.

Pricing methods

There are four important methods of pricing: (i) Cost-plus or full cost pricing. (ii) Pricing for a rate of return. (iii) Marginal cost pricing. (iv) Administered pricing. and (v) Going-rate policy.

Full Cost Method

Cost-plus or full cost pricing is a method commonly adopted by the businessmen to fix a price of the product. He calculates the cost of production per unit and adds a margin of profit to it. In other words, the producer adds a certain percentage of profit which he considers as fair to his cost in order to arrive at a price which is acceptable to the consumers. This procedure is known as cost-plus pricing.

Cost-plus pricing means the addition of a certain percentage of profit to the cost of production to arrive at a price. For example, the cost of production of a product is Rs. 10. If the management decides to have a mark of 100 per cent, then Rs. 10 is the addition to the cost. Hence, the price is Rs. 20 per unit of the product. Here two elements make up the price: one is the average cost or cost per unit and the other is the mark-up (profit). These two components are found in the cost-plus pricing.

A clear analysis of profit is known only from the cost analysis. Moreover, cost is the base on which is grounded the percentage of profit which the manufacturer wants to arrive to the price of the product. The computation of cost of production of a commodity is a difficult thing. There are three different methods of computing cost. According to Joel Dean, there are three different concepts of cost components used in cost-plus pricing. They are : (a) the actual cost, (b) the expected cost and (c) the standard cost.

(a) Actual costs are those costs which are actually incurred by the firm in order to produce a given commodity. They are also called *historical cost.* Actual costs include wage bill, raw-material costs and overhead charges at the current output rate. The prices of these materials prevailing in the latest period will be taken into consideration to determine actual costs.

(b) The expected cost is a forecast of the actual expenses for the pricing period. Suppose the company wants to introduce a new product six months from today, the company first determines the cost at the prevailing prices. Then the prices of various products are projected for the next six months and thus the expected cost is calculated.

(c) Standard cost refers to a normal cost determination at some normal rate of output at a given level of capacity utilisation. To calculate the standard cost, the capacity of the plant is considered. Supposing the plant is running at 60 percent capacity - if the plant works at 80 percent of the capacity, then the cost may be normal or optimum. This optimum is taken into consideration in calculating the standard cost.

Though these three methods are available to calculate cost, each company follows one of the methods. Again, a firm may first arrive at costs based on the three methods and then decide upon the one which suits it best. Each method gives a different figure and as such different prices emerge.

The firm, after arriving at the cost, records a fair rate of profit which is added to it and determines the price. What is fair rate is difficult to say. But a fair rate of profit is assumed to be between 10 and 15 percent of the cost.

Limitations

(i) The cost-plus pricing ignores the demand side of the problem. This method takes into account only the costs and a certain rate of profit.

When a firm starts producing a new product, it should take into account the willingness of the consumers to buy it.

(ii) It fails to consider the importance of competition and as such, it ignores the existence of competitors completely. In fact, any pricing of product should take into consideration the price of the products of the rival.

(iii) When a firm manufactures and sells multiple products, there is bound to be some common costs. These costs are allocated arbitrarily. When costs are not allocated precisely, then the method cannot become valid.

(iv) This method is totally based on conventional accounting system. It ignores the future costs in the pricing decision. It considers only the past and the present costs. Moreover, opportunity cost is very important in determining the price. Thus, the cost-plus pricing method does not make use of economic tools altogether.

Uses

Despite these limitations, this method is very popular among many producers in India. In India, the publishing industry uses cost-plus pricing in fixing the prices of various publications. Cost of production is first assessed and a certain percentage of profit is added and the selling price is fixed. This percentage is called *mark up*. Sometimes pricing of the product by this method may result in making the price to be prohibitive. When such a firm has to face competition, it finds it very difficult to sell its product in the market. In such cases, it has to abandon the cost-plus pricing and bring the price to the level of the rivals. In order to do so, it has to reduce some costs. This means that cost-plus pricing will have to be modified suitably.

In India, cost-plus pricing method is extensively used. It is because of two specific advantages. Firstly, there is prevailing a seller's market in India, which makes it possible to pass on the additional costs to the buyers. Secondly, this is easy and has tacit approval of the government in fixing the prices of the product of all public sector industries.

Rate of Return Pricing

The cost-plus pricing method has led to a controversy with regard to fair rate of return. Some businessmen argue that a decent percent of return on investments is fair, but some others do not accept this conclusion. Therefore, the word *'fair'* is an ambiguous word.

Under this method, the price is determined by the planned rate of return on investment which is expected to be converted into a percentage of the mark up. The profit margin is determined on the basis of the rate of production and the total cost of a year's normal production. Then, the capital turnover is computed by taking the ratio of invested capital to the annual standard cost. Then the mark up percentage of profit is obtained by multiplying capital turnover by the goal rate of return. Let us take the following example :

Say, the capital turnover is Rs. 0.9 lakh. The desired rate of return is 27 per cent. Now –

% mark up = Capital turnover x desired rate of return

= 0.9 x 27 = 24 percent

Now, 24 per cent is the mark-up. Or it may also be found out by this method :

$$\frac{\text{InvestedCapital}}{\text{Standard Cost}} = \frac{\text{Earnings}}{\text{Invested Capital}} = \frac{\text{Earnings}}{\text{Standard Cost}}$$

American firms start with a rate of return which they consider satisfactory and then fix a price that will allow them to earn that return when their plant is running at 80 percent utilisation. They determine the standard costs as standard volume and add the margin necessary to return the target rate of profit over the long run.

While defining the rate of return, it is held that it should cut across business cycles and should be determined on the basis of standards of reasonableness. This method is essentially the cost-plus pricing method but an improved one. Since it builds price on cost which is standardised, it develops a profit mark up related to a rate of return

Marginal Cost Pricing

Under cost-plus pricing and rate of return pricing, the prices of products are determined on the basis of total costs. (variable + fixed costs). Under marginal cost pricing, fixed costs are ignored and pricing is determined on the basis of marginal costs. Marginal cost means cost of producing additional units of the product. The firm uses only those costs which are directly attributable to the output of the specific period. The price so determined must cover the marginal cost and the total cost will have to be covered in the long run. Price based on marginal costs will be much more aggressive than the one based on total costs. Further, when a firm has a large unused capacity, it should explore the possibility of producing and selling more - it should cover the marginal cost. The real difficulty is to know the marginal cost.

Advantages of Marginal Cost Pricing

Under marginal cost pricing, price are never rendered uncompetitive merely because of higher fixed overhead costs. If the variable costs are higher, the prices also will be higher, but they can be controlled in the short period and thus make the price competitive.

Marginal costs reflect more accurately the future as distinct from the present cost structure.

Marginal cost pricing permits a producer to resort to aggressive price policy than is possible under full cost pricing. An aggressive pricing would lead to higher sales and by increased marginal physical productivity and lower input factor prices, marginal cost can be reduced.

Marginal cost pricing is very much useful over the life cycle of a product.

Marginal cost pricing is more effective than full cost pricing because it helps in solving short run problems. That is, under the conditions of change, marginal cost is the most suitable method of short run pricing. In the short run pricing, only marginal costs are covered and fixed costs are completely ignored.

The only difficulty in marginal cost pricing is ignorance of the marginal cost technique. In a period of business recession, the firms using marginal cost pricing can overcome the recession by lowering the prices and thereby allowing the sales to increase. With the existence of idle capacity and the pressure of fixed costs, firms successfully cut down prices to a point equivalent to marginal cost and earn a fair rate of return in the period of crisis.

Going Rate Pricing

The going rate pricing is opposite of full cost or cost-plus pricing. The going rate policy means, adjusting its own price policy to the general price structure in the industry. This policy is adopted where it is difficult to measure the costs. Though the firm has complete freedom to fix its own price, it will not do so, but instead, it tries to adjust its own price policy with the price prevailing in the market. The going rate pricing is adopted when the price leadership is very well established. When firms want to avoid the tension of price rivalry in the market, they adopt the going rate pricing. This is very easy and there is no need for a firm to take the trouble of calculating costs and demand.

(Many big firms in America have adopted this policy of price leadership.)

Guidelines for Price Fixation

Some guidelines for price fixation have been given by Bates and Parkinson in the book *'Business Economics'*.

(i) It is necessary to know the costs incurred in relation to output and also to distinguish between prime costs and overhead costs.

(ii) In the beginning, prices should cover prime costs and later on the price should cover the entire costs.

(iii) The firms must know the prices of the products sold by other firms. The costs incurred must be comparable to the costs of the other firms for the same amount of output.

(iv) If the demand for the product of a firm is sluggish, then it will have to reduce the price a bit in order to improve its position.

(v) If the costs of raw-materials and labour rise, the firm is compelled to increase the price.

(vi) If the costs are rising and the sales are sluggish, then the firm must be able to refrain from raising the price.

(vii) The capacity of the plant must be used to the optimum extent. Production should be concentrated on those products whose demand is high.

(viii) The firm by improving sales campaign, must build the image of the firm.

(ix) As far as possible, prices should cover the costs. Further, if the costs are higher than the costs of rivals, the firm in question is required to reduce the costs by means of better management.

(x) If the prices set by the firm are bringing good profits, then the firm should resort to expansion of production.

(xi) Prices should not go against the public interest.

(xii) If the company is making high profits by selling at a price, the rivals are sure to enter into the industry and compete away the profits.

Some Pricing Problems

The life period and its distinctiveness - pricing of a new product

In the production of a product, a distinction is made between perishable and non-perishable products. A perishable product does not last for a long period, whereas a non-perishable product has two characteristics, namely its life period and its distinctiveness. In a real situation, the life of a product does not extend beyond a particular period of time. In this case, non-perishability refers to the period of time for which a particular product lasts. This period of life lasts as long as the product is distinctive. A manufacturer introduces a new product into the market, which is substantially distinct from the existing product. This newness is its distinctiveness which lasts over a period of time, for the rivals try to bring the products which are identical to the company's products, so that they might serve as its substitutes.

In this sense, the so called distinctiveness is completely lost. That, distinctiveness of a product lasts only for a short time.

There are five stages in the lifecycle of a product. They are : (i) Introduction of a product through innovation, (ii) Growth of sales, (iii) Maturity, (iv) Saturation and (v) Decline.

When a new product is introduced in the market, which is distinctive in many respects, but owing to the lack of consumer awareness, the sales are minimum. In order to create interest in the product, a huge advertisement budget is necessary. There are high promotional costs while the volume of sales is low and the profit also is less and in fact, the firm may incur losses. These are the characteristics of the product in the first stage.

Then the product begins to make gradual progress and the sales increase. The firm starts making profits also. In order to maintain high sales, the firm is required to improve the quality of the product. This is the second stage of the product.

In the third stage, it gets maturity. Though the sales rise, the rate of growth is slow, because of the entry of rivals. Profit margin also diminishes inspite of good sales.

The next stage in the lifecycle of the product is the saturation stage. Sales reach a particular level here and it remains there for long.

When the substitutes emerge in the market with better quality and price, the sales of the existing product starts declining.

The life cycle of a product is always short. It is due to several factors like continuous research for product development, improvement of the product made by several companies and the emergence of competitors. If one company offers a better product, the rivals also imitate the product strategy and try to produce much better products than the previous company. If a competitor makes better improvement, the sales of his product increases and thus makes good profits.

When the distinctiveness of the product fades, the pricing discretion enjoyed by the firm no longer holds essence.

Perishable Product

When a product is perishable, it means that its distinctiveness is lost. This is so when new products develop a distinctiveness and protect themselves from the attack of the substitutes. This results in *product degeneration.* Viewed from this angle, every product has a degeneration cycle. When a new product is launched in the market, the distinctiveness of the existing product starts declining. At this stage, it itsef becomes a target of compètitive encroachment. New rivals enter the field and their innovations reduce the extent of distinctiveness between the first product and the product of the rivals. As a result of this, the distinctive product gradually degenerates and becomes a footpath product. In such cases, the pricing policy needs to be carefully determined to take care of the cyclical changes.

Degeneration

A pricing policy should also take into consideration the degeneration aspect of the product. The degeneration of a product arises as a result of the negligence of technical and economic factors. The technical factors relate to the improvement of the quality and design of the product. The economic factors relate to the market acceptance and the entry of rival firms. Market acceptance is conditioned by cultural lags. For example, when power based mixies were introduced for the first time in the city markets, the housewives accepted them on the ground that it relieved them from physical torture they experienced from conventional grinders. When more competitors entered into this market with better performance and price concessions, the mixies became '*footpath*' products. The problem that arose then was how to price those products.

Pricing of a New Product

If the new product is with high distinctiveness among the existing products, then the fixation of the price should be based on the demand, the market target and the promotional strategy.

In the case of pioneer products, the estimation of their demand is very difficult. The estimate of demand for such products should be studied in the following manner :

(i) Whether the new product is accepted by the consumers.

(ii) At what price it is acceptable.

(iii) If three or four prices are fixed, what would be the volume of sales at each price and

(iv) What would be the reaction of the manufacturers of the substitutes.

Product Acceptability

It is based on the willingness of the consumers to buy the product. The willingness to buy depends upon a factor that is whether it would meet their requirements. If it does not meet the needs and requirements of the consumers, the product should be improved to serve the purpose. Supposing the new product is a strategic alternative, then it should be found out how many consumers would buy the new one in place of the old one.

Range of Prices

It is very important to assess the action of the consumers at different prices. For this, a market research will have to be undertaken. There are specialised market research institutions which can undertake this survey. The core question that arises is at what prices different quantities of the product are demanded. There are some practical difficulties as regards the price that consumers are willing to pay for the product. It is possible to find out the reaction of the consumers at different prices at different places through substantial market research.

Expected Volume of Sales

The next important task is to determine the anticipated volume of sales at different prices. This depends upon demand elasticity and cross elasticity. If the product introduced is a pioneer, it is very difficult to estimate the demand. If the consumers refuse to accept the product when it is brought into the market, then the whole exercise of determining the expected volume of sales is a waste. If the product is going to be accepted, it would be worthwhile to assess price as well as cross elasticity. Supposing a company introduces a new product which satisfies the consumers, the demand would naturally rise and the company which introduced the product would also makes profits. Even other companies start producing and selling similar products with sufficient sales campaign, with the product being distinct, the sales of it will not be affected.

Reaction to Price

The assessment of the reaction of the consumers to the price is a very tricky task. The company which introduces a new product will have to monitor the activities of the rivals in order to find out the marketing strategies that they are going to adopt.

Product Testing

The acceptance of a new product by the consumer depends upon product testing and test marketing. It is the experience of trade and commerce that more than 80 per cent of the new products fail to click in the market. In order to make it acceptable, product testing is essential. Product testing refers to the various methods which are employed to assess the acceptance of products by the consumers. It is necessary to know from the consumers whether they are satisfied with the product. Therefore, some samples of a new product is to be released at different centres of the country to assess the reaction of the consumers. It is generally said that most of the new products are given a blind test. In this blind test, if the brand name is concealed and the reaction is known, the brand name might influence the consumers. When a new product is put to test with an established image and reputation, it becomes all the more necessary to find out whether the product is acceptable and whether it lives up to the image of the brand name of the concerned company.

Test Marketing

Market research is indispensable when a company wishes to produce a new product. The test market research may not guarantee the success of a new product, but it will reveal the actual position. The usefulness of test marketing has been upheld by E. J. Devis as follows:

'Test marketing is a complex operation. Its foundation in statistical theory is not popularly sound, but practical difficulties may prevent much improvement in this direction. Many of the predictions made on the basis of test marketing are too facile a basis and far more needs to be done to investigate the possibilities of improved predictive techniques. In general, test marketing is under-researched, with far too many organisations being content to measure one aspect of the end result through retail outlets and ignoring the possibilities of and the need for collecting other types of data as the test proceeds. Against all this, with the ever-increasing expense of marketing, there may be even less willingness on the part of a manufacturer to jump directly from pre-testing to the national launch. Consequently, test marketing is likely to remain. Test marketing can provide a great deal of knowledge and experience of a new product and it should give atleast a clear indication of a plan which is failing to meet its objectives.'

The pricing policy of a new product involves apart from the cost of production, the study of prices of the alternative products of the group to which the new product belongs. For example, if the new product is an household appliance, the prices of household appliances should be studied. The prices of the substitute products and their usage have to be known before pricing a new product. Let us take the following example:

Household product (Pressure cooker)

Product	Price	Weightage	Weighted price
	Rs.		Rs.
A	800	15	12,000
B	1000	20	20,000
C	1200	20	24,000
D	1500	30	45,000
E	2000	15	30,000
		100	1, 31,000

$$\text{Suggested Price is} = \frac{131000}{100} = \text{Rs. } 1{,}310$$

Weightage is given on the basis of the usage of the appliance. If, in a house only a bachelor lives, its usage is limited and therefore less weightage is given. In a big family, its usage is high, therefore high weightage is given. Thus, taking the total weightage price and dividing it by the weightage, the suggested price is arrived.

High Skimming Price

A skimming price is that where the initial price is high. Whenever a company introduces a new product, it spends a huge sum of money on advertisements. The company may put the product in attractive packages. Therefore, to cover all these costs, the company fixes a high price. If the new product which has no substitute also has a good usage, the product can be sold at a high price. The company is quite sure that in course of time, the substitutes are going to enter into the market. When it has no rivals, a high price is fixed for the product. When the substitutes enter into the market, then the price is reduced and thereby the challenge is posed. However, by the time the substitutes enter the market, it is not certain that this product will command a market value. It may lose to the product of the competitors. Therefore, an initial high price is suggested for a new product when it is introduced for the first time.

When a new product with a high skimming price is introduced, the demand may not increase all of a sudden. Therefore, promotional expenditure of a high magnitude will have to be incurred. Further, if the price is very high, many consumers may not buy it. Therefore, a potential market will have to be decided on the basis of elasticity of demand. If the demand is inelastic, a high price may be fixed. When this segment of the market is exhausted, then the second segment of the market will have to be tapped at a lesser price. For example, in the case of the publication of a text book, it is priced high. But the next paperback edition is priced low.

A high initial price may be useful if the production of the product requires high technical skill and it is difficult and time consuming for competitors to enter on an economical scale.

A Low Penetration Price

A low penetration price pertains to charĝing a low price in the beginning itself. If the price is low, it can penetrate into the market quickly. It is due to the fact that the consumers may buy the product at a low price. Before fixing the low price for the new product, a market research is necessary. In the high skimming price situation, the firm gets profit which may arise in the short run quickly but in the case of low penetration price, profits may arise in the long run. One way this is advantageous, for it is possible for the product to establish itself firmly in the market. If the price is raised afterwards, the demand is not going to fall.

The objective of low penetration pricing is to keep the rivals away from entering into the market with substitute products. The low price of the products prevents competition. If the price is set low, the margin of profit also is low and thereby new - comers are not going to venture into the production of this product. A low penetration price is advantageous when the productive capacity of the plant is high. A low price is sure to capture the entire market and production price is profitable because large quantity can be sold. In the case of a multi-product firm, it is not the margin of profit that matters. If the potential market is large, the big companies by selling the product at a low price, drive away many small companies.

Private Costs and Social Costs

In the study of cost analysis, modern economists like Richard-D-Lipse and others have identified private and social costs and examined their relevance in the pricing of goods and services.

Private cost measures the opportunity cost to the firm of the resources that it uses. The opportunity cost is based on the alternatives that are available to the firm. If the firm uses a resource for which it has absolutely no alternative use, then the private cost is zero. Private cost is usually based on the market value of the factors currently purchased by the firm and the price that could be obtained by selling to outsiders the services of factors owned by them.

Social cost means the opportunity cost to the whole society of the resources that the firm uses. The opportunity cost is based on the alternatives available to the whole society. If a firm uses a resource for which the society has no alternative uses, then the social cost is zero. It is the value of the resources in its best alternative uses.

Implications

The private consumption activity creates social costs that neither the producer nor the consumer is willing to pay for it. Pollution is a fine example, where the air, lakes and the earth inherit the dirt created by manufacturing and consumption activities. *Progress means more refuse* and *polluted streams.*

An increase in the consumption of automobiles requires a facilitating supply of streets, highways, traffic control and parking space. The protective services such as the highway patrols must also be available, so must those of hospitals. Thus, the need for balance becomes very clear. The use of privately produced vehicles has on acceleration, got out of line with the supply of related resources. The result has been hideous road congestion and its attendant consequences on health and well-being of the people.

Divergence between Social Cost and Private Cost

When the firm is calculating the profitability of alternative production plans, it will have to estimate the revenue gained from selling the output and the cost of production. In assessing the cost of production of a given output, the firm must estimate the opportunity cost of required factor services. The opportunity cost to the firm will normally be related to the market prices of the factor services. If the market prices of the resources used reflect adequately their alternative uses of the resources from the whole society's point of view, then the firm's decisions will be based on a consideration of the value of the alternative uses of these resources in the whole society.

The divergence between the private cost and social cost is one of the most important reasons for intervening in a free market economy. It is because such a divergence ensures that not even perfect competition would lead to an optimum allocation of resources. In perfect competition, marginal cost is equal to price. Then the cost of producing the last unit produced which measures the value of the factor services in other uses is just equal to the market value of the goods produced, which measures the value to the consumers of the output of the resources in their present use. If the marginal social cost exceeds the marginal private cost, then the value to the society of the resources in alternative uses would exceed the value in their present use. Thus, social value could be increased by transferring the resources to other uses.

The social value of resources in alternative uses is measured by social costs, the value to the firm is measured by private costs. If the two do not coincide, the firm will base its decisions about the allocation of resources on considerations that do not reflect the interest of the society as a whole. Let us take an example:

A factory discharges its waste into a river resulting in pollution, which destroys the fish living downstream and forces several communities to instal costly water pollution treatment plants and to build swimming pools, since the river is no longer safe for swimming. The private cost to the factory of using the river as a waste disposal is zero, since there is no alternative use of the river to the factory and no price is to be paid for this privilege.

The social costs consist of the fish that are destroyed and the resources used in the purification plants and the construction of swimming pools (plus the cost incurred by a host of other consequences of water pollution.) The social cost of using the river to dispose off the waste may well be greatly in excess of the social cost of having the factory's waste disposal in a chemical treatment plant. Yet, there will be no incentive for the private firm to adopt what is socially the least cost method, since the private cost of alternative methods do no reflect the social cost.

Let us take another example. An industrial complex discharges smoke into the atmosphere. The private costs is zero, social costs emerge when the prevention done on a large scale is enormous. The cost to the society is very great.

When social cost exceeds private cost, a tax on the production of goods by industries which cause pollution may bring private costs more in line with the social costs.

Pricing Concepts

Pricing is an important element in marketing mix. Determination of a right place for a product is very essential in a sound marketing mix. Right price can be determined either by research or by test marketing. A study of pricing involves a study of pricing concepts which serves as a guide for executive decision making and control. The various concepts of pricing which helps in decision making are:

(i) Peak load pricing,
(ii) Pricing over life cycle of a product,
(iii) Pioneer pricing,
(iv) Product line pricing,
(v) Transfer pricing.

Peak Load Pricing

There are certain products which cannot be stored and demand for them varies over time. For example, demand for electricity is high during the day time and low during night time. It is high in a cold country and low in a hot country. But, it is high is desert countries for electricity is needed for airconditioning and cooling. In cold countries, it is needed for room heating. There is some exception in demand for some commodities as mentioned above. In the same manner, demand for telephone is more during day time and low during night time. If electricity and telephone are offered at a constant price, it would result in great pressure on demand during one time phase and excess capacity during the other time phases. Since these services are not storable, the capacity to be installed should depend upon that maximum demand, i.e., peak load demand. In the case of electricity and telephone and some postal services, the prices are high for the peak load period and low for the low demand period. During the nights, the demand is low and charges are also low. Such price differences change the demand from peak period to non-peak period.

In view of the high peak load demand, the installed capacity of the machines are put into maximum use. In view of the high prices in the peak load period, the costs is more then covered. Any loss in the non-peak period is covered by excess of earnings earned during the non-peak period. The prices are determined for both the demand functions in such a way that the entire costs are covered, i.e. both variable and fixed costs.

The peak load pricing involves flexible pricing over time, thereby an optimum combination of prices for the peak as well as non-peak is determined.

Pricing over the Life Cycle of a Product

There are some products which are constantly changing owing to strategic innovation. If a new product, an instrument or a process of production technique is developed, it will not be for a long period. In the course of a year or two, a new product is developed making the old one unpopular. Therefore, it can be said that most products have something of a perishable distinctiveness, whereby these products become ordinary commodities over a period of time. Joel Dean calls this a *'cycle of competitive degeneration'*. With the development of a new product followed by an innovation, the existing product loses its distinctiveness. At this stage, competitors enter the market with innovations and substitutes, making the original product to disappear from the market. The following figure shows different stages of a product, life cycle. It is stated that there are five different stages in the life cycle of a product. The innovation of a new product and its degeneration into a common product is known as life cycle of a product.

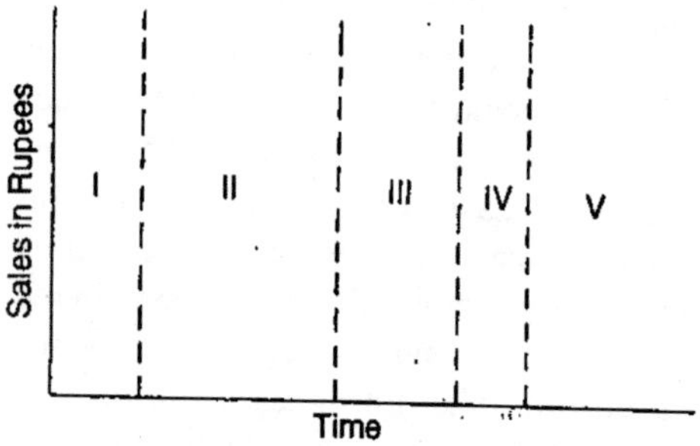

Sales revenue curve

I. Introduction stage

II. Growth stage

III. Maturity stage

IV. Saturation stage

V. Decline stage

When the product enjoys distinctiveness, the producer enjoys monopoly power and it could be vice versa, under certain situations proving detrimental to the producer. In this stage, he can withstand competition. As the product moves from one stage to another stage, there is improvement in the beginning and after reaching the maximum, the product becomes insignificant. In order to save itself from the stage of insignificance, he also takes up innovation. Either he improves the old product or he produces a new product.

Introductory Stage

In this stage, the firm develops a new product through and advertisements innovation. The product is put into the market with all necessary propaganda. But the demand for the new product in the beginning is very slow. At this stage, the firm incurs higher promotional costs, but the sales revenue is so low, and eventually it cannot cover any costs fully.

Growth Stage

In this stage, there is rapid expansion of sales because of the effect of sales promotion undertaken in the introductory stages. In view of increased sales, the company earns good profits after covering the entire costs.

Maturity Stage

When the product enters the maturity stage of growth, the volume of sales goes on increasing, but the rate of growth is rather slow. This is because all those who need the product, have already purchased it and the number of new customers for the product is low. The firm spends considerable amount on sales promotion to boost its sales. But there is only a replacement demand in the market as against new demand. Maturity stage is a stage of optimum growth. It cannot go on forever. During this period, there emerges an innovation. This innovation results in the development of a better product. Consequently the demand for the old product starts declining. Then the product enters the fourth stage called *saturation.*

Saturation Stage

Saturation point is defined as the declining posture after reaching the zenith in the demand for the product. At this point, the firm is producing the product at a higher cost in view of high promotional expenditure. Since the sales are declining, the firm is not in a position to cover any costs. On the other hand, it starts incurring losses. Finally it enters the stage of decline.

Decline

Decline is the last stage of the life-cycle of the product. The sales of the product falls significantly in view of the emergence of the rival product with better quality and appearance. When the competitors enter the market with limitations, then the existing product loses its distinctiveness.

Causes for Growth Cycle of the Product

There are many reasons for the rise and fall in the growth of a product. Where there is no competition for the product, a new product commands a great demand, sales and profit. When the alternatives emerge as a result of innovation, with better image and prices, the original product loses its distinctiveness.

When the distinctiveness of the product fades, the prices of the product decline. Throughout the life cycle of a product, we find change in demand, price, promotion expenses, cost of production and distribution. Therefore, the pricing policy of such products must also be suitably modified to adjust the various phases of the product.

Pricing of the Product at the Maturity Stage

In the introduction stage, the price of the product is generally low. But when the product experiences growth, the price also rises. When it reaches the maturity stage, the price of the product must also be stable. When the demand for the product starts declining and the replacement demand also is more than the new demand, the technology for the production of the product is the same for all firms and finally with the emergence of substitutes and imitations, the distinctiveness of the product is eroding, the price of the product also has to be altered. In the later maturity stage, the firm is required to take stock of the situation and change the price policy. In other words, the firm is required to bring down the price to the extent the demand elasticity of the product permits.

Pricing of Public Utility Product and Services

Pricing of public utility products and services like electricity, railways, telephones, etc. poses some special problems. These undertakings are natural monopolies and they are not meant for making monopoly profit. Since enormous investments are made for generating and supplying electricity, it must earn sufficient revenue to meet all costs of production and distribution. Technology of production and distribution enable the undertakings to achieve economies of scale, so that large firms can produce at much lower costs than small units.

Generally, full cost pricing is followed in the case of public utility products. Further, the enterprises are also required to pay a certain agreed dividend to the government for providing investment capital. Hence, they have to fix a price which assures fair returns for the investments made.

Multi - Product Pricing

Modern industrial concerns are producing many products. They are called multi-product producers. The multi-product firm is classified into several types :

(a) *A joint product firm* : A firm manufacturing soaps can easily produce various by-products. Soap is the main product, glycerine is another product, and cosmetics are also produced in such firms.

(b) *Firm producing related products* : A shoe manufacturing company produces various kinds of shoes for ladies, for children and gents. Since the product is raised from the same plant and uses the same labour and raw materials, there exists some sort of inter-dependence.

(c) *Firm producing unrelated products* : A firm manufacturing refrigerators also produces washing machines, vacuum cleaners, etc. A company producing steel almirahs, produces refrigerator, watches, etc. These products use different facilities, raw-material and manpower. These firms diversify into different unrelated products mainly to take advantage of goodwill and sales network.

Pricing of the products of a multi-product firm requires the study of the following relationships:

Demand Relationships

If the different products are either subsitutes or complements, a change in the price of one product affects the demand for a related product, according to their cross elasticity.

Cost-relationships

When the multiple products are produced with the help of the same production facilities, some costs are directly chargeable to the products and some costs are common to all. For example, if the raw-material is different, its price is charged to the product while the space, the rent, the administration and the sales services are common to all the products.

Production Relationships

If the multiple products of a single production process are availabel, then a primary product along with several by-products can be produced either through fixed or variable proportions.

Capacity Relationship

If a firm has excess capacity or idle capacity, this can used to produce one or more additional products. The cost of fixed factors can be shared between other products.

Product Line Pricing

Product line pricing refers to pricing of a group of products which are related either as substitutes or complements. The cross elasticity of demand is the important factor in determining the price of product line.

Substitute goods

Supposing the company is producing substitute goods, then the market is segregated on the basis of elasticity of demand. Each product in the product line competes 'in house' with each other. There are a good number of firms producing substitute goods and competing internally and externally. If the price of a substance good is favourable, it pushes the sales of that product as against the sales of another product.

The pricing of substitute products is generally determined by two methods. One is the mark-up method in which the producers use a margin i.e., pricing in the proportion to costs. The second method is to price the product varying the size of the margin with the level of costs. If the product is costlier, the margin also is higher and hence the price also is high.

The weakness of these two methods is that they do not take demand and competition into consideration. The decision of costs among the products is done arbitrarily and hence the pricing also reflects the arbitrariness.

Complementary Goods

In the case of complementary products or joint products, the demand inter - relationshios is complementary. The degree of complement takes two forms :

(i) Fixed proportions - for example, cotton and cotton seeds or hides and meat.

(ii) Variable proportions - for example, passenger and freight services in the case of railway services.

In the case of complementary goods, a fall in the price of one results in an increase in the demand for other goods. In such cases, cross elasticity is negative. Generally, the sellers lower the price of one (hide) in the hope of selling the complementary product (meat) at a higher price. In the case of joint products, since the costs are common to both, their allocation to each item is difficult.

In the case of joint products, of fixed proportion and group of products, they are one package so far as production is concerned, but they are priced separately. For example, cotton is priced higher than cotton seeds. The allocation of cost is not made to each individual product but priced differently with a view to earn maximum profits.

In the case of joint products with varying proportions, the total cost is apportioned to each product. The optimal price-output combination for the joint products would require simultaneous cost-revenue relationships.

Price of Multi-products - General Considerations

Pricing in multi-product firms is not an easy job, because in the production of several products in a firm, there are facilities which are commonly used in all such cases. There is a greater amount of inter-dependence between the production of different products. The following considerations are used in the pricing of products:

(i) Pricing in the case of products which are different widely and have no element of inter-dependence, is done separately on the basis of cost and demand functions. It is like the pricing of a single product.

(ii) In the case of joint products, the basic consideration of pricing is that the total cost is recovered by selling the main product and the by-product. The joint products are of two kinds : (a) where proportion of main products and by-products can be varied, (b) where the proportion cannot be varied. In case of the former, the producer manipulates the share favourable to him. In the fixed proportion case, the prices are determined on the basis of demand. One product (for example, raw cotton) commands a high price and the seeds are sold at a lower price. In all, the total price should cover the total cost.

(iii) In the other case of goods, the production is done using some common facilities. The price and output determination in case of such products depend on the contribution of each product to the fixed costs.

Transfer Pricing

In a large sized firm, several products are produced using different processes of production. In such business organisations, the work is divided among several sections or departments. For all practical purposes, each section is an independent unit. This results in the transfer of goods, services and even money from one section to another section or from one unit to another unit. Many large sized companies have this inter-company transfer of goods. For example, in a huge automobile company, production and marketing of trucks, cars, two-wheelers, engines and so on are organised in a separate manner. The managerial decisions taken are also different. In other words, each unit enjoys considerable autonomy. The units transfer goods among themselves. The prices that units change affect the performance of the other units. If transfer prices understate or overstate the values and costs, the decisions of the units would go counter to the company's corporate objectives. The price and output decisions of other departments are influenced by the transfer price. It affects profitability also. The rules observed in such pricing are as follows:

(i) Each division must be treated as an autonomous unit.

(ii) Intra-company transfers should be priced at their marginal costs.

(iii) The inter-transfer of goods are meant for meeting the requirements of inter-dependent divisions of a big company.

For example, pig iron produced in one division is meant for the steel making division of the same company. In such cases, the marginal cost of the product of a division is determined by its own cost.

For calculating the transfer price, one of the following three methods are followed: (i) Market price method, (ii) Cost basis and (iii) Cost-plus basis.

Market Price Basis

In the case of transferred products, the appropriate price is the market price. This is the most suitable system of the pricing of transfer goods. If the market price is preferred, it makes the inefficient division to be alert and efficient. If the product is homogeneous, it is easy to ascertain the market price. But there are differences in the quality of the product or services, and then the market price is required to be adjusted to cover all such factors.

Cost Basis

Cost consideration is made in the case of products produced by one division and meant for sale to another division of the company. For example, if there is a separate maintenance department, then the cost of service or maintenance is assessed on the basis of costs incurred by the department in keeping the assets of other departments in good condition. In other words, the goods meant for inter - divisional transfer should be priced at the level of the marginal cost of production. This pricing policy will maximise group profits.

Cost-plus Basis

Under this method, the pricing is based on the actual cost plus some percentage of profit. The transferring division adds a certain percentage of profit just to inflate the profits of the company. Normally, this division incurs the cost, so that the amount of profit added to it will cover the unexpected losses which may occur in future. Thus, transfer pricing by helping the individual divisions to maximise the profits, also maximises the profits of the company.

Price Discounts and Price Differentials

Price discounting is a normal practice found in large-scale marketing of the products, maybe agricultural raw materials or finished products. The discounts are given generally to buyers of goods who are called *distributors*. Such discounts are called distributor's discounts. They are price reductions given by manufacturers to wholesale buyers. Wholesalers in turn, offer discounts to retailers. The discounts which are given to dealers and retailers and distributors are called *trade channel discounts*. The discounts result in differential pricing, which has become an accepted practice in price policy.

Kinds of Discounts

There are different types of distributor's discounts determined on the basis of experience. Generally, there are three kinds of price discounts shown to the distributors:

(i) On the basis of position of the buyer,

(ii) A price list drawn to show discounts to different type of distributors and

(iii) A single discount combined with supplementary discounts.

Discounts are offered to the distributors on their market position. For example, if a distributor commands a large portion of a country's market like the whole of South India commencing business from Deccan, the discount is generally higher than the regional distributor. The discount pattern followed in practice is five percent to retailers, three percent to local distributors and two percent to regional distributors. The net prices are shown on the package of products. This includes the discounts at different trade levels.

Determination of Distributors Discounts

Distributors are direct buyers of products from manufactures. They perform some important functions such as offering the product to the retailers on credit with a view to clear the product from the godowns. They maintain an organisation with men and equipments in order to deliver goods and offering free services whenever required. For example, the distributors of TVs, refrigerators and other durable household equipments maintain technicians to provide free servicing, which is one of the conditions of sale. This free servicing for a specific period forms a sort of discount.

Trade discounts cover the operating costs and the normal profits of the distributors. These distributors undertake sales promotion and get higher discounts. The rate of discounts depend upon the type of services offered by the distributor. The discount must be such that, it should cover the entire operating costs, and also bring a certain amount of profits to the firm.

Most of the manufacturers, either by custom or practice have been following a fixed discount structure. In the case of high priced luxury goods which are slow moving, the rate of discount is high. But those companies which face stiff competition offer discounts twice as high as those given by market leaders. Apart from a discount, the dealers also get price advantage.

Trade channel discounts are used to achieve profitable market segmentation. In order to make effective sales of certain products, the market has been divided into sub-markets. If there is a main distributor in a region, he provides for sub-markets. If there is a main distributor in a region, he provides for sub-dealership in different places of his region. These sub-dealers in turn may appoint local dealers who supply the product to the retailers.

Since demand elasticities in these sub-markets are different, the prices are also different. The discount structure is arranged in such a manner, that it becomes possible to have different prices suitable for each sub-markets. For example, in the case of components, prices would not influence demand. The demand for a car tyre does not depend upon the price, but it depends upon the need. If the need persists, the owner has to buy the product even at a high price. But the dealers have to maintain adequate stock at the local level for which an attractive discount is required to be given. The bulk buyers of the components are the manufacturers and the producers are required to offer higher discounts. The quantum of discounts given to distributors and dealers depend upon the price elasticity of demand for goods. In the case of replacement goods such as tyres for cars and other automobiles, the manufacturers have to give huge discounts to dealers. Here, the consumers prefer to buy a product for which they have preference and price has no effect on them. In order to shift the demand from one preferred product to an alternative product, the dealers also have to offer discounts. The dealers in such cases discriminate prices between the old customers and new customers. They charge somewhat higher prices to the old customers and lower prices to the new customers.

The discount facility has given rise to several problems in the pricing of products. The main problem is whether to fix a high price and produce products of high quality or to fix a low price and produce goods of low quality. Whenever the discounts are offered, they become the item of cost and as such the price will be naturally high. Discounts are indispensable until the product becomes popular. When the product becomes popular, its demand increases sufficiently, making it possible for the company to reach an optimum capacity.

The manufacturers often depend upon the goodwill of the distributors. If the distributors do not show any interest in the brand product, the manufacturers are put into difficulties. The distributors have, by experience, the capacity to judge whether the quality of the product and its price are favourable or not. Therefore, the manufacturers have to satisfy the distributors and dealers more than the consumers, as consumers are guided by the dealers. If the dealers say that the product 'X' is better than product 'B', then the consumers prefer 'X' product. It is therefore, very important for the manufacturers to secure the goodwill of the distributors. This can be done by not only supplying the products of good quality with reasonable price, but also offering substantial discounts. If the product is a highly advertised one, then the dealer's influence on the consumers is limited. In such cases, the dealers have to be content with a small percentage of discount.

Quantity Discounts

Quantity discounts are price concessions offered to the distributors on the basis of the quantity of the product purchased. Quantity discounts are related to the size of a single purchase. The size of the lot purchased may be measured either in terms of physical quantity or the value of the product. In case of homogeneous products such as refrigerators, scooters or cars etc., it is the physical quantity considered. In the case of heterogeneous products, which are difficult to add, like furniture and scientific instruments, the money value of these products is preferred. Therefore, the quantity discounts are related to either physical units of the products or the money value of the products. High discount is offered if the dealer buys a bigger lot size. The main objective of quantity discounts is to encourage the dealers to buy the product in large amounts, thereby, the manufacturers can reduce their cost of selling, packaging, delivery, etc.

It is stated that quantity discounts was examined by Monopolies and Restrictive Trade Practices Commission. Initially, the MRTPC Commission agreed with the grant of high discounts to large orders in many cases referred to it. But later on, the Commission came to the conclusion that this practice distinguishes between larger buyers and small buyers ultimately coming to the conclusion that this practice is unsound.

Cash Discounts

Cash discounts are price concessions offered when the payment is made promptly. For example, if the dealers make the full payment within the specified period, a discount of two percent is allowed. Firms offer cash discounts with a view to improve the liquidity position and to minimise bank borrowing.

Cash discount is a very good device. It eliminates the accumulation of credit. If the buyers make payment on receipt of the consignment, the manufacturers are also willing to offer higher discounts. If the buyers decide to purchase the product on credit, they have to forego the discounts also.

It is necessary to compare the benefit of cash discount with that of the cost of cash discount. The rate of cash discount must be lower than the benefits which the firm gets by offering these discounts.

Price Differentials

An important aspect of price differential is price discrimination. In open price discrimination, the producer divides the market into several sub markets and charges different prices in each market, depending upon the elasticity of demand for the product. If the demand for the product is inelastic, he charges a higher price.

Time Differentials

There are different ways of discrimination of prices. One such discrimination is that of *time differentials*. The producers take the advantage of change in demand elasticities over a period of time. The demand for a product may be high in a particular season, for example, the demand for woollen goods is high in winter, while the demand for cotton cloth is high during summer. Let us take up another example : Demand for telephones is higher during day time than during the night. There are two cases of time differentials. (i) Clock time price differential and (ii) Calendar time price differential.

Clock Time Price Differential

Suppose demand elasticities change during a day, sellers can charge different prices at different points of time during the 24 hour period. Such a price differential is known as *clock time price differential*. It's object is to charge a higher price when the demand for the product is inelastic and a lower price when the demand for the product is elastic. The common examples are telephone services and the differences between morning shows and afternoon shows in cinema houses. In the case of telephone services, day time charges are higher than night time charges. It is due to its inelastic demand during day time, that the charges are high and at night time, the demand is elastic and hence the rates are low.

The following conditions are to be fulfilled if the clock time differentials are to become profitable:

(i) Buyers must have a definite preference for buying a product at a particular time.

(ii) The seller must be in a position to offer his product at a lower price in the slack period.

(iii) The product offered for sale is not a storable item either wholly or in parts. If the product is a storable one, the buyers buy it when its price is low and use it whenever it is required.

Calendar Time Price Differentials

In the calendar price differentials, the period of sale of a product or a service is more than 24 hours like days, weeks, months, etc. For example, swimming pool charges and charges for hotel accommodation on hill stations differ on the basis of seasons. During winter, the charges are low and in spring, they are higher. The seller of these services charge higher prices in spring in view of its inelastic demand. Taking this opportunity, the sellers of the services exploit the consumers.

The economics of pricing points out that the pricing of product or services must be related to cost. The prices are differentiated during a whole period of a year or so in such a manner that higher cost of maintenance must be overcome by charging a higher price during seasons.

Use-price Differentials

Price discrimination is made by the public utility organisations like electricity organisation, railways etc. on the basis of use of the services. Railways are used to transport different commodities and they can be used not only for long distance travel but also short distance travel. Charges for these uses are different. The sellers of these services divide the market into different segments and charge prices according to the demand.

In order to make use of price differential effective, the demand elasticities for the product or services must be different.

Geographical Price Differential

Price discrimination is practised by sellers on the basis of buyer's location. Such discrimination is called *geographical price differential.* For example, at the place of production of a commodity, the price of the product is low, while at different centres of the nation, the price is high. The price of the product at the point of production is known as FOB Price (i.e. free on board), while the latter is a delivered price. The delivered price includes the cost of shipping the goods.

FOB Pricing

It indicates that the buyers have to pay the transport and handling charges and they are responsible for any loss of goods during the transport. Sellers charge uniform price to all categories of buyers at the point of production. The sellers do not make any discrimination between a buyer of large quantity and small quantity. But they have to bear the entire transport cost. It is the responsibility of the buyers to arrange for their own mode of transportation. If the sellers take up the responsibility of transportation, then they include the transport charges in the price of the commodity.

In order to practice FOB Pricing, the sellers have to fulfil the following conditions :

(i) If the transport cost is small when compared to the production cost of the commodity, the sellers will sell outside the place of production or local market.

(ii) The fixed cost must not be very high to force the sellers to go out searching for customers in distant markets.

(iii) If the firm sets up plants at different demand centres, it can cater to the regional market needs easily without bothering about excess production.

Uniform Delivered Pricing or Postage Stamp Pricing

It implies that the seller charging uniform price for his product without looking into destination of the product, is called *'Postage Stamp Pricing'.* In the case of postage stamp pricing, the seller sells the product at a uniform price at all centres of a country. The quoted price includes the transport cost also.

Postage price is quoted in two ways : (i) the seller sells the product at a single price all over the country and (ii) secondly, a uniform FOB Price is quoted and the buyers are allowed to deduct a certain percentage from the price towards the freight charges. In these two cases, there is a certain amount of discrimination.

Postage pricing is commonly practised by sellers in selling popular brand products and having wide national markets. For example, most of the soap manufacturing firms sell their brand soaps at a uniform price all over the country. They advertise the prices of their products in newspapers. For example, the Bata Shoe Company sells its different brand shoes at a uniform price all over the country. Most durable goods are sold like this.

Postage stamp prices are very suitable when the transport cost is insignificant to their actual cost of production. Goods like clothes, cosmetics, soft drinks, electrical and electronic equipments, radios, typewriters are some examples for postage pricing. This pricing gives the producer easy access to all markets regardless of the location.

Zonal pricing

Many a times, the producers, instead of charging a uniform price in all regions of the country, differentiate between zones. They divide the country into several zones and the price in each zone is different from the other zone. This is known as *zone pricing.* This is done with a view to cover transport charges. Zonal pricing is preferred when the transport cost on goods is too high. If the transport cost is high, the producers fix different prices for different zones.

Base Point Pricing

A major production centre for a particular product is chosen for pricing, which consists of a factory price and transportation price. This is called *base point pricing*. A delivered price is quoted on the basis of base point. In other words, a base point price includes mill price or ex-factory price and transportation costs. The transportation cost, which is taken into consideration, is not the actual freight charge, but transportation charge from a designated centre.

A seller of the product may use single base point pricing or multiple base point pricing. Under the single base point, all sellers quote a uniform price irrespective of their locations. In the case of multiple base point pricing, two or more producing centres are chosen as base points. The seller then quotes a delivered price which includes mill price and transportation charge from the base point to the buyer's nearest point. Base point pricing is used extensively by heavy machinery manufacturers.

Pricing Strategy for Multiple Products

Pricing of a product is a difficult task, for several aspects have to be looked into. In recent years, the producers have to take into consideration several aspects like competition, advertisement and the quality of the product to fix a reasonable price for their products. In modern times, the firms are producing several products which may be related to the main product or unrelated to the main product. The multiplicity of the product by a firm creates three kinds of relationships :

(i) Demand Relationship

When a firm is producing different products, either substitutes or complements, it has to see how a change in the price of one product affects the demand for others.

(ii) Costs Relationship

When multiple products are produced within the same plant and machineries, some costs are directly chargeable to each product, while other costs are common to all.

(iii) Capacity Relationship

If the firm has idle capacity, it can produce one or more additional products. When a new product is produced, the fixed costs are shared among several products which alter the optimal output and price structure of all products.

A multi-product line can be classified into:

a) Joint product firm, b) firms producing unrelated products and c) firms producing relating products.

(a) A joint product firm is one where a main product and a by-product are produced. For example, in a sugar factory, sugar is the main product and alcohol is a by-product. Let us take another example. In soap factories, soap is the main product and glycerine the by-product.

(b) There are firms producing unrelated products. For example, a company manufacturing steel almirahs and refrigerators is also manufacturing locks and soaps. These products are made using different raw-materials. The firm producing multiple products which are unrelated to each other, take advantage of the goodwill of the company and the marketing network. If a firm adds one more product, the marketing of it may be done by the existing network.

(c) A firm is producing many related products, for example, a cotton textile firm is producing yarn, cloth and apparel. These various products are produced from the same plant. They are very inter-dependent.

Product Line Pricing

Product line is a group of products which are related to each other. They may be subsitutes or complements. The means of determining the prices of these related products is that of studying the cross elasticity of demand.

Pricing the product belonging to this line involves determining the proper relationship among the prices of the members of the product group. In pricing of these products, the producers want to cover full allocated common and overhead expenses. The specific technique is to price the products in proportion to costs. This method does not take into consideration demand and competition.

The pricing of such products may also be done by varying the size of the margin and the level of costs. If the product produced by the firm is costly, then the margin also is higher. This approach also fails to take into account the demand and competition. The allocation of costs to joint products is done arbitrarily, resulting in prices which reflect the arbitrary allocation of common costs. The main consideration in pricing of these products is that the firm should get a higher margin of profit after covering all costs. The cost structure of the product line is as follows. For example, supposing a biscuit manufacturer produces two types of biscuits - the first category needs more labour but less material cost per packet while the other brand needs more materials than the first one. The cost structure for these two varieties of biscuits is as follows:

	Biscuit 'A'	Biscuit 'B'
Material cost	4	2
Labour cost	2	3
Over cost	1	2
Full cost 1 + 2 + 3	7	7
Incremental costs (1 + 2)	6	5
Conversion cost (2 + 3)	3	5

The pricing can be worked out as follows:

Full cost pricing	10%	7.70	7.70
Incremental cost pricing	10%	6.60	5.50
Conversion cost Pricing (2 +3)	90%	5.70	4.50

Some Problems in Product Line Pricing

There are some problems in pricing of the products in product line. There are two approaches to tackle the problem:

(i) There is a practice of charging a uniform price irrespective of size differences. For example, products of the same quality are priced uniformly. The shoe manufacturing companies fix a uniform price for the shoes of same quality. In such cases, the sizes are not taken into consideration.

(ii) There is another approach namely charging prices on the basis of sizes. In such cases, quality of material, labour used is the same, but prices vary according to the size. For example, jute sack manufacturers fix a lower price to cement bags and higher price for sugar bags. But it is not so in the case of products like toothpastes and other packed products like oil and tooth paste. Groundnut oil of five kgs is cheaper per kilogram than smaller tins. The same thing is found in advertising also. If a producer takes one full page advertisement, it is cheaper than a small space advertisement.

Special Order Pricing

In the pricing of products produced specially for a consumer, the producer takes into consideration the full cost of producing this. The full cost includes a certain percentage of profits also. In special order pricing, the producer, though he enjoys monopoly, cannot exploit the consumer. If the producer quotes a high price, he may lose the order. If the producer has idle capacity of plant and machinery, he maybe forced to accept the lowest price. If the alternative is idleness, he may charge a price equal to incremental costs. The incremental revenue must exceed the incremental cost of producing the special order product. If the plant is not idle, then he quotes a price which covers his full cost plus a certain percentage of profit.

Pricing of Spare Parts

Every producer of durable goods produce spareparts for replacing the wornout parts. When the capital good is to be repaired, then the broken parts will have to be replaced. In such circumstances, prices of spare parts pose some problems. Pricing of spare parts involves the considerations of the following aspects:

In case of parts produced by the original manufacturer of capital goods, he enjoys a monopoly and he charges a high price. If there are alternative spare parts almost similar to original products, then the original producer of spares cannot charge a monopoly price. If the prices of the spares of original producer are very high, the buyers may not buy them from him. They may go in for alternatives. In the case of manufacturers, they may start producing the spare parts. For example, large manufacturing companies have their own workshops and research departments. They may fabricate the spares. Now many ancillary industries have specialised in producing components to machineries. In fact, the producers of capital goods buy the components from the ancillary industries. In such cases, the prices of the spares are lower than the prices of original spares manufactures. Therefore, the prices of spares are generally kept at reasonable level. However, the manufactures of these spares follow certain thumb rules to fix the prices for the spares:

(i) Full cost of producing the spares plus a reasonable profit will be the basis of pricing the spare parts.

(ii) Spare parts are priced sometimes according to their weight after making adjustment for the complexity.

(iii) The sum of the price of all the parts taken individually should not exceed twice the price of the equipment as a whole.

(iv) The prices of different spare parts should have consistency among themselves.

Normally, the prices of the spare parts which are available in plenty are low and further those spares can be produced easily and will be priced low. Japan by producing and exporting spare parts of their capital equipments at lower prices is making large amount of profits. Many automobile manufacturers are also selling parts at lower prices and thus making good profits.

Pricing Leases and Licences

There are companies leasing the equipments on lease rent to the manufacturers. If the manufacturers find that obtaining an equipment on lease is profitable, they are not going to buy a new machine. The lease rent is charged on the basis of the capacity of the user. That is perfect price discrimination followed in all such cases. If the equipment is used for different purposes, the benefits accruing to the users also differ. A person is going to make a high profit from using it. He is naturally charged a higher lease rent. The minimum rent is fixed by the leaser on the basis of cost of the equipment, its servicing charges, depreciation, etc.

Royalty is levied when a patent is given for use. The royalty and licence charges are determined, keeping in mind various considerations :

(i) The expenses incurred in developing a patented product are basically sunk cost. They cannot be used for any other purpose. Hence they are not relevant in determining the patent fee.

(ii) The minimum rent is determined on the basis of incremental cost of operating the licensed patents.

(iii) The upper limit of the royalty takes into account the benefit of the product to the license and

(iv) In between these two limits, royalty is determined taking into account the possible competition, infringement of the patents and the intervention of the government in the high royalties fixed.

For example, in the case of patents offered for copying, the incremental cost of producing is taken into consideration in determining the royalty.

Product Line Balancing

Producing multiple products is the order of the day. Prof. Nickerson in his book *'Managerial Cost Accounting and Analysis'* said that it is like a family in which all children are not born with same facility and aptitude. In the same way, the products produced by a firm are unrelated, the production of which is done with a view to make high profit. There are some more profit-intensive products and some others are less profit-intensive products. In pricing the whole range of products, the producer takes into account the whole range of products. The producer takes into account several considerations.

(i) In the case of widely different products which have no interdependence, pricing for each product is done separately on the basis of its cost and demand. The firm may give up producing loss making products and concentrate on products which are giving good profit.

(ii) In the case of a joint product firm, the basic consideration is to recover the total cost by the sale of the main product and the by product.

(iii) In the case of products which are inter-dependent, the output and price determination depend on the contribution of each product to the fixed costs.

Product Line Diversification

Product line diversification arises whenever there is excess production capacity in a firm. In such cases, the firm thinks of adding a new product to the existing products. If it adds a new product, no additional cost is involved and it can sell the product at a reasonable price and thereby remove the unutilised capacity of production.

Excess capacity may occur for several reasons. It may occur whenever the firm makes over optimistic demand for its product. If the firm cannot sell that much of production, then there exists excess capacity. Excess capacity may arise due to seasonal variations in the demand for product. Companies producing goods which meet seasonal demand, find excess capacity in out of seasons. In such cases, companies producing goods which meet seasonal demand start producing a new product. Excess capacity may also occur due to cyclical fluctuating in sales. It may occur when there is change in demand for the product. In such cases, the companies produce new products to make use of the unutilised capacity of the plant and machinery.

Diversification

Many companies are adding new products to their existing product line. For example, a company manufacturing sugar production machinery may take up producing earth moving equipments or textile yarn or cloth making machinery, etc. Diversification is considered to be profitable in such circumstances. The main goal of such diversification is to make maximum profit from the present investments. If the net return from the new product covers the incremental costs, the companies are highly satisfied.

There are many examples found in the present industrial set up to justify the diversification. For example, a company which commenced as a sales organisation, after some time, took up the production of that product. The Godrej company which was producing almirahs, subsequently took up the production of typewriters. In all such cases, the objective of diversification was to maximise profits.

Consideration for Diversification

Diversifications mean producing one or more products to the existing products in the same plant. Diversification is taken up when the existing products are facing stiff competition and their future prospects are not good. Many companies take up diversification owing to political, social and economic compulsions. It may also be taken up to avoid the various restrictive regulations of the government. The Indian Tobacco Company

(ITC), a cigarette producing company in course of time, diversified its activities into hotel business, paper boards manufacturing, marine products, etc. In fact, many companies have diversified their activities and are earning enormous profits.

Diversification is undertaken to make the best use of the existing marketing network. For example, Indian Express was publishing only English language newspapers and now it is publishing many regional language newspapers, weeklies, film newspapers, business newspaper, etc.

A company may take up diversification with a view to derive advantage of the concessions offered by the government.

Companies, while taking diversification, must justify their action by showing economic advantages. It is not desirable to launch diversification far the sake of adding a new product. The management has to examine all possible advantages and disadvantages before adding a new product to the product line. If the diversification does not involve additional investment and additional capital expenditure, it is sound. Otherwise, diversification tends to result in additional costs.

Scope of Diversification

Any company can diversify its activities. But the scope of diversification is limited to companies which have excess of production and marketing capacity. There are certain factors which restrict the scope of diversification.

(i) The Costs

The costs play an important place in the diversification of the company. If the diversification does not result in additional costs, it is permitted. If a company producing sugar can diversify to make use of the byproducts available in the factory, it does not require additional costs.

(ii) Demand

Demand for the product is very essential for diversification. A firm having earned reputation for safeguarding and maintaining the quality of products may take up adding another product to the existing products. It will be easy for that firm to sell the new product without any difficulty. Sometimes, manufactures of high quality goods start producing a new product using the byproduct produced in the company. When the quality product is sold in the company's name, the company can sell the new product in its own name and can thus sell the product easily. If companies producing similar goods under different brand names amalgamate themselves, even then the products can be sold under the same brand names. The firms producing consumer goods will have to study the consumer's preferences before undertaking the production of them. Their preferences are so very uncertain because they are choosy and buy different types of goods. The firms have to spend a considerable sum of money on advertisements in order to attract the consumers and to retain the loyalty of the consumers.

Need for Market Research

Market research is very necessary in order to assess the potential demand for the products. It is one of the ways of forecasting demand. If the company adds a product without considerable market research, it may have to incur heavy losses.

The consumer's social and economic background play a decisive role in consumer's demand. Most of the consumers in India, even in urban areas do not use foreign system of eating foods. If an Indian company takes up producing household appliances which are being used in foreign countries, they may find lack of demand and finally incur heavy losses. It is because that the Indian consumers have very little need for them. Even the price does not influence them to buy the products. For example, there are packaged fast foods being produced by several firms. Demand for these products may be found in metropolitan cities like Mumbai, Delhi, Chennai, etc. but it is very low in many urban places. As such, a through market research is to be undertaken before embarking on the large scale production of new products. With strategic market research, the consumers are accepting these products in a big way.

Alternative Approach

There are three alternatives for the firms which are facing uncertain demand for new products. They are improve, buy or drop. If the firm finds that the demand for its product is very low and not picking up even after heavy advertisement and publicity campaign, then it has to decide any one of the three alternatives mentioned above. Improvement means redesigning the shape of the product and introducing improvements to please the consumers. When the existing product is obselete or out of fashion, the firm is required to change the shape and appearance of the product. This can be seen in many consumer durable goods like refrigerators, washing machines, television sets or automobiles, etc. For example, Godrej has improved the refrigerators in order to accomodate more things. This improvement may satisfy the consumers and the demand may pick up.

Then, there is another alternative, namely buying a product. It means, that the companies buy the product if the price of the product is low. The advantage in buying is that it will help in large scale production. The third alternative is to drop the product from production. If the production of a new product does not assure a reasonable profit, then it is better for the firm in stopping its production. In relation to the production of a new product, if the demand is uncertain, it is better for the firm to stop producing the product. Many a time, producers are reluctant to eliminate the product on the ground of sentiment. And care must be taken to produce an attractive and user friendly commodity which satisfies the consumers. If the company finds it unable to sell the product, then it is better to drop the product instead of incurring more losses.

Retail Pricing

Generally, price determination is made by the producers of products. Retailers have very little say in the matter. However, retailers also incur some costs and they also add their costs to the pricing of the products. The costs that are incurred by retailers are storage and handling etc. Sometimes, retailers, while selling a particular product, influence the buyers to buy other products also. In the case of many products, the retailers have no chance of adding anything to the price marked on the product. Many manufacturers of brand products fix the retail price. Further, the producers suggest a price and this appears in the form of 'price not to exceed.....' and as such, the retailers sell at the price marked on the product. Nowadays, the governments are fixing the retail prices of certain commodities like sugar, vanaspathi, etc. Alternatively, the trade associations may fix the prices of certain products. There is what is called what the traffic will bear in terms of pricing. It means charging the consumer as high a price he is prepared to pay. Sometimes retailers also fix the price on these basis.

There is another method of pricing by retailers namely, pricing in accordance with terms of sale. In this case, the actual price is higher than the invoice price. If the retailers provide some services like home delivery and credit facility, then an additional price is added to the retail price. Sometimes, old stocks are sold at reduced rates.

The retailers generally are satisfied with low margin in view of high turnover. But it is not so in the case of departmental stores. The percentage of margin in such stores varies between 10 percent and 15 percent. If there is stiff competition in the market, then the percentage of margin is within five percent.

The Package Commodities Regulation Order 1975

This order maintains that no person shall pre-pack for retail sale or cause to be pre-packed for retail sale any commodity, unless each retail package in which such commodity is prepared, bears thereon a label securely affixed, a declaration as to the name of the commodity, the quantity, the date of package and the price. The producer may state ex-factory price plus central excise and further states that it excludes States taxes. Sometimes the maximum price at which the commodity is sold may be mentioned on the package, which includes all taxes, transport charges, commissions, etc. Thus, the manufacturers have several options such as ex-factory price, FOR, destination price, sales price exclusive of all taxes and retail sale price inclusive of all taxes, etc. If the retail price is mentioned on the package of the product, the retailer has to sell at the price itself. The authority to fix the retail price is the manufacturer of the product. The price that is mentioned on the package is the maximum price and not the minimum price. Supposing the price falls owing to various factors, the retailers are required to sell at the reduced price if they want to sell more.

Re-sale Price Maintenance

Prof. G. C. Allan defines resale price maintenance as the stipulation by a supplier so that his retailers shall resell particular goods at prices fixed by him or for not less than those prices.

Resale price maintenance means selling the branded products at a uniform price. The manufacturers of branded products fix and stipulate the price of the products at which the product is to be sold by the individual retailer. This is done to maintain a uniform selling price of branded products at different outlets. Since such a price is handed down from the producer to the retailer, it becomes a kind of vertical price control.

There are two types of resale price maintenance. One is called collective resale price maintenance and the other is individual retail sale price maintenance. Under the collective resale price-maintenance, the manufacturers of different brand products collectively fix a resale price and notify it as a condition to all traders who buy products from them. Any retailer who reduces the price of the branded product, is removed from the manufacturer who maintains control over his own resale price. The resale price of manufacturers of similar products may differ. Retailers can search for alternative sources of supply of the product. Collective price maintenance is highly effective in the sense, it controls at the very source of the supply of alternative products.

Resale priced maintained, whether individual or collective, does not allow competition to exist among the distributors and the price is stabilised which attract the consumers. If a dealer reduces the price of a product, it does not increase sales and on the contrary, the consumers may feel that the quality of the product is not good.

Advantages

Resale price maintenance has several advantages. It enhances the reputation of the firm keeping the price uniform and stable. It does not allow indiscriminate selling of high priced products. It maintains the quality of the product. It eliminates unfair competition. It prevents excessive profiteering. It safeguards the interests of the consumers by enforcing the stability of the price of the product. It promotes fair trade practices. It enables the manufacturer to maintain his reputation in the market.

Disadvantages

The resale price maintenance has the following disadvantages too. The practice of resale price maintenance prevents competition and supports the formation of monopolies. In India, under Section 39 of the MRTP Act, all kinds of resale price maintenance are considered as void *ab initio*. If the manufacturers keep the high price and by withholding the supply of the product or products, it results in the exploitation of the consumers. That is why resale price maintenance is not allowed in India under the MRTP Act. It encourages inefficient dealers to survive for long periods. The resale prices are set generally at a higher level and as such prevent the efficient distributions with lower overheads to sell at lower prices. The policy of resale maintenance is being debated seriously in Western Countries like USA, West Germany and Great Britain.

Dual pricing

Dual pricing is a system in which two types of prices are prevailing for a product. Under this system, one price is fixed and controlled by the government and the other price is to be determined by market forces. The price fixed by the government is fairly static while the other price is fluctuating. In this system, a certain percentage of output is brought under government pricing and the balance is allowed for private pricing. In the dual pricing system, both socialist pricing and capitalist pricing co-exist. Government of India introduced this system in the case of products like sugar, cement, etc. The dual pricing is still being practised in the sale of sugar in India. Fifty or sixty percent of the output is brought under public distribution system through fixed prices, while the balance is sold at market prices. The Government's fixed price is always less than the market price.

The price fixed by the Government under the dual price system covers the cost of production and allows a reasonable amount of profit. Since there is another price which is higher than the controlled price, the manufacturers get a higher amount of profit. The dual system is practised so as to protect the weaker section of the society from higher price for the essential commodity. All consumers are assured of minimum requirements at the controlled price. If the consumers require more than the minimum, they have to pay a higher price for the product. The demand under the dual system is regulated by two prices. Under the controlled price system, demand is regulated while under the open market price system, price establishes the equilibrium between the demand and supply.

Administered Prices

Administered prices are the prices of commodities fixed by the government to prevent price escalation, black-marketing and shortages in supply. The Government may adopt administered prices for essential commodities like steel, cement, fertilizers and petroleum products etc. In the case of petrol, the Government has fixed the price and the retailers have to sell it at that price only. In the case of the other commodities, the government has reserved the right of allotment to users and the products are sold at the administered prices.

The objective of administering the prices of some essential commodities is to prevent any sudden rise in their prices and to ensure reasonable prices to the users. It is because of the importance of raw-materials like steel, cement, fertilizers etc., and their prices must be stabilised at a reasonable level. If the prices of these commodities are allowed to rise or fall, the production of final commodities is affected. Administered prices denote a pool price while the production units are given an assured price called *retention price.* These retention prices may be the same for all units or may be different to different units. The administered prices are fixed on the basis of the cost of production plus a certain amount of profit. Administered prices are advantageous both to the users and to the producers. When there is a change in cost of production, the administered prices are also changed. The costs of many articles like steel, cement, etc. are worked out by the Bureau of Industrial Costs and Prices in India.

Pricing in Public Utilities

The term public utilities refers to services provided by the Railways, water supply, electricity, telephone and Posts and Telegraphs (P&T), etc. All forms of transport are also included in the term public utilities. Public utilities are run either by the government department or government formed corporations. They render services in the interest of safeguarding the public from private sector exploitation. The commodity or service rendered by such industries is so essential to the economic life of the people and hence these services are considered as necessities.

The product of public utilities are different from the product of other industries. The products of public utilities are services rather than tangible commodities. The transport services provided to the city commuters by the Government Road Transport System, the Railway facility, water supply, telephones, etc. are all services which are meant for the entire community. In all these cases, the services are punctual and effective and they have more value than products. Constant and reliable supplies of these are the criterion. Since the public utilities are in the nature of rendering essential services, these products cannot be stored. Water and gas supply, telephone services, P&T services cannot be stored to render stability in production and distribution. The nature of public utility services can be stated as follows:

(i) They are monopolistic in nature. Monopolies are created by the act of the government and competition is prevented with a view to avoid wastage. Even if competition is allowed, it may last for some time in the beginning but later on it may become a monopoly by means of amalgamation and integration. If the monopoly is allowed in the private sector, it will exploit the consumers and therefore, the government takes the monopoly of these services.

(ii) *Large scale operation* : Public utility services are nationwide in character. They operate on a large scale which in turn, enables the company to device internal and external economies. Consequently, the average cost falls and the service can be rendered at no loss and no profit basis.

(iii) The demand is inelastic for the public utility services. If the prices of the services are increased by limiting the supply, it results in the exploitation of the consumers. The services are so important that the consumers will not reduce demand, even if the prices of these services are high. For example, the railway travel, telephone services etc. These essential services enjoy the inelasticity of demand.

Large Fixed Investments

Huge investments will have to be made in the case of public utility service industries. The cost of construction and maintenance of different transport services are very high. Huge investments are required in the railways. Providing track, construction of bridges, tunnels, installation of signals, rolling stock, etc. cost enormous sums of money. In the case of supply of electricity, main costs relate to the construction of transmission lines. Further, in all public utility services, some unused plant capacity will be maintained in order to meet occasional peak demands. Extra plant capacity is maintained in order to meet unforeseeable contingencies. This involves huge investments in plants and equipments.

Decreasing Cost

In such public utilities, in view of the surplus capacity of plants, it is possible to increase the output at an decreasing average cost. When the output is increased, the cost per unit also falls. But, when the plant is over utilised, then the averaged cost is bound to rise.

Price Discrimination

In most of the public utility services, price discrimination is practised. The utilised can charge different prices to different types of consumers. Electricity Boards, Water Supply Boards are charging high rates to industrial users and low rates to domestic users. In the case of bulk consumers, the rates are lower than small consumers. The railways too are following price discrimination. High rates are charged for short distances and the low rate for long distances.

Welfare Principle

The main objective of public utility services is to provide services on - profit and no - loss basis. Their main consideration is to promote the welfare of the community. Since the goal of public utilities is to promote community welfare, they charge low prices to poor people. Utility services are available to the people at cheaper rates. In fact, water supply to the people is done without any price. Water Boards provide public taps for this purpose itself. In times of scarcity, these services are owned by government. Electricity supply, water supply are provided by the state governments, while posts and telegraphs and railways are provided by the Union Government. In foreign countries like the United States of America, utility services are provided by private companies but they are all controlled by statutory regulations.

Pricing Policy

Since the main objective of public utilities is to promote social welfare, it cannot adopt maximum profit principle. Further, the pricing policy of public utilities is based on the principle of no profit and no loss. As such, in practice, they follow one of the following principles : (i) Fair rate principle, (ii) Average cost pricing and (iii) Marginal cost pricing.

Fair Rate Principle

The fair rate principle states that public utilities must get a fair rate or reasonable rate of return for the investments made. A return of six to nine percent or around 10 per cent is considered as a fair rate. This principle is adopted in order to make the utility concern cost-conscious and to make it work efficiently. The capital investment is first assessed and the expected returns to be obtained is calculated. The fair rate is decided on the basis of the following grounds :

(i) Original cost less depreciation,

(ii) Current replacement or reproduction cost less depreciation,

(iii) Capitalised market value of firm's assets.

If there is no change in the price level, the utility concern follows the first two methods. If the prices rise, then the firm follows the second principle and accordingly, the rates are also increased with every rise in prices. The principle of capitalised market value of the firm's assets is not practised in most of the cases. The best method practised in all countries is that of the principle of replacement costs.

Marginal Cost Pricing

Marginal cost pricing method is advocated by Professor Montgomery and Professor Lerner to the pricing of the public utility services. In competitive conditions, the firms follow marginal cost pricing to determine the prices. According to marginal cost pricing, the price of the products should be equal to marginal cost. The utility company produces maximum output when it equates the marginal cost to the prices of service. The prices of service is not uniform for all the users. What is followed generally in a monopoly utility organisation is that marginal cost is equal to average price and not the marginal revenue. In the case of a private monopoly, which is not utility organisation, is that the marginal cost is equal to the average price and not the marginal revenue. When MC is equal to MR, the firm maximises its monopoly profits. The public utility is not concerned with monopoly gain. If the cost is equal to the revenue, the organisation is highly satisfied. Hence, the monopoly utility organisation fixes the prices of the service in such a way that marginal cost is equal to the price.

The principle of marginal cost pricing is severely criticised by economists on the following grounds:

Firstly, this principle does not recognise the importance of long period problem. This principle holds good when the problem is of a short period only. But, public utility services are not short period phenomenon. Its importance in the long period is more than short period. Secondly, in a large utility monopoly company, the marginal cost is negligible when it produces on a large scale. On this ground, no public utility service can be supplied free of cost as the marginal cost is very low. Calculation of marginal cost in a large public utility monopoly is also very difficult in view of many where the overall cost is not ignored, even though they form a significant proportion of the total cost. Hence, the marginal cost principle is not accepted in the pricing of service of a monopoly public utility firm. Further, when the public utility firm produces a product or service under deficits, it is covered by public taxation. Price is not going to be increased to cover the losses.

Average Cost Principle

In the average cost principle, the firm is equating price with the average cost. When the utility firm is working under increasing costs, the equality of AC with price is beneficial to the firm. When the firm is working under decreasing cost, equality of AC with AR will result in lesser output. If this principle is practiced, the concept of public welfare has to be abandoned.

Actual Pricing

Actual pricing practice followed in most of the public utilities firm is that of what the traffic can bear. This principle is known as *value of service principle.* Each category of consumers is charged a price that it is able to pay according to its demand for service. The consumers are divided on the basis of the elasticity of demand. If the demand is inelastic, higher rates are charged. Lower prices are charged where the demand is highly elastic. Thus, the public utility organisation practices the discriminatory pricing and thus renders useful service to the community.

The commissions and tribunals of public utilities take various factors such as the production cost, the administration cost, fair return on capital in determining the prices for services. More than that, they also look into promotional aspects namely the social services that each firm renders. Sometimes, the authorities may fix the price of a utility concern arbitrarily without looking into cost aspects.

General Considerations in Pricing and Price Forecasting

Pricing of a product is a complex problem and there is no readymade formulae which can be immediately applied to solve the problem. However, several general considerations have been suggested to serve as guidelines in the pricing of products. Some of them are stated as follows :

(i) *Nature of Corporate Objectives*

Before taking up the technical function of the pricing of a product, it is absolutely necessary to know the objectives of the firm. These objectives might be the maximisation of profit, maximisation of sales to get a large share in the market etc. Every firm has fixed a target rate of profits and the concerned authorities have to achieve this objective in the manner of pricing of the product. While fixing the price, it is also necessary to examine the impact of pricing on other policies and the growth of the firm.

(ii) *Nature of Competition*

This is another consideration which the management of the firm has to bear in mind, namely whether the firm is facing perfect competition, imperfect competition like monopoly, monopolistic competition, etc. In the case of perfect competition, the firm has to accept the price and the firm has no option in this. The pricing of the product becomes very important when the firm is facing imperfect market. Since the product is not homogeneous, the pricing of the product is to be related to its utility. Thus, pricing policy must be governed more by this relative aspect than by its absolute price.

(iii) *Promotional Policies*

Pricing of the product is also governed by the promotional efforts of the company. The sales campaign plays a very important role in the sale of the product. The pricing of the product should also take care of the promotional policy of the company.

(iv) *Co-ordination in Product Line*

There are many channels in the sales of the product and the pricing should establish proper co-ordination among producers, distributors and retailers. The interests of the producers and the distributors must be identical, otherwise, the purpose of pricing will be defeated. The price fixed by the producers must be accepted by sales channels.

(v) *Pricing Routine Function*

Pricing of product is no doubt based on some systematic studies. Generally, it is not done arbitrarily. Yet, it becomes a routine function in the sense, that instead of following its own independent policy, it may mechanically follow the prices fixed by its competitors. If there is a wide difference between the prices of alternate product, firms with higher price find it difficult to sell the products in the market. Therefore, firms fix the price as it is prevailing for similar products in the market.

If a firm is manufacturing a large number of products, it adopts a definite pricing method for some products, while for others, not very significant, it may mechanically fix the price of its products.

If the firms find it very difficult to get adequate and reliable data on the demand aspects, then they prefer to rely on the mechanical formulae.

Adoption of mechanical formulae will be helpful in fixing the price sometimes and the firms prefer to use this formulae rather than following a complicated device.

External Factors

The external factors which influence the pricing policies of firms are the elasticity of demand and supply of product, the trend in the market, the purchasing power of the people of the country, the inflationary or deflationary position prevailing in the country and the government tax and public expenditure policies. The government action on prices is very important in this respect. If the government enforces price control on many articles of general consumption and industrial uses, the firms have no discretion in this matter. The government control may be direct or indirect. In the direct control, the government announces the prices of the products and all the sellers have to strictly follow the government control may be direct or indirect. In the direct control, the government announces the prices of the products and all the sellers have to strictly follow the government price regulation. The government may enforce price regulation in the interest of primary producers like cotton, jute, sugar-cane growers. In the same way, the government may regulate retail sale prices of essential commodities with a view to safeguard the consumers. Besides, the government and the firms too have to study the economic condition prevailing at particular times, such as depression or recession or boom. Thus, the firms are required to look into these various factors before fixing the prices of their products.

General Objectives of a Pricing Policy

The objectives of pricing of products are many. While fixing the price of the products, the firms have to look into objectives. These broad objectives are as follows:

(i) To achieve a given rate of return for the entire product line,
(ii) To maintain or to increase the market share of the product,
(iii) To maintain price stability at a desired level,
(iv) To follow a price policy which meets all market conditions and
(v) To prevent new firms entering into the industry.

There are no doubt certain advantages and disadvantages in achieving each objective. However, the firms have to make a compromise between the two extremes. If the firms aim at maximising profits, they have to keep a high price to the products. If the prices are high, the sales of the products might be affected and the firms cannot maximise profits. If the price is high, it is impossible for the firm to get a greater market share. If the price of the product of a firm is high, it encourages the rival firms to complete this product. All these are conflicting objectives. Therefore, it is better to follow the suggestions given by Kotler in pursuing a pricing policy.

(i) A firm may not fix a price which achieves the maximum returns, but would rather fix a price which gives it a smaller but satisfactory rate of return.

(ii) Often, firms are found to fix a price which gives maximum profit on the entire range of products rather than price on one product and very low profit on the rest of the product line.

(iii) The firms which face the problem of liquidity, fix prices at a level which would ensure rapid cash recovery.

(iv) Some firms fix prices in such a manner that they can capture a larger share of the market and

(v) The product which has a high value for some of the buyers is sometimes sold at a high initial price to take advantage of the situation known as *market skimming*.

Apart from what has been stated above; there are managers who want to avert risk by following safe-pricing policies. There are some others who love to take risk, follow unorthodox pricing policies. Some managers follow old techniques of determining prices. All these peculiarities can be seen in the manufacturing unit.

Role of Costing in Pricing

While determining the prices of the product, the importance of cost cannot be ignored. They add some percentages of profit to the average cost and thus determine the price. This gives the impression that the price is determined by cost. But this is clear contradiction of the equilibrium rule of the firm, namely MC = MR. Actually in practical life, costs play a minor role in determining the price. The managers have to see apart from costs, other things such as market situations, demand factors and finally the determining factor, then there will be different prices for the same product since different costs prevail for many firms.

Some mangers take note of market conditions, demand for the product and the cost in determining the price. If the demand for the product is inelastic, the producers may increase the price, even though there is no change in the cost. Sometimes, the prices remain the same even if there is change in cost of production. It is because that the managers are guided by the market situations.

It is seen in the business world that given the price, the producers *'tailor'* their products in accordance with the preference and purchasing power of the buyers. In order to do this tailoring, the producers find out ways for selling the product at a price which gives profit. It has been observed that the producers instead of increasing the price when the costs rise, change the quality of the product. In conclusion, it can be said that if the price is determined on the basis of costs, the firm definitely gets a profit. But we have seen that a good number of firms are being wiped out from the business world, which is entirely due to continued losses. If the price fixed by the firm is lower than the cost, then the firm is sure to incur losses. Whatever may be the other factors, the costs cannot be ignored. It is absolutely necessary that the price should be higher than the cost. At what percentage it should be higher is determined by the other factors such as market situations and the demands.

Yet, costs play decisive roles in determining the products. It prevents the managers to lower the price in the hope of selling more and also it determines whether or not a product is worth including in the product line on the basis of its profitability rate.

Costs no doubt are an important factor in determining the price. Among the several types of costs, there is a question to be answered here as to which type of cost the managers have to cover. In the case of short periods, if the firms cover all the variable costs, it is sufficient. Short period is so small a period that the firm should not think of covering the fixed costs. While in the long run, the firm must not only cover all costs but costs should also earn a target rate of profits.

Elasticity of Demand

The price elasticity of demand plays equally an important role in pricing of a product. If the demand for the product is inelastic, the firms can increase the price and earn a target profit. If the firm, with a view to increase scales, reduces the price, the result will be utterly defeating. This is because quantity demanded of inelastic product remains the same after price reduction.

When the demand for the product is elastic, a fall in the price will result in the increase in sales. If the firm rises the price, the sales are sure to fall. The loss of sales is more significant than the benefits of rise in price. The following table explains the effect of change in price when the demand for the product is elastic and inelastic.

If the demand for the product is elastic, the firm should not increase the price. If the demand for the product is inelastic, it can increase the price. According to the above table, the effect of change in price, when the demand is elastic is that sales and profit fall. On the other hand, when the demand is inelastic, the sales fall marginally but profit is more than the normal profit.

Effect of Price Reduction

Price		Product X Elastic Demand	Product Y Inelastic Demand
Initial Price	Rs. 20		
	Units sold	2,000	2,000
	Sales Revenue	Rs. 40,000	Rs. 40,000
	Cost	30,000	30,000
	Profit	Rs. 10,000	Rs. 10,000
Change in price to Rs. 18			
	Units sold	3,100	2,100
	Sales revenue	Rs. 55,000	Rs. 37,800
	Cost	45,000	31,500
	Profit	Rs. 10,800	Rs.6,300

Effect of Increase in Price

Initial price Rs. 20			
	Units sold	2,000	2,000
	Sales Revenue	Rs. 40,000	Rs. 40,000
	Cost	30,000	30,000
	Profit	Rs. 10,000	Rs. 10,000
Change in price to Rs. 22			
	Units sold	1,400	1,900
	Sales sold	Rs. 30,000	Rs. 41,800
	Cost	21,000	28,000
	Profit	Rs. 9,800	Rs. 13,300

Price Forecasting

A manufacturing unit generally comes across some problems regarding the change in prices of raw materials and other factors of production and the prices of finished products. A change in the price of the product may be due to the change in the economic conditions of the country, but at times, prices of certain commodities change even though there is economic stability in the country. Whatever may be the reason for a change in price, the firm must be in a position to foresee these changes in prices, then it will not be possible for it to adjust its prices to cost changes and it may also experience losses. Therefore, the producers and sellers and these persons involved in the commodity markets must make price forecasts if they want to grow in business.

Impact of the Nature of Commodity and its Market

The dealers in products are required to know the nature of the commodity and its market for the forecasting of prices. It is because prices of different commodities fluctuate differently, depending on the demand and supply conditions. McNair and Meriam say that an understanding of supply and demand conditions of the commodities is essential for price forecasting.

The main reason for price fluctuations is the differences in the nature of commodities and their markets. The understanding of the nature of the commodity is necessary in price forecasting. The main things to be known in this context are as follows :

(a) It is necessary to know whether the product is the main one or the byproduct. If it is a byproduct, its supply depends upon the main products. Therefore, a byproduct is linked with the main product and byproducts are not produced for their own sake. For example, the production of oil cake depends upon the production of oil. Therefore, in making the price forecast of a byproduct, the cost aspect need not be taken, because they are products for their own sake. If the supply does not respond to price changes, then prices of the byproducts will automatically fluctuate.

(b) The price forecasting must take into account the changes in the price of the related commodity. For example, the prices of manufactured goods depend upon the current prices of raw materials. If the prices of raw materials rise, the manufactures can forecast the rise of the manufactured goods.

(c) If the supply of a commodity is unpredictable, the price forecasting is uncertain. If there is striking of oil in the Kaveri delta, then the supply can be predictable and price forecasting may also be made with certainty.

(d) The extent of competition in the market also determines the extent to which price forecasting can be successfully made. If there is a dominant firm in the industry, its price policy will become the base for price forecasts. If there is severe competition in the market, the price forecast is not easy.

(e) The price setting of some products is made not only by domestic users but also international users. For example, the prices of some raw materials like rubber are set in the world markets. In such cases, forecasting the prices for domestic raw materials will be very difficult. The prices of minerals and metals generally fall in this category.

(f) If there are tariffs and other barriers for the free flow of international trade, the firm has to take into account the import duties in forecasting the price of internationally traded goods.

(g) The nature of the elasticity of demand is to be understood in forecasting the prices. If the demand for a commodity is elastic, any change in supply does not matter much on the price. If the demand for the commodity is inelastic, the supply of goods will have an impact on its price.

(h) The influence of supply on the price of a product is to be studied in price forecasting. There are many agricultural commodities whose supply depends upon climatic factors. The supply of these commodities cannot be changed because their prices have risen. For such commodities, the price forecaster has to analyse the supply position. In the case of manufactured products, the supply can be adjusted to the demand. The basis of price forecasting for such commodities is the demand.

Importance of data on the Commodity Markets

Commodity data regarding the actual production of the year, the previous year's stocks and the demand for the commodities are all necessary for price forecasting. There are some commodities the demand for which is only seasonal. Therefore, business, firms have to maintain sufficient stocks to meet an increasing demand whenever it arises. In the case of agricultural commodities, it is necessary to maintain sufficient stocks to meet unforeseen situations. While in the case of capital and durable goods, heavy inventory is not necessary. So, seasonal variations have limited impact on price in the case of manufactured articles. Therefore, the maintenance of data is necessary for price forecasts.

Normal stocks

Normal stocks are stocks which are maintained by the businessmen to meet immediate demand. Stocks maintained for three or four weeks are considered normal stocks. These stocks are necessary and would be useful whenever the supply channels experience setbacks. Supposing there is transport bottle-neck owing to floods or strike or transport workers, normal stocks become insufficient and the prices tend to rise. But, it becomes sometimes difficult to quantify normal stocks.

Consumer stocks

Data on commodity stocks are obtained from producers, wholesale dealers, retailers, stockists, etc. But they do not say anything maintained by consumers. Consumers too generally maintain stock of some goods of importance. They maintain a stock of grains of one month's requirements at home. The manufacturers also maintain stocks of raw-materials of two to three weeks of requirements. These stocks also influence price forecasting and hence they should also be taken into consideration.

Seasonal Stock Variations

In the case of agricultural commodities like wheat, millets, pulses, oil seeds, cotton and jute, production is seasonal while consumption is throughout the year and as such the seasonal stock varies. In the harvest season, the stock increases while in the sowing season it diminishes. As such, prices fall during the harvest season, while prices rise during sowing and growing seasons. In the same way, there are commodities, the consumption of which is seasonal while the production goes on throughout the year like woollen cloth. The price variations between the seasonal and non-seasonal stocks depend upon the cost of maintaining the stocks.

Demand and Supply Conditions of Commodities

The knowledge of future demand and supply conditions of the commodities is essential in forecasting of prices. While estimating the demand and supply of commodities prevailing at the time of making pricing forecast, it is also essential to estimate future demand and supply of commodities for a specific period, say three months, six months, one year, etc. If the forecast is being made for six months, then the probable supply and demand conditions during the coming six months have to be estimated carefully.

While making estimates of future demand for commodities, the following factors have to be noted:

(a) The consumption of commodities in the past three or four years has to be obtained, for this would give an idea of future consumption. In the case of durable commodities, past consumption is not a guide. In the case of non-durable commodities, past consumption will be a reliable guide. In the case of durable goods, past consumption is not a guide. In the case of durable goods, low demands in the past often indicates a high demand in the future.

(b) In order to assess the demand for consumption of goods, the purchasing power of the people has to be known. In addition to the purchasing power of the people, the employment situation in the country also must be taken note of. If the disposable income of the people is high, then the demand for consumption of goods will also be high. As regards the industrial commodities, the liquidity position of industrial buyers and the conditions in the capital market have to be studied.

(c) In order to forecast the price of the products, it is necessary to take into consideration, the propensity to consume by the people. It is also necessary to study whether the willingness to buy depends upon the price

or not. If the price of the product is low, the consumers may not buy. Even if the price is high, the consumers may not buy. If the buyers come to know that the prices of the products would come down, they may not be willing to buy at low prices. Thus, willingness to buy has to be intensified in order to induce the consumers to buy the commodities. This is possible only when the employment increases and good payments are made.

While estimating the prospective demand, the forecaster is required to look into the past behaviour of demand, the purchasing power of the people and the propensity to consume.

Prospective Supply

The following factors have to be considered in estimating the prospective supply:

(a) It is necessary to compare the actual production with the productive capacity in the industry in order to assess the excessive capacity. If there is any additional demand for the product, it can be met by using the excessive capacity which can be done at lower costs and such a rise in price can be checked. Therefore, the firm must ascertain any excess capacity in the industry before any forecasting.

(b) The supply of a product always is determined by the price of the product. If some firms are producing the product at higher costs than others, a low price of the product will make those firms to suspend production. As a result of this, the supply of the product falls. The high cost firms compare the price with the variable cost of production. If they find that the price is higher than the variable cost of production, then they start producing and as a result, total supply would again rise.

(c) The production forecasts of agricultural commodities made by the Department of Agriculture and Statistics has an impact on market prices. Good crop reports lead to a decline in price and vice-versa.

Thus, a sound knowledge of supply and demand of product help the forecaster in estimating a realistic price structure.

The Typical Price Changes

Prices of products change, i.e., the rise or fall according to certain situations. The changes in prices over a period of time are due to economic and non-economic factors. The non-economical factors are also called seasonal price fluctuations. The economical factors are *cyclical* changes.

Seasonal Changes

Demand for certain commodities will only be seasonal. For example, umbrellas are required during rainy season. Ice-creams are used only in summer seasons. Woollen clothes are used only in winter. These are seasonal commodities. Fruits of certain types are grown only in certain seasons. Normally in seasons, when the supply is more than the demand, price falls. Or it may also be possible that the demand may rise during the seasons and consequently, the prices may also rise. These fluctuations are common in agricultural commodities where they cannot be stored for longer periods. In the case of manufactured articles, seasonal variations have a limited impact on prices for they can be stored.

Cyclical Changes

During business cycles, prices of all commodities fluctuate. In the boom period, prices of all commodities rise very significantly, while during the period of depression, prices of manufactured articles, shares and stocks fall more steeply than agricultural commodities. During the periods of business cycles, prices fluctuate, but the intensity of fluctuations differ between products. If the supply of the products cannot be adjusted to demand, the prices fluctuate violently. Thus, in order to make reliable forecasts, it is necessary to study the nature of economic conditions prevailing at a period.

Further, the prices of certain products fluctuate with products in the same way but the prices of some of the products fluctuate earlier or later than for the products in the economy. In other words, some products are early movers while some others are late movers. While making price forecasts, the knowledge of fluctuations of general economic conditions and their impact on the economic scene is quite useful.

Questions

1. What is meant by 'Pricing policy'.
2. What are the objectives of pricing of a product.
3. What is the utility of cost-plus pricing.
4. What are the advantages and disadvantages of marginal cost pricing.
5. What do you mean by 'transfer pricing'?. How is transfer price determined.
6. Explain the pricing policies of a life cycle of a product.
7. What are the unique problems in multi-product pricing.
8. Distinguish between skimming price and penetration pricing.
9. What is product line pricing. What is peak load pricing.
10. What are the general considerations of the Pricing Policy.
11. Describe the factors which help price forecasting.
12. Discuss the problems that the management faces while pricing of new products.

13. Comment on the various types of discounts and the effects of each on sales.
14. Explain the pricing approaches in the following cases :
    i. When products differ in size.
    ii. When order has been placed for a specific design of a product
    iii. When products are complementary.
15. How do you determine rent on an equipment given on lease.
16. Define the following:
    i. FOB Pricing
    ii. Postage stamp pricing
    iii. Cyclical pricing
    iv. Resale price maintenance
    v. Penetration price
    vi. Administered prices.

❖✻❖✻❖

CHAPTER 14

PROFIT MANAGEMENT

NATURE OF PROFIT

Profit is the reward of the entrepreneur rather than on account of the entrepreneurial function. Profit differs from the returns on other factors of production such as land, labour and capital. Profit is a residual income and not contractual income. Land, labour and capital are used in contracts where they receive pre-determined income, whereas profit is the amount of money received by the firm after meeting all costs and contractual payments. A company may receive higher profits or no profits, but it is not so in the case of land, labour and capital.

In ordinary language, the term *'profit'* is understood as an excess of income over costs. But in economics, profit is regarded as a reward for entrepreneurial function of risk-management and better management. The entrepreneur earns profit because he manages risk for his price-output policies which may prove to be incorrect in view of the future business movements. Schumpeter has assigned to the entrepreneur the role of an innovator and profits as a reward for his introducing innovations. Prof. F. H Knight has emphasised the uncertainty in the economy as a factor which gives rise to profits and bearing uncertainty is the task of the entrepreneur. There are some economists who have accounted profits as non - functional income. J. M. Keynes has expressed the view that profits resulted from the favourable movements of general price level. If the general price level rises, with the costs being unchanged, then the businessman earns profits. Professors Joan Robinson, E. H. Chamberlin and M. Kalecki have associated profits with imperfect profits, competition and monopoly. According to them, greater the degree of monopoly power , greater is the profit. As a matter of fact, profits arise from all these sources. Prof. B. S. Keinstead observed that profits originate from monopsoly successful innovations and a correct estimate of the uncertain future. He has said that, 'Profits may come to exist as a result of monopoly or monopsony, as a reward for innovation, as a reward for the correct estimate of uncertain factors, either particular to the industry or general to the whole economy.'

It is necessary to understand that profits are residual incomes left after the payment of contractual rewards to the other factors of production. The entrepreneur cannot undertake the production of any commodity without using the factor inputs such as land, labour and capital. He pays rent to the land, wages to the workers and interests to the capital. In fact, the entrepreneur makes payment to these factors well in advance of the realisation of the value of the output. What is left after paying contractual rent to land, wages to workers and interest to the capital borrowed, is called *profits*. The profits are non-contractual income and therefore they may be negative or positive, whereas the interest is always positive. It should be noted that pure profits of the entrepreneur are found by substracting from the gross residual income the imputed values of rent and interest on the self-owned land and capital employed by the entrepreneur and also the imputed wages for his work of routine management. Business profits are, therefore, specially contingent upon the successful management of risks. Modern industry is faced with a number of uncertainties. The entrepreneur receives a reward for combining the factors of the production to meet economic needs of the people faced with various uncertainties. He gets profits because he selects the risks and manages them skilfully.

Analysis of Gross Profits

Generally, profits refer to gross profits. Gross profits stand for the total earnings of the entrepreneur. It is a mixture composed of several elements. From the total receipts of business must be taken out the monies paid to various factors of production engaged on a contract basis. Thus, the rent, wages and interests have to be deducted out of the total earnings of the entrepreneur. Gross profits include the following items :

(a) Interest on entrepreneur's own capital.
(b) Rent of land owned by the entrepreneur.
(c) Entrepreneur's wages of management.
(d) Reward for the risk taken by the entrepreneur.
(e) Gains as a superior bargainer.
(f) Monopoly gains and windfall profits.

Net Profit

Net profit is the pure profit which is the amount that accrues to the entrepreneur for bearing the risk. It is inseparable from all businesses under a system in which production is done in the anticipation of demand. Pure profit is that profit made exclusively for bearing risks. Net profit is the income received by the entrepreneur after all the factors of production are paid off. The concepts of gross profit and net profit can be analysed as follows :

Gross profit : Total Revenue – Total explicit cost
(cost incurred in hiring factors of production)

Net profit : Total gross profit – Total explicit cost plus total implicit cost.
(cost for his own labour and capital)

The following example makes the above concept clear.

Total revenue of a company manufacturing cloth = Rs. 10 lakhs.

The explicit cost incurred for production are :

(a) Rent of factory premises	=	Rs. 50,000
(b) Interest on bank loans	=	50,000
(c) Wages and salaries	=	2,50,000
(d) Raw-materials	=	2,50,000
Total explicit cost or paid cost :		6,00,000

The implicit cost of the firm :

(a) Wages for the personal labour of the entrepreneur	60,000
(b) Interest on his own capital	10,000
(c) Depreciation of machinery and equipment	50,000
(d) Taxes paid to the Government	1,25,000
Total implicit cost	2,45,000

Now, 1) Gross profit = Total Revenue - Total explicit cost.
Rs. 10,00,000 - Rs. 6,00,000
= Rs. 4,00,000

2) Net profit = Gross profit - Implicit costs
Rs. 4,00,000 -Rs.2,45,000
= Rs.1.55.000

In a big company, all costs are explicit costs. The large firm calculates gross profit by taking difference between total revenue and total cost. Then the depreciation and taxes paid are deducted from the gross profit to calculate net profit.

The meaning of net profit is shown more clearly though the following chart :

Net Profits

1. Payments for risk and uncertainty
2. Reward for bargaining ability
3. Reward for innovations
4. Monopoly gains
5. Chance gains

Payment for Risk and Uncertainty

When an entrepreneur starts a business, he takes certain risks. The most important risk is that of production in anticipation of demand. Sometimes, the product does not meet the requirements of consumers, the sales are bound to fall and he may incur losses. If the sales rise more than his expectation, he may get profits. For risk bearing, he is rewarded. This reward is included in net profit.

Reward for Bargaining Ability

The entrepreneur having good bargaining power, purchases raw materials at reasonable prices. He makes suitable arrangements to store the raw materials properly. By proper inventory building, he maintains the supply of raw materials as regular. He hires labour at normal wages and borrows working capital at reasonable rates of interests. Thus, he controls explicit costs. It means that the bargaining ability of entrepreneur brings good net profit.

Reward for Innovations

Entrepreneurs are always looking for some good changes. Whenever there is an invention or an improvement, he will be the first person to put it into reality. He may discover a new source for his raw-materials or he may explore a new market for his profit. All these are innovations. As a reward for this, he gets net profit.

Monopoly Gains

When an entrepreneur captures the entire market by eliminating competition, he gets monopoly profit. When there is no competition, he becomes a monopolist. By increasing the price, he sells the product for which there is no substitute. Thus, he gets more profit. This is called *monopoly* gain.

Chance Gains

Sometimes an entrepreneur gets windfall profits. This is due to the sudden rise in prices. This is also included under net profit.

FUNCTIONS OF PROFIT

Profit is an essential factor for capital formation. Whenever a firm gets profit continuously over a long period, its economic strength increases. The entrepreneur will be in a position to make great improvements of his business. This will be an incentive for hard work and innovation. Peter Drucker says that profits serve the following objectives of the business. Profit reflects the level of performance of the firm. It indicates the soundness of the business. A higher profit suggests tat the firm is being managed efficiently. Profit is a true measure of performance. It shows that the organisation is in sound financial condition.

It serves as a premium which covers the costs of business firm. Profits indicate the economic strength of business. The company can stay on in business and produce the product continously. Profit is thus stated as the cost of being and staying in business. The management of a company is required to provide for these costs by earning sufficient profit.

Ensuring of the supply of capital is the most important function of profit. A certain percentage of net profit is set apart for innovation, better management and modernisation or the renovation of business.

The fundamental objective of a firm is to ensure its own survival. In order to survive, it should earn a substantial profit. When a firm is making good profits, it can make changes whenever required. It can plan for reasonable growth. It is stated that profits are a natural concomitant of the growth of business overtime. In fact, profits are essential as a means to an end. They are not an end in themselves although essential for the continuity and growth of the firm.

Accounting Profit and Economic Profit

Accounting profit is defined as the revenue realised in a given period after providing for expenses incurred during the production of a commodity. Accounting profit is also called *Residual Profit.* For the business firm accounting profit is very important. In the balance sheet of a firm, accounting profit occupies an important place. The accountant deducts explicit costs from the revenue in order to determine profit. But this attitude does not satisfy the economist. The economists say that both explicit and imputed costs (i.e., the cost that would have been incurred in the absence of self owned factors) are to be deducted from the total revenue to determine economic profits. The entrepreneur's wages, interests on his own capital, rent for the use of his own premises are to be taken into consideration in calculating economic profits. Thus, the profit arrived at after deducting both explicit and imputed costs may be called *economic profit.* From the managerial point of view, economic profit is very important because this alone shows the viability of a firm. A firm may show accounting profit but it may incur economic losses. Such a firm cannot be considered viable.

Theories of Profit

Several economists have contributed significantly for the development of the theories of profit. Prof. F. H. Knight pointed out that, 'perhaps no term or concept in economic discussion is used with a more bewildering variety of well established meaning than profit.' According to Prof. Knight, profit is the reward for uncertainty bearing. Even before Knight. F. B. Hawley and A. C. Pigon had pointed out that entrepreneurs earn profits, because they have to bear risks in business. Prof. F. Walker, the American economist developed the rent theory of profit originally propounded by Senior and J. S. Mill Prof. Taussig propounded wage theory of profit. Prof. Clark developed the dynamic theory of profit. Prof . F. Hawley, an eminent American economist, advocated risk theory of profit. Modern economists like Chapman, Stonier and Hague applied marginal productivity theory for determining profits. Thus, there are many theories of profit. All these theories individually advocate one aspect of entrepreneurial functions for the emergence of profit. But, it is a fact that profits arise because of all the functions of the entrepreneur. Let us study some of theories briefly:

Profit as Rent of Ability

This theory was originally propounded by N. W. Senior and J. S. Mill, the noted English economists. But Prof. F. A. Walker fully developed the rent theory. Walker pointed out that different pieces of land earn rent in accordance with their fertility. In the same way, able entrepreneurs earn more profit than normal entrepreneurs. Walker regards profits as the rent of ability. He states that just as there are different grades of land based on fertility, there are different grades of entrepreneurs. Those firms which are managed by marginal entrepreneurs earn no profit. Their revenue is equal to the cost of production. Such firms earn no loss and no profit. These firms are called firms managed by marginal entrepreneurs. But there are entrepreneurs who are very efficient and bright, who command extraordinary organising ability. The case of such firms is similar to that of best grade lands. Such firms earn more profits than mediocre firms. Profits are thus like rent and like rent they do not enter into price. Profits are a surplus between firms managed by the two grades of entrepreneurs.

Wages of management are not profits and the marginal entrepreneur earns the wages of management. Wages of management have to be paid because of maintaining the given supply of entrepreneurs. Such wages enter into cost of production and hence price. But profit is a surplus which arises between firms managed by entrepreneurs with different abilities. Hence this theory is called *rent theory* of profit.

Criticism

Rent theory of profits suffers from the same weakness as Ricardo's theory of rent. Rent and profits are not similar, but Prof. Walker considered them as similar. Critics have shown that rent and profits are two different things. Rent is positive but it is not negative. In the case of profit, it is both negative and positive. An entrepreneur may earn losses also.

Secondly, this theory does not explain the real nature of profit. It merely provides as best a measure of profit.

Thirdly, profits according to Walker, are earned by able entrepreneurs. But this way of argument has been challenged by many economists. They say, that even marginal entrepreneurs earn profit, because profit is earned due to risk taking and uncertainty bearing.

It is wrong to say that profits do not enter into price. They may not enter in the short period, but they must be covered by price in the long run. In fact, normal profit enters into cost. If the entrepreneur does not earn normal profit, he will have to close down the production. Therefore, profits enter into price in the long run.

Fourthly, the concept of the marginal entrepreneur brought about by Walker is absurd. According to Walker, marginal entrepreneurs are those who earn no profit. Since the concept of no rent land does not exist, the concept of no profit entrepreneur also does not exist. If the entrepreneur does not profit, he ceases to be called an entrepreneur.

Fifthly, rent is a fixed item and it is known as surplus but in the case of profit, it is unknown. An entrepreneur does not know whether he earns profit or not. Profit is due to the uncertainty of future and also due to innovations. From the above discussion, it can be concluded that Walker's theory of profit does not explain scientifically the causes for the emergence of profit.

Dynamic Theory of Profit

This theory is associated with the name of the American economist J. B. Clark, who says that in a static world, nothing changes. It means that the size of the population, the amount of capital, the quantity and quality of human wants, the methods of production, technical knowledge, the organisation of business, etc. remain the same. In such an economy, economic activities of the previous year are simply repeated in the current year. In a static economic world, demand and supply remain unchanged. The prices paid to the factors of production are equal to marginal productivity and there will not be profits to the entrepreneur. In a static society, the incomes, tastes and fashions of the people remain unchanged. Prof. Knight comments, 'In a static state, each factor secures what it produces, since cost and selling prices are always equal, there can be no profits beyond wages for the routine work of supervision. In a stationary state, everything is known and knowable. There is no risk and no uncertainty and hence no profits.'

Profits arise when selling prices of the goods exceed their cost of production. In a competitive long term equilibrium, price equals average cost of production (including normal profits, which are in fact wages for routine supervision and management) and therefore no profits are made. If no changes either in the conditions of demand or in the conditions of supply occur, competitive equilibrium will persist and therefore no profits will be earned by the entrepreneur.

Having explained the conditions of a stationary state, Prof. Clark now explains the characteristics of a dynamic economy. He says, 'We are not living in a stationary state. Ours is a dynamic world and some changes are taking place constantly in our state. A clever entrepreneur sees the change, arranges the production in such a manner that he will get profit. Either by invention or otherwise, he lowers the cost and makes profit. In the changing world, opportunities for the clever entrepreneurs are immense and by turning the situation in their favour, make profit. It is only because the world is dynamic, that it is possible for them to make profits.'

J. B. Clark mentions five types of changes that occur in a dynamic economy which give rise to profit. These five changes are changes in the quantity and quality of human wants, changes in the methods and techniques of production, changes in the amount of capital and changes in the forms of business organisation. These changes are constantly taking place and bring about a divergence between price and cost and thereby rise to profits, positive or negative. If the demand for products increase due to the increase in income, change in tastes of fashions and preferences, the price of production will rise and if the cost of production remains the same, profits would accrue to the entrepreneurs. If the entrepreneurs adopt new techniques of production, the cost may go down. Discovery of new raw-material may result in costs going down. If prices remain constant or do not fall, the firms would receive profits.

Apart from the above changes mentioned by Clark, economists have said that there are other changes which occur in the economy. These changes are called *innovation* and *exogeneous* changes. Innovations are introduced by entrepreneurs themselves. The entrepreneurs earn larger profits whenever they introduce innovations. These innovations will reduce the cost of production or increase in the supply of goods. The entrepreneurs earn large profits whenever innovations are successful. When these innovations are spread out, some new firms come into existence and old firms adopt them. Consequently, more output is produced. This results in the fall of prices, increase in demand, more sales and more profits. But new innovations are being continuously introduced by the entrepreneurs and profits continue to arrive out of them.

Exogeneous changes arise whenever changes external to firms or industries take place in the economy. These changes affect all firms or all industries in the economy. For example, war may break out or inflation or deflation may occur resulting in the rise or fall in prices, changes in monetary and fiscal policies may take place. These will affect production, income and consumption. All these changes affect either the cost or demand of the products and give rise to profits, positive or negative as the case may be.

Thus, profits arise as a result of changes. But Professor Knight says, to 'Dynamic changes give rise to a peculiar form of income in so far as the changes and their consequences are unpredictable in character. It cannot then be the change which is the cause of profits, since if the law of change is known, as in fact is largely the case, no profits can arise. The connection between change and profits is certain and always indirect. Change may cause a situation, out of which profit will be made, if it brings about ignorance of the future'. Professor Knight further added that, only unpredictable, unforeseen changes and uncertainty about the future, give rise to profit. He does not recognise dynamic changes as the cause of profit. It may be pointed out that if there is no change, there will be no uncertainty about the future and therefore no profits. Thus, the factor of change is fundamental in bringing profits into existence. Therefore, in an economy where nothing changes, there can be no profits, there is no uncertainty about the future and so there are no risks and no profits.

Innovation Theory of Profits

Professor Joseph Schumpeter, an American economist, propounded the theory of innovation as the cause of profit. Successful innovations like important dynamic changes have been upheld by Professor J. B. Clark. But Schumpeter has singled out the importance of innovation for the emergence of profits. In fact, innovations are possible only in dynamic economies. Schumpeter added that the main function of the entrepreneur is to introduce innovations in the economy. Profits are reward for performing this function. Now, what is innovation, has a very wide meaning. An innovation means an application of inventions. Any new policy adopted by an entrepreneur either to increase output or increase the demand for the product is called *innovations*. According to Schumpeter, discovery of raw-material or new technique of productions, resulting in lowering the cost of production or improving the quality of the product is innovation. He classifies innovations into two categories.

The first type of innovations are those which reduce the cost of production, in other words, which change the production function. In the first type are included the introduction of a new machinery, new and cheaper techniques or processes of production, exploitation of a new source of raw-material, a new and better method of organising the finance. The second type of innovations are those which increase the demand for the product, in other words, which change the demand or utility functions. In this category are included the introduction of a new product, a new variety or design of the product, a new and superior method of advertisement, discovery of new markets, etc. If these innovations are successful, that is, if it achieves its aim of either reducing the cost of production or enhancing the demand for the product, it will give rise to profits. Profit emerges because of successful innovations. If the cost of production falls owing to innovation, the price of the product falls and thereby the entrepreneur will be in a position to sell more. Schumpeter makes it very clear that profits accrue not to him who introduces it. Whenever any new innovation is contemplated to be introduced, it always calls for the new combination of factors or allocation of resources.

The profits which arise as a result of innovation are not permanent. They are temporary and tend to be competed away as others imitate or adopt it. When an innovation is going to be copied by other rival firms, they either cease to be innovations or lose their novelty. When an entrepreneur introduces a new invention, he is in a monopoly position first, for a new innovation is confined to him only or when it is patented, the original innovator will enjoy it. But in a dynamic world, the superior entrepreneurs continue to make innovations and enjoy the profits thereof. When after sometime, others adopt it by making suitable improvements, then profits to the original innovator would be annihilated. But, Professor Stigler observes, 'these profits may exist for a considerable time, because of the ignorance of other firms. More important, the successful innovator can continuously seek new disequilibrium profits, since the horizon of conceivable innovations is unlimited.'

It should be noted here that profits are both the cause and effect of innovations. Profits serve as a necessary incentive for making innovations. Hence, profits are a cause of innovations. Since innovations result in profits, profits are the effect of innovations.

Criticism

Schumpeter's innovation theory is also subject to criticism by many economists. Schumpeter restricts the function of the entrepreneur to that of innovation only. But innovation is not the only function but it is one of the functions of the entrepreneur. He does not mention in his theory the important facts like risk taking and uncertainty bearing for the emergence for profit. Another deficiency in this theory is that profits are only of short period in nature. But in fact, if the profits are temporary, no entrepreneur will stick to the production process. Therefore, it can be concluded that innovation theory is only partially true. However, Schumpeter has upheld the role of an entrepreneur in introducing innovation in getting profits.

Hawley's Risk Theory of Profits

In the modern industrial system, businessmen invariably take risk in business. The greater the risk, the higher is the profit, which induces the business people to start business. Professors A. C. Pigon and F. W. Hawley have said the entrepreneurs earn profits, because they bear risk in the industry. Hawley says that profits are the reward for risks and responsibilities that the entrepreneur subjects himself to it. Drucker has mentioned four kinds of risks, replacement, proper rise, uncertainty and obsolescence. Replacement is called depreciation, which is calculable, but it becomes the item of cost. Risk of marketability of the product and uncertainty are not costs but are charges against profits. They may be called cost of staying in business. Physical risks like fire and accidents can be provided against by insurance and therefore are included in the costs. There are certain risks which cannot be foreseen. It is for undertaking these risks, which cannot be foreseen, that the entrepreneur is rewarded by profits.

Such unforeseen risks are inflation, deflation, changes in income, tastes of the people, etc. No insurance company will pay compensation for these risks. If there is any loss, the entrepreneur will have to bear it. If there is any profit, he will be very happy. This is the effect of risk taking. Therefore, the entrepreneur is rewarded in the form of profit for risk taking.

Criticism

This theory considers profit as a reward for taking risks in any business venture. But critics point out that high profits made by the entrepreneur cannot be attributed to the element of risk. They are not at any rate in proportion to the risk undertaken. On the contrary, Carver says that profits arise not because of risks undertaken, but because of reducing them. In other words, it is said that profits are made not because of risks which are borne but because of risks which are avoided. Prof. Knight has added that profits arise not due to all risks but they are only for unforeseen risks.

Thus, Hawley's risk theory is partially valid for risk taking in a fundamental function of the entrepreneur for which reward is profit.

Uncertainty Bearing Theory

Of all the theories of profits, the theory propounded by Professor Knight is the most striking for he upholds uncertainty bearing the main cause for the emergence of profit. In his book *'Risk Uncertainty and Profit'*, he has said that there is intense relation between uncertainty and profit. He has elaborately discussed the distinction between risk and uncertainty and predictable and unpredictable changes. According to him, dynamic changes give rise to profits in so far as changes and their consequences are unpredictable in character. He adds that, only those changes which cannot be predictable give rise to profits and subsequently, profits arise because of uncertainty of the future. If the future conditions are foreknown in the present, the entrepreneurs make adjustments and see that the prices are equal to costs. But entrepreneurs are ignorant about the future and produce under the conditions of uncertainty and thus earn profits. In the modern period, entrepreneurs are undertaking and thus earn profits. In modern period, entrepreneurs are undertaking production under the conditions of uncertainty. In advance, they have to make estimates of the future demand for the product and other factors which affect price and cost. The entrepreneurs arrange for the supplies of factors of production at fixed prices in advance itself. They realise the value of the output after it has been brought to the market for sale. Between the time of contract for the supply of factors and realisation of the sale producers, many changes may take place which are either positive or negative. That is, uncertainty about the future conditions of demand and supply give rise to profit which are either positive and negative. If the entrepreneurs make correct anticipations, they get positive profit, while the anticipation proves to be incorrect and they have to suffer losses. Thus, profit is a residual and on-contractual income which accrues to entrepreneurs because of the fact of uncertainty.

The next important aspect in the theory is the question of what changes cause uncertainty. As has been said above, there are two types of changes taking place and are responsible for the conditions of uncertainty. First type of change that causes disturbances is due to innovations (for example, introduction of a new product and a cheaper method of production). These innovations not only create uncertainty for the rivals who are affected by them, but they also involve uncertainty for the entrepreneur who introduces them, for one cannot be certain whether a particular innovation is successful or not.

The second type of changes which causes uncertainty are those which are external to firms and industries. These changes are changes in the fashions and tastes of the people, changes in government policies and laws, especially taxation, wage and labour policies and laws, movements of prices as a result inflation and deflation, change in the incomes of the people changes in production technology, etc. All these changes cause uncertainty and bring profits-positive or negative into existence. Thus, it can be concluded that entrepreneurs who work under the conditions of uncertainty bear an uncertainty and earn profits.

In this connection, Professor Knight makes a distinction between insurable risk and non-insurable risk. Because of the changes which are continuously occurring, entrepreneurs face some risks. But all risks do not cause uncertainty and give rise to profits. It is only non-insurable risks that cause uncertainty and entrepreneurs earn profit for bearing these risks. The question that arises is to distinguish between insurable and non-insurable risks. The entrepreneurs face risks of fire, theft, accident, etc. which cause them huge losses but they are insurable risks which means the loss is covered by the insurance company. The insurance premium is included in the cost of production. In the case of insurance risk, uncertainty does not arise and therefore such risks do not give rise to profit.

But there are risks which cannot be insured and therefore, these risks have to borne by the entrepreneurs themselves. The non-insurable risks relate to the outcomes of price and output decisions to be taken by the entrepreneurs. Whether it will pay them to increase the output, reduce output and what will be the outcome in terms of profit or loss, etc. have to be decided. And also, they have to decide whether to increase the price or decrease the price and on such a price will there be profit or not. For taking all these decisions, he has to guess about demand and cost conditions and there is always risk of suffering losses as a result of decisions. No insurance company will pay compensation against such losses. It is therefore clear that non-insurable risks which cause uncertainty and these alone cause profit. Knight thus says, 'It is uncertainty distinguished from insurance risk that from effectively gives rise to the entrepreneurial form of organisation and to the much condemned 'profit' is an income form.'

Criticism

The uncertainty bearing theory has been criticised by many economists on the following grounds :

(i) Uncertainty is not the only factor that limits the supply of entrepreneurs. Lack of funds, lack of opportunities and the presence of economic friction are some of the factors which restrict the supply of entrepreneurs.

(ii) Uncertainty bearing is not the only function of the entrepreneur. His main functions are initiating production, coordinating and factors arranging the sales of the product for which he gets profit.

(iii) Uncertainty bearing cannot be considered as a factor of production. It is an element of real costs which means exertion, abstinence, sacrifice, etc. as distinguished from money costs.

(iv) In recent years, managerial economists have stressed on the importance of better management. According to them, uncertainty bearing and risk taking have no relevance. Able managers have to reduce uncertainties to the barest minimum. Profit is the result of good performance.

All these theories of profit emphasise only one aspect of the entrepreneural functions. In fact, profit arises due to the overall performance of the entrepreneurs. Professor Samuelson aptly sums up 'Profits are the bait, the carrots dangled before us enterprising donkeys. Losses are our penalty kicks. Profits go to those who have been efficient in the past, efficient in making things, in selling things and in foreseeing things. Through profits, the society is giving the command over new ventures to those who have piled up a record of success.' Again, the 'profits are the report card of past' the incentive gold star for the future and also grubstake for new ventures.'

Profit Objectives

Modern business firms are always profit oriented. In fact, profit seeking is the motive stressed upon by all businessmen. The success of the enterprise depends upon profit making. The volume of profit made [illegible] regarded as the primary measure of success.

In economic theory, we find that the fundamental aim of any business is to maximise profits. Doubts have been raised in recent years about whether profit maximisation is the only motive which governs the behaviour of the rational entrepreneur or whether it is the best policy for him. This assumption does not always hold good. Profit is no doubt necessary without which the economy cannot attain stable growth. Keeping profit in view, the modern business people have placed other objectives in the forefront.

(a) Profit is a means to an end, the end being growth and development both in micro and macro economic terms.

(b) Attainment of leadership in the industry, for which a satisfactory level of profit consistent with the capital invested, work force employed, volume of output produced, etc.

(c) Facing potential competition and restricting the new entries. If a firm or two or three firms are earning supernormal profits or large profits, rivals may enter into the industry and compete with the existing firms. Therefore, reasonable profit which guarantees their survival and growth is sufficient. According to Joel Dean, 'Competitors can invade the market as soon as they discover its profitability and find ways to shift the patents and make necessary changes in design, technique, etc.'

(d) Preventing government interference is another objective in seeking reasonable profits. If the government comes to know that the firms are earning huge returns, they may resort to high taxation. Again, high profits may be taken as an index to monopoly power and to prevent the growth of monopolies, the government interference through price control, profit regulation, etc. will be called for.

(e) Maintaining consumer's good-will is another objective of the modern business for which the firms have to restrict the profit. By keeping low profits, the firms may seek the goodwill of the consumers. Consumer goodwill is valued so much in these days that the firms are satisfied with small profit. In his address to the General Body of ITC., Mr. Huskar said, 'We are concerned with out ultimate customers, who are paramount, who are final judges of the quality of the company's products who must be given what they want, must be continually satisfied and must be provided the very best value for their money.' For this purpose, the firms would like to keep a low profit margin.

(f) Whenever trade unions come to know that the firms are declaring higher dividends to the shareholders, they demand higher wages, bonus, etc. To avoid such happenings and to maintain cordial industrial relations, the firms keep the profit margin at a reasonable level. This is referred to as 'Wage consideration'.

(g) Liquidity preference means maintaining comfortable case positions to meet the day-to-day transactions. The managements, in order to give greater importance to financial soundness, keep less profit and maintain high cash levels.

(h) Avoiding risk involves keeping the profit margin at a reasonable level. Risk element is high under profit maximisation. To minimise risk, it is better to keep the level reasonable. It is worth seeing what Ford, the ace manufacturer of cars, says in this connection. Ford looked upon profits as a part of the game. He thought his main aim was to provide the large volume of employment at the highest possible wages and sell the car at the lowest possible price. Ford said, 'that his company was organised to do as much good as we can everywhere and for everybody concerned. To make money and use it, give employment and send out the car where people can use it.' This sums up the objective of great companies.

Maximising long run profits or a steady flow of profits for a long time has been highly criticised by many managerial economists. As Peter Drucker says, it is the first duty to survive. Therefore, the guiding principles of business economies is not maximisation of profit, but it is the avoidance of loss. Professor Galbraith has said, 'Self interest will lead the techno-structure to prevention of loss ahead of maximum returns for loss can destroy techno-structure while high revenues accrue to others.'

Profit Maximisation Vs Security Motive

The concept of profit maximisation has been subject to lot of criticism. Classical economists held that the entrepreneurs' attempt to maximising profits is a rational behaviour. Doubts have been raised by some economists in recent years about whether profit maximisation is the only motive of the entrepreneur.

It has been held that in deciding about his price and output policy, the entrepreneur does not aim at maximising profits at a particular point of time, instead, he tries to have a steady flow of profit for a long time. In other words, the entrepreneur wants secured profits in order to continue in manufacture of products. Professor Rothschild observes, 'Profit maximisation has until now served as the wonderful master key that opened all doors leading to an understanding of the behaviour of the entrepreneur. It was always realised that family pride, moral and ethical considerations, poor intelligence and similar factors may modify the results built on the maximum profits assumption, but it was rightly assumed that these disturbing phenomena are sufficiently exceptional to justify their exclusion from the main body of price theory. But there is another motive which cannot be so lightly dismissed and which is probably a similar order of magnitude as the desire for maximum profits, namely the desire for secure profits.'

According to Professor Rothschild, the assumption of profit maximisation is no doubt valid to the situation of perfect competition or monopolistic competition. Under monopolistic condition, the aim of the firm is to secure monopoly profits. In the case of oligopoly, Rothschild says that the assumption of profit maximising is not sufficient. Here is both the desire for achieving a secure position as well as the power to act on his desire.

Prof. Baumoul's Sales Maximisation Hypothesis

After challenging the assumption of profit maximisation, Professor Baumol has put forth maximisation of sales as the ultimate objective of the firm. He says that the firm tries to promote sales not merely as a means to further its other objectives, namely operational efficiency and profits, but for the businessman, 'sales have become an end of themselves.' Therefore, he declared that sales maximisation is a valid assumption about the behaviour of the firm.

He said, while maximising sales, the businessmen will not disregard costs incurred on output and profits to be made. If the sales of the company increases, it then means that the businessmen are not only covering costs but also making a usual rate of return on the investment. If the management were to get the reasonable profit, they would be satisfied. They do not insist more. He further adds that, 'so long as profits are high enough to keep stock-holders satisfied and contribute adequately to the financing of the growth of the company, and the management will bend its efforts to the augmentation of sales revenues rather than to further increase in profits.'

Satisfaction or Utility Maximisation

Baumol's theory of sales maximisation as a rational behaviour of the entrepreneur is considered as an alternative to the theory of profits maximisation. Under this contention, the entrepreneurs produce more and sell the product at a lower price which will come near to the welfare maximisation of the consumers. Another alternative to the theory of profit maximisation is that of utility maximisation propounded by economists like Benjamin Higgins, Mekin Reder and Tibor Scitovsky. If the entrepreneur is supposed to maximise his satisfaction, then it is not only the satisfaction which he gets from material goods which are obtained with the money profits earned from putting in entrepreneurial activity, but also the satisfaction which he obtains from leisure at his dispensation. Professor Hicks says that leisure or quiet life is an essential ingredient of an individual's welfare. But more work put in by the entrepreneur, the less leisure he will be able to enjoy.

It is said that the entrepreneur would get maximum satisfaction where his net profit is optimum.

Donaldson and Lorsch said that career managers prefer policies that favour long term stability and growth of their firms which are possible only when they get maximum current profits. Top managers seek the maximisation of wealth, the more the wealth, the greater the assurance of the means of survival.

PROFIT POLICY

It is generally held that the main motive of the businessman is to make profits. The amount of profit that a firm makes show its efficiency. The profit that a firm makes should not be at the point of exploitation of consumers. It is also believed that the firm while making maximum profits, should also satisfy the requirements of the consumers. In the modern period, the concept of social obligations has been thrust upon the businessmen and as such they have to sell the product at a reasonably low price. The firms should earn profits for their own survival and growth. The firms should generate sufficient surplus for introducing modernisation. All these aims constitute the profit policy.

Aims of Profit Policy

The businessman seeks to pursue many objectives. No doubt profit making is the main objective, yet it is not the only objective. A firm makes profit provided, the product produced by it satisfies the consumers, that the firm can sell more and make more profits. If it makes sufficient profits, the firm can give good dividends to the shareholders, attractive salaries to the workers etc. The firm can fix a target rate for profits. Target rate of return is that rate which helps the firm to mobilise the capital required by the business. If there is any need to issue fresh equity capital, it should show to the public that it is getting adequate returns. The adequate rate is also the rate of profit earned by other companies in the same locality.

There is a problem in determining the criteria of rate of return. Several criteria have been stated to determine the suitable rate of return. They are :

(a) Competitive rate of profit is that profit which is closely related to the rate of profits of similar firms. It should be slightly different from the size of profit of other companies.

(b) Historical rate of profit is the rate of profit determined on the basis of past earnings. It should be sufficient to attract fresh capital. The firm has to examine the historical rate of profit on equity capital in the past dividends to shareholders and the degree of competitive men in the market.

(c) The rate of return on investments should protect the interest of present shareholders, so that the firm does not face any problems in raising fresh share capital.

(d) The rate of profit should be such that, there is a surplus after paying the dividends to the shareholders with a view to provide funds for further development.

In quantitative terms, the rate of profit should be 10 and 15 per cent after taxes. In the case of industries with heavy capital investment, a moderate rate of return of eight per cent is recognised as the adequate rate of profit. In India, majority of the firms keep a 12 per cent post-tax return on net worth.

The question of return in a certain percentage of capital employed is a controversial subject. Some businessmen associate this concept with capital and risks involved. In industries where there is great risk, they keep a high percentage of return. Thus, the concept of reasonable rate of returns is very difficult to define. A rate of return beyond 15 per cent of the total capital employed is considered to be optimum. Most of the professional managers of big companies achieve this objective by means of superior management design, research and marketing. They do not resort to price increase with a view to get the higher rate of returns.

Consideration of Other Objectives

The managers of most of the companies insist on adequate profit as a necessary means to achieve other objectives including social and moral objectives. Profit making is no doubt necessary. In addition to adequate profit, the firms often pursue multiple and even contradictory goals. Cyert and March in their book *'Behavioural Theory of Firms'* have discussed five aims which represent the main operative organisational goals. They are: production goal, inventory goal, sales goal, market share goal and profit goal.

The firms want to maintain the manufacture of products at a stable level. They do not allow violent fluctuations in production. They also assure a certain percentage of production as inventory to prevent the fluctuation in prices. Sales goal is considered as very important from the point of view of stability and the survival of the firm. At the same time, modern business managers want to capture a high percentage of the share of the total market for the product. Top management may insist on it because of the comparative performance measure aspect which is contained in it.

In order to achieve these objectives, Cyert and March said that managers keep an optimum rate of profit.

Social Responsibility of Business

Modern business cannot function effectively in a welfare state if it arbitrarily determines a high rate of profit. Society permits for a reasonable rate of profit. Social thinkers in recent years have emphasised on the social responsibility of business. The concept of social responsibility is defined as the obligation of the business community for the well being of the people, the state and the environment in which they operate. The business community is required to safeguard the health and wellbeing of the society. The business organisations are required to produce to the maximum extent possible. The business people should have concern for the public. They should give priority to the goals set by the government for the betterment of the people. They are required to solve many social and ecological problems such as urban congestion, environmental pollution, industrial discharges into river waters, depletion of natural resources, etc. It is also the responsibility of the business people to cooperate with the government in the eradication of poverty, unemployment, regional backwardness, etc.

They have certain responsibilities with regard to consumers, investors, employees and the government.

The producers by manufacturing products of high quality and fixing reasonable prices can discharge their moral obligations towards the consumers. The products must have a utilitarian value and their consideration is not solely on profit but on profit with services being extended to the consumer.

The obligation towards the investor involves in providing reasonable dividends to shareholders and to see that industry grows with stability. They are required to safeguard the assets and properties of the business

They are also expected to look after the employees very well. It means, the payment for the services should be equal to the marginal productivity of the workers. The management should motivate the workers to discharge their duties sincerely and honestly. They should seek the cooperation of the employees in running industries.

Their responsibility to government is immense. They are required to follow rules and regulations of the government. They have to pay due taxes on time. They have to cooperate with the government in various development activities.

These are various ways in which business community can discharge their responsibilities.

Issues in Profit Measurement

Many aspects of profit have been analysed in previous paragraphs. However certain other issues which have direct bearing which have direct bearing on profit have been discussed in the following paragraphs. The other issues are:

(a) Profit and Depreciation

(b) Capital gains and losses

(c) Profit maximisation Vs Profit Optimization.

(d) Reasons for limiting profits.

(e) Standards of reasonable profits.

(f) Profits for Control.

Profit and Depreciation

While analysing the concept of net profit quantitatively in the beginning of this chapter, depreciation has been considered as one of the essential aspects of determining the divisible profit. Divisible profit here refers to the net surplus available for distribution to the owners of the company. Net surplus is equal to gross earnings minus of depreciation and tax. In accounting terms - it is "Profit after depreciation and tax". Therefore, in order to arrive at true profit, depreciation is considered as a vital deduction out of gross earnings.

To determine the periodic nett income, the cost of using the long-term assets should be properly calculated and charged to the P&L A/C of each year during which the assets are to run in the books of accounts. The use costs are called by different names such as *Depreciation, Depletion, Amortisation,* etc.

In the case of tangible assets, *Land* has unlimited life and hence there is no necessity for creating use cost against it.

Assets like building, plant, equipment, tools, furniture, fixtures and vehicles are having `use costs' and hence have depreciation.

Natural resources like oil, timber, coal, mineral deposits are also exploited and their `use cost' is termed as Depletion which refers to the systematic and rational allocation of acquiescing cost to the future periods in which the revenue is derived from that asset.

Intangible assets like patent, copyrights, trademarks and goodwill will have the use cost called Amortisation. In these cases also, there will be rational allocation of costs to future periods in which benefits contribute to the revenue.

Whether it is depreciation, depletion or amortisation, the charge is definite against profit. If the use costs are not charged, profit will be inflated and real profit will not be arrived at.

The Institute of Chartered Accountants of India defines depreciation as "a measure of wearing out, consumption or other loss of value of a depressible asset arising from use, effluxion of time or obsolescence through technology and market changes. Depreciation is allocated so as to charge a fair proportion of the depressible amount in each accounting period during the expected useful life of the asset. Depreciation includes amortisation of assets whose useful life is pre-determined."

Therefore, many factors like obsolescence, effluxion of time, wear and tear, change in technology, cause depreciation and the use cost of assets have to be rationally allocated to future periods on the basis of utilisation of assets each year. "The main emphasis in depreciation accounting is on the computation of periodic charges to be allocated as an expense and to be matched with revenues reported in each period."

The relevance of depreciation in profit analysis is that it has to be set aside before arriving at divisible profit. *"Depreciation accounting is a system of accounting which aims to distribute the cost........of tangible capital assets, less salvage (if any) over the estimated useful life of the unit in a systematic and rational manner. It is a process of allocation, not of valuation."* (AICPA-USA). From this definition, we understand, that depreciation is related to the expected benefits derived from the assets and it is possible to measure the benefit.

Depreciation attempts to measure the value of benefit, the asset has provided during a given accounting period and not an attempt to measure the value of an asset at any given time. The benefit is valued as portion of the cost of assets. This means, "The balance sheet value of depressible asset is that portion of the original cost which has not been allocated as a periodic expense in the process of income measurement."

Depreciation charged to the P&L A/C will not itself provide fund for replacement of a depreciable asset. But the charging of depreciation to income "ensures the maintenance intact of the original money capital of the enterprise". Depreciation is not identified with cash or any other specific asset. A rational allocation of use cost is made and charged against revenue before arriving at disposable profit.

Depreciation is not a valuation process. Valuation considers depreciation as the fall in value of an asset over a period of time. However the depreciation does not arise due to fall in value, but rather from the process of ensuring a return on capital invested. Even in periods of appreciation in value of an asset at a point of time, there will be depreciation. The increased value is not brought into books of accounts. The increase in value may be a temporary phenomenon. Therefore it cannot be accounted in the middle and unless it is realised. Interim fluctuation have to be ignored as the assets are bound to reduce to below scrap value. Hence the rational and scientific allocation of the cost of assets against the revenue over the period is called for.

Several factors influence the section of depreciation method. There are different methods of charging depreciation and which method needs to be followed is influenced by the following factors.

(i) Legal Provisions;

(ii) Financial Reporting;

(iii) Effect on managerial decision

(iv) Inflation;

(v) Technology and

(vi) Capital Maintenance

Legal Provisions : Statutes provide that fixed assets are to be depreciated, for eg., the J.S. Companies in India must charge depreciation before arriving at divisible profit. Even the rate of depreciation cannot be arbitrary. The Income-Tax rules provide the rate of depreciation to specific assets. These have to be followed.

Financial Reporting : Financial response like P&L A/C, B/S etc., should present true and fair profits as well as the position of assets. Since depreciation is a recognised charge against revenue, it would be reflected in financial reports. Hence an appropriate method has to be adopted.

Effect on managerial Decisions : Charging depreciation against a depressible asset may be due to the proper recognition of revenue in a given period. But another aspect to be looked into is that it checks the cash outflow. Saving tax by charging depreciation is a short-sighted argument. But saving the interest of the enterprise by the manager is the real pressure behind depreciation. It also increases the financial flexibility. This aspect is kept in mind while selecting the method.

Inflation : At times the rate of depreciation will not be sufficient to meet the replacement cost because of the increase in the price of the asset. The rate of deprciation may be very less and hence periodic revisions are essential as inflation (increase in the price of asset at the time of replacement due to short supply) forces to raise the price at a later date. Therefore, the method of depreciation should have flexibility.

Technology : Another major factor that influences the method of depreciation is `technology'. Enterprises don't know when their technology adopted in production process becomes outdated. Commercial life of machines is decided by technological progress. Today the life of a machine is no longer an engineering concept. Particularly in case of computers, technology becomes outdated at a faster rate. Therefore, the method of depreciation to be charged by the company should be capable of recovering the use cost, at a faster rate. An industry which is exposed to fast technological progress will have to adopt a flexible depreciation policy. A fixed rate of depreciation will force the entity into liquidation. Therefore, during the highly revenue oriented period, higher depreciation is required. This will provide cushion for replacing the assets quickly.

Capital Maintenance : If the method of creating depreciation is based on historical costs, and the current revenue is higher at high price prevailing due to inflation, the income or profit derived may be fictitious. This type of income measurement and maintaining only financial capital during inflation results into the erosion of real capital of the business. In other words, creating less depreciation will result in the payment of dividend which is not actually earned and the payment in such case may be out of capital.

The following factors determine the method of depreciation to be adopted. However, depreciation policy should be flexible. As per Indian Accounting Standard, 6, "a change from one method to another method providing depreciation can be made only if the adoption of a new method is required by statute or for compliance with an accounting standard or if it is considered that the change would result in a more appropriate preparation or presentation of the financial statements of the enterprise."

Thus, depreciation has its influence and impact on profit of an enterprise and is a definite charge against revenue.

Capital gains and losses

This issue is not directly connected with profit maximisation. It is mainly concerned with capital or wealth maximisation. Even before analysing the concept of capital gains, let us know about the concept.

Capital gains refer to the profit derived from setting the assets. Can this profit be recognised as a profit which forms a part of business profit? No, this is not a revenue profit and does not recur regularly. Since it is profit derived out of capital items, it is treated differently in the business operations.

It is no doubt a surplus obtained from one of the business activities. But it cannot be used for declaring the dividend as in the case of revenue profits. Capital gains normally are shown in the balance sheet and forms a part of equity. The profit so derived has to be used for writing out capital losses. If any surplus is left over, it may be used for declaring the bonus shares, if the rules of the firm provides for it. Otherwise, it will be continued in the firm as a capital gain under the head *Capital Reserve.*

Similarly, capital losses cannot be charged to the revenue profit heavily. It is written off propitiatingly charging to the revenue profit. The expenses like cost of issue of share, debenture preferential share etc., under writing commission, preliminary expenses are all heavy capital expenses and are not charged to the P&L A/C of one year. They are proportionately charged and written off over the years. Hence it is essential that capital losses are treated differently from that of revenue expenses. The loss on sale of an asset can be directly charged to the revenue account, if it is not heavy. What is heavy loss and what is not is decided by the value judgement.

While determining the capital loss or gain, depreciation on that asset is also considered. Look to the following example.

A building, whose cost of construction was Rs.5 lakhs was sold for Rs.6 lakhs after 5 years of construction. As per generally accepted accounting principles, it was depreciated at 5% flat per annum. In this case, capital gain is as follows:

Cost of the building	Rs.5 lakhs
Less. Depn @ 5% Flat for 5 years (5 x 5%)	1.25 lakhs
	Rs. 3.75 lakhs
Sales Proceeds	Rs. 6.00 lakhs
Capital gain	2.25 lakhs

Capital gains and losses are treated separately and these items are not mixed with revenue profit.

Profit maximisation and optimisation

The terms *'Maximisation'* and *'Optimisation'* are confusing ones. Here an attempt is made to distinguish between these terms.

The concept of 'maximisation' will be a myth. There is no limit for earning profit. Unless a standard is fixed, the concept cannot be properly understood. Profit maximisation can be measured, if a comparable parameter is provided. Otherwise it will be simply a usage without any specific position. The following example will throw light to understand the concept.

Supposing a T.V. Manufacturing firm is willing to maximise the profit. The firm is producing to the full capacity and is having shift competition in the market. However, the product is sold in the market with certain distribution strategies. How to maximise profit in this context? The only way to assess the maximum of profit is to know the industry profits and compare the profit of the firm with that profit to know the level of maximisation. Supposing the T.V.industry in making 15% per annum.This firm can take this as a parameter to know the concept of maximisation. If the firm is earning only 10% p.a., it has not maximised its profit. Any earning beyond 15% (industry profit) will be the maximisation. Thus only with certain standards, the concept of maximisation can be understood.

The term `optimization' of profit refers to reaching the normal earning level. If the firm, on an average, is earning a percentage of profit every year, the firm's profit is said to be epitomised. The profit earned is 'best or most favourable', and may be called `optimum' profit. The concept of favourable profit depends upon the environment in which the firm works. In the existing business environment, if the firm makes a reasonable profit, the profit is said to be epitomised.

The concepts `maximisation' and `epitomisation' in a real sense have no meaning, unless they are quantified and standards are set to measure these levels. However, it may be only an academic exercise to distinguish between these two terms.

Reasons for limiting profit

Earning of excess profit is not prohibited. But it is not possible to earn super profits. Every business firm works with the aim of earning huge profits. But there are several uncontrollable factors which restrict the firm to earn maximum profit or super profit. When we analyse the profit curve of an enterprise for a long period of five to ten years, we observe that the firm will be earning only normal or optimum profit or even below the optimum level. Continuous earning of super profit even by monopoly firms will not be possible as uncontrollable factors influence such profits to come down. In real situations, profit earned will be a normal profit. The reasons for earning normal profit are as follows:

(i) Threat of entry of rival to the market.

(ii) Government policies on tax matters, quote policies, monetary policies etc.,

(iii) Resource crunch.

(iv) Disturbance in distribution channels.

(v) Market behaviour

(vi) Consumer behaviour and to retain customer goodwill.

(vii) Rapid change in production technology.

(viii) Weak promotion policy of the firm.

(ix) To keep labour cool

These are the major factors which cause the reduction in profit. One or some of the above factors come in the way of making extra profit or even to earn optimum profit.

Firms also don't wish to earn super profits for long. They want to limit the profit as they have to stay long in the business. They have social responsibility and ethics. This prevents them to aim only at profit maximisation. Society will not pardon the business houses, if they squeeze the consumers. After certain fluctuations in earning in the initial years, the firms get stabilised in their business operations and make only normal profit. But there will be steady growth of profit. Abnormal situations rarely arise. Since each firm is interested in the longevity of the enterprise, they restrict profits to a certain limit. This limit may marginally change each year, because of the growth in business volume or due to price fluctuations. Super profit is a temporary phenomenon, even in monopoly firms. As the consumer resistance begins, they are forced to bring down the price. Therefore, they feel the pulse of the market and bring down the profit margin.

Thus, limiting the profit is both a natural and forced phenomenon.

Standards of reasonable profits

Let us know as to what reasonable profit is? Reasonable profit here refers to the profit which gives a fair return, on capital employed. The term *fair* may refer to a certain quantity in the existing circumstances. As we have discussed in previous paragraphs about `optimum profit', we can consider that 'industry profit' can be taken as the fair profit to be earned by the firms. Industry profit is the average profit earned by a group of firms producing identical products. If an individual firm's profit reaches the level of industry profit, then it can be said that the firm is earning a reasonable profit.

To determine and earn the reasonable profit, we have to set certain standards. Profit standard can be in the following forms:

(i) Standard in the form of aggregate rupee terms.

(ii) Standard in the form of percentage of sales.

(iii) Standard in the form of 'Return on Investment'.(ROI).

Which standard of these standards is appropriate its uses: If the firm depends upon its uses and if the firm has to avoid competitors, the ROI is the relevant standard that the firm can adopt. If it has to satisfy the customers, keeping certain margins over unit cost is the standard to be adopted.

The ratio of profit to sales as a standard is not a viable one. This ratio varies widely in many firms with different production plans, and the varied turnover, different composition of capital etc., will be inappropriate having the same ratio of return on invested capital. As every investor looks at net profit, ROI is the most important standard that can be adopted.

Standard Setting

Setting a standard for earning reasonable profit is not to influence the standard setting. They are as follows:

(i) Attracting Outside Capital : The firm's profit earning should be that it should attract outside capital. Investors invest in firms which are making good profits, declaring reasonable dividend every year and maintaining sufficient reserves to plough back in times of necessity. While setting the standard, this aspect has to be considered. The focal point in this issue of attracting outside capital is that profit earning should be steady and normal. This, of course, is influenced by factors like capital structure of the enterprise, cost of capital, rate of retained earning, the financial decisions of the management etc., and outside capital should be capable of making good profit.

(ii) Role of Internal Resources : Internal resources here refer to retained earnings. How far the firm can depend upon the retained earning to finance a desired rate of growth without seeking external funds is important. Maintaining high reserves to plough back to improve the business operation is not that desirable. High plough-back does not have public acceptance. The feelings is that all earnings should be distributed to shareholders. This means there should be of high dividend pay-out. If all the earnings are retained or heavy retention of earnings reduces the dividend payout, it affects the shareholder's interest. Maybe their holdings may sell at premium in the stock market. But their intention is not selling the equity for premium. Equity holders expect a good dividend for which a good portion of earnings have to be earmarked.

Retained earnings can be used for business expansion or maintenance which may result in additional revenues to the firm. This may enhance the rate of dividend to equity holders. Retained funds will be under the exclusive control of the management. But the management may not properly utilise it. If all or major portion of earnings are distributed to the share-holders, they will have the choice to increase their portfolio. They can use their dividend earnings in acquiring equities of other firms of their choice. Maintaining retained earnings at a higher scale remains a debatable point. However, it is one of the factors which influences the standard setting for earning reasonable profits.

(iii) ***Normal Profit :*** Another standard that can be considered for earning a reasonable profit is 'maintaining normal profit over the normal years'. If the firm's average profit for previous years is taken as an indicator, if the earning capacity of the firm and if investors confidently invest in the firm as per the indicator, then `normal profit' can be taken as one of the standards for earning reasonable profit. But how to fix the normal period and normal profit? In a developing economy like ours, the economy will be oscillating and there will be no price stability. It will have its impact on the firms. Therefore which is a normal period and which is an abnormal period cannot be strictly assessed. However, average profits of previous years can be considered as a standard to indicate the reasonable earning capacity of the firm.

These standards can be considered for earning reasonable profits. Ultimately, the factors that decide the profit earning capacity of the firm are situational analysis and quick and sound business decisions. Which standard has to be chosen depends upon the factors like avoiding competition, maintaining liquidity for business operations, keeping the human force at work happy, preparing sound long-term growth plans etc., Standards are hetrogenous and the choice of a standard depends upon its purpose and its persuasive values.

Profit for control

'Profit for control' is a concept which recongnises profit centres in the organisation and each centre is made to work actively to contribute to the overall profitability of the firm. Identifying profit centres and fixing responsibilities to centre heads to contribute so much profit to the total profit of the firm is profit for control.

It is a thinking that workers who work at different levels of organisation do not think of profit concept of the firm. They always work in their ambit without considering the cost of their operations. The waste or idle working hours or slackness on the part of workers will contribute to the increase in cost of production and it will have a bearing on the profit earnings of the firms. To check attitudes of workers like (i) spending heavily on perfection of production over work without recognising cost and usefulness of such operations, (iii) lack of incentives for bottom line workers for their creativity and innovations, and making them feel that they are insecure, will hamper the profit earning capacity of the firm.

The firms have now recognised these problems and are restructuring managerial operations to see that every worker identifies with his work and ultimately with the organisation. In the process, the functional organisation system has emerged and profit centres are created in the organisation. Each functional manager (marketing, finance, production, human resources etc.,) will be fixed with the responsibility of his functional department and is delegated with certain authority to make his department viable.

These functional bosses have to prepare periodical reports about their revenue, expenditure and operations and submit to the top for appraisal.

How to fix the profit standard for each department is a point to be examined. There are two ways of setting standards for the functional departments. (i) Setting profit goals in terms of net profits for the firm and (ii) Confirming profit goals to the contribution to the total profits determined by cuts and revenues of that centre or department.

Fixing profit standards to the first method is not feasible as it is very difficult to measure the overall revenue cost of the firm by individual departments. The reasonable approach is to take into account only the cost and revenue of that functional department and fix the standard. Each functional executive should be given the widest discretion in pricing and promoting to reach his profit goals. While determing the profit goals, some of the general overheads can be proportionately charged to functional departments as the operational aspects of the firm is an integrated activity and each department is interlinked. So many activities take place in the general interest of the firm and expenses on these activities may be proporationately charged to each department while setting "controllable profits".

Thus, 'Profit for Control' involves indentifying work magnitude of each department and costs incurred thereon, fixing profit standards for each department, considering the cost and revenue of each department, receiving periodical reports to measure the work in terms of profit and adopting corrective measures to achieve optimum profit/targets set for each department.

This is a control technique adopted to achieve operational efficiency in each department.

Profit Planning and Forecasting

Profit is indispensable for the health and well being of the business. The sign of healthy business is to make continuous profit in the midst of various risks and uncertainties. These uncertainties arise on account of the diverse nature of competition, uncontrollable cost elements and the continuous technological developments and so on. Modern businesses have to withstand various shocks which they face in society. If the prices of products are high, the businessmen have to face consumers' resistance. If the prices fall, then they may not incur good profits. In these days of technological developments, many products become obsolete. If the scope of market segmentation and product differentiation is great, the risk of product obsolescence also increases. If such a scope is less, the risk of price competition increases. At the same time, the risks involved in product competition is greater than price competition. Therefore, business in such an economic environment is very risky. These risks will have to be covered by means of accurate business planning and strategic operations.

Profit planning is an integral part of business policy and planning. Profit policy is programmed through profit planning, which gives a concrete shape to the profit policy of the firm. It is a sign of good business which can make profit consistent with myriad of risks and uncertainties in business. These risks and uncertainties are faced boldly with profit planning.

Profit planning is achieved through the control of internal and external factors which exert pressure on profits. In other words, some planning at a particular level of profit has to be made. The question now arises how the pressure on profits is avoided. The pressure on profit is exerted by sales revenue and the total costs arc production. Infact, sales revenue, prices per unit of the products sold and the total costs are inter-related. The relationship between sales revenue and the cost of production and other items is stated as follows:

P (Profits) = I (Sales Revenue) – C (total cost of production)

I (Sales Revenue) = S (volume of sales) × (Price per unit)[u]

C = (Total cost of production) = R (Price per unit of input) × L (Volume of inputs.)

The relationship is summarised in the following equation :

$P = I - C ; I = S \times u ; C = R \times L.$

Then $P = (S \times u) - (R. L).$

Under perfect competition, since the prices of outputs and inputs are given to regulated profits, volume of sales (S) or the volume of inputs (L) have to be manipulated. If the firm wants to increase profits, it will have to either increase the volume of sales or reduce the volume of inputs.

Under imperfect competition, prices are different, products are different and the firm can manipulate the price of the product and prices of the factors of production. Profits may be regulated by means of employing sophisticated techniques like Break-Even Analysis, Profit-Volume Analysis and Linear Programming.

Break-Even Analysis

The break-even analysis (BEA) is defined as an important technique in the study of relationship between costs revenue and profit at various levels of sales of a firm. Joel Dean says that BEA. presents a flexible projection of the impact of volume of output upon costs revenue and profits. As such, it provides an important bridge between business behaviour and economic theory of the firm.

When a firm breaks even, it means that it has not made profit nor incurred loss in its operations. In order words, break-even point (BEP) is defined as *the point at which the level of output and the level of revenue is equal to the cost of production and marketing.* This is also called no profit and no sales point. The object of BEA. is not just to determine the break even point but to understand the financial relationship between cost, revenue and the rate of output. The revenue and expenses situations at different levels of output or sales of a firm are drawn in a map and this is called *break-even chart.*

Break-Even Chart

Break-even charts are being used in recent years by the managerial economists, company executives and government agencies in order to find out the break-even point. In the break-even charts, concepts like total fixed

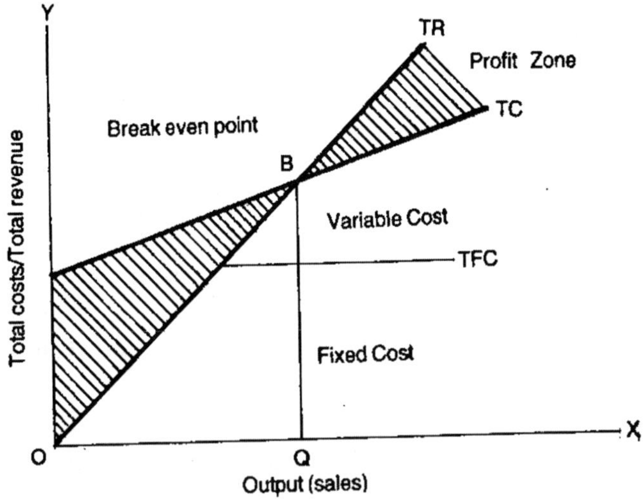

cost, total variable cost and the total cost and total revenue are shown separately. The following diagram illustrates the typical break-even chart.

In the above diagram, the volume of output or sales is measured along the OX axis and the costs and revenues are measured along the OY axis. For the sake of simplicity, assuming constant factors, linear revenue function is drawn. Similarly, a linear total cost function is drawn. It is composed of total fixed cost which is represented by (TFC) on the chart. The variable cost function is assumed to change linearly in a constant proportion to the change in output.

In the above chart 'B', the break-even point is the point at which total revenue equals total cost at the level of output 'Q'. So, the net profit is zero at the level of output OQ. The area between TR and TC depicts the profit function. It means that the firm incurs loss when it produces output below

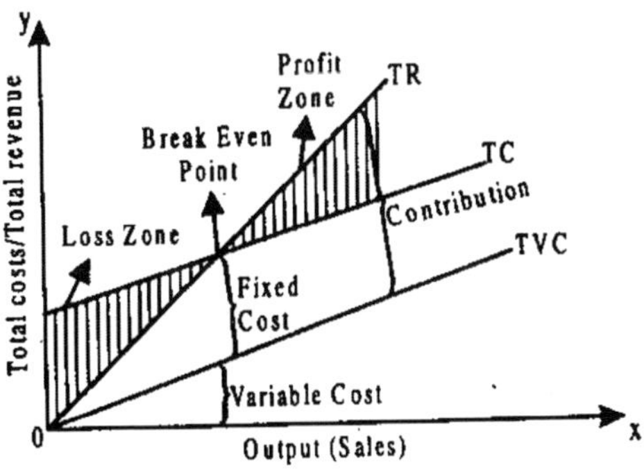

OQ. OQ is the level of output where the firm makes neither profit nor loss. When it expands output, it makes profit.

The break-even chart can also be represented in an alternative form where the contribution to fixed cost (contribution margin) and profits is clearly depicted.

Prof. F. V. Gardner in his book *'Profit Management and Control'* considers that the break-even chart is an excellent instrument panel for the guidance of businessmen in determining the profitable output and controlling his business.

Break even point can be determined either in terms of physical units or in terms of sales value of the output (money terms).

BEP in Terms of Physical Units

Break even point may be determined either in terms of physical units or in money terms (sale value of the output). The break-even point in physical terms is determined by a formula as under

$$\text{BEP} = \frac{\text{TFC}}{\text{P} - \text{AVC}} = \frac{\text{Total fixed cost}}{\text{Price per unit} - \text{Average variable cost}}$$

P - AVC means the contribution margin per unit.

Taking into consideration the contribution of per unit cost and revenue, BEP is located at the level of output at which the price per unit or average revenue is equal to average cost. That is the selling price should cover average variable cost in full and a part of fixed cost. The price of the unit in excess of the average variable cost is regarded as contribution margin per unit which contributes towards the fixed cost. Thus, the BEP is reached at a point where sufficient number of units are sold so that its total contribution margin becomes equal to the total fixed costs.

Let us consider the following examples :

Suppose the fixed costs of a factory are Rs. 20,000 and the variable costs are Rs. 4 per unit and the selling price is Rs. 8. per unit. The break-even point would be:

$$\text{BEP} = \frac{\text{Rs.}20{,}000}{(8-4)} = 5000 \text{ units.}$$

If the company sells 5000 units, it would not make any loss or profit. Let us work it out it as follows :

Sales = Rs. 40,000

Cost of goods sold :

1. Variable cost 20,000
2. Fixed cost <u>20,000</u> <u>40,000</u>

Net profit Nil

It may also be arrived at by applying the above formula :

$$BEP = \frac{\text{Total fixed cost (TEC)}}{\text{Price per unit - Average variable cost}}$$

$$BEP = \frac{\text{Rs. } 20{,}000}{\text{Rs. } 8-4} = 5{,}000 \text{ units}$$

Break even point is reached when the firm sells 5000 units. When 5000 units are produced, the total revenue will be Rs. 40,000. The total cost

FC + VC

= Rs. 20,000 + Rs. 20,000 = Rs. 40,000

Thus TR = TC, so there is no profit and no loss.

Net profit is zero, which is the break - even point.

Break Even Point in Terms of Sale Value

The above method holds good when a firm is producing only one product. But, in many cases, a firm is producing more than two products. It may be called multi-product firm, BEP is calculated in relation to the total sales expressed in terms of money. In this case, we decide the fixed cost by the difference between sale value and the variable costs. That is BEP is a point where the contribution margin (Sale value - variable costs) would be equal to fixed cost. For example, if the sales are Rs. 400 and the variable costs of these sales are Rs. 280 and the contribution margin ratio (400 – 280) / 400 i.e. 0.3

The formula for calculation BEP is fixed cost/sales value - variable cost.

For example : Sales Rs. 12,000

Variable cost = 800 12,000

Fixed cost = 4000

Let us take up a problem :

AB firm produces four products. Sales value is Rs. 40,000. Variable costs are Rs. 12,000.

Fixed cost is Rs. 28,000. Calculate the BEP.

$$BEP = \frac{\text{Total fixed costs}}{\text{Contribution ratio}}$$

Contribution ratio is measured as :

$$CR = \frac{TR - TVC}{TR} \frac{4000 - 12000}{40000} = \frac{28000}{40000} = \frac{7}{10}$$

$$BEP = \frac{TFC}{CR} = \frac{28000}{7/10} = \frac{28000 \times 10}{7} = 40000$$

The break-even point is reached when the firm's sales value is Rs. 40,000. At Rs. 40,000 sales value, there is no profit and no loss.

Problem No. 2

The fixed costs of a factory is Rs. 15,000 per year. The variable costs per unit of the product is Rs. 3 per unit. The selling price is Rs. 5 per unit. Find out the break-even point.

$$BEP = \frac{\text{Fixed costs}}{\text{Contribution ratio}} \text{ (Selling price - variable cost per unit.)}$$

Let us find out the units of the products produced.

$$\frac{15{,}000}{5-3-2} = 7500 \text{ units.}$$

That means, the company would not make any profit or loss at a sales volume of 7500 units.

Sales = 7500 units x Rs. 5 = 37, 500

Costs of goods sold at Rs. 3/-

	Rs. 22,500/-
Fixed costs	Rs. 15,000/-
	Rs. 37,500/-
Net profit is	Nil

BEP of a company manufacturing multi products :

Product	Selling price	Variable cost per unit	% share of each product to total sale
A	Rs. 5	3	20
B	Rs. 8	5	25
C	Rs. 10	6	30
D	Rs. 12	7	25

The capacity of a firm in terms of Rs. is one lakh. The fixed costs are Rs. 15,000. Calculate BEP.

Solution : $$\text{BEP} = \frac{\text{Fixed costs}}{\text{Contribution ratio}}$$

In this case, the fixed costs are Rs. 15,000.

The contribution ratios have to be calculated.

Contribution ratios of each product is the difference between selling price per unit and its variable cost.

Contribution ratios of each product :

A = Price – VC	Rs. 5 – 3	= 2
B = Price – VC	Rs. 8 – 5	= 3
C = Price – VC	Rs. 10 – 6	= 4
D = Price – VC	Rs. 12 – 7	= 5

The contribution ratios will have to be expressed as percentage of prices.

$$A = \frac{5}{2} \times 100 = 40 \qquad B = \frac{3}{8} \times 100 = 37.5$$

$$C = \frac{5}{2} \times 100 = 40 \qquad D = \frac{5}{12} \times 100 = 41.66$$

To obtain contribution ratios for each product, the contribution percentage has to be multiplied by the percentage share of each product.

A. 20% x 40% = 8%

B. 25% x 37.5% = 8%

C. 30% x 49% = 12%

D. 25% x 41.66% = 8%

Total = 36%

This 36 per cent is the contribution of all products.

$$\text{Now, BEP} = \frac{\text{Fixed cost}}{\text{CR}} = \frac{15{,}000}{36\%} = \text{Rs. } 42{,}000$$

If the firm makes a sales revenue of Rs. 42,000 per year, it can make no profit and no loss.

Managerial Uses of Break-even Analysis

(i) The BEA provides a microscopic view of the profits of the firm. Based on the analysis, the management can chalk out the plans, ·grammes and policies pertaining to the development of the firm. Suppose a firm wants to know the volume of sales required to achieve a certain amount of profit, BEA may be utilised. Then the following formula will have to be used :

$$\text{Volume of sales necessary} = \frac{\text{Fixed costs} + \text{Profit(Target)}}{\text{Marginal contribution per unit}}$$

Let us take up the following example :

Fixed costs Rs. 15,000. The profit target is Rs. 5,000.

Selling price is Rs. 5 per unit. Variable cost : Rs. 3 per unit.

$$\text{Then, } \frac{15{,}000 + 5000}{CR = 2} = \frac{20{,}000}{2} = 10{,}000 \text{ units.}$$

If the firm sells 10,000 units, it can make a profit of Rs. 5,000.

(ii) The break-even profit helps the management to know at a glance the profits generated at different levels of sales. The BEP can be used in determining *'the safety margin'* regarding the extent to which the firm can permit a decline in sales without causing losses. The formula to determine 'safety margin' is :

$$\text{Safety margin} = \frac{\text{Sales} - \text{BEP}}{\text{Sales}} \times 100$$

Taking the above examples,

$$\frac{50{,}000 - 37{,}500}{50{,}000} \times 100 = 25\%$$

That is, the firm can afford to lose sales up to 25% of the present level before incurring a loss. 25% is the safety margin.

3. The break-even analysis is very much helpful in decision making pertaining to price policy, sales projection and capital budgeting.

4. In modern business situations, many times firms may be faced with the problem of reducing the prices of their products. Whenever the firm reduces the price, there will be a reduction in the contribution margin (towards fixed cost). This means that, to remain at the same level of profit, the firm has to increase its output. The firm cannot assume that a fall in price will result in a rise in sales. Assuming there is no change in sales, the firm has to calculate the increase in volume of output in order to remain at the same level of profits, following a reduction in the price. The following

formula can be used :

$$\text{New volume of sales necessary} = \frac{\text{Total Fixed cost} + \text{Total Profit}}{\text{New Selling Price} - \text{Average Variable cost}}$$

Let us take the following example :

If FC of a firm is Rs. 10,000, profit target is Rs. 22,000, selling price is Rs. 10 per unit and variable cost is Rs. 5 per unit, then the total volume of sales necessary, using the earlier formula is 6,400 units; given the target profit of Rs. 22,000. Suppose the firm decides to reduce the selling price from Rs. 10 to Rs. 9 per unit, then the new volume of sales necessary using the above formula would be :

$$\text{New volume of sales necessary} = \frac{10{,}000 + 22{,}000}{9 - 5}$$

$$= \frac{32{,}000}{4}$$

$$= 8000 \text{ units.}$$

Thus, after reducing the price from Rs. 10 to Rs. 9 per unit, if the firm wants to maintain the target profit of Rs. 22,000, it has to increase sales from 6,400 units to 8,000 units. In other words, a reduction in price by Re. 1 should be followed by an increase in sales volume by 1600 units, if the firm has to maintain the same profit level.

Limitations of BEA

(a) In the BEA, everything is assumed to be constant. This implies a static condition. But costs and revenues may change over a period of time, making the projection based on the past data wrong. As such, BEA is useful in situations of stable and slow moving entities.

(b) Since BEA is based on many assumptions which do not hold good in practice, we assume cost and revenue functions are linear. We assume again selling price as constant, etc. In fact, the linearity of cost and revenue functions are real only for a limited range of output.

(c) The break-even analysis is based upon the accounting data, as such, it neglects imputed costs, takes arbitrary depreciation estimates and considers inappropriate allocation of overhead costs. In order to make the best use of BEA, a good accounting system is to be followed.

(d) The BEA regards profit as a function of output only. It fails to consider the impact of technological change, division of labour, improved productivity, etc.

(e) It assumes horizontal demand curve which means, any quantity is sold at one price which can be true only under the conditions of perfect competition. Hence, to be realistic, calculations have to be made at several price levels. Thus, several total revenue curves are required instead of one. It is so because in the real world, there is imperfect competition prevailing. Otherwise, the demand schedule will not get its due weight.

In view of these limitations, the use of BEA is very much restricted. The BEA is very simple and easy to understand and hence, it is very much used by the management.

Profit Forecasting

Profit forecasting is indispensable for profit planning. Profit forecasting means projecting the future profits, assuming the factors like growth of the size of the business, the pricing policies of the firm, the cost control policies, depreciation policy and so on. It is also necessary from the point of view of economic health and stability of the firm to project for certain years the growth of sales, increase in costs and consequently the profits also.

Joel Dean points out three approaches to profit forecasting.

(i) Spot Projection means projecting the entire profit and loss for a specified period, say five years, seven years or ten years. The projection of profits and loss statements for this period depends on the projection of sales, costs and prices of the same period. Since profits are surpluses resulting from the forces that shape the demand for the company's products and govern the behaviour of costs, their prediction is subject to wide margins of error, from the culmination of errors in forecasting revenues and costs and from the inter relation of the various components of the income statement.

(ii) Break-even analysis identifies functional relations of both revenue and costs to output rate with profits related to output as a residual or surplus.

(iii) Environmental analysis relates company's profits to key variables in the economic environment, such as the general business activity and general price level. It is based on the movement of business cycles.

The profit forecast is intimately related with variables like the growth rate of output, changes in prices, wages, material costs and productivity or factors of production. All these are inter-related to the aggregate business activity of the nation.

In practice, these approaches are used in combination to project future profits.

Questions

1. What is profit? What are the functions of profit?
2. 'Profit is reward for successful innovation'. Explain.
3. Distinguish between gross profit and net profit.
4. Distinguish between economic profits and accounting profits.
5. Explain the role of risk and uncertainty in the origin of profit.
6. 'Profit is the reward for risk taking.' Explain.
7. Comment on dynamic theory of profit.
8. Distinguish between risk and uncertainty.
9. What are the objectives of profits?
10. Explain Baumol's Sales Maximisation Hypothesis.
11. Comment on the social responsibility of business.
12. Explain the concept of break-even in profit planning.
13. Explain the break-even analysis and its limitations.
14. What is meant by the term 'profit forecasting'?.
15. Discuss why profit maximisation is not always the aim of business.

CHAPTER 15

THEORIES OF WAGES

Wages are the remuneration paid to the factor of production 'labour', for the services rendered by it in the process of production. Benham has defined wage as, *'a sum of money paid under contract by an employer to a worker for services rendered.'*

Distinction between Nominal and Real Wage

Nominal Wages refer to wages paid in terms of money. The reward received by labour in cash is called *nominal wage* or *money wage*. Real wages, on the other hand, refer to the amount of necessities, comforts and luxuries and other facilities which workers could enjoy by working at a job. Since the money received by labour commands the necessities, comforts and conveniences and the purchasing power of money, to a large extent determine the real wages of a worker.

Factors Determining Real Wages

Let us briefly discuss the factors determining real wages :

(i) Purchasing Power of Money : As and when the value of money changes, the purchasing power of money also changes. Purchasing power refers to the amount of goods and services which a unit of money can purchase. This varies with the general price-level and index number of commodity prices. A rise in general price-level will mean a fall in purchasing power and consequently a decline in real wages. Money wage may be high but real wage is less if there is inflation in the economy.

(ii) Method of Payment : Normally workers are paid in the form of money. But in some occupations besides money remuneration, subsidised or free lunch, free housing facilities, free transport facilities etc. may be provided to the workers. Any benefit extended by non-monetary methods, forming part of wage, is a real wage earned by the worker. The wage earner would consider all these aspects to prefer a particular kind of work to another.

(iii) Subsidiary Earning : To find out the real wage of the workers, we have to take into consideration extra earning possibilities. For example, professor can make extra earnings from tuitions. A worker in a dairy farm may get free milk everyday. These are all subsidiary earnings in the work and these incomes should be considered in deciding the real wages of a worker.

(iv) ***Nature of Employment :*** Some jobs are of a routine nature while others are more demanding and tiresome. The conditions under which the worker performs his duties is also an important factor in the determination of real wages. Working conditions include not only the number of working hours and working days but also the recreational, educational and other facilities provided by the employer. Conditions of employment thus affect the real wage estimates of a worker.

(v) ***Regularity of Employment :*** Regular employment with low wages will be preferred to irregular work with high wages. In comparing real wages of the worker, due allowances must be made for differences in permanency and regularity of work.

(vi) ***Future Prospects :*** The prospects of promotion and higher wages may induce a person to work for low wages. Due allowance, therefore, should be made for the present value attached to the anticipated increased earning in the future.

Theories of Wages

From very early times, economists have formulated theories explaining wage determination. A consideration of the earlier theories inspite of their defects and short-comings will help us in understanding the modern explanation of wages. The early theories are briefly discussed below :

The Subsistence Theory of Wages

This theory was formulated by the physiocrats who maintained that the wages of labour always remained at the subsistence level. Just as the value of a commodity under free competition is determined by its cost of production, so also the value of the commodity labour is determined by its cost of production, which was taken to be the subsistence level of the worker. According to this theory, the labourer should be paid just enough to live and perpetuate his clan. The theory is called the *'iron law of wages'* by Lassalle. According to this theory, if wages exceeded minimum subsistence level, population would expand resulting in an increase in the supply of labour, until wages were again at bare subsistence level. If on the other hand, wages fell below the level of subsistence, there would be a reduction in the population and supply of labour, until wages were raised to the subsistence level.

Criticisms of the Theory

The theory has been criticized on the following grounds :

(a) It is wrong to assume that a rise in wages above the subsistence level is immediately followed by a growth of population which pushes wages down to the level of subsistence again. It is more natural for the labourer to think of improving his standard of living, instead of increasing the number.

(b) The theory is too pessimistic and does not consider the role of efficiency of labour in determining wages. In most cases, workers may be more skilled, better qualified or more enduring. With an increase in efficiency, labour productivity also increases resulting in higher wages.

(c) The theory neglects the demand side and considers only the supply side of labour. In determining the price of anything, both demand and supply should be considered together.

(d) The theory ignores the fact that labour is heterogeneous. If all labourers must get only the bare necessaries of life, all must get the same amount of wages. But then there are many differences in wages as between regions, trades and persons.

(e) The subsistence theory of wages was used by the capitalists in the 19th century, against trade unions and against their attempts to raise wages. The theory asserted that wages estimated in food and necessaries would be absolutely constant and rigidly fixed for all time, and thus implied that there was no sense in trade unions agitating for higher wages. The fact that, historically workers in industrialised countries have been able to secure high wages and enjoy a high standard of living, is probably the greatest criticism of the subsistence theory of wages.

The Wages Fund Theory

This theory was first propounded by Adam Smith, but was later given final shape by John Stuart Mill, in his *'Principles of Political Economy.'*

According to the theory, every employer sets apart a given amount of capital for the payment of labourers, known as the 'Wages fund'. It is called a fund because it is almost unchanged and constant. Since it is constant, wages will depend directly upon the size of labour force - i.e., wages will vary inversely with the size of labour. If labour force increases because of an increase in population, the fund remaining the same, wage per labourer will go down. The opposite will happen when labour force contracts

Thus :

$$\text{Wage Rate} = \frac{\text{Wages fund}}{\text{No. of labourers}}$$

According to Mill, a rise in wages will be possible only under two conditions, either the wages fund must increase or labourers must restrict their numbers.

The advocates of this theory believed that a rise in wage would in the end be counteracted by an increase in population. Further they argued that trade unions could not succeed in raising general wage rate. For, if wages rose in one country, they were bound to fall in another, because the total wage fund was fixed.

Criticism of the Theory

(a) In the first place, the theory does not explain the principle behind creating wage funds. It depends on the arbitrary will of the producer which makes the theory highly illogical.

(b) Further, the theory ignores the efficiency of labour and consequent difference in wages in practical life. If labour is more productive, it is entitled to a higher wage.

(c) The theory is unscientific, for it assumes a fixed wages fund first, and then considers the determination of wages later. In fact, we should find out the wages per worker in the first instance, and from it calculate the wages fund.

(d) The theory has completely ignored the way in which the wage fund is distributed. It has also ignored the influence of trade unions in collective bargaining.

Mill himself became aware of these defects and abandoned it altogether in the next edition of his book.

The Residual Claimant Theory

This theory was put forward by the economist F. A. Walker in his book *Political Economy*. According to this theory, labour gets the residual portion after all the other factors have received their remuneration. Firstly, rent is deducted and rent must come out before the question of wages is considered. Secondly, remuneration for the use of capital must be deducted. The third and last deduction is the profits, the remuneration of the entrepreneur. After these three shares being taken out of the product of industry, 'the whole remaining body of wealth is the property of the labouring class.'

This theory takes into consideration, the possibility of increasing wages by increasing the total produce. In this respect, it admits the efficiency of labour and also the theory sounds a little optimistic.

Criticisms

(a) This theory is defective because, in practice, labour is not the residual claimant but it is the entrepreneur who has a claim over the residue.

(b) Secondly, the theory ignores the supply of labour, in the determination of wages. It does not take into account the relative scarcity or abundance of labour in the determination of wages.

(c) According to Walker, rent, interest and profit are fixed by economic considerations, independent of the volume of output produced which implies that these payments are of a fixed nature. In other words, when output is increased,the share going to the factors of production other than labour remains constant. But this is not true because all these incomes, particularly profits accruing to the organisers change, with the change in output.

In view of the above defects, this theory too has been rejected by the economists.

The Marginal Productivity Theory of Wages

The general theory of distribution has been extended to wages and has come to be known as Marginal Productivity Theory of Wages. The theory is based on the following assumptions:

(a) Firstly, there is perfect competition in the market for the factors of production.

(b) There is homogeneity in the units of labour.

(c) It operates in the long period under static conditions.

On the assumption of the above conditions, the theory states that at any given time, wages shall be equal to the marginal productivity of labour.

Labour is demanded in the labour market because it is productive. An employer will be willing to pay the labourer more if he helps him to produce more and earn high profits. The theory states that wage rate is determined by the demand and supply of labour and it is in equilibrium when wages are equal to marginal productivity.

In every business, there is a point beyond which it is uneconomical for the employer to engage additional labour. At this point, there is a certain product ascribable to labour. According to this theory, wages tend to equal this marginal product i.e., the product of the least productive worker. The last labourer employed produces just enough to cover his cost to the producer. Assuming that all labourers are equally efficient, they will receive the same wage. i.e, the wage representing the product of the last labourer employed.

Suppose 100 machines and 1000 labourers produce 10,000 units of a commodity and keeping other things constant, one more labourer is employed. Now 100 machines and 1001 labourers produce 10,005 units. i.e, the marginal productivity of labour is 5 units. Further, suppose that each unit of the commodity could be sold at Rs. 5/ unit, the value of the marginal product would be Rs. 25. This means that each labourer will get the full value of the marginal product i e., Rs 25. If the labourer does not get the full value, he moves away to another job. Because of this, mobility and equality between wages and marginal productivity is established.

Criticism

(a) The assumptions of the theory viz. perfect competition, mobility of labour and homogeneity of factor units are unrealistic.

(b) Secondly, this theory is static. All factors are assumed to be constant. But in practical life, labour is not of the same quality; and remuneration does not remain constant.

(c) Further, it should be noted that productivity of labour is also the function of wages. Less productivity may be the result of low wages.

(d) Finally, it has been argued that the theory does not explain the determination of wages. It does not consider all forces which influence the supply of labour. Actual determination of wages depends on institutions like trade unions, employees' associations, minimum wages regulations etc.

Modern Theory of Wages

Modern theory of wages gives a satisfactory explanation of wage determination. It takes into consideration not only the productive aspect but also the demand and supply of labour in the labour market, in determining the wage rate. Hence this theory is also called *'Demand and supply theory.'*

According to this theory, the price of labour, just like the price of any other commodity, is determined by the market forces of demand and supply.

Wage Determination Under Perfect Competition

Demand for Labour

Demand for labour is a derived demand. The elasticity of demand for labour also depends on the elasticity of demand for goods which it produces. The demand for labour depends on the price of other competitive and complementary factors. For example, labour and machines compete with each other for being engaged in a particular line of production. If prices of machines are higher than those of labour, the employer would prefer to employ more of labour. Thus, its demand would increase.

Another fundamental factor governing the demand for labour is its productivity. The demand price of labour depends upon productivity i.e., marginal revenue product of labour. The higher the productivity of labour, the greater will be the demand for it from the employer. The employer would keep on engaging more and more labourers so long as their contribution to production is more than the wages paid.

But the moment wages become equal to marginal productivity of labour, further employment of labour is stopped. Since all labour is assumed to be homogeneous, what is paid to the last labourer will be paid to all the others. Hence, wages = marginal productivity.

The demand for labour is illustrated in the following figure:

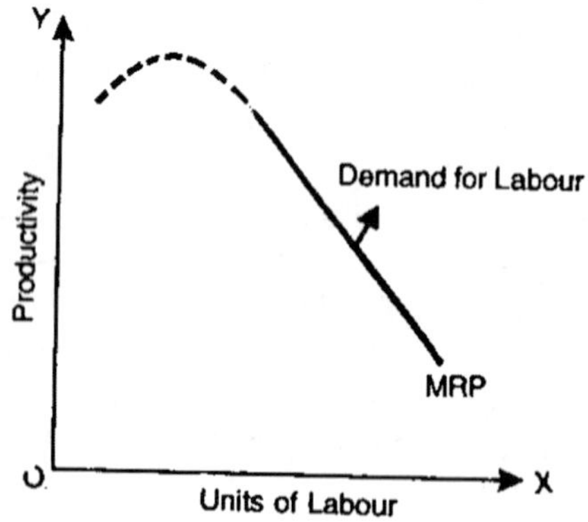

Fig. 1

In this figure, the Marginal Revenue Productivity (MRP) curve declines as more units of labour are engaged. The MRP curve of the firm constitutes the demand curve, which slopes downwards and its location or elasticity depends on the factors already discussed. In order to arrive at the market demand and supply curve, the following assumptions are made.

(i) The number of workers and employers are large.

(ii) Both workers and employers act independently and there are no monopoly elements.

(iii) Labour is perfectly mobile between firms or regions.

(iv) There is one price for service of labour.

Supply of Labour

Supply of labour refers to the number of workers who would offer themselves for employment at different wage rates. To a firm under perfect competition, the supply of labour is perfectly elastic. At a given wage rate, the firm can employ as many workers as it likes.

But for the whole industry, supply of labour is not elastic. If it wants more labour, it can attract labour from other industries only at a higher price. Even at a higher price, supply may not be forthcoming because it depends on various conditions apart from remuneration. It depends on population, geographical conditions, occupational distributions, education, training etc. The workers may prefer to work less and enjoy leisure with increased income. In such a case, the supply curve for labour will be backward sloping after a certain stage. A categorical statement cannot be made that the supply of labour will be greater, with higher wages. However, normally we assume an upward sloping curve.

Determination of Wages

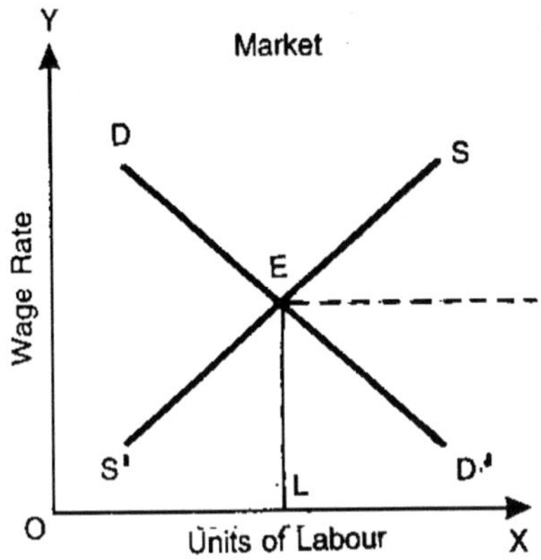

Fig. 2

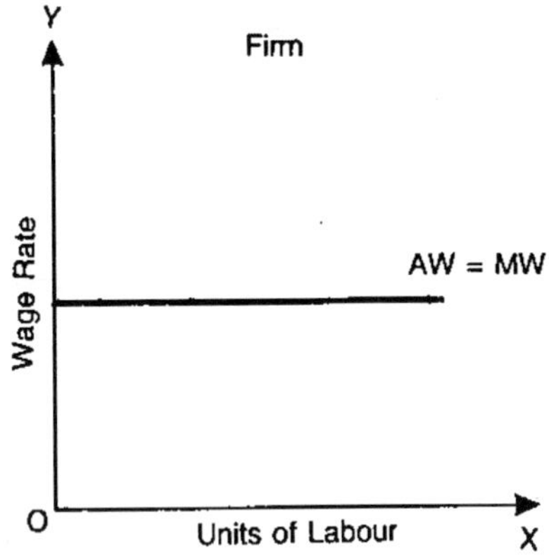

Fig. 3

Figure 2 shows the demand and supply of labour in the market. The equilibrium point is 'E' where wage EL and the quantity of labour demanded and supplied is OL units. Once the wage is determined for the entire industry, each firm accepts the wage as given. This is shown in Fig. 3. No worker will be prepared to work for less. The supply curve will be horizontal and this represents the average wage and marginal wage (AW = MW) of the labour of the firm.

Relation between Wage and Productivity

Every employer will stop employing labour at the point where marginal cost of labour is equal to marginal revenue product. (MW = MRP). This is true in both short and long periods.

As far as average wage and average revenue product is concerned in the short-run, there are three possible alternatives :

(i) The wage can be higher than ARP in which case the employer will incur loss.

(ii) The wage can be lower than ARP in which case the employer will incur loss.

(iii) The wage can be equal to ARP, where the employer will neither secure a profit nor incur a loss.

In the long-run under perfect competition, profit and loss in employing labour will be eliminated. The ARP will be equal to wages. We have already seen that wage is equal to MRP in all periods. So, we reach the final conclusion that in the long-run, under perfect competition, the wage of the labourer will be equal to ARP and MRP of labour. This is illustrated in Fig. 4.

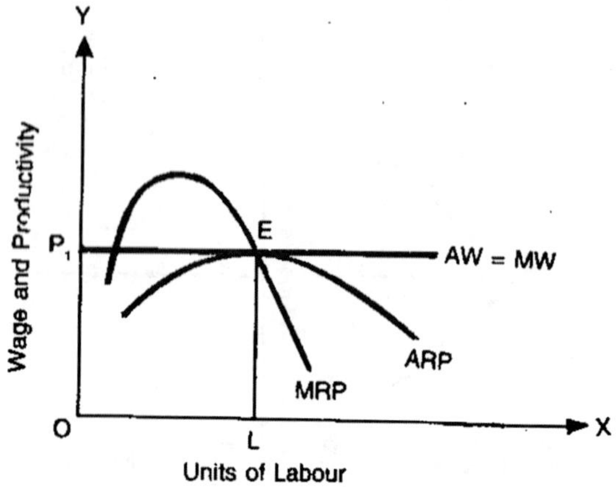

In the above fig. OP is the wage and MW = MRP, AW = ARP. So at equilibrium, wage = ARP = MRP. The total wages paid to labour is equal to $OLEP_1$. The total revenue product of labour is also equal to $OLEP_1$. So under perfect competition when wages are made equal to ARP and MRP, there is no exploitation of labour.

Wage Determination Under Imperfect Competition

In the actual world, in most cases, labour markets are imperfect. Either the employer or the trade unions become powerful and may dictate terms and rates of wages.

Under imperfect competition, the employer will face a rising supply curve which implies that he can attract additional workers only by paying more wages. The supply curve of labour can also be called the *average cost* of labour. Since average wage curve is rising upwards, the corresponding marginal wage curve will also be rising at a greater rate. Fig. 5 illustrates the shape of the two curves under imperfect competition.

In Figure 5, the employer is in equilibrium at point E where MRP = MW. The employer will demand OL units of labour. At E, MRP is at a higher level (i.e. EL in the Fig.), but the wage for a worker is at a lower level i.e. LR and whenever wage is lesser than MRP, there is exploitation of labour. The exploitation is equal to ER for the worker. Total revenue product in the figure is OLQP. Total wages paid is OLRS. So exploitation of labour is equal to PQRS, as shown by the shaded rectangle.

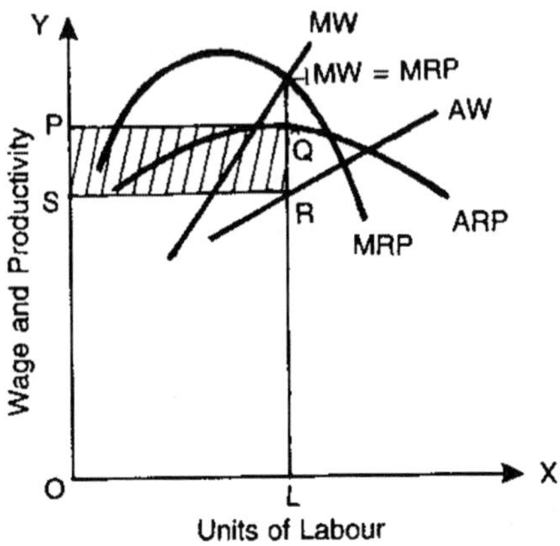

Trade Union Movement in India

Trade unions are associations of workers who voluntarily come together to promote their welfare and protect their welfare and their interests through collective action. According to Sydney and Webb, trade union is *'a continuous association of wage earners for the purpose of maintaining and improving the condition of their working lines.'*

Early Development

The trade union movement in India started in the first part of the 20th century, although the seeds of the movement were sown with the formation of the Bombay Mill Hand's Association in 1890, whose pioneers were Mr. Lokhande, S. S. Bengalee and others who were successful in promoting worker's welfare, by forming trade unions and organising strikes.

Trade Union Movement during 1920s

With the end of the I World War, a modern Trade Union movement took permanent roots in India. The first All India Organisation, namely the All India Trade Union Congress (A.I.T.U.C.) was set up in 1920 to promote worker's interests and to unite the smaller unions. The A.I.T.U.C took the responsibility of spreading the movement to regions where it had not penetrated.

Trade Union Act, 1926

In 1926, the government passed the Trade Union Act, which had far-reaching effects on the movement. This Act laid down the rules for registration which enhanced the status of the unions. The Act conferred on the Unions certain rights and privileges and they now enjoyed a certain amount of protection from law suits and criminal prosecutions for their activities in furthering an industrial dispute.

The registered unions were not allowed to use their funds for political purposes and they were required to submit an annual audited statement of accounts.

Towards the end of the 1920s, there was a major split in the trade union movement since leaders differed in their ideologies. The Communists established their hold over A.I.T.U.C, and the Moderates established the All India Trade Union Federation.

The 1930s started with an unfavourable climate and brought a lull in the trade union activity. The serious economic depression aggravated the effect. There was widespread retrenchment and strikes of this period aimed at maintaining wages and preventing retrenchment. But just before the II World War, unity in the movement was brought about.

The Trade Union Movement during II World War

The II World War created a controversy and the trade union leaders again split on the question of participating in the war. The nationalist leaders wanted to strengthen the national movement and overthrow the British, whereas the Communists following the Russian Communist Party wanted to help the British fight the Nazis. This caused a sharp rift in ideologies and the Trade Union movement witnessed a split again. The government used the Defence of India Rules and prohibited lock-outs and strikes and referred all industrial disputes to conciliation and adjudication. But the deteriorating economic conditions made workers conscious of the need for making organised efforts for securing relief. This resulted in a marked increase in the number of both trade unions and organised workers.

Post-Independent Period

After Independence and Partition, the country was plagued with growing unemployment. A series of strikes swept the country and the number of strikes and man days lost during this period were the highest recorded in the country. The disunity was aggravated by the starting of three central organisations during this period. The India National Trade Union Congress (I.N.T.U.C.) was started in 1947 and was controlled by the Congress Party. The Praja Socialist Party started the Hind Mazdoor Sabha (HMS) in 1948 and the United Trade Union Congress (U.T.U.C) was formed in 1949 by some radicalists. All these organisations have been working for the betterment of labour.

It may be observed that the movement is more widespread and has taken deep roots. It is now better organised and is on a more permanent footing.

Defects of the Trade Union Movement

According to V. V Gire, the Trade Union Movement in India suffers from the following defects:

(i) Predominance of small sized unions - nearly 3/4[ths] of the unions have less 500 members.

(ii) The unions suffer from poor finance on account of both small membership and small subscriptions.

(iii) They suffer from the absence of full-time paid officers.

Apart from these, there are other serious defects which have to be mentioned. They are:

(i). Leadership has been provided by outsiders specially professional politicians. Naturally, the welfare of the workers are often ignored and trade unions are used to promote the interests of the political parties.

(ii) Most unions have concentrated on the organisation of strikes to bargain with the employers. They have ignored beneficial activities like provision of medical and sickness relief, educational and cultural activities etc.

(iii) Finally, the nature of the working class has adversely affected the efficiency of the trade unions. For example, illiteracy, ignorance, migratory character and differences between workers in caste, creed, religions, language etc. has rendered the trade unions inefficient.

Measures to Strengthen the Movement

A strong trade union is necessary to safeguard the interests of labour and help in achieving the targets of production. The following measures may be adopted to strengthen the trade union movement.

(i) *Unity Amongst Workers:* All those who believe in the Trade Union Movement should join hands to form a single central organisation to represent all their demands. The alternative will be for all trade unions with different affiliations to come together, on the basis of a common programme including methods, objectives and procedures.

(ii) *Removing Unhealthy Political Influence:* Trade unions must be removed from the influence of political parties which are prepared to sacrifice the interests of the working class to serve party ends. The workers must be made to realise the utter uselessness of party politics in trade unionism.

(iii) *One Union One Industry:* Multiplicity of unions in a single establishment leads to inter-union rivalries. This weakens the power of collective bargaining and reduces the effectiveness of workers in securing their rights.

(iv) *Working Class Leadership:* Trade union leadership has almost been provided by outsiders who are professional agitators and who are interested in using workers as pawns in their political game. It is essential that trade unions should be taken over by workers themselves. The setting up of the Asian Trade Union College at Calcutta to train young men from working class in trade unionism, has been welcomed.

(v) *Conscious Trade Union Leadership:* It is necessary for the trade union leaders to acquire a full understanding of the constitutional and legal rights available to the unions. Personal integrity, patience, understanding and courage are some qualities which a trade union leader must possess.

(vi) *Awareness of Workers:* Trade unions must inculcate in the workers, a sense of responsibility and discipline. Every worker must be made to understand fully his duties and responsibilities first, and then his rights and privileges.

(vii) *Greater Benefits from Unions:* Indian trade unions are operating more or less like strike committees. The moment the remedy is obtained the interests of the workers sag, and such a state of affairs should be avoided. Trade unions should provide certain benefits to the workers such as compensation for accidents, medical aid, education, thrift etc.

Besides, maintenance of strike funds by the unions is a necessity, which would be used to help workers during strikes as *'strikes pay.'* This will ensure strength and loyalty of the members to the union.

Industrial Disputes in India

Industrial disputes refer to conflicts or frictions between the employers and workers. From the side of workers, conflicts take the form of protests like strikes, go-slow tactics, gheraos, demonstration etc. On the side of employers, conflicts take the form, retrenchment, dismissals, lock-outs etc. Any kind of conflict results in tensions and loss of production and a decline in national income. It is therefore, necessary to know the cause of industrial disputes and the measures to settle them.

Causes of Industrial Disputes

(i) *Demand for More Wages and Allowances*

In recent years, wages have not been rising in proportion to the rise in prices. The Indian industrialists have not been following an enlightened policy in the matters of paying wages. Most industrial disputes were due to demand for high wages.

(ii) *Demand for Bonus and Increase in Bonus*

There is an increasing feeling among the workers that they should get a greater share in the profits of industrial concerns. Non-acceptance of this by the employers has been a source of friction among the employers and employees.

(iii) *Demand for Improved Working Conditions*

This may take the form of lesser working hours, better safety measures in the workplace, canteen facilities, leaves etc. which are also responsible for industrial conflicts.

(iv) *Retrenchment of Workers*

Sometimes workers may be retrenched for some reasons such as closing down of some sections of the industry, recession in the industry etc. This would be opposed by the workers resulting in industrial disputes.

(vi) *Other Causes*

Among the other causes, mention may be made of the failure of the employers to recognise trade unions, conflict between rival unions for representation, insult to trade union leadership, introduction of rationalisation of the factory etc.

Settlement of Industrial Disputes

Industrial disputes lead to several unpleasant consequences and so efforts should be made to settle disputes and promote better industrial relations. With this objective in mind, Government of India passed the Industrial Disputes Act of 1947 which was amended in 1956.

The machinery for the settlement of industrial disputes, outlined by the Act is as follows:

(i) *Works Committees*

These are joint committees of employers and employees which attempt to remove the causes of friction and promote good relation between the parties. Industrial establishments with 100 or more workers may be directed to constitute such a committee by the government. On June 30 1987, such committees were functioning in 560 establishments.

(ii) Conciliation Officers

Conciliation officers are appointed by the Government for particular regions and industries. It is the duty of these officers to bring together both the parties and resolve their differences. Then they send a report to the government about the success or failure of their efforts in settling the disputes.

(iii) Board of Conciliation

Board of Conciliation appointed by the government for settlement of disputes consists of a chairman who is an independent person, and two or four persons representing the employers and employees. It takes up any case, referred to it by the government. It reports to the government about the success or failure including the steps taken and reasons for the failure to bring about a settlement.

(iv) Court of Enquiry

Whenever the conciliation officers or Board of Conciliation fail to settle a dispute, the matter is referred to the Court of Enquiry. The Court consists of one or more independent persons. The court will investigate the dispute and submit its report to the government, the case will then be referred to the Industrial Tribunal for adjudication.

(v) Labour Courts

Labour courts have been set up by State governments to go into the disputed orders of employers, dismissals, suspensions of employees, legality of strikes, lock-outs etc. Labour courts settle matters speedily and report to the government.

(vi) Industrial Tribunals

Industrial tribunals are of two types

(a) State tribunals are set up by state governments and headed by a high court judge. They adjudicate disputes relating to wages, bonus, etc.

(b) National tribunals are appointed by the Central government for adjudication of the industrial disputes involving matters of national importance. The adjudications of these two tribunals are binding on the parties concerned.

(vii) Joint Management Council

The government has recommended the setting up of the Joint

Management Council consisting of the representatives of the employers and workers in each establishment. The workers' participation in management helps them to understand the problems of the industry and help them contribute towards the creation of better industrial relations.

(viii) Code of Discipline

A code of discipline was evolved in 1958, at the Indian Labour Conference, by the national trade unions and leading organisations of employers. This code seeks to avoid strikes and lock-outs and voluntarily agree to maintain and create an atmosphere of mutual trust and cooperation. All grievances and disputes are to be settled by mutual negotiation and conciliation.

Conclusion

The above machinery for the settlement of industrial disputes is being effectively utilised in recent times and has contributed to better industrial relations.

Minimum Wage Controversy

A national wage policy in the narrow sense, deals with the problems of the level or structure of wages or both, with specific objectives of obtaining better levels of living for workers in the organised sector. In the broad sense, it includes the formulation of guidelines for fixation of wages for all categories of workers, both organised and unorganised. Thus, a wage policy is directed to influence wages across the board, so that the broad social objectives of living wages, a fair wage and reduction in sharp inequalities in wage payments can be obtained.

Minimum Wages Act, 1948.

The Minimum Wages Act, 1948 came into force form 15th March 1948 and was amended several times, the latest being the 1993 amendment.

According to the Act, the minimum wages must provide not merely for the bare subsistence but also for the preservation of efficiency of the worker, and so it must provide for some measure of education, medical requirements and amenities. The capacity of the employer to pay is not a consideration in fixing wages.

Thus, the minimum wage was prescribed as the lower limit and the upper limit was set by the capacity of the industry to pay. The National Commission on Labour (NCL) very categorically stated: 'Among the competing claims on value-added in industry, *'the first claim is of the worker for a basic minimum wage irrespective of any other consideration. Beyond this, however, in the determination of wage differentials, the capacity to pay becomes relevant.'*

The Chakravarty Committee also recommended that the minimum wage should not fall below the poverty line. However, minimum wages should be suitably adjusted taking into account variations between different centres and regions.

The Bhoothalingam Study group in a very forthright statement mentioned: *'the real minimum wage can only be the absolute national minimum, irrespective of sectors, regions or states, below which no employment would be permitted.'*

With such loud pronouncements, the study group recommended a minimum wage of Rs.150 per month at 1978 prices, as against the recommendation of Rs.200 by the Chakravarthy Committee at 1974 prices. Obviously, the recommendations of the Study group were considered to be regressive by the Trade unions. But the fact remains that there is a need to prescribe a basic minimum wage supported by steps for its reinforcement.

Questions

1. What do you mean by wage. Distinguish between real wage and money wage.
2. Briefly explain the subsistence theory of wages.
3. Explain residual claimant theory of wages.
4. Give an explanatory note on marginal productivity theory of wages.
5. Explain the modern theory of wages
6. Briefly explain the Trade Union Movement in India.

❖❄❖❄❖

CHAPTER

16 ECONOMIC OPTIMISATION

For a consumer, normative science helps in determining the appropriate consumption level, given his objective of maximising satisfaction and the constraint of spending due to the limited purchasing power he possesses.

For a producer, on the other hand, managerial economics as a normative science, assists in taking a decision to produce most appropriate units of a product to maximise profit, with the limitations he has in procuring raw material, technology, skilled labour and other infrastructure facilities.

These two roles of normative science is considered as economic optimisation. In other words, *'Economic Optimisation strikes a balance between the objective and constraints and provides the optimum solution.'* For a consumer, it indicates an optimum consumption level for the purchasing power at his disposal to get maximum satisfaction. Similarly, it indicates the optimum production level with the given resources to maximise profits to the producer.

Concept

Economic optimization refers to the fixing of value which can be minimum or maximum for attaining an objective. There may be a single objective or a number of objectives and they also differ from organisation to organisation.

An enterprise, for example, might have the single objective of optimising profits. In this case, the firm will have to decide about the inputs and their values to be employed in the production process to get optimum output which brings optimum profit. These inputs may be under the control of the firm and only by varying the controllable inputs (these are called choice variables) and the firm may produce optimum output and attain its objective of earning optimum profit. In the process, the firm may encounter certain problems (constraints) which may have to be solved.

Similarly, another enterprise may have multiple objectives like utilising resources, providing more job opportunities to people, optimising profit etc. But there may be constraints too. If all the objectives are to be implemented, the cost of capital maybe more which increases the cost of production. Therefore, solution for such constraints has to be found out. The firm can enter the capital market and get the required capital at the least possible costs or it may raise the capital by balancing debt and equity and thus make the cost reasonable.

Thus, the concept of economic optimisation involves both objectives and constraints of our enterprises and helps in securing the desired results. In the process, the objectives and constraints are analysed, problems are identified, solutions are arrived at and implemented to attain the optimum level of operation.

Process of Economic Optimization

The problem of economic optimization involves the following processes:

(i) Analysis of Objectives and Constraints

The firm must have some control over the variables which determine the achievement of the goal. If profit making is the objective of the firm, then at least some factors which determine profits like production cost, selling costs etc. must be under its control. Generally, all firms enjoy control over at least some of the constraints which determine profits. The firms have to identify these variables and use them effectively to achieve the goal.

(ii) Identification of Problems

The firm must identify whether there is only one factor which determines the achievement of the goal or a number of factors. If it is the former, it is called *single factor* optimization problem. Otherwise, it is a *multi-factor* optimization problem.

Further, the firm may have to optimize, both when it has constraints and also when it has no constraints. Sometimes, the constraints may arise within the firm and sometimes they may arise due to external factors.

A firm optimizing under constraints may further be faced with the problem of producing to the extent of availability of the factors. It may be forced to produce a limited quantity due to limited factors at its disposal. In other words, the quantity produced is equal to the amount of factor availability. This is a case of *'equality constraint.'* Sometimes the firms may optimize by producing output either equal to or less than the available amount of factors. This is a case of *'inequality constraints'*.

(iii) Arriving at Solutions

Taking all the above discussed problems into consideration, the firm tries to attain optimization. Solutions are arrived at by trying to strike a balance between the objectives of the firms and the limitations they face.

Thus, the optimization problem may be depicted in the following manner :

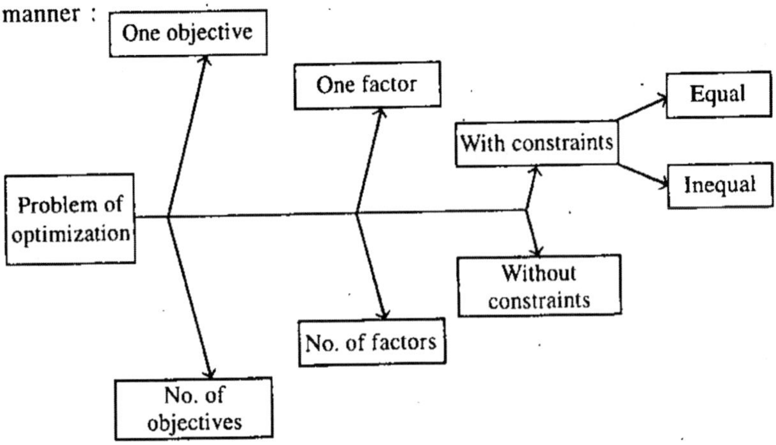

(iv) *Requirements for Solving Problems of Optimisation*

Before a firm can optimise, it is necessary to have one objective factor (which is important in attaining the goal) under its control. It must also be possible for the firm to express this factor in a form suitable for analysis.

But we must remember that if this factor has a fixed value, then there is nothing left for the firm to optimise. For e.g., if the Government of India fixes a certain quota for importing washing machines to a dealer in India and also fixes the selling price of these machines in India, then the dealer has no problems of optimization. He has no control over the factors viz., quantity and price of washing machines, which determine profits. However, if the government allows the dealer to import any quantity or allows him to fix the selling price, then he is faced with the problem of attaining optimum profits.

Another problem faced by the firm is to derive a relationship between the factors which determine the goal and the goal itself. We can arrive at a relationship between these two by using tables, graphs or equations.

For example, we may consider the following function :

$$P = f(Q)$$

where, P = profit

q = output (quantity)

The above function does not reveal whether there is a direct or inverse relationship between the two, we may have to further specify the relationship between the two by expressing it as $\frac{\Delta P}{\Delta O} > O$ for a direct relationship and $\frac{\Delta P}{\Delta O} < O$ for an inverse relationship.

The usual relationship between profit and output may be expressed in a tabular form:

Output (Q)	Profit
0	–40
1	15
2	35
3	50
4	60
5	68
6	73
7	68
8	60
9	50
10	35
11	15
12	–5

The above table can be graphically represented as follows:

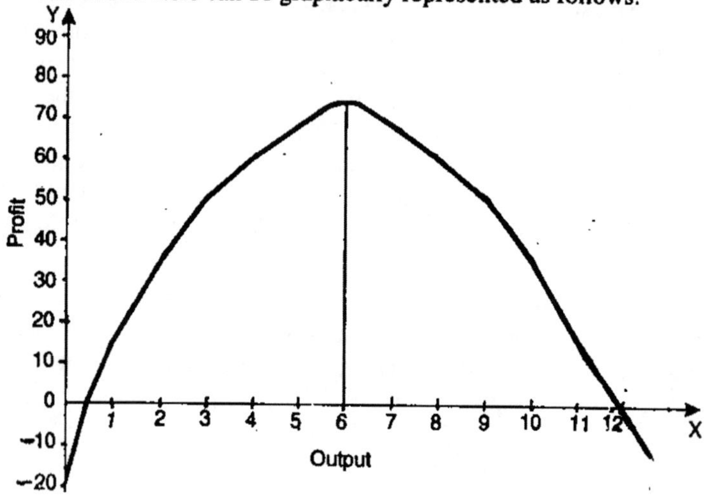

From the tabular form of the profit function, it is clear that profit reaches maximum level at the 5th unit of output. We can also obtain the average incremental profit (AIP) for the different levels of output. If this is done, the output at which profit is maximum is the one at which AIP is the least before turning negative. AIP is nothing but change in profit divided by change in output. Since output changes by one unit each time, AIP = Δ, where Δ denotes change.

Output	AIP
1	25
2	20
3	15
4	10
5	8
6	5
7	–5
8	–8
9	–10
10	–15
11	–20
12	–15

Thus, when AIP is the least i.e., 5 before it turns negative, profits are maximum.

To conclude, the discussion on economic optimisation, is a concept which tries to explain the situation where the consumer, with his limited purchasing power, strives hard to get maximum satisfaction by consuming the goods and services provided by producers according to his taste prefrence and fashion on the one hand and the producer working hard to produce optimum output with the limited resources at his command on the other. It explains the optimisation of goals of both the producer and the consumer.

Questions

1. What do you mean by economic optimisation.
2. Give a note on economic optimisation.

❖✻❖✻❖

CHAPTER 17

CAPITAL BUDGETING

MEANING

Capital as a term refers to that part of man's wealth which is used in producing further wealth which yields an income. Capital is a produced means of production. The term is generally used to mean capital goods such as plant and machinery, tools and accessories, stocks of raw materials, goods in process, energy means etc.

Capital plays an important role in the economic development of a country. It is impossible to think of production without capital. Capital mobilisation is very important before organising production. At the same time, the entrepreneur is required to formulate a budget of capital disposition. Capital budget is an estimate of expenditures involved in procuring plant, machinery, raw materials etc. Capital budget is a blueprint of a company's financial policies, plans and performance. At the same time, it is an index of performance. Based on this performance, the budgeting technique is developed. Capital budgeting is defined as a management function in designing and carrying through a systematic investment programme.

Forms of Capital Budgeting

Capital budget takes several forms. The management of a company has to decide the following things :

(a) Whether to buy a new plant or build a new factory or buy one which is functioning.

(b) Whether to replace the existing machinery by a new one or to improve it by suitable repairs and conditioning.

(c) Whether the equipment is to be imported or to be acquired within the country.

(d) Whether to buy new or second - hand machinery.

(e) Whether the new equipment should be purchased outright or should be acquired on lease.

The capital budget should contain the following informations :

(a) a list of investment proposals, (b) the estimated cost of proposed projects, (c) the likely earnings of these proposals, (d) the paȳ back period and the expected rate of return. All these information are necessary for the preparation of a capital budget.

A capital budget should be flexible enough to accommodate itself to the changing conditions. Since capital budget is essentially a process of planning hence the resources should be used in the best possible manner.

The following is an example of a capital budget of a company in Bangalore, manufacturing PVC pipes:

Sl. No.	Item of expenditure	Proposed amount In Rs. Lakh	Justification
1.	Extruders 2	Rs. 20.00	These machines are indispensable, for setting up a PVC Tube unit.
2.	Injection moulds 10	Rs. 2.00	
3.	Cutting Machine	Rs. 0.20	
4.	Grinding Machine	Rs. 0.20	
5.	Moulding Machine	Rs. 2.60	
	Total	Rs. 25.00	

Investment on the above machinery is called *capital expenditure.* The capacity of the machinery depends upon the probable sales of different sizes of tubes. If the firm is small and there is centralisation, the capital budget is prepared straight away. If it is a large company and there is decentralisation, the capital budget is prepared department wise and then a consolidated budget for the entire company is prepared.

The capital budget contains the following information :

(i) A description of the proposals,

(ii) A proposed investment outlay,

(iii) The likely savings of earnings,

(iv) The expected life of the project,

(v) The pay back period,

(vi) The expected rate of return.

The above information is necessary in order to evaluate the investment proposals and monitor its progress.

Types of Capital Budgets

A modern industrial organisation is so complex in character that an elaborate budget is to be formulated. This contains various details. If an organisation is engaged in both production and marketing, its capital budget should show all the details. The method of preparing capital budget depends upon the activities that a firm performs. Generally, the following approaches have been suggested to prepare the capital budget.

(i) the expedient or last resort approach,

(ii) the product mission approach and

(iii) the functional approach.

The expedient approach is an adhoc way of incurring capital expenditure - whenever exigency arises, capital expenditure is incurred. If a crisis arises, some effort is put to tide over the crisis. As such, this approach is known as *planning* for a crisis. This kind of approach is generally followed by public sector firms and government industrial concerns. This is not capital budget in a real sense.

In the second approach focussing in modern times, firms generally do not satisfy in the production of one product. They want to manufacture many products. Generally, they are called *multi-product* firms. For example, a pharmaceutical firm produces several drugs and vitamins and tonics. In such firms, the capital budget is prepared for each separate item. A machinery for drug manufacturing cannot be used for vitamins manufacturing. The investment of capital requires a conscious and deliberate planning of existing resources with a view to achieve the broad objectives of a company.

Functional mission approach deals with the type of service rendered in the production and marketing of a product. When the product is produced or marketed, it involves services. Any innovation introduced would add to the services. The rendering of service depends on the resources available with the company. In other words, the available resources must be used in such a manner that it should lead to the rendering of service. This is the functional approach of budget.

Need for Capital Budgeting

Capital budgeting is indispensable for establishing and running industrial organisations. In modern times, huge capital is required to set up a plant, which will have to be raised from the financial market. If the generation of profit from investments is not sufficient, then the firm incurs substantial loss. While committing large expenditure for a project, the management will have to make a proper study of its future profitability. This calls for capital budgeting.

Capital budgeting is necessary in order to secure adequate return from investment for this purpose, higher operating costs are to be reduced and idleness of the machinery should be avoided. Investment decisions, therefore, should be done carefully through capital budgeting.

When capital expenditure is incurred on a project, there arises the long term nature of fund commitment. When once such a huge investment is made, it cannot be reversed or transferred to some other use. The investment is sunk and the mistake cannot be rectified. Therefore, if a realistic capital budgeting is made, all these uncertainties can be avoided.

If capital budgeting is done systematically, it results in losses to the firm. Any investment made on plant and equipment will bring returns only in the long run. Therefore, correct decisions will have to be made after capital budgeting.

All these arguments show the importance of capital budgeting. Capital budgeting is very necessary whenever long term investment is required to be made. Capital budgeting is one of the areas of managerial decision taking.

Nature of Capital Budgeting

Capital budgeting involves the following three things :

(i) The amount of resources required for capital expenditure,

(ii) The availability of monetary resources and

(iii) The allocation of available money to the various competing projects.

Supply of Capital

There is a problem of mobilising sufficient capital for investments. This is called *supply of capital.* The supply of capital comes from sources namely internal and external. The sources of internal resources are: (i) depreciation collection and (ii) retained profits. The external resources are receipts from the sale of shares and debentures. The management has to do considerable exercise to forecast how much money can be raised internally. If the companies build up funds like depreciation fund, reserve fund and undistributed profits fund, then the company can take up necessary capital investment. If a company decides to expand production or modernise the industry then it has to go the capital market by means of selling additional shares and debentures. In the capital budgeting, an elaborate future forecast is required to be made.

Demand for Capital

The capital is required either to replace the existing machinery or to set up a new plant or to expand the scales of operation. The company has to make a list of capital equipments needed during a certain period. An inventory of capital equipments reveal the capital needs of the company. In other words, the inventory shows when such a machinery is to be replaced or modified and so on. Machinery is subject to wear and tear and for which depreciation is to be allowed. In the initial period, the old machinery is conditioned and afterwards, it will be replaced by new machinery. The question which arises is that at what stage the existing plant is to be replaced. There are some machineries which would become useless. When the machine becomes unproductive, it becomes obsolete. Obsolescence has a different connotation as well. Some techniques which are in vogue today may become obsolete tomorrow. A superior technique needs to be introduced to be incorporated in capital budgeting. When a company wishes to diversify production, there is a need for additional funds.

Capital Rationing

Capital is a scarce resource and also it has a cost. Whenever a certain amount of capital is invested, the most important point to be considered is to find out suitable returns on investment. The management will have to take correct decisions regarding this aspect. If the investment yields a reasonable rate of return, then only the management takes a decision on investment. In effect, it is a measure to determine the cut-off point in capital budgeting.

Since the capital is scarce, it should be utilised in such a manner that it should bring a reasonable rate of return for a long time to come. It means that it should be utilised only in profitable industries. The prospective return differs from industry to industry. In capital intensive industries, the rate of return is low. In consumer goods industries, the rate of return is high. In India, public industries have been set up to create proper infrastructure in the country. Those investments have resulted in creating infrastructure while the rate of return is not even reasonable. The private sector industries consider the rate of return which is very reasonable.

Investment Criteria and Investment Appraisal

Capital investment decisions are based upon whether the management wants to install new equipment or to replace the existing ones. Whenever there are technological changes, the old machinery has to be replaced by new ones. When a new equipment is to be purchased, an appraisal will have to be done for the cost of the new equipment - this is an important factor for decision-making. This appraisal has to be made in respect of incremental cost and not the full cost.

There are several methods for evaluating the profitability of investments. These methods provide a yardstick by which alternative projects may be measured and projects may be ranked after an appraisal. These methods are:

Pay Back Period Method

The pay back method is used to find out in how many years, the investment is got back. It is measured in terms of monetary value. There are two aspects in this method - one is the amount of investment on new equipment, plant or machinery and the expected annual returns. The total investment is divided by the annual return to determine the pay-back period.

$$\text{Pay back period} = \frac{\text{Amount invested}}{\text{Annual return.}}$$

Supposing the investment on a plant is Rs. 2 lakh and the annual return is Rs. 25,000, the pay back period is : 2 lakhs + Rs. 25,000 = 8 years. This means the initial investment is recovered in eight years. By calculating pay back period, we can rank the projects on the basis of profitability. Let us assume that a firm has four investment proposals with relevant data :

Investment Proposal	Initial Investment	Life in Years	Amount of cash flow
A	Rs. 2,00,000	15	Rs .25,000
B	1,50,000	12	30,000
C	1,20,000	10	20,000
D	1,00,000	10	10,000

Pay back period is to be calculated and ranked. This is as follows :

Investment Proposal	Initial investment	Life in years	Annual earnings	Pack back period	Ranking
A	2,00,000	15	25,000	8.0	4
B	1,50,000	12	30,000	5.0	1
C	1,20,000	10	20;000	6.0	2
D	1,00,000	10	16,000	6.3	3

On the basis of the pay back period, investment proposal 'B' is considered to be good. The pay back period emphasises quick cash return flow. Where liquidity is considered very important, the pay back period is used. This method is used by American companies when they want to invest in other countries. If a particular project does not pay itself within five years, then this project is considered not viable.

Advantages of Pay Back Period

This method is very simple to calculate and easy to understand. It enables the management to judge the length of time the funds are blocked and risks involved in various projects. This method is useful in selecting industries without much risk and less gestation period. By looking into project profiles, it is possible to select less risky projects. By this method, it is possible to reject those proposals which suffer from uncertainty and risk. However, it favours those proposals which yield more in a short period.

Limitations

The pay-back method of evaluation suffers from some limitations. Though the project profile may say that the pay time is very short with high profitability, but in reality, it may not be so. Profits may be comfortable in the beginning but after some time, it may dwindle, resulting in longer pay back period. This method may not approve the projects with long gestation periods. But these projects may show high prospects of growth. Liquidity may be a good sign for a viable project but the growth aspect cannot be turned down. Generally, a firm makes investments not only with a view to get profit but also to establish itself permanently. A project not only earns profit in the pay back period, but also earns through the existence of the project.

Let us take up an example to show how the returns plays an important role in the selection of the projects:

Proposals	I year	II year	III year	IV year
A	25,000	25,000	10,000	5,000
B	15,000	15,000	20,000	30,000

Suppose a firm has two investment proposals with an investment of Rs. 50,000. In the above example, proposal 'A' has 2 years and B has 3 years of pay back period. On this basis, the firm selects proposal 'A'. Actually proposal 'B' yields Rs. 80,000 in the 4 years period as against Rs. 65,000 yielded by proposal 'A'. On this basis, proposal 'B' is better than 'A'. It means that the pay back period does not allow the firm to select a project which gives low returns in the initial period but high returns afterwards.

There is however a preference to the pay back method owing to certain inherent advantages.

According to George A Christy, when the life of a project is greater than twice the pay back period, the reciprocal of the pay back period is a close estimate of the true rate of returns. Prof. Harter Thomas observes that professional managers use the pay back method as a means to demonstrate their ability to generate quick profits. Shorter the pay back period, greater is the realisation of investment capital. Therefore, the pay back approach is very much used in these days of technological developments.

Rate of Return Method

This is another method of evaluating the project. This method is based on the financial statement of the firm. This method aims at providing us with an estimate of the rate of returns. It does not consider the time as spent. It considers the average rate of return over the life of the project. In order to find out the average rate of returns, the total net income is divided by the average investment over the life of the project. The formula for calculating the average rate of return is as follows :

$$\text{ARR} = \frac{\text{Estimated net profits}}{\text{Capital employed}} \times 100$$

Let us take up the following example.

Suppose : Initial investment is Rs. 2 lakhs.
Gross annual cash flow is Rs. 40,000.
Depreciation is Rs. 20,000 and
Net annual cash flow is Rs. 20,000.

$$\frac{\text{Net annual return}}{\text{Original investment}} \times 100 = \frac{20{,}000}{20{,}000} \times \frac{100}{1} = 10\%$$

There is a diversity of practice in measuring the capital invested. Some firms take only the initial investment to calculate the rate of returns. Some other firms take average amount invested over the life of the project. The average amount is calculated by adding the initial investment and scrap value and this method is considered to be more realistic.

The formula for calculating average rate of return is as follows :

Initial Investment + Scrap Value If the scrap value is zero, then average rate of return is only half of the initial investment. The average rate of return is the net annual cash flow divided by half of the original investment. Taking the previous example, the ARR is :

$$\text{ARR} = \frac{\text{Net annual cash flow}}{\frac{\text{Intial investment}}{2}} \times 100$$

$$= \frac{20{,}000}{\frac{20{,}000}{2}} \times 100 = 20\%$$

It shows that the average rate of return under the second version is double the rate under the first version.

Project Appraisal

Let us apply the above formula to the five proposals under consideration. We assume that the scrap value is zero. Annual depreciation is calculated by dividing the initial investment by number of years. Net annual cash flow = gross annual cash flow - depreciation. ARR is calculated on an average and not on initial investment.

Ranking of the proposals using ARR method :

Proposal	Initial investment Rs.	Life in years	Annual cash flow Rs.	Depre-ciation Rs.	Nett annual cash flow Rs.	ARR %	Rank-ing
A	3 lakhs	20	75,000	20,000	55,000	50	III
B	2 lakhs	15	60,000	9,000	51,000	60	II
C	1.5 lakhs	10	50,000	8,000	42,000	66.6	I
D	1 lakhs	6	20,000	5,000	15,000	40	IV

As shown in the above table, proposal 'C' is viable: his second best. Project D is least preferred.

This method is very simple to calculate and easy to understand. The chief limitation is that it does not take into account the time value of money. It gives the same importance of money received now and the money received in future. Secondly, the expected rate of return is misleading because it ignores year by year pattern of profits.

The Net Present Value Index (NRI) Method

The two methods explained earlier, which are also known as traditional methods of investment appraisals, suffer from a major defect, namely ignoring the time value of money. The net present value index method removes this defect while calculating the profitability of project proposals.

In this method, the value of the time is considered very important. Money received at present is more valuable than the equivalent amount of money received next year or the year after. The reason is that money received today can be invested to earn a certain rate of interest. Value of money will not remain the same in future. For example. Rs. 1,100 next year if the rate of interests is 10% (Principal Rs. 10,00 + interest Rs. 100 = Rs. 1100). In the same way, Rs. 1000 received next year is not equal to Rs. 1000 this year, but it is worth less than the 1000. In other words, Rs. 1000 of next year will have to be discounted by an interest rate of Rs. 10 per cent.

$$\text{Present value (PV)} = \frac{R_1}{1+r}$$

in which R_1 = value in the first year, r = rate of interest.

For example, if R_1 is Rs. 100 and r is 10 percent, then the present value of R_1 is

$$\frac{100}{1+10\%} = \frac{100}{1+0.1} = \frac{100}{1.1} = \text{Rs. } 99.91$$

It means Rs. 100 of the next year will be equal to Rs. 90.91 of this year. Hence, the present value of a future income to revenue is its value discounted at rate of interest known as the discount rate. This formula can be extended to find out the total present value of the stream of annual returns or cash flows over a number of years.

$$\text{TPV (Total present value)} = \frac{R_1}{1+r} + \frac{R_2}{(1+r)^2} + \frac{R_3}{(1+r)^3} ....+ \frac{R_n}{(1+r)^n}$$

The net present value of an investment proposal is the difference between the total of present values of the estimated annual cash flows over the life of the project and the initial investment of the project. If the net present value is positive, it is profitable, if it is negative, it is not profitable. For example,

Initial outlay of project	= Rs. 2 lakhs
Life of the project	= 5 years
Scrap value of the present asset the at end of 10 years	= Rs. 10,000
Net cash flow : First year	= Rs. 10,000
Second year	= Rs. 49,000
Third year	= Rs. 54,000
Fourth year	= Rs. 55,000
Fifth year	= Rs. 47,000
Rate of Interest	= 10%

The management has to compute the present value of next benefit or cash flow at discount rate of 10%.

Year	Net cash flow	Discount factor at 10%	Present value CPV
I year	Rs. 35,000	0.91	Rs. 31,850
II year	Rs. 49,000	0.83	Rs. 40,670
III year	Rs. 54,000	0.75	Rs. 40,500
IV year	Rs. 55,000	0.68	Rs. 37,400
V year	Rs. 47,000	0.62	Rs. 27,140
			Rs. 1,79,560

Now, the initial investment = Rs. 20,00,000
Scrap value at the end of 5 year = 10,000
Present scrap value (Rs. 10,000 x 0.62) = 6,200
Present value of investment
(2,00,000 – 6,200) = 1,93,800
Net present value = Gross present value - present value of investment
= Rs. 1,79,560 – 1,93,800
= –14,240

In this case, the net present value is negative and hence the project is not profitable.

Ranking of the Proposals

When there are a number of investment proposals, we have to compute the present value of cash flows of all the proposals. We have to calculate the net present value index (NPVI) by using the following formula :

$$\text{NPVI} = \frac{\text{Gross present Value of the proposal}}{\text{Initial investment}}$$

If the index shows once the higher side, the proposal is profitable. The proposals have to be ranked in accordance with their net present value index.

Let us now apply this formula and find out the NPVI and then say whether the proposal stands at the highest rank or not.

1 Proposal	2 Initial invest-ment	3 Annual cash flow	4 Life in Yrs.	5 Profit factor at 10%	6 Gross PV (3 x 5)	7 NPVI 6 + 2	8 Ranking
A	3 lakhs	75000	20	8.5	637500	2.15	II
B	2 lakhs	60000	15	7.7	462000	2.31	I
C	1.5 lakhs	50000	10	6.1	305000	2.01	III
D	1 lakhs	20000	6	4.3	86000	0.86	IV

On the basis of the above table, proposal 'B' is the most profitable proposal followed by A and C. If any project has NPVI less than one, the project will have to be rejected outright.

Discounted Cash Flow Method

Discounted cash flow method takes into account the fact that the money received today is more valuable than the same amount received next year. In the investment of capital, time factor plays an important role. This method therefore gives greater importance to the time value of money in calculating the profitability of the proposals.

The process of adjusting the face value of future cash flows to their present value by means of imputed interest is called *discounting*. The imputed rate of interest is the rate of return. The imputed rate of return calculation that takes into consideration the time value of money is called the *discounted cash flow method.*

The discounted rate is that interest rate which when applied to a series of future cash flows, brings the sum of their present values to the same level as the original investment. The rate of interest is usually found with the help of present value tables, though it can also be calculated with the help of a more complicated arithmetical formula which is as follows:

$$C = \frac{R_1}{1+r^1} + \frac{R_2}{(1+r)^2} + \frac{R_3}{(1+r)^3} + \dots\dots\dots \frac{R_n}{(1+r)^n}$$

Where C is initial investment or purchase price of the capital equipment, R_1, R_2, R_3 is the income stream of projects over different years and r = rate of discount.

For example, the purchase price of machinery is Rs. 1.64 lakhs including taxes and then the machine has a life of 5 years, with no scrap value, and the cash flow is as follows :

Year	*1*	2	3	4	5
Cash flow Rs.	30,000	40,000	60,000	50,000	40,000

The internal rate of return is to be calculated by the trial and error method. Discount the future income flows of Rs. 30,000, 40,000, 60,000, etc. to the present value by such a rate of interest that the total present values is equal to the purchase price of the capital asset. Since there is no objective method of finding a unique rate of discount, which will reduce the future income flows to equal the purchase price of the machinery, we have to follow a trial and error approach.

Year	**Annual cash flow**	**Present value of discount factor (at 8%)**	**Present value**
1	30,000	0.93	27,900
2	40,000	0.86	34,400
3	50,000	0.80	40,000
4	60,000	0.73	43,800
5	40,000	0.68	27,200
			TPV = 1,73,300

As per the assumption of keeping the discount factor at 8 percent, the total present value is equal to Rs. 1,73,300. But the gross present values are not equal to the present value of investment. Hence, the discount rate of 8 percent is discarded and a discount of 10 percent is assumed. Then, the position is

Year	Annual Cash flow	Discount factor at 10%	Present value
1.	30,000	0.91	27,300
2.	40,000	0.83	33,200
3.	50,000	0.75	37,500
4.	60,000	0.68	40,800
5.	40,000	0.62	24,800
			1,63,600
		or	1,64,000

At this discount rate, the present values of all future cash flows are almost equal to the cost of investment.

Computation of internal rate of return of a capital asset is to know the return from investment. In order to mobilise this amount of money, the firm has to pay a rate of interest to the suppliers of capital. This is the *market rate of interest.* The proposal will materialise if the interest rate of return is higher than the market rate of interest. In this example, if the market rate of interest is 12 percent, as this proposal yields only 10 percent, the investment is not worthwhile.

In the computation of internal rate of return of several projects, it is necessary to find out the pay back ratio or P ratio by using the formula :

$$\frac{\text{Initial Investment}}{\text{Annual cash flow}}$$

After the calculation of the pay back ratio, the range of expected rate of return and the exact value of rate of return have to be calculated.

To calculate the expected rate of return, the present value table has to be made use of. For example, for the proposal A, against 20 years which is the life of the project, locate the P ratio of 4.0. The range of return is 25 percent arrived by interpolation. The interpolation is done by the following formula:

$$r = r^2 - \frac{P - P_2}{P_1 - P_2}(r_2 - r_1)$$

Where, r is actual rate of return through interpolation,

r_2 = higher rate of return in the range,

r_1 = lower rate of return in the range,

P = P ratio

P_1 = P ratio corresponding to r_1 (lower rate of return)

P_2 = P ratio corresponding to r_2 (higher rate of return)

In the case of proposal 'A', the range of return is between 25 and 30 percent. By interpolation, the actual rate of return is 25.

Discounted Cash Flow Method vs. Net Present Value Index Method

Discounted cash flow method considers the time value of money. It considers the cash flows over the entire life of the project. The net present value index method also takes into consideration the time value of money. The pay back method has the merit of revealing that investment which pays itself back the quickest is the best. Quick pay back becomes very important in the case of firms with low liquidity. It is also of great significance when the obsolescence is high. The pay back period method and the accounting rate of return method also are very simple. But they ignore the time value of money.

The discounted cash flow method and the NPVI methods are no doubt very sound, but the discounted cash flow method is very much complicated and tedious, while the NPVI method is the simplest and the best. It is also to be noted that these two methods are used under various circumstances. The NPVI method is no doubt superior in situations involving unusual cash flow patterns. However, the NPVI method is to be supplemented by the pay back method. It is because the investments which pay itself back quickest is the best.

In conclusion, it may be said that the appraisal techniques are important tools in assisting managerial decision making. The management may not always select a proposal with high profitability. It may consider other issues like availability of resources internally suitable to the proposal. Therefore, management judgement will always play a role in the selection of the project. Even then the management cannot ignore the conclusion arrived at from appraisal techniques.

Of all the techniques, the widely used technique is the pay back period technique, while other techniques may be used to verify the viability of the proposal.

Questions

1. Define capital budgeting and give examples of capital budgeting problems.
2. What is meant by cost of capital. Explain how it is calculated.
3. Explain the various yardsticks for evaluating the profitability of project proposals.
4. Compare the internal rate of return and accountant's rate of return as methods of capital expenditure analysis.
5. What are the principal methods of ranking alternative investment proposals.
6. Discuss the significance of Discount Cash Flow in capital budgeting.
7. Write short notes on :
   a) Pay back period of appraising capital expenditure projects.
   b) Capital budgeting problems.
   c) Types of capital budgets
   d) Capital rationing.

CHAPTER

18

INPUT-OUTPUT ANALYSIS

INTRODUCTION

The starting point of Input - Output analysis is the inter- industry analysis propounded by the French Classical Economist Quesnay. Professor Leontief with some modifications improved and perfected this analysis. Professor. Lange in his book *Introduction to Econometrics* writes about input - output analysis as follows: *'It is described as a mathematical study of production structure of the economy, taking into account the interdependence of the various production sectors constituting the economy.'* Input-output analysis purports to predict the total production per sector given the amount that the consumers spend on production of each sector. In economics, it is called the analysis of inter-industry or inter-sector flows.

Input-output analysis means the inter-dependence of various sectors of the economy. It examines the relationship between input and output. Input means the factors of production like raw material, capital, etc used in the production of a commodity. For example, a firm is manufacturing soaps, one of the raw materials is the non-edible oil. Hence, non-edible oil is the input, while the soap is the output. Thus, all raw materials used in the production of various commodities are called *inputs* and the final commodities produced from the inputs are called *outputs*.

Characteristics

Input-output analysis studies the production structure or product mix of an economy consisting of a number of production structures. From the macro-point of view, the economy is classified into three sectors broadly like agriculture, industry and services. The production per sector is determined by supply and demand in each sector.

Input-output analysis take into consideration that all production sectors are mutually inter-dependent. It means agriculture supplies raw materials to industries and raw materials are inputs. Industry supplies agricultural machinery and fertilizers to agriculture. This means each production sector is conceived as receiving raw materials, i.e., inputs from other production sectors and the production sector in turn supplies its output as raw materials for other production sectors. The construction of input-output table is called *Transactions Matric.*

Thirdly, the input-output analysis is purely mathematical in character. It consists of several simultaneous equations to find out the values of some unknowns.

Methods of Input-Output Analysis

Preparation of an input-output table is the first important exercise in this analysis. In order to do this, we have to group all firms into a number of sectors. Number of sectors may exceed 250 in an economy. For practical purposes, these sectors have been reduced to some 30 or 40. For example, there are three principal sectors such as agriculture, industry and services. The industry sector can be classified into a number of sectors. Likewise, the services sector can be divided into number of sectors like banking, insurance, travel transport, hotel, etc.

Each firm must be placed only in one sector. If the firm is that of dairy farming, it should be included in the agricultural sector. Dairy farming can also be put in the industry sector. This is important strategically.

After classifying all firms into some significant sector, the transition table has to be formulated, showing how much each sector buys from the other sector in a given year. For example, if the motor industry buys steel from the iron and steel industry, this is delivery from industry to industry.

If a farmer buys agricultural machinery, then the delivery is from industry to agriculture. The following is the input-output table showing transactions in crores of rupees per year.

Input-output Table

[In crores of Rs.

From Sector	To sector			Final demand	Total output
	Agri-culture	Industry	Services		
Agriculture	250	300	100	400	1050
Industry	300	800	200	2500	3800
Services	100	600	300	1500	2500
Primary output	400	2100	1100		4400
Total	1050	3800	2500	4400	

The above input-output table shows how much each of the sectors bought from others sectors and how much they delivered to the various sectors in a given year. The annual value of agriculture output is Rs. 1050 crores and Rs. 250 crores worth of output, i.e., 26 percent of the total output went from agriculture itself, i.e., the farmers purchased from farmers themselves. Rs. 300 crores of agriculture output was delivered to industries. The test of the agricultural production went to the service sector.

In the above table, we find that the consumers made purchases worth Rs. 4400 crores (400 + 2500 + 1500). The question now arises as to how did consumers get income to buy this amount of goods and services. They have got income in the form of wages, rent, profits and interest. Businessmen also received money in the form of profits. Shareholders received income in the form of dividends. In short, consumers earned income by working in different sectors and they in turn spent the income on goods and services. The total value of the output under this sector was Rs. 1050 crore. Out of this, Rs. 650 crore is accounted for by the purchases of the agricultural sector, Rs, 3250 crore from its own sector, Rs. 300 crore from the industrial sector and Rs. 100 crores from the services sector. The Rs. 400 crore may be referred to as sector income and it includes the incomes of those who give their labour and capital to this sector. The technical term for the sector income is *primary input*, which includes items such as imports and depreciation and with the addition of primary input, the transaction scheme appears as above.

Assumptions

The input and output analysis assumes the following :. (i) Prices remain unchanged and (ii) constant returns to scale. The Matrix of coefficients remain the same.

Calculation of Coefficients

From the transactions matrix, coefficients can be calculated. Inputs from the transactions matrix can be converted into coefficients. An input coefficient may also be called as *input requirement unit of output*. The calculation of technical coefficient or input coefficients is as follows:

As shown in the above table, total production in the agricultural sector is Rs. 1,050 crore. To produce this amount of output, it is necessary to purchase agricultural goods worth Rs. 250 crore, industrial goods worth Rs. 300 crore and services worth Rs. 100 crore. If we divide these amounts by the total production of Rs. 1,050 crore, we get 0.2, 0.3, 0.09 respectively. These numbers represent the delivery of the three sectors to agriculture per crore of rupees worth of agricultural production. In other words, agriculture production of Rs 25 crores of agricultural input, 0.3 crores of industrial input and 0.09 crores of services. In the same way, we have to divide various input deliveries to the industrial sector by the total industrial production :

300 ÷ 3800 = 08 ; 800 ÷ 3800 = 0.2 ; 600 ÷ 3800 = 0.16

In the same way, we have to divide various input deliveries to the service sector by the total production in the service sector and we get the following :

100 ÷ 2500 = .04 ; 600 ÷ 2500 = 0.24; 300 ÷ 2500 = 0.12

These ratios are summarised as under :

From sector	**To sector**		
	Agriculture	**Industry**	**Service**
Agriculture	0.20	0.08	0.04
Industry	0.39	0.20	0.24
Services	0.09	0.16	0.12

The nine ratios so obtained are called the *technical coefficients*. It means a unit of output of a sector technically requires a certain percentage of input from each sector.

Applicability of Input-output Analysis

The input-output model is used intensively in economic planning. The input- output table reveals a sort of giving and taking. For the sake of understanding, we have taken only three sectors in the example. Normally there are several sectors. In such cases, grouping of industries is done and coefficients will have to be calculated.

The input-output model is being used in all planned economies. It has worked well in the centralised economy of USSR. In India, this input-output analysis has been made use of. The Planning Commission in India has developed 89 sectors for the purpose of planning. The input-output model can also be extended to the micro level. If the manager of a company has a dynamic marketing manager, he never fails to grab any opportunity. Supposing, a company is manufacturing motor tyres, the company produces all types of tyres. The total output of the industry is Rs. 250 crore. The position is as follows :

Industry group is X. The total output of the industry is Rs. 250 crore. The output of the industry by the end of the year is Rs. 300 crore. The pertinent question that has to be answered is what is the output that the industry can sell to other industries. With the following table, the question is answered.

Saleable output of Industry 'X'

[Rs. in crores

Receiving Industries			Final demand	Total Output
X	Y	Z		
$\frac{25}{250}\times 300$	$\frac{50}{250}\times 300$	$\frac{75}{250}\times 300$	$\frac{100}{250}\times 300$	300

The position of the industry is as follows :

Receiving Industry	Present share	Future share	Increase in share
X	25	30	5
Y	50	40	10
Z	75	90	15
Final Demand	100	120	20
	250	300	50

The proportion of various types of tyres is as follows :

Types of tyres	% production	Output to the total of Rs. 250 Crores	Output of the total of Rs.300 Crores	Increase
Car tyres	30	75	90	15
Bus tyres	10	25	30	5
Scooter tyres	35	88	105	17
Moped tyres	20	50	60	10
Others	5	12	15	3
Total	100	250	300	50

From the above table, we find that the production of car tyres is of the value of Rs. 75 crores. From this, we have to find out the value of the tyres used by X industry and how much is being sold on Y and Z industries. At the same time, we have to find out the consumption of tyres by X industry from the future production of worth Rs. 90 crores. The calculation is shown here under :

Output of Industries X, Y, Z of car tyres :

Rs. In crores

Industry	Existing outputof all tyres	Multiplier	Existing output of car tyres	Future output	Increase
X	25	$\frac{25}{250} \times 75$	7.5	9	1.5
Y	50	$\frac{50}{250} \times 75$	15.0	18	3.0
Z	75	$\frac{75}{250} \times 75$	22.5	27	4.5
Final Demand	100	$\frac{100}{250} \times 75$	30.00	36	6.0
Total	250		75.0	90	15.0

The output of X sold to industry Y is its input. The total sale of the output that X sells to Y is the value of Rs. 15 crores and the future sales will be Rs. 45 crores. The increase will be Rs. 18 crores. Supposing there are six firms selling their output to industry X and Y and their market share is as follows :

Market shares of 6 firms

[Rs. in cores]

Firm	% Market share	Present sales	Future sales
A	20	3.0	3.6
B	20	3.0	3.6
C	15	2.3	2.7
D	15	2.3	2.7
E	20	3.0	3.6
F	10	1.4	1.8
Total	100	15.0	18.0

The manager of Firm 'A' s total market share is 20%, the sale value is Rs. 3 crores. If he has to maintain 20% share, he has to sell Rs. 3.6 crores worth of tyres. This is how input-output analysis is helpful to business managers.

Questions

1. What is input-output analysis. Explain with an example.
2. What are the main features of input-output analysis.
3. Discuss the uses and limitations of input-output analysis.
4. Explain the techniques used in input-output analysis.

❖❋❖❋❖

CHAPTER

19

NATIONAL INCOME ANALYSIS

Meaning and Definitions

The study of National Income Analysis has gained greater importance since the outbreak of the 'Great Depression' in the thirties and in this century. Keynes *'General Theory of Employment, Interest and Money'* was a pioneering work in this direction. The subject further gained importance as a result of quest for rapid economic development in under-developed countries. The factors on which employment in a country depends upon includes investments which in turn depends upon investment on various activities. Investments in turn depends upon the aggregate demand for goods and services. Investment is also the function for the future rates of profit.

The main problem that is required to be investigated is that, what determines the level of output in a given period. The volume of output of employment in a country depends upon National Income.

National Income is generally defined as income of the nation. The national income reveals the nature of economic activity in a country. National Income data provides an idea of a country's aggregate economic activity.

Alfred Marshall, defines National Income as: Labour and capital of a country acting on its natural resources, produce annually a certain 'net' aggregate of commodities, material and immaterial including services of all kinds. The word 'net' means that from the gross volume of the output, the depreciation must be deducted.

Pigou has defined National Income as that part of the objective income of the community including income derived from abroad which can be measured in money. Prof. Fisher says that national income refers solely to services received by ultimate consumers, whether from the material and human environment.

Thus, the concept of national income has three interpretations. It represents the income, consumption and saving of the people of the community.

Keynes, concept of national income is entirely different. According to him, the Gross National Product refers to the total value of the output produced in a year. If the user's cost or depreciation value of capital equipment is deducted, we get Nett National Product (NNP).

National Income is also defined as the aggregate factor income which arises from current production of goods and services of a counrtry. The nation's economy refers to the factors of production supplied by the people of that country. Prof. Pigou has defined National Income as *'National Dividend is that part of the objective income of the community including income derived from abroad which can be measured in money.'* Prof. Irving Fisher defined it as *'The National Dividend or Income consists solely of services as received by ultimate consumers whether from their material or from their human environment.'* Thus, a piano or an overcoat made for me this year is not a part of this year's income but an addition to capital. Only the services rendered to me during this year by these things are income. Thus, National Income is measured not by its annual production but by annual consumption.

Thus, National Income is the sum of all incomes in cash and kind accruing to factors of production in a given time. It is also the values of net outputs arising in several sectors of the nation's production. It is also the sum total of all consumer's expenditure, government expenditure on goods and services and net expenditure on capital goods.

National Income is expressed with reference to a period of time, namely a year. This is because National Income is a flow and not a stock, i.e., income generated every year and at different rates and their period is mentioned during which income is generated. It is measured and shown with reference to a year as an *annual flow.*

Concepts of National Income

There are five concepts of National Income, namely

(i) Gross National Product, (ii) Net National Product, (iii) National Income, (iv) Personal Income and (v) Disposable Income.

(i) Gross National Product (GNP)

GNP is defined as the total market value of final goods and services produced in a year. The gross national product is the basic social accounting measure. It includes all economic productions in the economy during a year.

Two points must be noted in calculating GNP. Firstly, it is a monetary measure. There is no other way of adding up the different sorts of goods and services produced in a year except with their money prices. But, in order to know accurately the changes in physical output, the figure of gross national product is adjusted for price changes by comparing to a base year.

We must take into account the money value of the final goods (and services) produced in the economy to avoid double or multiple counting, since most of the goods pass through several stages in production before reaching the market. Many parts and components are sold by potential companies which are used in a final product. These goods are called *intermediate goods*, which enter into yhe production of other goods. For example, bread is a final good, flour is an intermediate product. Motor car is a final product. Steel and its components used therein are intermediate goods. Thus, intermediate goods are to be excluded and only the value of final goods alone should be taken into the calculation of GNP.

Secondly, the money value of currently produced goods must be taken into the calculation of GNP, because it is a measure of country's productivity during a year. If certain goods produced in 1991 are not sold till 1992, they would be part of the GNP of 1991 and not 1992.

Another important thing to be noted in this connection is that the non-productive transactions should be excluded. The non-productive transactions are transfer payments such as old age pensions, unemployment compensations, grants or gifts, etc.

In the gross national product, the depreciation or replacement value of the used capital goods is not deducted.

Calculation

In calculating GNP generally, two methods are employed. One is the expenditure or output approach method, the other is the income approach method. Expenditure approach method involves in calculating the value of the final goods consumed. Most of the goods produced in a country are consumed. But there are some goods which remain unsold. If unsold stocks are regarded as having been bought by the producers who hold them as inventories, then the monetary value of the total national production would be equal to the national expenditure.

Under this expenditure approach, the following categories of expenditures are added in order to find out the GNP.

(a) **Personal Consumption Expenditure :** This includes those expenditures made on durable and non-durable goods produced in a country during a year. This also includes the expenditure on services, such as transport, education and medical. Expenditures made on houses are treated as investment rather than consumption expenditure. Expenditure on household equipment such as motor car, refrigerator, television, etc. forms the consumption expenditure on durable goods.

(b) Gross Domestic Private Investment includes private investment on capital goods such as buildings, machinery, plant, equipment, etc. Such investments are made by business firms. Houses are also included in this category of expenditure, because they are durable and that they represent capital goods. If a business firm purchases a secondhand machinery, it is not investment. In the same way, if a person purchases already constructed houses, this is not investment. Purchase of existing shares and stocks also is not investment for purposes of national income accounting.

(c) Government Purchase of Goods and Services : The governments both at the centre and states purchase from the market consumer goods such as paper, stationary, machinery, equipment, etc. for their enterprises. In addition, the government incurs expenditure on payment of salaries to Military Personnel, Police and Administration, etc. Government also pays old age pension, unemployment doles, etc. If the payments are not made for currently produced services, they are not included in GNP.

(d) Net foreign investment arises from international transactions like imports and exports. If there is positive surplus, it is added to GNP. If there is negative deficit, it is deducted from GNP.

It is thus clear that if the entire production of a country is purchased at market prices, the amount so spent will represent the gross national prlduct of a country. If the expenditures of the above four categories are added, we get the GNP.

Income Approach to GNP

The expenditure made by the people of a country on goods and services produced in a country during a year becomes the income of the various factors, which collaborated in the production of these goods and services. The factor incomes are grouped into following categories:

(a) Wages and salaries (b) Incomes of company business
(c) Rental incomes of persons (d) Corporate profits
(e) Incomes from net interest.

The wages and salaries received by the employees, both government and private sector firms during a year plus certain contributions such as provident fund contribution made by the employers. This includes the income earned by self-employed persons, rental incomes earned by individuals on agricultural and non-agricultural property, corporate profits earned by joint stock companies before the payment of taxes and dividends to shareholders. The net interest earned by individuals from sources other than the organs of the government are to be added to get national product.

An aggregate of all the five categories of incomes will not be equal to the GNP as estimated by the expenditure method. The reason is that a part of the total expenditure incurred by the community does not become available to the factors of production in the form of incomes. There are two such leakages - one is that of indirect taxes levied on goods and services by the government, second is the depreciation on plant and machinery, buildings, etc. The expenditure by households on goods and services includes indirect taxes levied by the government. The income from indirect taxes goes to the government. In the same way, depreciation is not the income of any factor of production. While calculating GNP by Income Method, we have to add indirect taxes and depreciation.

The two approaches are shown in the following table :

Expenditure Approach –

(i) Personal consumption expenditure plus

(ii) Gross domestic private investment plus

(iii) Government purchases of goods and services plus

(iv) Net foreign investment.

Total = Gross National Product.

Income Approach –

(i) Wages and salaries of employees plus

(ii) Incomes of non-company business plus

(iii) Rental incomes of persons plus

(iv) Corporate profits plus

(v) Income from net interest plus

(vi) Indirect taxes plus

(vii) Depreciation of capital goods.

Merits of the Two Approaches

Gross national product is the most frequently used concept. Whatever may be the approach used, the result is the same. But some allowance will have to be made for all errors and omissions. Hence, in actual practice these two methods are used in combination with one another in order to get accurate figures.

GNP is a better index of the country's actual production and employment. It is also statistically simple for it does not take into account the problem of depreciation. But it is not a net measure of the nation's economic performance. It is only a gross measure. In order to get net measure, we have to examine another concept called *net national product.*

Net National Product

In the net national product concept, the net value of goods and services produced in a country in a year is considered. It means that in the production of goods and services, there is the consumption of capital goods such as equipment and machinery. The capital goods like machinery wear out or depreciate in value as a result of its consumption or use in production process. This consumption of fixed capital or fall in the value of capital due to wear and tear is called depreciation. In order to get Net National Product, the value of depreciation has to be deduced from gross national product. Net National Product then means the market value of all final goods and services after providing for depreciations. NNP is also referred to as National Income at market prices. It is a better concept than GNP, because it makes proper allowance for depreciation. NNP is helpful in the analysis of long run problems of maintaining and increasing the supply of physical capital in the country.

Net National Product = Gross National Product – Depreciation.

National Income

National Income is also called National Income at Factor Cost. There is also a concept called national income at market prices. National income at factor cost means the sum of all incomes earned by the suppliers of resources for their contribution of land, labour, capital and entrepreneurial ability which go into the year's net production. In other words, national income at factor cost shows how much it costs to society in terms of economic resources to produce the net output. The term national income refers to national income at factor cost. The difference between the national income and national income at market prices is that indirect tax and subsidies cause market prices of the products to be different from the factors resulting from it.

For example, a motor car costs Rs. 2 lakhs which includes excise duty of Rs.20,000. The market price of the car is Rs. 2 lakhs while the factors engaged in production get Rs.1.80 lakhs. Thus, the value of national income at factor cost would be equal to the market prices minus the indirect taxes plus subsidies. The concept of national income is very important in economics for it throws light on the distribution side of the national output. It tells us how the national income is distributed among the four factors of production in lieu of the services rendered by them. As such, it is closely related to economic justice.

Personal Income

Personal income is that income actually received by the individuals or households in a country during the year, from all sources. Actually, the whole national income earned by factors of production in a year is not available to them. For example, the companies have to pay corporate taxes before the distribution among shareholders. Further, a part of the corporate profits is retained by the companies. Further, the workers and salaried employees have to make social security contributions out of their wages and salaries. To the extent of these deductions, the amount available to them is reduced. Further, the government may give some social security benefits such as old age pensions, unemployment etc. to the people. Such payments are not given for any productive work. They are known as *transfer payments.*

In order to derive personal income, the following three types of incomes namely social security contributions, corporate income taxes and undistributed corporate profits have to be deducted from national income. Transfer payments have to be added.

Personal Income = National Income – Social Security contribution, corporate income taxes and undistributed corporate profits + transfer payments.

The concept of personal income is a very useful concept. It indicates the potential purchasing power of households in an economy. It enables us to measure the welfare of the whole body of consumers in the country. The weakness of this concept is that it does not tell us clearly the actual amount of income available for the consumers to spend on consumption and services. To know this, we have to study another concept called *disposable income* of the household.

Disposable Personal Income (DPI)

The whole personal income is not available for the consumers to spend on consumption. The reason is that, out of the income received, the individuals have to pay personal income taxes. When this amount is paid, the available income is very much reduced. Therefore, that part of income which is left behind after the payment of direct taxes is called Disposable Personal Income. It is the disposable personal income which is spent by the individuals on consumption. At the same time, there is also saving. Out of the disposable income, the individuals save a part of the income for their security in future. Disposable income can either be consumed or saved. Therefore Disposable Personal Income = Consumption + Savings.

DPI = PI – Taxes

Real Income and National Income

National Income of a country is expressed in terms of money. But the value of money goes on changing over a period of time. This creates difficulties in comparing the national income over the years. To overcome these difficulties, the economists have introduced another concept called *real income*. When the national income is expressed in terms of the prices of a particular year it is called national income. The nominal income of a particular year when compared with the national income current prices, it is also called nominal income. The nominal income of a particular year, when compared with the nominal income of a base year, it will include the effect of two changes. (i) The change in the production of goods and services (ii) change in the price level. When price level changes, the national income of a particular year reflects the change in the price level, while the price level of the base year is constant. To make the comparison clear, the nominal income will have to be deflated. This deflating is done in the following manner. Supposing 1980 is kept as a base year in which price level is equal to 100. We have to calculate the real national income of the year 1992. The price level of 1992 will have to be deflated to the price level of 1980.

Thus, when the national income is expressed in terms of current prices it is called *nominal income*. When it is expressed in terms of constant prices or prices prevailing in the base year, it is called real income.

The concept of per capita income is used in economic writings and discussions as an index of changes in the standard of living of the people of a country. The per capita income indicates the changes in economic progress in terms of goods and services available per head of the population.

The formula for calculating per capita income is as follows:

$$\text{Per Capita Income} = \frac{\text{National income at constant prices}}{\text{Population}}$$

Relation of GNP, NI, Personal Income and Savings :

		Rs. Crores
GNP	...	50,000
Depreciation	...	– 5,000
Net National Product		45,000
Indirect Taxes		– 6,000
		39,000
Subsidies	...	+1,000
National income		40,000
Corporate profits		– 7,000
Dividends	...	+ 1500

Government and Business transfers	+ 2,500
Personal Income	37,000
Personal Direct taxes	– 7,000
Disposable Income [DPI]	30,000
Personal Consumption Expenditure	27,500
Savings	2,500

Estimate of National Income of a Country in a Given Year :

A : Income Method	Rs.Crores
Income: Wages, salaries, etc.	10,000
Profits (Public & Private)	5,000
Rent	2,000
Interest	1,000
Total Domestic Income ...	18,000
Less: Stock appreciation	–2,500
Residual error	–500
Net Property Income from abroad ...	1,000
GNP	16,000
Less Depreciation	– 1,500
National Income ...	14,500
B : Expenditure Method	
Consumer's Expenditure	11,000
Public Authorities current expenditure on goods and services	6,000
Gross Capital formation investment 5,000	
Domestic Expenditure at market prices	22,000
Plus Exports and Income from abroad	6,000
Imports and Income paid abroad	–2,500
Taxes on Expenditure	–10,000
Plus subsidies	+ 500
	16,000
Less Depreciation	1,500
National Income ...	14,500

Significance of National Income Estimates

The National Income of a country reveals the true picture of the economy. A rise in national income indicates a rise in standard of living of the people of a country. It also reveals the improvement of economic welfare. The national income estimate reveals the overall production in each year and thereby we can compare the real growth of the economy. If the growth is stagnant, measures can be adopted to increase the national income. Of the national income concepts, the per capita income occupies a very important place in comparative economics. It measures the average standard of living of the people. Economic welfare depends to a considerable degree on the level of national income and the average standard of living of the people. Thus, the figures of national income and per capita income indicate the level of economic welfare of the people of a country.

By comparing the national accounts of various periods, we will be in a position to know the nature of the economy. This is very important when the government of a country launches planning for economic development. Supposing national income is stagnant in a year or a period of two or three years, the government can initiate development through investments.

National income estimates show the contribution made by different sectors of the economy such as agriculture, industry, trade and commerce, etc. According to National Income figures of India, we will come to know that about 42 per cent of the national income comes from agriculture. This shows that agriculture is very important from the point of view of the economy.

National income estimate also throws light on the distribution side. This means how far the different categories of income such as wages, profits, rents and interest are contributing to national income. If the contribution of wages is higher than the profits, it indicates that the labour class are contributing more than the proprietor class.

National Income estimate also throws light on the three major aspects of the economy namely, consumption, savings and investment. Information regarding these things is necessary for promoting suitable economic policies. It is the rate of saving and investment that determines the rate of economic growth. Further, consumption plus investment constitutes the level of aggregate demand on which the level of employment and income depends.

The National Income figures are used to measure the economic welfare in different countries. A country is declared as a developed country or an under-developed country on the basis of the per capita income.

The formulation of planning for different sectors of the economy is based on the national income figures. By looking at the national income figures of various sectors, various states and we can say which sector needs more emphasis for development. From the national income estimates, we can also see the part played by the government in the national economy.

Infact, no development planning is possible without the complete study of national income estimates. National income estimates are very useful in formulating plans for the development of agriculture, industry and infrastructure, etc. Preparation of the Five Year Plans depends very much on the availability of data regarding national income, consumption, savings and investment, which are all provided by the national income estimates. Further, we can evaluate the achievements of the development targets laid down in the Plans from the changes in national income and various components.

As Prof. Samuelson has rightly said *'by means of statistics of national income, we can chart the movements of a country from depression to prosperity, its steady long term rate of economic growth and development and finally its material standard of living in comparison with other nations.'*

Questions

1. Explain the concept of National Income and discuss its relevance to business.
2. What are the different methods of measuring national income.
3. Explain the following concepts:
   (i) Gross National Product
   (ii) National Income
   (iii) Disposable Personal Income
   (iv) Real Income and National Income.
4. Explain the importance of National Income Analysis to business people.

❖❋❖❋❖

CHAPTER

20 BUSINESS CYCLES

Meaning and Definitions

The term 'business cycles' or trade cycles refer to fluctuations in production, employment and income of the people of a country. Business fluctuations are the peculiar phenomenon of a free economy. In a free economy, the role of the government in economic matters is very limited. Consequently, the investment, production and distribution of national wealth go on in an unregulated manner. If the entrepreneurs find that economic prospects are bright and profit realisation is high, investment increases. This leads to an upsurge in all economic activities. This upsurge cannot go on forever. The forces of pull operate desperately and the whole economy plunges in darkness. These economic fluctuations are known as business cycles or trade cycles.

James Arthur Estey in his book *'Business Cycles'* writes, 'These cyclical fluctuations are characterised by alternating waves of expansion and contraction. They do not have a fixed rythmn, but they are cyclical in that the phases of contraction and expansion recur frequently and in fairly similar patterns. These patterns are most marked in those countries which are built upon business rather than agriculture and have been particularly noticed in free economics for over more than one hundred years. A business cycle is a very complex economic phenomenon and it is associated with alternating periods of prosperity and depression. It is a common experience of businessmen who know that a continuous movement forward is a myth. Business moves forward in an upward direction for some period and afterwards, followed by downward swing and this goes on. There are upward swings and then the downward swing follows. These go on in an irregular manner. Every boom is followed by a slump and vice-versa. This is a *trade cycle.* The trade cycle simply means the whole course of trade or business activity which passes through all phases of prosperity and adversity.

Some Definitions of Trade Cycle

W.C. Mitchell defines trade cycle or business cycle as a series of fluctuations in the economic activities of organised communities. The adjunctive business restricts the concept of fluctuations in activities which are systematically conducted on a commercial basis. The noun 'cycles' bars out fluctuations which do not recur with a measure of regularity.'

Keynes describes the business cycle as, 'A trade cycle is composed of periods of good trade characterised by rising prices and low unemployment percentages alternating with the periods of bad trade characterised by falling prices and high unemployment percentages.'

Benham says that a trade cycle may be defined broadly as a period of prosperity followed by a period of depression. It is not surprising that economic process should be irregular, trade being good at some time and bad at others.'

Thus, a business cycle is an alternate expansion and contraction in the overall business activity as evidenced by fluctuations in the measures of aggregate economic activity such as gross product, the index of industrial production and employment and income.

The cyclical fluctuations cause economic crisis in the country, damaging all branches of the national economy. Sometimes, the cycles maybe confined only to individual industries or individual sectors of the economy. Whenever the cycle appears, it not only engulfs all prosperous sectors of the national economy, but also the international economy. Thus, cycles have world-wide implications.

Characteristics of a Business cycle

A study of the fluctuations of an economy will reveal two important characteristics. (i) It is cyclical in nature which means prosperity is followed by slump and (ii) It embraces all parts of the economy. Its general nature is *sychronism*.

(i) Trade cycles occur periodically at fairly irregular intervals. A trade cycle may occur once in thirty or forty years. The period of a cycle may vary from seven to ten years. It occurs periodically in a regular fashion. It means the prosperity is followed by depression. In other words, they occur alternatively. But these need not be uniform in the extent and magnitude of the trade cycle. Though the general structure of different trade cycles may be the same, they differ in rythmn.

(ii) The second characteristic is that it is all embarrassing. It means it affects the entire business world. If there is recession in one industry, it spreads to all industries in a short time. It not only affects one country, but it affects the economies of other countries as well. The Great Depression in 1929 is an example of this characteristic.

(iii) There are upward swings and downward swings like waves in the sea. Rising prices, employment, production and income are the features of the upward swing while fall in prices, unemployment, fall in production and income, etc. are features of the downward wing.

(iv) The process of the trade cycle is cumulative and self-reinforcing. The upward and downward movements are cumulative. When once the upward movement starts, it creates further movement in the same direction. If the prices start rising, the forces make the prices to rise further. This momentum will persist till the forces accumulate, alter the direction and create the downward movement. When the downward movement starts, it persists in the same direction leading to a worse depression.

(v) The cycles are similar but not identical. The common characteristics of the business cycles will be the same but they differ in intensity. 'A typical business cycle has all ups and downs but in one trade cycle, the upward movement may be steep while the downward movement may be short. The rythm may be rough and imperfect.'

Classification of Business Cycles

Prof. James Arthur Estey classifies business cycles into major and minor trade cycles.

Major business cycles are those cycles where fluctuations of business activity are very steep, leading to economic crisis. Crisis is mentioned to mean the major breakdowns that occur from time to time. Major cycles constitute the interval between successive major downturns of business activity or between major recessions. The duration of a major cycle may be 8 to 10 years. The up-swing of business in the major cycle is often interrupted by minor downward swings. Likewise, the downswing of a major cycle may be interrupted by minor upswings. These shorter cycles in major cycles are called *minor* cycles. The average duration of a minor cycle may be 2 to 3 years. These minor cycles often occur in all economies.

Phases of a Business Cycle

A typical business cycle is characterised by five different phases or stages. They are: depression, recovery (revival), prosperity (or full employment), boom (overfull employment) and recession.

Depression

Depression is a stage of a business cycle in which the business is at the lowest ebb. The entire economy is engulfed in depression. Depression is characterised by a sharp fall in production, increase in mass unemployment, falling prices, falling profits, low wages, contraction of credit by the banks and other financial institutions and a high rate of business failures. There will be all round pessimism and despair. The business failures result in closing down of factories and consequently large number of employees and workers face unemployment. In this period, bank credit is stopped and consequently money supply also is reduced. The purchasing power of the money goes on rising but purchasing power of the people remains very low, which is due to unemployment. Since the general purchasing power of the people is lost owing to unemployment, their demand for goods and services also falls. This affects the production also. The production of essential commodities continue at a low level but the production of capital goods is stopped. All construction activities come to an end. The consumer goods industries such as food and clothing continue to produce at a lower level. The production of capital goods fall to low levels. Since the costs are sticky and do not fall as rapidly as prices, the producers suffer a huge loss. Many firms will be closed down on account of accumulated losses. The fall in prices distorts the relative price structure. The prices of raw-materials and agricultural commodities fall greater than finished manufactured articles. The agriculturists are hit hard more than the manufacturers. The United States witnessed two longest depressions during 1873-78 and the 1929-33 Depression was considered as very severe.

Recovery or Revival

The conditions of depression were no doubt very severe. But, this stage of affairs will continue for three to four years. During the period of depression, prices and costs fall to a very low level with huge unemployment of labour and productive powers. Business activity settles down at a new equilibrium level of low prices, low costs and low profits. During this period, rays of hope appear in the minds of the business people and they feel that the economic situation was not as bad as it was in the crisis period. Pessimism which was seen in every walk of life during the initial period of depression will vanish. The business people will now find that the situation is better to start production. The industrial production picks up very slowly and gradually. As a result of this, demand for raw-materials, capital and labour also increases. Wages are low even for efficient workers, sufficient number of skilled workers are now available. Money is cheap and also the raw-materials. All these result in the demand for capital goods. The producers order for new machinery or repair the old machinery. Constructional and allied industries receive orders and they start re-employing the workers. When the workers get employment, they get salaries and wages. The suppliers of raw materials get revenue. The banks also start functioning seriously. They expand the credit. The pessimism and despair of the depression gradually vanish in the minds of the people. There arises optimism every where. Businessmen now start activities. These changes are the signs of recovery or revival. In the earlier stages, the recovery is slow, but gradually it improves. When the general atmosphere of hope prevails, new inventions also take place. This leads to innovations, application of new techniques to production and so on. The business has turned round the corner.

Prosperity or Full Employment

Revival once started, gathers momentum. The initial revival which was started in a humble way, picks up the speed and is now strengthened by numerous developments. The investment activity picks up, followed by expansion of credit by commercial banks. Stock markets also start functioning vigorously. Prices and profits also rise influencing further investment. Optimism grows and spreads far and wide. The period of prosperity also is called period of expansion. The period of expansion may last for five to six years. The expansion goes on without interruption and all those unemployed men and materials are absorbed in economic activities. The country is gradually experiencing the stage of full employment. During this period, the economic activities become hectic. In a matter of months, the progress reaches the highest point, resulting in high stocks, high commodity prices, high profits and overfull employment. This stage is now called *'boom'*.

Boom – or Overfull Employment

Boom is the final stage of a business cycle where the business activity expands very rapidly. Economy rises to new heights.

The prosperity phase of a business cycle is one where the economy attains maximum growth with full employment. If the economy is stabilised at the point of full employment, there will be a full employment equilibrium. At this point, all the resources are optimum employed. The business reaches maximum growth when there is optimism prevailing in all sectors of the economy and businessmen with the hope of earning more take up speculative activity. They continue to invest on various sectors of the economy. This puts additional pressure on the existing resources which are already fully employed, resulting in the sharp rise in their prices. The demand for labour rises but this demand is met by the existing workers, who leave the present job and take up a new job on higher wages. This situation is called *overfull employment*. Money wages rise, Profits increase and the interest rates also go up. The demand for bank credit also increases. Attracted by high profits, industrialists increase investment activity. The banks also meet their capital requirements at higher rates of interest. The resource owners also increase price of resources. Thus, everywhere there is jubilation. Professor Haberler has described this situation as 'a state of affairs in which the real income consumed, real income produced and the levels of employment are either high or rising and there are no idle resources in the economy'. If the economy is moving in an upward movement and if there are no checks, then the economy reaches new heights. The boom carries with it the seeds of self-destruction. As soon as prosperity reaches an ugly turn, the whole economy plunges into darkness. When the economy is driven to the boom, then cracks are seen in all sectors. This means costs gradually rise and overtake prices and profits. In the beginning, the situation goes unnoticed but soon it is recognised and now the boom conditions go beyond control. Now hastily set up firms collapse. No doubt, the signal of collapse warn the businessmen but they cannot halt the economy from disaster. The boom is inevitably followed by a burst.

Recession

Then starts the downward course. When profits are decreasing, the businessmen stop orders for capital goods. The government too applies the axe mercilessly. The bankers who had given loans liberally now demand for repayments. The stockists are compelled to dispose off the stocks in the market. But there will be no buyers of these goods. Prices start collapsing. This shakes the confidence of the businessmen. All activities are going to be reduced in the beginning and finally stopped. Unemployment appears in all industries. This leads to a fall in income, expenditure, prices and profits. This situation is called *recession*. The recession has a cumulative effect. Once it starts, it goes on gathering momentum and finally assumes the shape of depression.

The various phases of business cycle are shown in the following diagram.

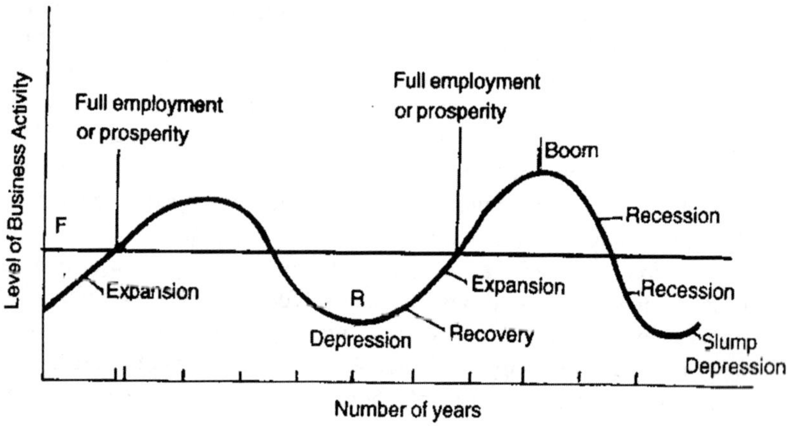

The various phases of the business cycle are explained in the above diagram, In this diagram, FE is the full employment line. Above this line, we see the boom and the recession, boom in the upswing and recession in the downswing. Below this line, we find two stages, depression and recovery. When the economy achieves recovery from the depression, there will be expansion of economic activity after some years. The trade cycle starting from depression moves to recovery or revival, expansion, prosperity or full employment and reaches the zenith called boom, which subsequently results in fall. If economy is stabilised at the full employment level, occurrence of boom can be prevented.

Theories of Trade Cycle

The theories of trade cycles explain their causes theoretically. These theories are classified into monetary theories and non-monetary theories. The non-monetary theories are the following:

(i) **Climatic theory :** Some economists have established the relationship between climatic changes and trade cycles. Changes in climate bring about changes in the agricultural production. If the rains occur systematically or periodically, the crops will become bumper and as a result of supply of, abundance of agricultural raw-materials, industrial and commercial activities also will rise further. If the harvests are poor, then the agricultural production also falls, resulting in rise in prices and so on.

One of the climatic theories is the *sun spot theory*. This theory was propounded by Stanley Jevons, a celebrated British economist. According to him, variations in the atmosphere of the sun, determine the fluctuations in economic activity. He said that at certain intervals, dark spots appear on the Sun, which affects the transmission of heat to the earth. This affects agricultural crops which in turn influences the level of business activities in the economy. When the agricultural production falls consequent upon the appearance of spots on the sun, the entire economy is engulfed by depression. The depression in the agricultural sector spreads to the entire economy which in turn depresses the entire economy. On the other hand, if there are no sun spots, agricultural production does not suffer but increases. The variations in production do not suffer but increase. The variations in the rainfall are so regular that the periods of poor harvests often alternate with periods of good harvests.

Modern economists do not accept the climatic theories of trade cycle. It is impossible to connect the occurrence of sun spots to failure of rainfall. It is quite possible that rainfall in India particularly is very irregular and uncertain. If the rainfall fails, it surely affects agricultural production. This in turn affects industrial production. In fact, the non-agricultural industrial countries suffer more from business cycle than do the agricultural countries.

(ii) Psychological theory : The pyschological theory was propounded by Prof. A.C. Pigou. In his work *'Industrial fluctuations'*, he has advanced an approach that business cycles are the outcome of the psychology of industrialists. Business fluctuations are the result of waves of optimism and pessimism among the businessmen and industrialists. If the businessmen and industrialists are optimistic about the growth of economy, they invest capital, organise production and as a result of these, income and employment rises. The economy moves towards expansion and prosperity. If the people think that the trade is good and going to remain good, this feeling radiates the entire economy to action. The entire business community becomes optimistic and carries on business activity in an intensified manner. This leads to the emergence of boom in the economy. Since the appearance of boom is an indication of future gloom, the business and industrialists now see some cracks in the economy. Soon the economy is clouded with pessimism with regard to future business prospects. The big industrialists communicate their pessimism to others and ultimately the entire business community becomes pessimistic. When they see business failures on a national basis, fresh investments are stopped and they curtail the production. This leads to the emergence of slump. Thus, the occurrence of boom and slump is entirely due to the alternating waves of optimism and pessimism on the part of the investors. This is all psychological.

The psychological theory has been commented on the ground that it does not offer any comprehensive explanation of the business cycle. The theory says that industrial activities are affected by the waves of optimism and pessimism. But the theory does not explain the causes for the same. In fact, the bright prospects in the economy make businessmen optimistic. There must be some cause for optimism and pessimism. Optimism and pessimism are not themselves self-generated. The main cause for the emergence of optimism in the economy is high marginal efficiency of capital, as pointed out by Keynes. If the marginal efficiency of capital is high, then the investors undertake fresh investments. This leads to chain of action in the economy. When the marginal efficiency of capital (future expectation of profit from the additional investment made) falls, automatically the businessmen become pessimistic about the investment and consequently, the downward trend follows. However, it highlights the changes in the psychology of businessmen which play an important role in the upswing and downswing of the economic activities. For example, a depression which has occurred further spreads to the entire economy causing pessimism in the minds of business people. The fact that psychological factors accentuate the business cycle cannot be undermined.

(iii) Over production theory : Some socialist economists say that over-production of all goods and services in an economy is responsible for the business cycle. The over-production results in disequilibrium in the economy. When the supply of goods and services exceed the demand, then such a situation is known as *over-production*. Over-production does not restrict to one commodity only. Over-production of industrial goods is mainly due to competition. Each firm expecting to capture the entire market produce as high as possible obtaining factor inputs even at higher prices. This causes over-production and the market is flooded with all sorts of commodities. When the demand for the supply fails to match, then the prices of goods start falling.

The competition which has resulted in over-production results in a rise in the prices of inputs. Since the supply of inputs is limited, the increased demand for inputs pushes their prices. Consequently, the cost of production also rises. As a result of over-production, the prices of finished goods fall and as a result of increased demand for inputs to produce more, the cost of production rises. As such, many firms start experiencing losses. In the course of downward swing, marginal firms collapse, while large firms incur huge losses. In fact, the entire economy witnesses depression.

The over-production theory highlights the peculiar competitive behaviour of business people. In fact, it is true that over-production induced by competition results in a depression. The theory does not tell why the depression comes fairly often. Since the business cycle is a complex phenomenon, it cannot be accounted to the competition aspect alone.

(iv) Under-consumption Theory : This theory is also known as over-saving theory which was propounded by J.A. Hobson and Major Douglas. According to them, there is too much of saving during boom and further addition to saving results in under consumption. The authors of this theory say that depression in an economy is due to the prevalence of inequality of incomes. The proprietary class have too much of income and their consumption of goods and services is low when compared to their income. On the other hand, the incomes of wage earners are low and as such though their propensity to consume is high, their actual consumption is low. This results in depression. Thus, too much of saving and too little consumption as against maximum production is the cause of business depression.

There is another version of the under-consumption theory. According to some economists, during the boom period, prices of commodities rise faster than wages resulting in increased profits to businessmen. This results in the shift of wealth in the form of profits and incomes in favour of rich people and capitalists as against the wage earners. The rich and the capitalists save more than the consumption and consequently over-saving takes place in the economy. Over-saving results in the increased supply of capital which finds its way to new investments. Since the incomes of the wage earners remain almost stagnant, their consumption also lags far behind production. The production rate increases at a more rapid rate than the expenditure on consumption, resulting in over-production, fall in prices and slump. When the slump appears in the economy, production is curtailed. Wage earners are thrown out of employment, which precipitates a crisis.

The under-consumption theory contains an element of truth. But, under-consumption itself cannot be the sole cause for the trade cycle. The trade cycle is a very complex phenomenon. It cannot be explained in terms of over saving or under consumption. According to this theory, savings find their way to the capital goods industries. This may not be so, for investment will be done only when there is profit. Investment is not made simply because capital is available. Therefore, it is the prospects of profits and not the availability of more capital which causes investment in an economy.

(v) Innovation Theory : Innovation theory was propounded by Joseph Schumpeter. According to him, innovations take place in a capitalist economy. Innovation means the application of inventions in the production process. When there are inventions or new techniques of production, the industrialists are eager to introduce them in their industries. According to Schumpeter, innovation means application of any of the following things.

(i) Introduction of new machinery.
(ii) Introduction of a new product.
(iii) Exploration of new market for the product.
(iv) Introduction of a new technique of production.
(v) Development of a new source of raw-material.
(vi) Introduction of changes in the forms of a business organisation.
(vii) Introduction of a new management system in the organisation.

An innovation in any one of the above things will result in expansion of economic activities. Those who undertake the innovation first, they are sure to make much headway over the others. Joseph Schumpeter says that innovations are generally found in capitalistic countries. It is because that leads to production of new products or use of better raw materials to produce a new product or improving the existing product or it may be anything which is something new. All these changes result in increased profit for the innovators.

Innovations are of two types :

(i) Greater waves of innovation (ii) Smaller waves of innovations.

According to Schumpeter, greater waves of innovation cause long business cycles while smaller waves lead to short business cycles. He further added that smaller waves of innovations go hand in hand with other innovations. It means that the innovations come in groups. It is because when there is an invention, the business people do not apply it and produce a new product immediately. In fact, the business people wait for several innovations which could be taken up by them together. When an innovation is introduced by an enterprising entrepreneur and when others find that this is giving profit to them, they also immediately adopt the innovation. As a result of these developments, the entire economy experiences the boom conditions.

Prof Schumpeter further explains how the upswing and downswing of the business cycle takes place in terms of innovations. He says, whenever innovation takes place, it causes disequilibrium in the existing economic system. This disequilibrium in the economic system continues till a new equilibrium position is established.

To begin with, Schumpeter assumes that the economy is in full employment. It means that all productive factors are put into optimum use and as such there is no unemployment in the economy. In such a situation, there is an invention of a new product. The enterprising entrepreneur, having seen the invention, decides to put into reality. He takes up the production of a new product through organising various factor inputs such as plant and machinery, raw-materials, labour and capital. All these result in the establishment of a new industry in the economy. Since all factors of production have been optimum employed, the new industry will have to draw factors from the existing industries by means of offering higher prices. Consequently, the prices of the inputs rise will increase the cost of production of the existing industries. The new industry is financed by bank credit. Since the factors employed in the new industry get higher rewards, their purchasing power would increase and they spend this income on goods and services. The demand for the product of the new industry rises along with the products of the existing industries. The existing industries now find that the new industry is making more profit on account of innovation. They also now resort to innovation. That means an innovation in one industry will spread to all industries in the course of time. This will create disequilibrium in the economy when all industries are contemplating on new innovations. The new innovations will be financed by bank credit. Consequently, supply of credit rises, demand for factor inputs also rises and the whole economy will be experiencing prosperity with high inflation. This process is called *upswing* of the trade cycle. Soon the boom situation appears in the economy with all firms producing the output with new innovations. This situation cannot achieve any stability. It is because the economy is producing much more than what it needs.

The severe competition among the industries results in full in the prices of the products and consequently the economy now swings towards depression. Fall in the prices of one industry soon spreads to other industries too. The fall in prices results in the reduction in output, increase in unemployment, fall in the purchasing power of the people and consequently all the industries, irrespective of whether that have adopted innovation or not, plunge in depression. This is the course of happenings in the downward swing of the cycle.

The innovation theory of the trade cycle has been commented on by some economists on the ground that the cause of innovation is not comprehensive. The commentators say that full employment economy is only a myth. Economy will always be less than full employment, particularly in a capitalistic society. Some factors are in a state of less than full employment. A discovery of new raw material or a new technique of production indicates that the economy is not in full employment. When the demand for a new raw-material arises and when it is used for the production of a commodity, it results in the increase of national output. An innovation will not lead to the withdrawal of productive factors from the existing industries. This in fact results in self adjustment amongst themselves. Secondly, the author of this theory says that the innovation is financed by bank credits which ultimately results in an inflationary situation. Since the innovation is resorted by the existing industry, a major part of the innovations are financed by withdrawing from the reserves kept by the industries for this sake. If this is so, innovations cannot cause inflationary pressures in the economy.

However, this does not mean that innovations are of no use. In fact, innovations give rise to large scale investment on capital goods industry, which itself will cause stimulation for further expansion in the economy. Therefore, it can be concluded that innovations provide stimulation for business activity.

(vi) Monetary Theory

Professor R.G. Hawtrey maintained that a business cycle is purely a monetary phenomenon. He said that variations in money supply are the main determinants of business activity and account for alternating phases of prosperity and depression. *'An elastic money supply is the root cause for the operation of a business cycle.'* Being elastic, the supply of money expands and contracts alternatively. When there is an expansion of money supply, economic activities will expand while contraction of money leads to contraction of business activities or depression.

In a capitalistic economy, most of the business is done on borrowed money. When business prospects are good, commercial banks provide loans by means of creating credit. When banks assure the business people of cheap and easy credit, they also expand their business activities. The banks build up a huge super structure of credit. This superstructure is maintained by means of offering cheap credit facilities. The expansion of money supply will be used for expanding economic activities. The producers borrow credit to expand production. The wholesale dealers use credit to build up stocks. The retailers use the bank credit to provide durable goods to consumers on credit. The consumers get the increased income and consequently their buying activity also increases. The effective demand of the community causes an upswing of the business cycle. When demand for goods and services of both producers goods and consumers goods increases, the producers and businessmen expand their operations by means of borrowing money from the banks. This huge business expenditure on factors of production increases their income, which in turn increases the demand for consumer goods. This further leads to an increase in the prices of all goods. The increase in prices stimulates the businessmen to produce and sell more. The production is further increased, providing still more purchasing power to the factors to be spent on the purchase of additional supply of commodities. This situation takes the economy to prosperity and boom. The banks which have provided enormous credit to the businessmen, traders and other producers soon find that they have crossed the limit. Probably, their reserve ratio has fallen dangerously low. In self defence, they apply the brake, namely stop further expansion of credit. The banks can create crisis within the rules set by the Central Bank. If the cash reservation falls, then they have to call back the loans given to the business people. This comes as a big shock to the businessmen who had hitherto been given very liberal loans. The sudden suspension of credit and compulsion of businessmen to repay the loans prove a bomb shell to the businessmen and traders release the stocks into the market. When the supply rises, the prices also fall suddenly. The stoppage of credit facilities make the producers to restrict production. This results in the retrenchment of the workers. When there is no buying activity of the consumers, the market is further depressed and prices start falling down. Business houses start experiencing huge losses. Some solvent firms experience great difficulties. The down-swing of the business cycle deepens causing depression in the economy. Thus, the monetary phenomena of hoarding and dishoarding, credit expansion and contraction cause the business cycle.

The monetary theory of Hawtrey emphasises on the role of banking institutions in stimulating the business activity in an economy. The banking institutions no doubt are commercial institutions and lend money on a rate of interest. If they get higher rate of interests, they lend money. They are required to function under the banking regulations. They themselves do not create crisis. The business people misuse the banking credit by using it for hoarding as against production. The banking institutions too become laxative when the economy is moving towards boom. In fact, the banking institutions prop up a boom by an over issue of credit and they accentuate the depression by withholding credit creation. But neither the boom nor the depression originates with them. The fault lies with the business people. But the fuel is added by the banks.

The theory exaggerates the role of bank credit in creating a trade cycle. Banks after all provide working capital. By working capital itself, business cannot expand to great heights. The big firms use their reserves and plough back profits for expansion and development. Bank credit performs the roles of stimulation in the economy.

The theory points out that withholding credit creation is responsible for depression. In fact, the business people themselves are not coming forward to use bank credit for running the business enterprises. Therefore, accusing the banking system for this havoc is not justified. And as such, a business cycle cannot be exclusively attributed to the misbehaviour of banking institutions.

(vii) Over-investment Theory

This is another version of monetary theory in which Dr. Hayek points out that excessive investment is responsible for the occurrence of business cycle. According to economists, followed by Dr. Hayek, they say that the boom is due to excessive investments and they regard the slump as the necessary corrective for the imbalances created during the boom.

When the rate of interest is low and the supply of bank credit is more, business people use this opportunity in promoting and developing capital goods industries. In fact, during the boom, the capital goods industries expand faster than consumption goods industries, while the capital goods industries suffer more than consumption goods industries during the depression.

Over-investment on capital goods industries during the period of expansion is entirely due to enormous credit provided by the banking system. Investment of capital goods increases because of the availability of sufficient credit at natural rate of interest. Hayek here makes a distinction between the natural rate of interest and market rate of interest. So long as the natural rate of interest coincides with market rate of interest, there is no imbalance in the economy and it is in stable equilibrium. The trouble arises when there is *discrepancy* between the two rates. Suppose the natural rate of interest is more than the market rate, the demand for credit for investment rises and to meet this demand, the banks create credit. This additional bank credit causes expansion in money supply and the consequence is the rise in the price level. If the market rate is more than the natural rate, the demand for bank credit falls and there will be contraction in money supply which will decrease the price level, resulting in depression.

According to Hayek, two factors are responsible for the business cycle. A low rate of interest encourages investment activities. The business people borrow increasing amounts from the bank and invest them to promote and develop capital goods industries. In the early stage of expansion, investment constitutes the up-swing of trade cycle. In this period, the businessmen are encouraged to adopt more and more round-about methods of production. When the economy reaches the full employment level, any further investment on capital goods industries will result in the shortage of resources. They are now forced to withdraw resources from consumption goods industries, through a process of forced saving. This happens because when the production of consumption goods is reduced, people are forced to save. While the supply of consumption goods falls, there results a sharp rise in their prices. The industrialists of consumption industries find it difficult to increase their production, since there have been diversion of resources to capital goods industries. There arises competition between capital goods industries and consumption goods industries, resulting in the rise in the prices of resources too. Thus prices of all commodities including factor inputs go on rising very fast, leading to a situation of boom.

The boom is soon followed by depression. During the short period of boom, production costs rise and soon the businessmen find their concerns are incurring losses. The businessmen become panicky and thus order for the stoppage of investments and production of capital goods. The reduction of investment and abandonment of production results in unemployment, fall in prices, income and thus the entire economy tends to be engulfed by depression.

The over-investment theory states that fluctuations in investment are the main cause of business cycles. According to this theory, if the investment is financed by savings, the fluctuation cannot occur. If the businessmen undertake investment from reserves, they can prevent the business cycles. If the investment is financed by a higher rate of interest, borrowing exclusively from the banks, then business cycle occurs definitely.

(viii) Modern Theory of Business Cycles

Modern theory of business cycles brings about a synthesis between monetary and non-monetary theory. This theory is also called acceleration and multiplier theory. Multiplier theory was advocated by J. M. Keynes. According to him, the operation of a business cycle is due to the fluctuations in the volume of investment and these fluctuations in investment are considered to be due to fluctuations in marginal efficiency of capital. When an investment is made on a project, it results in change in the level of national income. The change in investment will bring about magnified changes in the level of income and employment. This is the theory of the multiplier. But the multiplier alone does not cause a business cycle. Prof. Hicks has shown that interaction of the multiplier and accelerator causes fluctuation in a capitalistic economy. The business fluctuations are due to the combined effect of the multiplier and accelerator.

According to the theory of multiplier, whenever an investment is made, it will generate an expansion of employment and income, several times greater than itself. This is due to the multiplier effect. The increase in income will in turn create an increase in consumption. Increased demand for consumption goods induces more investment by a magnified amount on account of the operation of the accelerator. The original investment is called *autonomous* investment. The interaction of multiplier and accelerator causes employment output and the income to expand rapidly. This is the up-swing of the trade cycle. If the interaction is high, the combined reaction will also be high.In the normal circumstances, the operation is restricted. But in the abnormal situation, it becomes uncontrollable. That means, it takes the economy to the boom condition and alternately to the depression situation.

The up-swing of the business cycle cannot continue for ever. As soon as the economy reaches the boom, the down trend is inevitable. During the boom situation, as the incomes of the people increase, their marginal propensity to consume declines. Consequently, there arises disequilibrium between demand and supply. Decrease in consumption results in a greater decrease in investment also. Then the multiplier and accelerator start functioning in a reverse direction. When investment falls, incomes also fall, savings fall, which in turn results in fall in investment, income, demand for consumption and production goods. All these lead the economy to depression. Thus, Prof. Hicks says that the multiplier and accelerator together operate to cause fluctuations like prosperity and depression.

Control of Trade Cycles

Occurrence of the business cycle is a peculiar feature in a capitalistic economy. When the economy is progressively developing, all will be happy. Employment, income and consumption are all rising in a steady and stable manner. When the progress of the economy is very fast, its control becomes very difficult. The business cycle by creating cyclical fluctuations causes a great deal of harm to the smooth functioning of the economy. There are two ways of controlling business cycles - one is preventive measures and the other is curative measures.

The progress of the economy as a whole, must be carefully watched by the government, banking institutions and academic bodies like Universities. There are certain things like climatic changes which are beyond the control of human societies. But efforts must be made to use the climatic changes as beneficially as possible. If there are floods or droughts, a net work of irrigation systems must be provided to ensure normal supply of water to agriculture and other activities. If there are wars, earthquakes and epidemics, nothing can be provided against them. But their role in the trade cycle is insignificant.

One effective way of preventing business cycle is to adjust demand and supply, which can be done by means of collecting and disseminating statistics regarding national income, employment, consumption, production, saving and other things. If the prices are rising steeply, causes for such a situation have to be worked out and suitable action will have to be taken. The academic organisations may issue directives and warnings from time to time to prevent the occurrence of a trade cycle.

Economists have advocated certain measures to control the business cycles. They are :

(i) Monetary measures (ii) Fiscal measures and (iii) Administrative measures.

Monetary measures : Monetary measures are defined as the central banking action to control money supply and the rate of interest. Monetary measures embrace banking and credit policy relating to loans and interest rates as well as monetary standard and public debt. Monetary measures influence the credit base, the volume of credit and thus stabilise general price levels and economic activities of the country. Whenever the banks expand credit or even reducing the cash reserve ratio, then there arises an inflationary situation in the economy. Monetary inflation by leading to higher prices, higher profits and an optimistic outlook, strengthens the up-swing of the business cycle. When the inflation is within controllable limit, it can be tolerated. If it goes beyond the control, its cure becomes very difficult. Hyper-inflation should not be allowed to take place and at the same time, deflation too must be prevented. Inflation must be controlled by regulating money supply and deflation must be prevented by following a cheap money policy.

The bank credit policy involves two types of controls - one is quantitative controls and the other is qualitative controls. The quantitative controls by tightening credit supply checks investment in unproductive ventures. The qualitative credit controls seek to regulate particular type of credit. These controls are also called *selective* credit controls. The objective of selective credit controls is to stabilise bank advances for specific business schemes.

The central bank, apart from regulating bank credit, manipulates money supply too to prevent trade cycle. If the standard money circulation is reduced, the bank credit also is reduced automatically. The bank rate policy, the open market operations and changing the reserve ratios are followed to reduce money supply. The monetary policies are no doubt effective, they themselves cannot prevent or cure trade cycle. The success of the monetary policy depends upon the cooperation of the banking system. The banking institutions while granting credit, must see that the business people use the bank credit for the purposes for which such credits have actually been created. To make monetary policy successful, the fiscal authorities also have to fall in line with monetary authorities. Modern economists stress on fiscal measures to control business cycles.

Fiscal measures

Fiscal measures are those policy measures which the government adopts to control the operation of a trade cycle. Having realised that monetary policy alone cannot check the cyclical fluctuations, modern economists like Keynes and Hansen have suggested fiscal measures to be taken together.

Fiscal policy consists of (a) taxation measures, (b) public expenditure measures, (c) public borrowing. It is stated that the government should regulate the above activities in such a manner as to offset the cyclical fluctuations.

(a) Taxation Measures

In a system where the great majority of workers are in private employment, government's stabilisation policy consists in altering the general economic climate so as to mitigate or offset fluctuations in private business. Among the measures that a government may adopt to even out cyclical fluctuations, the most important are (i) altering the tax rate and tax structure to bring changes in the economy and (ii) changes in government contributing to the income stream through transfer payments like unemployment, insurance, social security benefits and so on.

Taxation measures include levying high rates during the boom and low rates of taxes during depression. Government tax revenue should be higher relative to the government expenditure in periods of high employment and relatively easy in periods of unemployment. During the period of high employment and high income, the government's transfer payments should be decreased. During the period of inflation, government should introduce different types of direct and indirect taxes.

High rates of taxation reduces money in the hands of the people and consequently, their spending is reduced and consequently stability is enforced. Lowering rates of taxation during depression and abolition of certain taxes would leave more money in the hands of the people who are encouraged to spend on goods and services which offset the decline in business activity.

(b) Public Expenditure

Public expenditure on infrastructure occupies an important place in public finance. During depression, economic activity is at a low ebb and there is enormous unemployment. Government expenditure programme during depression will provide more employment and consequently the propensity to consume of the people, increases. Therefore, the government expenditure programme is required to spend enormous sums of money on public works projects such as roads, canals, parks, schools and hospitals and so on. These public works projects by giving employment to the unemployed workers, provide them with purchasing power to buy consumer goods. This would help in offsetting the decline in effective demand and business activity. The funds to finance public works programme may be obtained by printing new currency or by borrowing from banks or by borrowing from the Central Bank. The public works expenditure of the state will thus perform the function of 'pricing the pump' of economic activity of the country. This is to fight depression. There is another equally important item of spending, namely public investments to stabilise the economic activity of a country. Private investment always depends upon the marginal efficiency of capital. Normally, during the period of depression, the marginal efficiency of capital is low and private investment also is not forthcoming. This is called *compensatory action* of fiscal policy. When the economy recovers and a wave of prosperity sets in, the government should reduce public expenditure. It should raise the existing taxes and levy new taxes to check private spending. Money circulation should also be reduced. The government should bring about surplus budgets during the period of prosperity.

(c) Borrowing

Public borrowing is another device in controlling the upswing of business cycle. It is through public borrowing that excessive purchasing power in the hands of the people is withdrawn. While during the depression, the government should borrow from those sections of the people who have surplus funds and provide for the government to increase public spending.

Administrative Measures

Monetary and fiscal policies themselves do not cure the upswing or downswing of business cycle. They shall be directed properly by the government administrations. The government should act promptly with the right type of taxation, monetary and public spending to check business cycle fluctuations. Since it is very difficult to expect prompt action by the administration, the economists have suggested some built-in stabilisers which are automatic in character. A built-in stabiliser is defined as an economic shock absorber which helps in smoothening the fluctuations on its own accord. One such measure is the progressive income tax devised by United States of America. This measure is so devised that during prosperity, tax rates are increased and during depression, tax rates are lowered. Such a progressive type of tax structure would automatically affect cyclical fluctuations.

There might be limitations in anti-cyclical measures. But they are indispensable to correct business fluctuations. During the period of depression, there might be enormous waste of money on public expenditure programmes but they are unavoidable. Further, owing to the immobility of labour, the policy of public works programme may fail to provide employment. For example, dam construction cannot absorb the unemployed textile workers. As far as possible, public works programme should be devised in such a manner as to absorb the locally unemployed labour. Public spending should stimulate indirectly private investments.

Questions

1. What is meant by trade cycle. Explain its different phases.
2. Examine the view that trade cycle is purely a monetary phenomenon.
3. What do you mean over-investment. Explain how does it cause business cycle.
4. Explain various measures followed in controlling trade cycle.
5. What do you mean by innovations. Explain innovation theory of trade cycle.

Short Answer Questions

1. Explain the role of marginal efficiency of capital in private investment.
2. Explain how does public expenditure programme help recovery of depression.
3. What are the objectives of monetary policy during boom.
4. What are fiscal policies. How far are they useful in preventing cyclical fluctuations.

❖✻❖✻❖

CHAPTER 21

INCOME, PRICE LEVEL AND EMPLOYMENT

Macro Economics

John Maynard Keynes' epoch-making book, *'General Theory of Employment, Interest and Money'*, published in 1936, disproved the classical theories, particularly the doctrine of *Laissez-faire.* Keynes clearly pointed out that there is no automatic adjustment or *'invisible hand'* as the classicists called it, to guarantee full employment in the economy.

Keynes' general theory touches all spheres of the economy and hence may be called *macro economics.* The determination of income and employment in the economy forms the most important aspect of macro economics and Keynes has dealt with these two aspects in great detail.

According to Keynes, the level of national income depends on the level of employment, and they are directly related. So Keynes stressed the need for increasing the level of employment.

According to Keynes, national income is composed of national consumption, national investment and national expenditure which is given by the equation $Y = C + I + G$. He said that employment in the economy depends on *'effective demand'* which in turn depends on consumption expenditure. Consumption in the economy depends on income and propensity (willingness) to consume.

Consumption Function

Consumption is the aim and end of all economic activity. Income is the most important factor which determines consumption. A major part of our disposable income goes towards consumption expenditure. It may be possible for investment expenditure to be zero in the economy, but consumption expenditure can never fall to zero, because of the simple fact that we have to exist. Generally, greater the disposable income, greater will be the consumption expenditure. But we cannot assume that consumption expenditure will be equal to income. According to Keynes, the psychology of the community is such that when aggregate real income is increased, aggregate consumption is increased, but not by so much as income. 'This observation of Keynes has come to be known as Consumption Function or Keynes' Psychological Law of Consumption.

Thus, Consumption Function is a brilliant tool in Keynesian analysis, which seeks to establish the relationship between income and expenditure. According to the Consumption Function, as aggregate income increases, the expenditure also increases but in smaller proportions. Again, as income increases, the additional income is divided between spending and saving, more so on saving i.e., what is not spent, is saved. And lastly, as income increases, both saving and spending increases.

The consumption function can be expressed in the form of a function in the following manner :

$$C = f(Y)$$

where C = consumption

Y = income.

At different levels of income, there will be different levels of consumption which can be measured by the average and marginal properties to consume. These two concepts may be briefly explained as follows :

Average Propensity to Consume (APC)

Average Propensity to Consume (APC) refers to the total consumption expenditure out of the given total income during a particular period. It is the rate of consumption to income and can be expressed as:

$$APC = \frac{\text{Total consumption}}{\text{Total Income}} = \frac{C}{Y}$$

Suppose the economy's aggregate income is Rs. 750 crores and its aggregate consumption expenditure is Rs 600 crores then,

$$APC = \frac{600}{750} = 80\ \%$$

Marginal Propensity to Consume (MPC)

Marginal Propensity to Consume refers to the change in consumption resulting from a given change in income. It is the additional consumption as a result of additional income. It is expressed as a ratio of change in consumption to change in income.

$$MPC = \frac{\text{Change in Consumption}}{\text{Change in Income}} = \frac{\Delta C}{\Delta y}$$

Where, ΔC = incremental change in consumption

Δy = incremental change in income

Suppose an economy earns an additional income of Rs. 250 crores, out of which Rs. 200 crores is consumed and the rest is saved, then

$$MPC = \frac{200}{250} = 0.8$$

The total income of the economy is divided into consumption and savings i.e., Y = C + S (Income = Consumption + Savings). We thus have average and marginal propensities to save. Average propensity to save means the amount of savings out of a given income and can be expressed as

$$APS = \frac{\text{Total Saving}}{\text{Total Income}} = \frac{S}{Y}$$

Marginal Propensity to save implies the amount of additional savings out of additional income which can be expressed as

$$MPS = \frac{\text{Additional Saving}}{\text{Additional Income}} = \frac{\Delta S}{\Delta y}$$

Since MPC and MPS taken together constitute one whole, we can find out one with the help of the other.

Thus, MPS = 1 – MPC

Consumption Schedule

Assuming *Cetirus Paribus*, the consumption schedule represents the amount of consumption and savings at different levels of income. The following is an imaginary schedule showing the division of income into consumption and savings, and the average and marginal propensities to consume:

Income (in Rs)	Consumption	Savings	%age APC	% of MPC
500	500	0	100	-
1000	800	200	86	.6
1500	1050	450	78	.5
2000	1250	750	72	.4
2500	1400	1100	66	.3
3000	1500	1500	61	.2

From the above table, we can see that as income increases, the expenditure also rises but the propensity or willingness to consume is declining. When the income is only Rs 500, the average propensity to consume is 100 percent, but as income rises to Rs. 3000, the APC has declined to 61 percent. The MPC also declines with increase in income.

A graphical representation of the consumption can be shown by taking income on x axis and consumption on y axis.

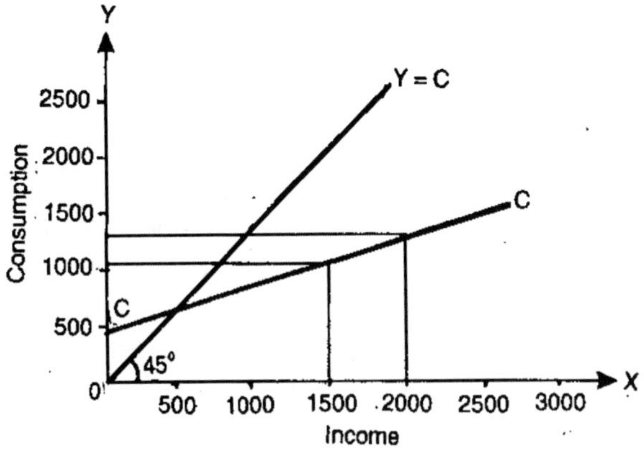

In the above figure Y = C, line is drawn at 45° angle denoting that it is a condition where the entire income is spent on consumption. The consumption function line CC is a straight line implying that as income increases, consumer demand also increases.

Factors Determining Consumption Function

There are certain important factors which influence the propensity to consume. The factors governing the consumption function can be studied under two heads viz, subjective factors and objective factors.

Subjective Factors

Keynes has distinguished between several subjective motives which influence consumption:

(i) An individual's present consumption is influenced by his forethought regarding unforeseen emergencies in the future for which he has set aside some income at present. This may be called the *'motive of foresight.'*

(ii) Present consumption of the individual may be influenced by his desire to provide for future requirements in relation to old age, education of his children, maintenance of his family etc. This can be called the *'precautionary motive.'*

(iii) Sometimes individuals may prefer to have smaller present consumption in order to enjoy and win appreciation for a larger consumption at a later date. This can be called *'calculation motive.'*

(iv) Sometimes, individuals may prefer to improve their standard of living gradually and this can be attributed to the *'Motive of Improvement.'*

(v) In order to enjoy the feeling of freedom and power to do anything one wishes, individuals may prefer to consume in lesser proportion to an increase in income. This can be called the *'Motive of Independence.'*

(vi) Consumption expenditure of individuals may be influenced by the need to be able to carry out speculative or business activities. This is called The *'Motive of Enterprise.'*

(vii) In order to leave a fortune behind, consumption at present may be restricted by an individual. This is called the *'Motive of Pride.'*

(viii) Lastly, consumption may be inhibited in order to satisfy the need for hoarding. This is the *'Motive of Avarice.'*

According to Keynes, the subjective factors do not change in short-run and thereby the consumption function remains stable.

Objective Factors

There are several objective factors which influence consumption. Some important ones may be considered here:

(i) *Income:* Money incomes of the individuals is by far the important factor that influences consumption. The relation between income, consumption and savings has already been dealt with.

(ii) *Price Level:* According to Keynes, a change in the price level affects the real income of the individuals although money remains constant. This affects the purchasing power and also consumption.

(iii) *Distribution of Income:* A more equitable distribution of income will increase the average and marginal properties to consume. This is due to the fact that the poor will have many unfulfilled needs clamouring for satisfaction and hence any additional income goes towards consumption expenditure.

(iv) *Fiscal Policy:* Progressive tax rates will reduce income inequalities which in turn help to increase the propensity to consume. At the same time, a reduction in indirect taxes will leave more disposable income which will help to increase consumption.

(v) *Rate of Interest:* According to Keynes, a rise in interest rates makes durable consumer goods more expensive especially when instalment purchases are made. This will discourage consumers from consuming more goods. A fall in interest rates will encourage consumption.

(vi) *Demographic Feature:* Generally, it is observed that large-sized families spend more than small-sized families. Again, urban-based families spend more than rural-based families. Professional people spend more than farmers and petty businessmen.

(vii) *Duesenberry Hypothesis:* According to Prof. Duesenberry, the consumption expenditure of individuals depends not only on the current incomes but also on past standards of living. This is because people find it difficult to adjust expenditure to changed conditions or incomes.

Again, 'individual's consumption depends not only on his absolute income but also on its size relative to others income'. It is natural for low-income groups to follow the consumption pattern of richer sections. This will make the richer section go in search of better goods. Thus, the mutual reactions will push up consumption expenditure which Prof. Duesenberry called it the *'Demonstration Effect.'*

Measures to Increase Propensity to Consume

The following measures may be advocated to improve the average and marginal propensities to consume:

(i) Government through its fiscal policies must aim to bring about a more equitable distribution of income.

(ii) Introduction of social security schemes such as old -age pension, health insurance etc. will help increase the purchasing power of the people.

(iii) An appropriate wage policy accompanied by a suitable productive policy would increase the propensity to consume. A mere rise in wages without improvement in productivity would lead to inflation.

(iv) Availability of easy and cheap credit facilities, encourage consumption. This is especially true in the case of consumer durable goods.

(v) Effective sales promotion techniques through advertisement and propaganda can influence the tastes and preferences of the people. This may increase demand and the consumption function of the economy would increase.

Aggregate Investment

Investment refers to the addition to capital assets like buildings, machinery etc. and also addition to stocks like raw materials and finished goods. According to Heilbroner, 'Investment, as the economist's result, is an activity that uses the resources of the community to maintain or add to its stock of capital wealth.'

Types of Investment

Gross and Net Investment

Gross investment refers to the total real investment, but part of the new capital is nothing but the replacement of depreciated capital. Hence this part should be deducted from gross investment to give net investments.

Net investment is that part of gross investment which represents the net addition to the total existing capital stock in the economy.

Induced Investment

Higher income levels of the people leads to greater effective demand, which in turn pushes up sales and profit margins. This induces entrepreneurs to invest more. Such a kind of investment which is income elastic is called as *'induced investment'*. It depends directly on incomes and given the marginal propensity to consume, an increase in income leads to an increase in investment and vice versa.

Normally induced investments are private investments since they are backed by profit motive. The following figure illustrates the direct relationship of income and induced investment:

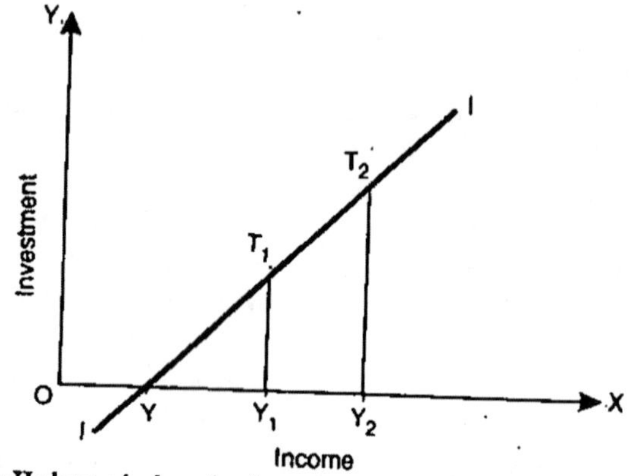

Figure II shows induced private investment at different income levels. When income is OY, investment is nil. As income increases to OY_1 investment also increases to $T_1 Y_1$ and when income further increases to OY_2, investment also increases to $T_2 Y_2$.

Autonomous Investment

Autonomous investment is independent of income levels and interest rates. Autonomous investments take the form of public expenditure by the government. It is dependent on factors like public policy, demographic composition, innovation etc. Examples of autonomous investments would be government investments on roads, railways, electric projects, dams etc.

Figure II indicates the autonomous investment curve which is horizontal to the x axis indicating that autonomous investment is income-inelastic. It remains constant at various levels of income.

Aggregate investment at any given point of time will be the sum of induced and autonomous investments.

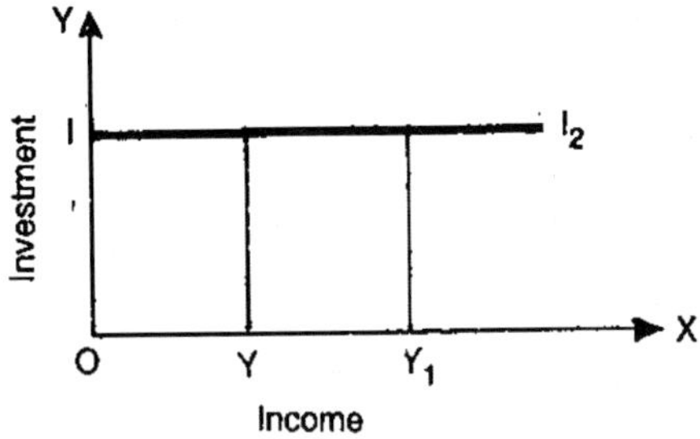

Multiplier Concept

'Multiplier' is an important concept developed by Keynes to analyse his theory of income and employment. Multiplier is defined as the ratio of change in income and changes in investment will lead to changes in consumption, which in turn will lead to changes in incomes. The Multiplier tries to measure the final change in income due to a certain initial change in investment. According to Prof. Samuelson, 'Multiplier is the number by which the change in investment must be multiplied in order to present us with a resulting change in income.' Thus, the final effect of an increase in investment on income is called the multiplier.

Working of the Multiplier

The process of the working of the multiplier can be illustrated with the help of an example.

Let us suppose that a businessman invests Rs.10 lakh in the course of expanding his business. This will result in an initial increase in incomes of those engaged in producing investment goods, by Rs. 10 lakh. Let us further assume that MPC is 0.5. Hence Rs. 5 lakh will be spent by these income recipients in the first round. This amount is again received as income by those engaged in consumer goods industries. This assumption is based on the logic that one person's consumption expenditure is another person's income. Those who have received Rs. 5 lakhs will spend 50 percent of it i.e. Rs. 2.5 lakhs (since MPC is 0.5) in the second round. Again, the process continues and in the third round Rs. 1.5 lakhs will be generated and so on.

Economists presume that each round takes about three months to materialize and this time interval between one round and the next is the multiplier period. As we move from one multiplier period to another, the initial expenditures give rise to gradually diminishing additions to income (when MPC > O but < 1). This process will continue till the total increase in income becomes so huge that it generates additional savings which is almost equal to original increment in investment.

The multiplier process may be illustrated in the following table:

We can see from the above table that an initial investment of Rs. 10 lakh leads to an increase in income by Rs. 20 lakhs assuming MPC = 0.5

The effect of the investment multiplier in generating income may be graphically represented.

Multiplier Period (in lakhs)	Initial Investment (in lakhs)	Increase in consumption (MPC = 0.5)	Total increase in Income (in lakhs)
0	10		10
1	10.	5	15
2	10	5 + 2.5	17.5
3	10	5 + 2.5 + 1.25	18.75
-	-	-	-
-	-	-	-
-	10	-	20.00

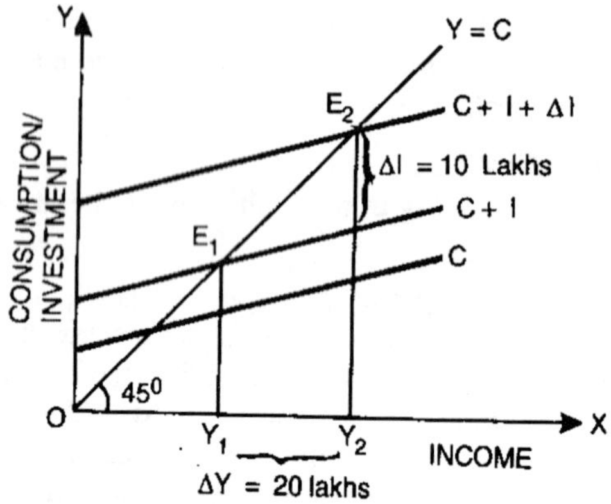

In the figure, C represents the linear consumption function curve which has a constant MPC of 0.5. The effective demand is given by C + I curve. The 45⁰ line indicates that Income = Consumption + Saving (Y = C + S). The original equilibrium is E, where C + I intersects the 45⁰ line.

An increase in investment is shown by C + I curve to C + I + ΔI curve. The difference between these two curves shows the extent of new investment (in our example it is Rs. 10 lakhs). This C + I + Δ I intersects the 45⁰ line at E_2 which gives the new equilibrium level of income of OY_2. The difference in income is shown by Y_1 Y_2 (which is equal to Rs. 20 lakh, in our example). It is infact, twice the initial investment indication that the multiplier co-efficient is 2.

MPC and Multiplier

The value of the multiplier depends on the consumption function and MPC. Greater the volume of consumption expenditure, larger is the volume of aggregate income and greater is the value of the multiplier.

The formula for the multiplier is :

$$K = \frac{1}{1 - MPC}$$

where, K = multiplier

MPC = marginal propensity to consume.

Since marginal propensity to save is 1 – MPC (as already explained in the earlier part of the chapter) the multiplier formula can also be written as :

$$K = \frac{1}{MPC}$$

In our example, we have assumed MPC = 0.5. Hence the value of the multiplier is,

$$K = \frac{1}{1 - MPC} = \frac{1}{1 - \frac{1}{2}} = \frac{1}{\frac{1}{2}} = 2$$

Hence the value of the multiplier is 2, and we have shown that an investment of Rs. 10 lakhs has led to Rs. 20 lakhs of aggregate income over a period. Algebrically, this relationship can be expressed as,

$$\begin{aligned} \Delta y &= K \cdot \Delta I \\ &= 2 \cdot 10 \text{ lakhs} \\ \Delta y &= 20 \text{ lakhs} \end{aligned}$$

Thus, given the MPC, we can calculate the multiplier by using the multiplier formula :

Value of MPC	Value of Multiplier
0	1
0.5	2
0.75	4
0.8	5
0.9	10
1.0	Infinity (∞)

Assumptions of Multiplier Concept

There are certain assumptions implicit in the Keynesian multiplier concept which may be stated as follows:

(i) It is assumed that MPC remains constant till increased investment results in increased aggregate income.

(ii) Only the original increase in investment is considered and subsequent induced investments (due to increase in consumption) have been ignored.

(iii) Fiscal and monetary policies are assumed to remain constant, so as not to influence the propensity to consume.

(iv) Multiplier effect is considered only when the economy is operating at less than full-employment level, when increase in investment leads to an increase in output, income and employment.

(v) The concept of multiplier is working under the assumption of a closed economy. The effect of international economic transactions on the domestic level of income and consumption is ruled out.

(vi) There is no significant time-interval between the receipts of income and its expenditure. Thus, the process of income propagation is assumed to be continuous.

(vii) Lastly it is assumed that the output of consumer goods should be responsive to changes in demand, if the multiplier is to work effectively. Otherwise, the propensity to consume would fall and this reduces the size of the multiplier.

Leakages in the Multiplier Process

Income, if it is not spent on consumption, is considered as leakage in the income propagation process. The operation of certain factors reduces the effect of the multiplier and these factors are called *'leakages.'* This leakage acts as a limitation to increase in national income. The following are some of the important leakages:

(i) *Savings:* Greater the volume of savings, lesser is the value of the multiplier.

(ii) *Debt Repayments:* When people use a part of their increased incomes to repay old debts, instead of spending it on consumption, that part of income is eliminated from the income stream.

(iii) *Hoarding:* If people prefer greater liquidity, then consumption expenditure falls and so also the value of the multiplier.

(iv) *Inflation:* With a rise in prices, the increase in income is lost on high prices. Consumption remains at the same level and hence value of the multiplier is less.

(v) *Import:* If imports exceed exports, the increased income resulting from increased investment, flows out of the country. This amount is not available for expenditure within the domestic economy.

(vi) *Taxation:* Heavy taxation reduces the multiplier effect by reducing the propensity to consume (of the people).

(vii) *Purchase of Stocks and Securities:* When people buy stocks and securities from their newly earned income, then to that extent their consumption expenditure falls, consequently value of the multiplier also falls.

To the extent that these above mentioned leakages can be avoided, the effect of the multiplier will be greater on the level of income and employment.

Limitations of the Multiplier Concept

(i) It fails to consider the effects of induced investments due to induced consumption and consider only the induced incomes.

(ii) It is a static phenomenon which shows how income gets propagated from one point of equilibrium to another. It does not tell about the actual sequence of events by which final increase in aggregate income is attained.

(iii) The assumption of MPC being constant is impractical. Practically speaking, MPC changes from person to person, place to place and time to time.

(iv) Keynesian Multiplier assumes a linear relation between consumption and income. But consumption is not the function of income alone but is influenced by a host of other factors.

(v) Keynes has given no empirical evidence of his multiplier concept. According to Haberler, 'Keynes offers no adequate proof, only a number of rather disconnected observations.' Hazlitt branded it as a myth and a worthless toy of monetary cranks.

Money and Interest Rate

Investment in any economy is determined by the marginal efficiency of capital (expected rate of return) and rate of interest. This topic deals with the determination of rate of interest.

According to the classicist, demand for and supply of savings determines the rate of interest. The rate of interest is determined by equality of and the interaction of saving and investment schedules.

But Keynes criticized the classical theory saying that they had ignored the changes in income level and their effect on savings and investment due to the 'multiplier effect.'

In his *'General Theory of Employment, Interest and Money'*, Keynes put forward his celebrated, 'liquidity preference theory' of interest rate determination.

Keynes defined interest as 'reward for parting with liquidity.' According to him, money is the most liquid asset and to make a person part with his cash (liquid asset), a reward has to be paid, and this reward is called *'interest.'* Greater the desire for liquidity, higher shall be the rate of interest demanded for parting with liquidity. Thus, interest becomes a purely monetary phenomenon.

Demand for Money

Keynes put forward three motives for preferring liquid assets (money) and the demand for money arises due to these motives, which are discussed below:

(i) *The Transaction Motive:* People prefer to hold money to meet the expenses incurred in the time interval between expenditure (outlay) and income (receipts from sales). The amount of money held for this purpose depends on the level income and the volume of business done.

(ii) *The Precautionary Motive:* People sometimes hold money in order to meet unforeseen contingencies. The amount of money depends on the nature of the individuals, his business activities and how easily he can borrow credit etc.

Speculation Motive

Sometimes, people would like to hold cash in order to take advantage of changes in the rate of interest. If an individual anticipates that interest rates are going to rise in the future, he may hold more cash, to take advantage of the situation. On the other hand, if he expects interest rates to fall in the future, he may prefer to hold less cash. Hence, there is a close relation between rates of interest and money held for speculative purposes.

Supply of Money

The supply of money in an economy at any specific period is given by the sum - total of all money - holdings. The supply of money can be controlled (unlike the demand for money) because it is in the hands of a single monetary authority viz. the Central Bank of a country. The rate of interest can be influenced by the supply of money, which in its turn, influences the demand for money (liquidity preference). Assuming *cetirus paribus,* higher the supply of money, lower the rate of interest and vice-versa.

Determination of Rate of Interest.

Rate of Interest is determined by the supply of money and demand for money. If the total demand for money is 'M' and the demand for transaction and precaution taken together is M_1 and demand of money for speculation is M_2 then, we get

$$M = M_1 + M_2$$

M_1 is not influenced by the rate of interest but by income levels. It is M_2 which directly depends on the rate of interest. So, it is M_2 which determines the actual changes in the demand for money at different rates of interest. On the supply side, the Central Bank fines the money supply and on the demand side, we have the liquidity preference. The rate of interest is given by the intersection of the two as shown in the figure.

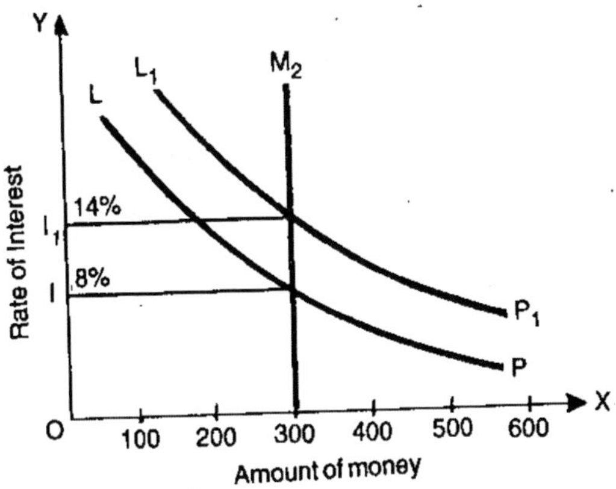

Suppose the Central Bank of a country creates a total amount of money (M) equal to Rs. 1000 crores. Out of this total of Rs. 1000 crores, an amount equal to Rs. 700 crores is held for transaction and precautionary motive (M_1). The amount for speculative motive (M_2) would be Rs. 300 crores indicated by the vertical line M_2 in the figure, showing the supply side of money, which is fixed. The demand for money to satisfy the speculative motive is shown by the Liquidity Preference curve, (LP) in the figure. Under given conditions, the demand for money (for speculative purposes) would fall if interest rate rises (they anticipate that it will fall in the future). The equilibrium rate of interest is shown by OI, i.e., 8 percent as at this rate of interest, supply of and demand for money are equal. If supply of money remains constant and liquidity preference of the people rises, the rate of interest would go up to OI_1, i.e.,14 percent.

Rate of Interest When the Supply of Money Changes

There is an inverse relationship between supply of money and rate of interest, holding the demand for money constant, as shown in the diagram given below.

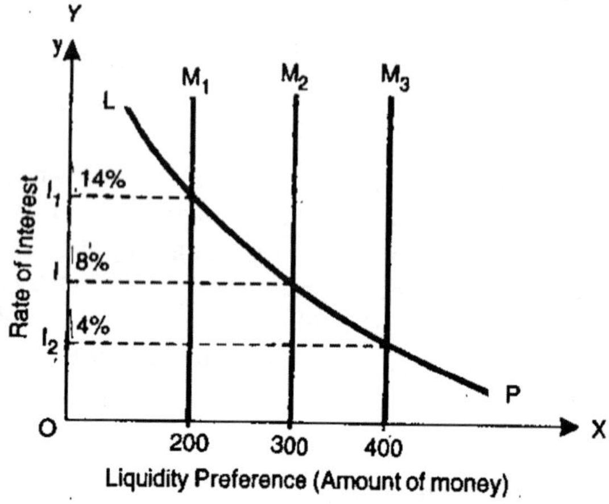

In the above figure, if supply of money increased from M_2 to M_4 (i.e., from Rs. 300 crores to Rs 400 crores), the rate of interest falls from I to I_2 (i.e.., from 8% to 4%) Conversely, if supply of money falls to M_3 (i.e. to Rs 200 crores), the rate of interest rises to I_1 (i.e., 14%).

Thus, in the Keynessian theory, the determinants of interest are demand for money for speculative purposes and supply of money by the Central Banking authorities.

Critical Evaluation of Keynes Theory of Interest

The major criticisms against the Keynes' liquidity preference theory of interest are:

(i) Hansen has maintained that the Keynesian theory, like the classical theory, is indeterminate. The theory only tells us the various schedule of liquidity preferences at various levels of income and not what the rate of interest should be.

(ii) Keynes ignores many powerful factors which determine rate of interest such as productivity of capital, thrift etc. when marginal productivity of capital rises, there is greater demand for investment which pushes up the rate of interest. Similarly, if people's MPC increases, savings decline and as a result, supply of funds in the economy decline, pushing up the rate of interest. Keynes ignored these factors and over-emphasized the monetary factors.

(iii) Keynes overlooked the fact that without savings, there would be nothing which could be parted for interest. According to Viner, *'Without savings, there can be no liquidity to surrender.'*

(iv) Keynes' theory does not hold good during a depression or a boom.

Contrary to Keynes theory, the rate of interest is low during a depression and high during boom period.

(v) The term 'liquidity' used by Keynes is vague. For instance, a person having money in the form of time deposits or short-term treasury bills, will obtain interest on them and also enjoy liquidity.

(vi) Lastly, Keynes' theory concentrates on the short-term and ignores long-term rate of interest.

IS - LM Analysis
(Modern Theory or Neo-Keynesian Theory of Interest)

The modern theory of interest put forward by J. R. Hicks and Hansen is an attempt to blend the classical and Keynesian theories of interest. They took into consideration the real aspects of the classical theory and the *'monetary'* aspects of the Keynesian theory and successfully combined the variables of savings, investment, liquidity preference and money supply.

According to this theory, there are four determinants of the rate of interests namely savings function, investment function, liquidity preference function and the supply of money function. The classical theory showed that the rate of interest is determined at that point where savings and investment are equal. Keynesian theory showed that the rate of interest is determined at that point where demand for money (liquidity preference) and supply of money are equal. All these four variables used by the classicists and Keynes, have been integrated with income to determine the rate of interest satisfactorily.

To arrive at the rate of interest, the modern theory uses two curves - the IS curve and the LM curve. The IS curve shows the equilibrium in the real sector (product market) and LM curve represents the equilibrium in the monetary sector (money market) the equilibrium of the real and monetary sectors give the equilibrium rate of interest. At this rate of interest, total savings will be equal to total investment, and total demand for money will be equal to total supply.

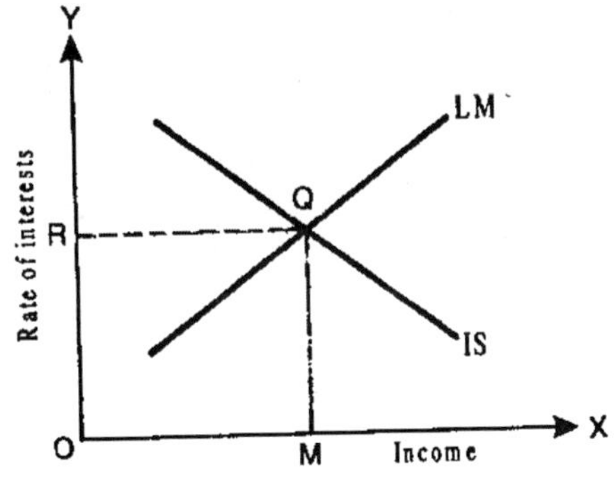

In the above figure, the equilibrium rate of interest is determined at the point of intersection (Q) of the IS and LM curves. Thus at OM level of income, the rate of interest is OR. LM curve has been drawn, taking the supply of money as fixed..

Aggregate Money Supply and Price Level

Keynes' theory of prices integrates the theory of money with the general theory of value and output. According to Keynes, an increase in money supply causes the increase in price-level indirectly through the rate of interest, income, output and employment.

The first impact of an increase in money supply will be on the rate of interest. As more money is available, the demand for it will fall, thereby pushing down the rate of interest. A fall in interest rates pushes up investments which in turn increases incomes. This pushes up employment and output and the process continues. During this process, costs of production rise thereby leading to an increase in prices. There are several reasons for a rise in the costs of production. They are :

(i) *Rise in Money Wages:* With an increase in output and employment the demand for labour increases, thereby empowering the trade unions with greater bargaining powers. This will result in wage rise.

(ii) *Scarcity of Inputs:* As output expands, due to scarcity of productive inputs in some sectors, the full employment stage cannot be reached by all sectors, simultaneously. Those sectors which have reached full employment will now face shortages of inputs, the prices of which soar, thus adding to the costs of production.

(iii) *Law of Diminishing Returns:* Due to the increased output, existing plants are over-worked and the law of diminishing returns starts operating. This pushes up the unit costs of production which results in increased prices of commodities.

Keynes assumed less than full-employment equilibrium in the economy. Under such conditions, an increase in money supply will mobilise resources resulting in greater employment and output. When the economy attains full employment equilibrium, additional money supply will result not in greater output but in higher prices. This marks the onset of true inflation in the economy.

According to this analysis, the relationship between money supply and prices is indirect, involving a complicated process through the rate of interest. Whether a fall in interest rates will lead to increased output, employment, income and thereby cause a rise in price level, depends on two main determinants of income viz., marginal efficiency of capital (MEC) and the propensity to consume. For example, if marginal efficiency of capital is less, then even though interest rates fall, investment, employment output and prices may not rise, with an increase in money supply. Similarly, if propensity to consume of the economy falls, then even if money supply increases, prices will not increase (due to the lack of effective demand).

Criticisms

(i) Keyne's theory is too general to help us in analysing the entire economy where the conditions of production are varied and the markets are too wide.

(ii) The theory does not take into consideration the effects of government policies and production and prices of commodities.

(iii) It is wrong to assume that the productive resources are responsive in supply, till full employment level is reached. In an under-developed economy, this is not true, because there are several bottlenecks in production and therefore an increase in money supply may not lead to increased employment and output.

(iv) The theory of money supply and price level, put forward by Keynes, holds good only when we assume that the determinants of income such as MEC and propensity to consume remain constant.

Questions

1. Explain the concept of effective demand. Discuss the relevance to the theory of employment and income.
2. What do you mean by consumption function. What factors determine the consumption function.
3. What is marginal propensity to consume. How is it related to the concept of 'Multiplier'.
4. Explain the changes in income responsible to changes in investment with the help of Multiplier.
5. Discuss the principle of Multiplier. What are its limitations.
6. Briefly explain the Liquidity Preference Theory of interest.

❖✻❖✻❖

CHAPTER 22

MACRO ECONOMIC POLICIES

Macro economics deals with the economy as a whole in terms of total consumption, total production, growth and other aggregate aspects. In this chapter, concepts like fiscal policy and monetary policy are discussed.

Fiscal Policy

Meaning and Importance

Fiscal policy refers to the policy of the government regarding public revenue, public expenditure and public debt. Fiscal policy tells the methods adopted by the government to earn revenue, to spend it and manage the deficit. It engulfs the fields of public finance, money and banking.

Prior to the Great Depression of the 1930s, governments all over the world (particularly in capitalist countries) played a passive role in economic activities. This concept of *'laissez - faire'* (non-interference of the government in economic activities) proved to be disastrous and had to be given up. The nation of 'Welfare State' was accepted by most governments. It was realised that the governments should actively involve themselves in economic activities to bring about economic growth and equality, through the adoption of appropriate fiscal policies. Today, fiscal policies of the government are used as powerful tools of public policy to achieve the goal of a welfare state.

The popularity of the fiscal policy since 1930s, according to Edward Shapiro, was due to the following factors:

(i) The failure of monetary policy in dealing with severe unemployment resulting from the Great Depression.

(ii) The influence of Keynes' 'new economics' with its emphasis on aggregate demand.

(iii) The increasing importance of public expenditure and taxation on the economy's total income and output.

Economists became increasingly aware of the growing disparities in economic conditions and maladjustments between consumption, production and distribution. They realised that the government should adopt appropriate policies to change, shape and direct the economic activities. Keynes believed that the government could raise or lower aggregate demand through appropriately designed policies relating to government spending, taxes and purchases.

Modern economists believe that the fiscal policy can be used to change aggregate demand in a such way and to such an extent that contributes to economic stabilization, especially in a developing economy. Where there is chronic unemployment of human resources and low rates of investment, fiscal policy can play a very important role. Its aim should be to promote the highest possible rate of capital formation without inflation.

Objectives of Fiscal Policy

The main objectives of fiscal policy in developed economies are, attainment of full employment and maintenance of economic stability. However, in developing economies, fiscal policy aims at increasing the rate of investment, reducing inequalities in income and wealth, reducing the levels of unemployment and controlling inflationary tendencies. The above mentioned objectives are discussed in greater detail below:

(i) **Attaining Full Employment**

An increase in government expenditure pushes up aggregate demand and through the multiplier effect, there would be multiple increase in national income and employment. The objective of full employment is achievable, given a sufficient increase in aggregate demand. The fiscal policy should be designed so as to increase aggregate demand by increasing public expenditure and reducing taxes.

(ii) **Maintenance of Price Stability and Economic Stability**

Fiscal policies of the government should be framed in a such a manner as to counteract the cyclical fluctuations i.e booms and depressions. During a depression, the appropriate fiscal policy would be to increase public expenditure and decrease tax rates. On the contrary, if there are inflationary pressures in the economy, the appropriate policy would be to reduce public expenditure and increase taxes, thereby reducing purchasing power in the hands of the people. This will help in achieving price and economic stability.

(iii) **Increasing the Rate of Capital Formation**

In a developing country where the levels of income and employment are very low, the fiscal policy must aim at increasing the rate of investment. This can be done by restricting consumption and pushing up the incremental having ratio. The government tries to achieve this through taxation and public borrowing.

But in a developing economy where incomes are low, raising revenue through direct taxes is very low. The government may have to resort to indirect taxes.

The second measure of raising resources through public borrowings has earned increasing importance in recent times. This is because both institutions as well as people who invest in government securities hope to receive incomes while their savings remain secure.

(iv) Developing a Socially Optimum Pattern of Investment

A socially optimum pattern of investment varies from country to country. In some countries, fiscal policy may have to aim at producing investment in social and economic overheads like transport, communication, power plants etc. In some other countries, investment in basic and heavy industries may come under the category of socially optimum investment.

(v) Minimising Inequalities in Income and Wealth

In order to reduce disparities in distribution of income and wealth, the government may design a tax structure which is progressive in nature. The indirect taxes should be heavy on luxury goods and light on necessary goods. As regards public expenditure, the government can undertake welfare activities like free medical, education, housing facilities etc. to the poorer sections of the population. Thus, by a sensible blend of tax policies and public expenditure policies, the government can minimise the inequalities of income and wealth.

(vi) Reducing Unemployment and Under Employment

The fiscal policy of the government can tackle the problem of unemployment and underemployment, with the help of specific public expenditure programmes. A public works programme of building roads, bridges, undertaking multi-purpose river projects etc. can provide employment to the urban unemployed population. Similarly, building of schools, hospitals, irrigation canals etc. during off-season can provide employment to the rural under-employed population.

Tools of Fiscal Policy

The chief instruments of fiscal policy are taxation, public borrowings, public expenditure and deficit financing. In short, the budgetary policy of the government is the major tool through which the government tries to achieve its objectives. We may discuss the major tool of fiscal policy and how they are used to achieve the goals of employment, growth and stability.

(i) Taxation

A suitable tax policy can act as an important tool in bringing about economic stability. Changes in tax rates bring about changes in the disposable incomes and levels of consumption of the people. During inflation, an increase in the rates of existing taxes and introduction of new taxes will reduce purchasing power and demand and thereby prices in the economy. During depression, a reduction in the tax burden will stimulate consumption and investment.

(ii) **Public Expenditure**

Public spending is another major tool of fiscal policy, which has far-reaching effects on income, output and employment in the economy. Whenever private investment is insufficient, the government should spend enough to fill the deflationary gap and restore full employment. On the other hand, if private investment is inflationary, the government should spend less so as to wipe out the inflationary gap. Thus, public expenditure can bring about an equilibrium between savings and actual investment.

Public spending is specially important in those areas where private sector is neither willing nor has the resources to invest. Therefore, the responsibility of building necessary infrastructure such as power generation, development of transport and communication, investment in basic and heavy industries etc. has to be borne by the government. This requires huge public expenditure and is called *'compensatory spending'*.

Sometimes, public expenditure is necessary to correct temporary maladjustments in the economy and to make it work smoothly. This helps the economy to have a continuous flow of economic activity and is called 'pump priming' method of public expenditure.

In modern times, the state has to fulfil certain social obligations such as free public health services, educational facilities, old age pensions, subsidies to the farming sector etc. Therefore, additional public expenditure has to be incurred towards the provision of these facilities.

(iii) **Public Debt**

Public borrowing is another important tool of fiscal policy through which the government raises loans from the public either in the form of voluntary loan or compulsory loan. Public borrowing and repayment can be used as an effective scheme to fight inflation and depression respectively. The government has to keep two things in mind while borrowing. The burden of public debt should be kept low and it should be done in those sections of the community who keep idle funds. The necessity to raise public loans arises often to help the government in the development process and build up the repaying capacity of public authorities.

(iv) **Deficit Financing (forced saving)**

Forced saving or deficit financing is a new weapon in the armoury of fiscal policy. In advanced countries, deficit financing occurs whenever there is an excess of public expenditure over revenues receipts. In other words, it involves the filling of budgetary gaps through loans. In developing countries, deficit financing literally means printing of more currency by the Central Bank and putting it into circulation.

During the times of depression, deficit financing could be used by the government to increase its public expenditure by initiating public works programmes. This would lead to an expansion in employment, consumption and investment and would in turn lead to further rise in employment income and consumption. In modern times, it is being increasingly realised that deficit financing can be used to reduce the intensity of business cycles and to deal with the problem of secular stagnation. These two tasks come within the purview of the 'compensatory fiscal policy.'

(v) **Budget Analysis**

Budget is an important fiscal tool which helps the government to fight inflation and depression and stabilise the economy. Various budgetary principles have been advocated from time to time. The 'managed compensatory budget policy' is considered to be the best fiscal policy in modern times. This policy consists in deliberately managing the budget to adjust public revenues, expenditure and debts in such a way so as to achieve full employment without inflation. According to this principle, if the economy shows signs of stagnation, the budget should take up compensatory spending and it should be a deficit budget. On the other hand, if there is inflation, a surplus budget is welcome. We should forget about balancing the budget as a separate goal.

Limitations of Fiscal Policy

Implementing the fiscal policies effectively has certain limitations and practical problems.

(i) Whenever legislative sanctions are required to bring about changes in tax structure, there may be administrative delays in implementing fiscal policies.

(ii) Effective implementation of fiscal policy involves accurately forecasting the future course of business cycles which is extremely difficult.

(iii) Existence of time lags between the initiation of the fiscal measure and realization of its impact reduces the effectiveness.

(iv) An increase in public investment may be followed by a decline in private investment.

(v) The fiscal policies may be inadequate in dealing with run away inflations and deep depressions.

Monetary Policy

Monetary policy refers to the measures adopted by the Central Bank of a country to control the money supply to achieve the objectives of general economic policy. According to R. P. Kent, monetary policy is *'the management of the expansion and contraction of the volume of money in circulation for the explicit purpose of attaining a specific objective such as full employment.'* In other words, monetary policy refers to those measures adopted by the Central Banking authorities to manipulate the various instruments of credit control which are at its disposal generally and both monetary and credit policies are clubbed together under the heading of 'monetary policy.'

Objectives of Monetary Policy

There have been changes in the objectives of monetary policy from time to time and they also vary from country to country. Sometimes, the monetary policy adopted by a country may have different objectives which are conflicting. In such cases, the country may have to compromise by setting definite priorities. Some of the major objectives of monetary policy may be discussed below:

(i) Price Stability

The 'Great Depression' of 1930s made all countries of the world realize the importance of price stability as the primary objective of monetary policy. When prices rise, the fixed income group gets adversely affected and when prices fall, the producers and businessmen get affected. It is now argued that price stability ensures steady growth in production and employment.

But price stability should not be confused with constant price level. There is a general consensus among economists that a mild inflation is consistent with price stability and that the slowly rising price level is really conducive for economic growth. The problem is to determine the rate of inflation that is 'safe'.

(ii) Stability of Foreign Exchange Rate

This is one of the traditional objectives of the monetary policy. When countries were on the gold standard, the aim of the monetary authorities was to regulate credit in such a way as to minimise fluctuations in foreign receipts and payments and thereby protect gold reserves. With the fall of the gold standard exchange rate, stability no more remains an important objective of monetary policy.

Today, most countries aim at maintaining a reasonable balance in their balance of payments. Accordingly, deliberate changes in exchange rates are now often resorted to in an effort to correct disequilibrium in the balance of payments.

(iii) Full Employment

Since the Great Depression and after the publication of Keynes 'general theory, the objective of full employment has gained importance. The monetary policy should aim at solving the unemployment problem by expanding consumption and investment expenditure. In order to increase the volume of investment, borrowings have to be stimulated by following the cheap money policy. This will increase the level of employment through the multiplier-acceleration effect. Once the level of full employment is achieved, monetary policy should aim at maintaining the full employment level, by equating savings and investment. If at any time, investment exceeds savings, there is the danger of inflation setting in. On the contrary, if investment falls short of saving, the economy may experience deflation and therefore, maintenance of full employment automatically ensures price stability.

In developing countries like India, since there is an imbalance between the supply of labour and supply of other resources like hand capital etc., full employment of labour is unfeasible. Therefore, such countries have to aim at 'optimum employment' instead of full employment in order to ensure highest national income.

(iv) High Rate of Economic Growth

The concept of economic growth implies a qualitative and quantitative increase in the volume of goods and services produced in the economy. For this purpose, the governments in developing countries through their monetary policy are trying to ensure adequate provision of credit for productive purposes. A large number of branches of commercial banks have been set up in the rural areas, and special institutions for providing credit to industries have been started in the urban areas.

The monetary policy in these countries allows money supply to slightly exceed the demand for money so that there is a small increase in price which is conducive for economic growth. However, this policy carries the inherent danger of giving rise to inflationary pressure in the economy.

(v) Equitable Distribution of Income

As regards this objective of achieving a more equitable distribution on income and wealth, fiscal policy is supposed to be more effective. But in recent times, the monetary policy is playing a 'supportive role' to fiscal policy in this respect. The credit policy can be organised in such a way as to provide more credit to the poor and needy, to help them purchase productive assets. Such a policy will also help in tackling the problems of unemployment and poverty.

Tools of Monetary Policy

In order to regulate credit in the economy, the Central Bank uses certain well known weapons which can be generally classified into:

(i) General or Quantitative and
(ii) Selective or Qualitative Methods of Credit Control.

General or Quantitative Methods of Credit Control

General methods are used to control the quantum of credit in general throughout the economy rather than the use of credit. The effects of general methods are all-pervading and affect the whole economy indiscriminately as a result of which even the productive investments would be hard-hit whenever there is credit contraction.

The three important general methods are discussed below :

(a) **Bank Rate Policy**

This is the oldest method of credit control first used by the Bank of England in 1839.

Bank rate refers to the rate of interest at which the Central Bank rediscounts approved bills of exchange. This policy works under the assumption that all other interest rates in the market invariably respond to changes in the bank rate. In a developed money market, this kind of relationship between bank rate and other market rates exist. Therefore whenever the Central Bank raises the bank rate (also known as dear money policy), all other interest rates rise and borrowings become less attractive and this results in contraction attractive and this results in the contraction of credits. A reduction in bank rate (also known as cheap money policy) on the other hand, reduces all other market rates of interest, thereby making borrowings more attractive and resulting in the expansion of credit.

Limitations of Bank Rate Policy:

(1) The effectiveness of bank rate policy depends on how far the commercial banks rely on the Central Bank for obtaining financial accommodation. Since most of the modern commercial banks have succeeded in becoming financially self-reliant, this method has failed to exercise the necessary control over the lending policy of commercial banks.

(2) In modern times, the required flexibility in the money market is lacking. As such, not only savings and investment but also the quantity of money and credit do not show adequate responses to bank rate.

(3) In most countries, a large, private market for reserve loans has emerged, which has succeeded in acquiring control over massive financial resources.

(4) Development of alternative and more effective methods of credit control have emerged in recent years, rendering the bank rate policy ineffective.

Open Market Operations

Open market operations refer to the buying and selling of government and other securities (in which it deals) by the Central Bank. This method exercises direct influence on the supply of money in circulation and the cash reserves of the commercial banks. Whenever the central bank sells securities, it intends to contract the quantity of money and credit by absorbing the purchasing power in the hands of the public. At the same time, it manages to reduce the cash reserves of the commercial banks and thereby reduce their capacity to create credit. On the other hand, whenever the central banks want to expand credit, it purchases securities. This will immediately put money into circulation, the cash reserves of the commercial banks will also go up thereby increasing their power to create credit.

Limitations of Open Market Operations

Although open market operations are one of the most widely used methods, it suffers from certain limitations:

(i) The effectiveness of this method depends to a great extent on the demand for and supply of government securities through which these operations are done. Many times, it so happens that when the central bank sells securities, the demand for them may be very less or non-existent. Under such circumstances, the Central Bank fails to exert the necessary influence on bank reserves and thus on their capacity to create credit. Conversely, when the central bank wants to purchase securities, it may find the supply of securities inadequate. Consequently, it cannot improve the supply of money and credit in the economy.

(ii) Open market operations become ineffective during times of depression when there is very little demand for credit by the borrowers for purposes of investment. During such times when the Central Bank purchases securities, only the liquidity position of commercial banks will improve without leading to expansion of credit in the economy.

(iii) Sometimes, this method may be rendered ineffective when people use hoarded money or income received from abroad, to purchase the securities. In such cases, the necessary impact on the reserves of commercial banks may not occur.

(iv) Lastly, the success of this method depends on the existence of a well developed money and capital markets in the economy. In many developing countries, the securities market is relatively under-developed. Thus the Central Banks of these countries do not have sufficient securities with them to conduct open market operations.

Variable Statutory Reserve Ratio

The Central Bank of a country enjoys the power to determine the statutory cash reserve requirements of the commercial banks. Under this policy, the Central Bank requires the commercial banks to maintain a certain percentage of their demand and time deposits as reserves.

An increase in the reserve requirements, implies that banks will be able to support lesser amounts of demand deposits. This will reduce the funds available for loans and hence lead to a reduction in credit. For example, if the banking system has Rs. 6,000 crores in total reserves and the legal reserve requirement is 8%, then the banking system can support Rs. 5,520 crores of demand deposits. Let us suppose that legal reserve requirement is raised to 9%. Now the banking system will be able to support only Rs. 5,460 crores.

Conversely, a decline in reserve requirements will imply that banks are now required to hold less reserves to support the existing amount of demand deposits. This means that the banks will now have excess reserves and this will help them to create more credit.

Selective or Qualitative Methods of Credit Control

The selective methods of credit control as distinguished from general methods are directed towards particular uses of credit. They operate by means of official regulations issued and enforced by the Central Bank. They aim at curtailing the flow of credit into unproductive channels and diverting them into productive channels of the economy.

Some of the important methods of selective credit control are:

(a) **Rationing of Credit**

The Central Bank may issue directions to commercial banks to restrict (ration) credit to certain sectors or sections of the population. This method is particularly useful in controlling inflationary pressures.

(b) **Direct Action**

This refers to forceful measures adopted against those commercial banks which have committed errors. The puritive measures used here are denial of re-discounting facility, charging penalty, fixation of quantitative credit ceiling etc.

(c) **Variable Margin Requirements**

This measure is used to thwart speculation and hoarding activities by traders. For instance, if traders hoard necessary commodities like foodgrains in an attempt to create artificial scarcity and thereby push up prices, then the Central Bank can raise margin requirement with respect to such goods. If the margin requirement is 50%, then the trader can get a loan of only Rs.10 lakhs against a security of Rs.20 lakhs. If the margin requirement is raised to 75%, he can get a loan of only Rs 5 lakhs against the same security.

(d) **Regulation of Consumer Credit**

This measure is resorted to only under severe inflationary conditions in an effort to restrict consumer demand for credit. For example, credit given for the purchase of consumer durables may be charged very high rates of interest to discourage borrowing for this purpose by the consumer. This results in a fall in demand and thereby a fall in the prices of these goods.

(e) **Moral Suasion**

This is a measure used by the Central Bank to put pressure upon the lending activities of commercial banks by urging them to voluntarily adopt certain restrictive practices.

(f) **Deficit Financing**

Deficit financing is a method adopted to cover the budgetary gap by resorting to loans from the banks in developed countries. However, in developing countries, resort is made to the Central Bank which merely prints more notes to cover the deficit.

In whatever way it is defined, deficit financing results in an increase in the level of expenditure of the community because it involves an increase in total money supply. Since there is creation of new money, it almost invariably results in inflation and as a result of deficit financing, the purchasing power in the hands of the people increases, but the production of goods does not increase simultaneously.

Limitations of Monetary Policy

As pointed out by Anthony. S. Campagna, 'untimeliness is one of the risks of the operation of monetary policy, and that risk is increased, the longer the lag between policy and response.'

(i) There is usually a noticeable time lag between recognition of the 'need' for action, which is by way of monetary policy, and actual implementation of the policy decision. Such lags occur due to the simple reason that monetary authorities can only alter the money market conditions, but it is the other economic units like firms, consumers, government etc. that must alter their plans keeping in view the changed money market conditions. Adding to this is the unreliability of forecasts,generally at a particular point of time, some sectors of the economy will be expanding while others may be contracting. Thus, it is very difficult to determine just where the economy is operating.

(ii) In recent years, the participation of a large number of financial intermediaries in money and capital markets and over which the Central Bank has no control, has rendered the monetary policies ineffective.

(iii) Sometimes, the Central Bank is faced with contradictory objectives particularly in the case of developing countries - for instance, attainment of economic growth and stability are the twin objectives of monetary policy. But the attainment of one may be possible only at the cost of the other. Economic growth requires a continuous but low rate of rise in price-level, in the order to keep the inducement to invest active.

But, often mild inflationary trends tend to develop into severe inflationary pressures and thus may come in the way of economic stability.

(iv) The most serious limitation of monetary policy arises from the fact that the money and capital markets are under-developed and unorganised. This makes it very difficult for the government to expand or contract money supply or to raise or lower the costs of borrowing in the private sector.

(v) Lastly, the ineffectiveness of the instruments of credit control which have already been discussed, limit the success of monetary policies.

QUESTIONS

1. What do you mean by Fiscal policy. Distinguish between fiscal policy and monetary policy.
2. What are the objectives of fiscal policy.
3. Give an explanatory note on tools of fiscal policy.
4. What do you mean by Monetary Policy. Briefly explain the various objectives of monetary policy.

❖✻❖✻❖

CHAPTER 23

BALANCE OF PAYMENTS

Meaning

The balance of payments of a country is a systematic record of all international economic transactions of that country during a given period, usually a year.

Balance of payments accounting of any country uses a double entry system of recording accounts with the rest of the world. Thus, the balance of payments account is divided into transactions giving rise to payments (or debit) and receipts (or credit). In the accounting sense, thus, the balance of payments of a country must always be in balance. In other words, the balance of payments as a whole must necessarily balance. This means the total receipts of a country are necessarily equal to its total payments, if receipts include not only the volume of goods exported but also the volume of gold or other monetary reserves exported in order to obtain purchasing power over that part of imports which is not covered by normal commercial exports.

In other words, debit or payment side of the balance of payments account of a country represents the total of all the uses made out of the total foreign exchange acquired by the country during a given period, while the credit or receipts side represents the sources from which this foreign exchange was acquired by this country in the same period. The two sides as such necessarily balance. If in the actual balance of payments account the credits and debits do not balance, the balance is usually achieved by adding an item called errors and omissions.

Structure of Balance of Payments

A balance of payments statement is tabulated to summarise a nation's total economic transactions undertaken on the international trade account. It is usually composed of two sections: (i) the current account, and (ii) the capital account.

Current account mainly consists of two sub-groups: merchandise or the trade account and the invisible account.

In the trade or merchandise account, only the transactions relating to goods are entered. That is, all goods exported and imported are recorded in the trade account.

The invisible account usually comprises the services account and the gifts or charities account. The services account records all the services rendered and received by residents of the nation. It consists of such items as banking and insurance charges, interest on loans, tourist expenditure, transport charges etc. Similarly, the gifts or charities account consists of all those items which are received or given away free by residents of the nation. It may be in kind or in cash. It goes without saying that these are all referred to as invisible transactions in the balance of payments theory and therefore recorded in the invisible account. It is interesting to note here that the International Monetary Fund (IMF) includes the following items as invisible transaction :

(i) International transportation of goods, including warehousing while in transit and other transit expenses.
(ii) Travel for reasons of business, education, health, international conventions or pleasure.
(iii) Insurance premiums and payments of claims.
(iv) Investment income, including interest, rents, dividends and profits.
(v) Miscellaneous service items such as advertising, commissions, film rental, pensions, patent fees, royalties, subscription to periodicals and membership fees.
(vi) Donations, migrant remittances, legacies
(vii) Repayment of commercial credits.
(viii) Contractual amortisation and depreciation of direct investments.

Capital account, on the other hand, deals with payments of debts and claims. It consists of all such items as may be employed in financing both imports and exports, namely, private balances, assistance by the international institutional agencies and specie flow, and balances held on government account. Accordingly, we shall have private capital account, international institutional capital account, specie account, and government capital account. Balances in these accounts may rise or fall from year to year, depending upon the movements or fluctuations in other items on capital account.

Items of balance of payments account may thus be summarised in Table 1.

It should be noted that the two accounts - current and capital - in the balance of payments should necessarily balance. The surplus in the trade or current account must be equal to the deficit in the capital account or the deficit in the current account.

Table 1

Balance of Payments

CURRENT ACCOUNT	CAPITAL ACCOUNT
1. Merchandise - Exports and imports a) Private b) Government 2. Non - monetary gold movement 3. Foreign travel 4. Transportation 5. Insurance 6. Government, not included elsewhere 7. Investment income 8. Miscellaneous 9. Transfer payments a) Official b) Private	1. Private (non - banking) loans a) Long - term b) Short - term 2. Banking (excluding Central Bank) 3. Official (including Central Bank) a) Loans b) Amortisation c) Miscellaneous d) Reserves (including changes in the foreign exchange assets of the Central Bank)
Total current Transactions Error and Omissions	Total capital and Monetary Gold

For instance, if India is importing more goods than its exports of goods and services to the foreigners, it will have a deficit in its current balance of payments. This she will have to pay either by gold and other assets or by borrowing from other countries. These are credit items in the capital account of the balance of payments. Therefore, the current and capital accounts together will balance each other.

Balance of Payments and Balance of Trade

There is a marked distinction between the concepts of balance of trade and balance of payments. Balance of payments is a wider concept than the balance of trade. In fact, balance of payment includes in its structure, the notion of balance of trade.

As we know, a country may export and import many items, both visible and invisible. Balance of trade refers only to the value of imports and exports of goods, i.e., visible items because it is an open trade between the countries and can be easily certified by the customs official. On the other hand, balance of trade is only a partial study of the balance of payments. It simply refers to the difference between the value of exports and visible imports.

This is what is represented in the trade or merchandise account section of the current account in the balance of payments statement. Thus, balance of trade is nothing but a major component of the balance of trade or merchandise account, the invisible account which is again composed of services sector and gifts and charities account comprising varieties of invisible items, plus the record of capital account.

Balance of Payments Always Balances

Since the balance of payments statement is drawn up in terms of debits and credits based on a system of double-entry book-keeping, if all the entries are made correctly, total debits must equal total credits. This is because two aspects (debits and credits) of each transaction recorded are equal in amount but appear on the opposite sides of the balance of payments account. In this accounting sense, balance of payments of a country must always balance.

In other words, debit or payment side of the balance of payments account of a country represents the total of all uses made out of the total foreign exchange acquired by the country during a given period, while the credit or receipts side represents the sources from which this foreign exchange was acquired by this country in the same period. The sides as such necessarily balance.

It should be noted that the two accounts - current and capital - in the balance of payments should necessarily balance. The surplus of the trade or current account must be equal to the deficit in the capital account or the deficit in the current account must be equal to the surplus in the capital accounts. Thus, the balance of current account need not be equal but can show a surplus or a deficit. There is, however, a corresponding surplus in the balance of capital account. As a result, the credit and debit sides of the balance of payments are exactly balanced.

To illustrate the point, an imaginary account of a country's balance of payments is represented in the following table:

Country's Balance of Payments Account

Credit (Receipts)		Debit (pay...ents)	
I) Current	Rs (crores)	Transactions	Rs (crores)
1. Merchandise trade (goods exported)	2000	8. Merchandise trade (goods imported)	4000
2. Services exported	1000	9. Services imported	1000
3. Income from foreign investment	3000	10. Foreign income from investment at home	1500 1500
4. Unilateral receipts	500	11. Unilateral payment	
Sub total	6500	Sub total	7000
II) Capital Transactions			
5. Long - term borrowings	1500	12. Long term lending	1000
6. Short term borrowings	1000	13. Short term lending	500
7. Sale of gold /assets	1000	14. Purchase of gold / assets	1400
Sub total	3500	Sub total	2900
		15. Errors and omissions	100
Grand Total	10000	Grand Total	10000

As already stated, the balance of the current account need not be equal but can show a surplus or a deficit. In the table, the balance of current account shows a deficit of Rs. 500 crores. However, there is a corresponding surplus of Rs. 500 crores in the balance of capital account. As a result, the credit and debit sides of the Balance of Payments Account are balanced.

Disequilibrium In the Balance of Payments

Although in the accounting sense, the balance of payments accounts must balance, it need not be in equilibrium. Suppose a country's balance of payments shows a deficit in the current account, its credit balance in the capital account must be large enough so that total debits equal total credits. In other words, when a country is facing a deficit in the current account, it has to either borrow capital on a short term as long term, or it has to export gold or receive donations from foreigners so that its credit in the capital account is equal to the extent of its deficit in the current account.

Hence, we may simply consider the balance of payments as the difference between receipts from and payments to foreigners by the residents of the country. A country's balance of payments is said to be in disequilibrim when there is either a 'surplus' (favourable) or 'deficit' (unfavourable) in the balance of payments. A country enjoys a 'surplus' balance of payments when total receipts exceeds total payments. Conversely, a country's balance of payments is said to be unfavourable when total payments exceeds total receipts in a particular year.

Causes of Disequilibrim

A country may experience a disequilibrium (either surplus or deficit) in its balance of payment either for a short period or for a long period. The nature and intensity of disequilibrium vary from country to country. The following are some of the important causes producing a disequilibrium in a country's balance of payments:

(i) Business cycles or trade cycles may cause cyclical disequilibrium.

(ii) Structural disequilibrium may be caused when heavy investment programmes are undertaken by developing countries. These countries tend to import capital goods for rapid industrialization while they may not be in a position to export much because they are basically primary producing countries and also because domestic requirements may increase.

(iii) Structural disequilibrium may also be caused due to increasing self-reliance on the part of both advanced countries and also poor nations. The advanced countries have become self-reliant in foodstuffs, raw materials etc., thus, affecting the exports of poor agrarian countries. Similarly, the advanced countries are also experiencing a decline in their exports due to the tendency of poor countries to become self-reliant in manufactured goods.

(iv) Rapid growth of population leading to increase in imports and decrease in the capacity to export may cause disequilibrium in the balance of payments, especially of developing countries.

Measures for Correcting Disequilibrium

Disequilibrium in the balance of payments may be corrected either through monetary or through non-monetary measures.

The following monetary measures may be used:

(i) **Deflation**

Deflation refers to the contraction in the volume of the home currency which would result in a fall in prices, and rise in the value of the home currency. When prices fall, exports become cheaper and imports become costlier. Thus, the volume of exports increase and volume of imports decrease and the disequilibrium (deficit) would be set right.

(ii) Depreciation

When the rate of exchanges of one country falls in terms of another country, it is called 'exchange depreciation.' Suppose 1 Re = 60 pence and India experiences an adverse balance of payments with regard to British pounds, then the demand for the British pound will rise. This results in a rise in the value of pound in terms of the rupee. To correct the disequilibrium, the rate of exchange of the Indian rupee in terms of pound has to be depreciated from 1 Re = 60 pence to 1 Re = 40 pence. This makes Indian goods cheaper for Britain and British goods become costlier for India. This encourages India clearing the deficit in the Balance of Payments(BoP).

This method works automatically and is suitable to correct a mild disequilibrium. This method can be successful only through the co-operation of foreign countries, which should not retaliate by depreciating their currencies as well. Moreover, depreciation may initiate inflationary pressures due to an increase in money incomes and rise in domestic prices.

(iii) Devaluation

Devaluation refers to the deliberate reduction in the external value of a country's currency in relation to the currencies of all countries or in terms of gold or in relation to the currencies of selected countries.

This is an extreme measure resorted to by the government to correct a serious and fundamental disequilibrium in the balance of payments. The direct and immediate effect of devaluation is stimulation of exports and reduction in imports. The distinction between devaluation and depreciation is that the former implies an official and deliberate reduction in external value of the currency announced by the government whereas the latter stands for automatic reduction in the external value of a country's currency brought about by market forces.

Devaluation will be successful only if the demand for imports and exports is fairly elastic. There should also be no change in the cost price structure in the devaluing country. Again, the foreign countries have to fully co-operate with the devaluing country by not raising their import duties or giving export concessions or by devaluing their own currency so as to multiply the favourable effects of devaluation to the country under consideration.

(iv) Exchange Control

Another effective method of correcting disequilibrium used by governments is exchange control.

According to this method, the foreign exchange earned by the exporters have to be surrendered to the Central Bank which will in turn be distributed among the licensed importers. This helps in controlling the volume of imports and keeping it within the limits of export earnings.

But exchange control is only a temporary measure and not a permanent solution to correct a basic disequilibrium in the balance of payments.

The non-monetary measures include:

(i) Import Duties and Quotas

In order to discourage imports, heavy import duties may be imposed especially on selected items of conspicuous consumption.

The government may sometimes fix quotas and thereby restrict the quantity of imports. This method can be used to eliminate or reduce the deficit in the balance of payments.

(ii) Export Promotion

The government may introduce policies and programmes which encourage exports, whenever the country is facing a deficit. Duties on exports may be reduced and incentives as well as subsidies may be given to exporting industries.

Questions

1. Distinguish between balance of trade and balance of payments. What information do you hope to get about the economic position of a country from its balance of payments.
2. Give an explanatory note on structure and components of balance of payments.
3. Explain the causes for disequilibrium on the balance of payments.
4. Explain the remedial measures adopted to correct the disequilibrium in balance of payments.

❖✻❖✻❖